CESARE BORGIA

SARAH BRADFORD

CESARE BORGIA

HIS LIFE AND TIMES

MACMILLAN PUBLISHING CO., INC.

NEW YORK

For Tony, Miranda, Annabella and Edward

Macmillan Publishing Co., Inc.
866 Third Avenue, New York, N.Y. 10022

Library of Congress Cataloging in Publication Data
Bradford, Sarah.
Cesare Borgia, his life and times.
Bibliography: p.
Includes index.
1. Borgia, Cesare, 1476?-1507. I. Title.
DG797.82.B65 1976   945′.6′060924 [B]   76-18925
ISBN 0-02-514400-6

First American Edition 1976

Printed in the United States of America

CONTENTS

ILLUSTRATIONS

ACKNOWLEDGEMENTS

My grateful thanks are due to Dr Cecil Clough for his generosity in providing me with suggestions and material and for his critical reading of my manuscript, to Dr Michael Mallett for his help with the bibliography, to Professor Nicolai Rubinstein for his monograph on Lucrezia Borgia, to Dr J.P.C. Kent for his information on contemporary coinage, and to Professor Douglas Johnson for his advice on French sources. In Navarre, my special gratitude goes to Don Vicente Galbete, director of the Diputación Foral de Navarra, whose unstinting kindness and cooperation enabled me to visit every site connected with Cesare in Navarre and to consult the archives of Pamplona and Viana, and who obtained for me much unpublished material. My personal thanks are due to my editor, Christopher Falkus, for the enthusiasm and work he has put into this book, to my agent, Jacintha Alexander, for her support and confidence, and to Peggy Munster for lending me the cottage at Bampton where the last draft of the book was written.

AUTHOR'S NOTE

Currency values: inflation has made difficult any valid equation between the values of fifteenth-century coinage and today's money. The gold coins mentioned in the text, Italian ducats and florins, French écus and livres, were worth roughly the equivalent of between one third and one half of a modern gold sovereign; e.g. an écu of Louis XII weighed about 3·5 g and in its own day a coin of this weight would have been worth about 4s 6d in English money of the time.

Military terminology: a *condottiere* was a mercenary captain whose contract, *condotta*, with his employer obliged him to provide a number of men for an agreed period of time in return for a stipulated sum. By the end of the fifteenth century the condottiere's cavalry force would consist of squadrons of twenty-five lances, each lance comprising five to six men, the man-at-arms, i.e. the heavily-armoured cavalryman, and his necessary attendants.

31 Britannia Road, sw6
1 November 1975

THE BORGIA LEGEND

CESARE BORGIA's name has been a byword for evil for over five centuries.

He was born, the illegitimate son of the Spanish Cardinal Rodrigo Borgia, later Pope Alexander VI, into a world which has been called 'the Golden Age of Bastards'. The princely courts of fifteenth-century Italy swarmed with the rulers' children struggling for a career through war, the Church, marriage or, not infrequently, assassination. 'The wicked custom of poisoning men', wrote the great Florentine historian Guicciardini, 'is a common practice in many parts of Italy.' Life was short; time pressed on ambitious men.

Wielding the sword and backed by the power, wealth and prestige of the Papacy itself, Cesare at twenty-seven became the most feared, hated and envied man in Italy, earning himself the reputation of the terrible Valentino'. Each of the princes and states in turn felt themselves menaced by his growing ambition, and his threat to the Italian political establishment generated a sense of shock and outrage which formed the basis of the Borgia legend.

This legend arises from the pages of contemporary accounts of the Borgias, the stuff of a sinister reputation that has shadowed them, and Cesare in particular, down the ages. Cesare was accused of murder, rape, incest, robbery and treachery – much the same charges which were levelled at his father the Pope. There were elements of truth in these accusations, but contemporary reactions to the Borgias were not based solely on moral grounds. It was an age in which the standards of public and private morality were far from strict: double-dealing and intrigue were regarded as an integral part of the game of politics and war, political assassination was common, and Alexander VI was not the first pope to have had a hand in it.

Most of the Italian lordships were founded upon violent conquest, and violence remained very much a part of political life. In the cities of Italy the factions fought each other bloodily in the streets, the Baglionis against the Oddis at Perugia, the Orsinis against the Colonnas in Rome. The pursuit of the vendetta, either as an act of personal vengeance or by the use of hired assassins, was an accepted custom; Cellini in his autobiography boasted of the many fatal brawls in which he had been involved.

Violence and murder were equally common in the private lives of the Italian signorial families. Sigismondo Malatesta of Rimini had two of his wives murdered: one poisoned, the other suffocated. Francesca Manfredi of Faenza lured her husband into her bedchamber on the pretext of being unwell and had him stabbed there by concealed assassins; when they bungled the job she coolly stepped forward, a fifteenth-century Lady Macbeth, and finished him off with a dagger thrust in the stomach. In July of 1500, in a bloodbath known as 'the Red Wedding', half the feuding Baglioni family of Perugia murdered the other half in their beds, a massacre which was quite overshadowed in contemporary chronicles by a single act of violence committed by Cesare at the time.

Sexual licence applied to laymen and clerics alike. The great lords had numerous mistresses who might be of noble or common birth, courtesans or married women, and broods of bastards who were brought up at their courts side by side with their legitimate children. The great churchmen behaved in the same way: Pope Sixtus IV's nephew, the flamboyant Cardinal Pietro Riario, kept a mistress whose shoes were sewn with pearls; of the Renaissance popes both Innocent VIII and Julius II as well as Alexander VI had illegitimate children A thriving population of whores serviced the swarming clerics in Rome, and the conventual orgies described in Aretino's *I Ragionamenti* were not figments of the author's imagination. Incest and sodomy were accepted, though officially frowned upon: Gian Paolo Baglioni of Perugia received ambassadors while lying in bed with his sister; Sigismondo Malatesta, whom Pope Pius II called 'the worst scoundrel of all the men who have ever lived or ever will live, the disgrace of Italy and the infamy of our times', was alleged not only to have committed incest with his daughter but to have attempted sodomy with his son. Yet it was for heresy, not sexual misdemeanours, that the same Pope later excommunicated him.

Why then has Cesare Borgia come down to us as the archetype of criminality? The hostility of his Italian contemporaries towards him and his family can be partially explained on the grounds of their Spanish blood. Italians disliked and despised all foreigners, whom they regarded as 'barbarians', and Spaniards most of all – with good reason. In Italy, where the Aragonese dynasty ruled Naples and Sicily, Spanish soldiers of fortune had already displayed that combination of courage, pride, endurance, ferocity and greed which was to drive the conquistadors on their bloody progress through the New World. From the pages of Aretino it is clear that the Spaniards in Rome were looked on as a kind of Mafia, and it is probable that the great families of Italy saw the Borgias in that light. *Marrano*, 'secret Jew', was the epithet most commonly thrown at Spaniards in Italy, and one which Cesare's enemies frequently used to describe him.

Racial prejudice, however, is an insufficient explanation for the devil-figure which Cesare represented to his contemporaries; it is their constant references to his 'dangerous nature' which give us the clue. Cesare Borgia was a dangerous man, with one quality above all which made him so: a driving ambition which was the key to his whole life, the underlying theme of his complex character. He was one of those rare men born with a superlative ambition to which all else was subordinated, a quality which makes a man a maverick among his fellows, and a threat to the normal tenor of their lives. Moreover Cesare deliberately created his own myth by calculated acts of terror, veiling his life in a secrecy which gave his sudden brutalities and lightning moves added impact.

Cesare's character was bewildering in its contradictions: he was a brilliant student, a man of lucid intelligence, possessed of notorious charm and eloquence – 'of his mind and tongue he makes what use he wills', one despairing envoy wrote of him. He was strong, athletic, an expert horseman and a skilful military leader. Even his enemies never denied his personal courage: 'In war he was a good companion and a brave man,' a French fellow officer recorded of him. He was also totally amoral, vengeful, treacherous and deceitful, 'the great dissembler' as Machiavelli described him, a man apparently incapable of deep and lasting human affection – except perhaps for his sister, Lucrezia. His complexities baffled even that acute observer Machiavelli, who saw the careful picture he had built up of Cesare shattered in an hour, so that he doubted whether it had been the truth or simply a mirage.

And so, to find the reality behind the myth, one must look beyond the kaleidoscope of contemporary impressions, sort out the distortions, and evaluate the man himself according to the facts – as far as they can be known after five centuries have passed. Cesare Borgia was above all a political animal, and it is in the context of contemporary politics that his story must be told.

I

THE STAGE

CESARE was destined to play his part in the limelight of the international stage. Fifteenth-century Italy was the centre of the civilized world, her cities far surpassing those of northern Europe in artistic achievement, learning, living standards, economic and political sophistication. But the glamour of Italy was only part of her attraction; early in the century the popes had returned to Rome from Avignon, and in a Europe still acknowledging the Roman creed the Eternal City was thus once again the focus of Christendom. Religion and politics were closely intertwined; the pope as spiritual ruler of the Christian world exercised enormous influence in international affairs and the action of the Papacy was central to the political calculations of the secular powers.

Yet Italy as a political entity did not exist; the Italian peninsula was a patchwork of independent states jostling for power and survival, a game in which the five major players, Venice, Milan, Florence, Naples and the Papacy, used the smaller princedoms as pawns on the political chessboard.

The ruling families of these minor states held absolute sway over their subjects, maintaining an outward appearance of independence which belied their real status as clients, victims and vassals of their greater neighbours. The Estes of Ferrara, the Gonzagas of Mantua and the Montefeltros of Urbino led cultivated lives in exquisite surroundings. They patronized the arts not only from private taste but for public prestige, often supplementing the revenues stretched by this extravagance by fighting as mercenary captains, condottieri, in the incessant quarrels of the other Italian powers. Yet despite their many palaces, their paintings, silks and jewels, their stables of stud horses and strings of hunting dogs, there was unease behind the glitter. The movements of the major powers beyond their frontiers could threaten their very existence; they were small floes in a shifting pack, at the mercy of political forces over which they had no control.

The greater Italian states, Venice, Milan, Florence, Naples and the Papacy, coexisted in an uneasy balance of power maintained by mutual jealousy rather than common interest. In Guicciardini's words, they were 'full of emulation among themselves, they did not cease to observe assiduously what the others were doing, each of them reciprocally aborting all the plans whereby any of the others might become more powerful or renowned'.

Venice and Milan, outstripping the other states in financial and military resources, regarded each other with a deep hostility. Venice, the great city on the Adriatic, ruled by an intelligent and ruthless oligarchy, enjoyed a political stability which led other Italians to call her enviously 'the Immortal'. She maintained an overseas empire and a web of international commerce stretching over the known world, with the resources of a vast naval armoury, an efficient and ubiquitous spy service carried on by her diplomats and agents, and the indus-tries – silks, jewellery, sweetmeats, Murano glass – which supplied the luxury needs of Europe. Traditionally Venice had observed a serene neutrality towards Italian affairs, but since the fall of Constantinople in 1453 her overseas empire had been gradually dwindling under the attacks of the Turks, and there were now signs that she was turning a predatory eye towards the Italian mainland to compensate for her losses overseas.

Milan, whose territories marched with those of Venice, naturally looked on her expansionist tendencies with distrust. The duchy of Milan straddled the rich countryside of Lombardy; the city itself with 300,000 inhabitants was larger than either Paris or Rome, and the revenues of the Milanese state, drawn from its industries of silk, armoury and agriculture, were only slightly less than those of France and England. All power was in the hands of Ludovico Maria Sforza, known as il Moro from his emblem, the mulberry, who ruled in the name of his nephew Gian Galeazzo. Ludovico was intelligent and cul-tivated, the patron of Leonardo da Vinci and Bramante, and a man of considerable personal charm. But he was also vain, an inveterate intriguer with a fatal tendency to overestimate his own cleverness and underestimate his enemies – and insatiably ambitious. 'A man born for the ruin of Italy,' commented the historian Paolo Giovio, and in-deed Ludovico's ambition to become the acknowledged Duke of

Milan was to have disastrous consequences for himself and his country.

Florence, the citizen republic on the Arno, could not be compared with Milan either in lands or in wealth, deriving her strength from Tuscan industry, the cloth trade and her role in the international banking system, and her prestige from the Medici family, whose leader, the brilliant Lorenzo, controlled the affairs of the city with a wise and subtle hand. But despite the genius of her artists and the industry of her merchants and artisans, Florence was militarily weak, and the stability of her civic system less assured than it outwardly appeared.

Far to the south of Florence, the kingdom of Naples represented the explosive potential of an already unstable situation. For over two centuries the succession to the Kingdom had been disputed between the Spanish kings of Aragon and the French dukes of Anjou, a quarrel which had been temporarily resolved in favour of a junior branch of the Aragonese royal house. But the King of Naples, the cunning and cruel Ferrante, did not rule a united people; his barons were divided between the partisans of the Angevin claims and those who supported the Aragonese, so that the succession question remained a smouldering issue for the future. Indeed, 'the Kingdom', as it was known, had always been the magnet for foreign invaders, and it was against the backdrop of an international scramble for Naples that Cesare Borgia was to make his career. Moreover, the question of Naples involved the Papacy, since the pope was feudal suzerain of the Kingdom and had the right to the investiture of the candidate to the crown: as such he would be the official arbiter in any quarrel over the succession.

The Papacy itself was, geographically, politically and spiritually, the centre of the Italian firmament. In Rome the Renaissance popes lived in a style indistinguishable from the courts of contemporary monarchs. Even as early as the twelfth century, St Bernard of Clairvaux had rebuked Pope Eugenius III for adopting the outward signs of the imperial rather than the apostolic succession: 'The pope is decked in gold, mounted on a white horse, surrounded by troops and officers... In this you have succeeded not to Peter but to Constantine ...' The Renaissance popes employed this imperial splendour as a deliberate policy aimed at reasserting the prestige of the Papacy after the humiliating years of exile at Avignon, when General Councils of the Church had attempted to limit papal power. The first of the great building popes of the Renaissance, Nicholas v, told the cardinals on his deathbed that he knew the faith of the masses to be fragile because the people lacked instruction, therefore it was important to consolidate their faith by the spectacle of material grandeur. Nicholas v (1447–55), Sixtus iv (1471–84) and later Julius ii (1503–13) conceived their ambitious reconstruction of Rome as the resurrection of the imperial city, the outward symbol of the pope's empire as the successor both to Peter and to Constantine.

The popes were absolute masters of the city of Rome, from which they derived a considerable part of their revenues. Although the city retained a façade of limited autonomy, with its own senator and civil service, and shared in the administration of justice with the papal court, financial affairs were entirely in the hands of the pope's officials. The pope stood at the apex of a court comprising palace officials, secret chamberlains, grooms, clerks, secretaries and guards, a household which in the time of Sixtus iv cost some 30,000–40,000 florins a year to maintain, and a vast and expanding bureaucracy, the Curia. The Curia comprised three main financial departments: the Chancery, headed by the vice-chancellor, the most important figure in the hierarchy after the pope himself, wielding such profitable instruments as papal bulls, briefs and admonitions, with which the pope regulated the affairs of Christendom; the Camera, which administered the spiritual and temporal income under the direction of a cardinal chamberlain; and the Datariat, which was concerned with the revenues from the sale of offices, fees for dispensations and annulments. Other departments included that of the apostolic penitentiary, responsible for issuing absolution for sins and remitting penances, and the Rota, a court of justice headed by the cardinal vice-chancellor. The official revenues of the Papacy in the late fifteenth century amounted to some 300,000 ducats per annum, which already made it one of the richest of the Italian powers, but to this must be added incalculable (since unrecorded) sums available to the pope from gifts and other sources dealt with through what was known as his secret treasury, and administered by a private treasurer.

The only constitutional check on the absolute power of the pope was provided by the College of Cardinals, but the popes, in the manner of secular politicians, reacted to opposition from this quarter by packing it with their partisans, often their own relations. The strength of the pope vis-à-vis his cardinals was the same as that of a king of France or of England in relation to their great barons; he was the source of patronage, of the offices and benefices which enabled the cardinals to maintain their splendid style of living. As princes of the Church they were expected to live like worldly princes; Paolo Cortese in his book *De Cardinalatu*, the ecclesiastical equivalent of Castiglione's *The Courtier*, specified that a cardinal should be rich and noble by birth, magnificent in himself and liberal with his money, and inhabit a superbly decorated palace. Such palaces, some of which were more lavishly equipped than the Vatican itself, required huge households, on average some 150 persons; the financial strain of keeping up appearances on such a scale was considerable. Burckhardt, the great historian of the Renaissance, wrote of 'the secret misery of prelates who, notwithstanding heavy debts, were forced to live in a style befitting their rank'. At the court of Rome, as elsewhere, prestige depended on expenditure and credit could be raised on status and expectations, with the result that even the highest ranking cardinals were often deeply in debt. It was therefore vitally important that a cardinal should belong to the inner circle of 'Curia cardinals' close to the pope; the vice-chancellor, head of the Papal Chancery, received 6000 ducats a year from his office, as did the apostolic penitentiary, the chamberlain probably even more. Cardinals known to be influential with the pope could become 'cardinal protectors' of secular states, and in return for acting in the interests of their secular clients received rich benefices, pensions, and subsidies. Thus the pope stood at the apex of the power pyramid, while the cardinals and officials scrabbled for position on its slopes.

While the pope ruled the Roman court as an absolute sovereign, he enjoyed one advantage over secular princes in the spiritual weapons at his disposal. Excommunication was still feared; for a city the laying of a papal interdict could mean the loss of its trade, for a lord the endangering of his state, since both would then be open to attack by their enemies while their friends were forbidden to help. The granting of dispensations for marriages and annulments could be used to extract considerable sums of money and concessions from secular princes, and as a potent and profitable form of political blackmail.

But the pope's personal enjoyment of this unique position was brief; the road to the Papacy was a long one, and most popes when elected were on the threshold of old age. The ephemeral nature of this power was the main reason for the rapacity of papal relatives, who saw the urgency of grabbing what they could while the going was good, and for the anxiety of the pope to see that his family was sufficiently endowed during his lifetime to enable them to maintain their position after his death. Since the way to the Papacy led through the College of Cardinals, the princes of Italy aimed at a cardinal's hat for their younger sons at the earliest possible age, so that they might, through long years of accumulated wealth and seniority, stand a strong chance of changing the hat for the papal tiara. For this they intrigued and bribed their way through the labyrinths of the papal court, prepared to go to almost any lengths and pay any price to obtain the prize. Their understanding of the dual nature of the Papacy, its spiritual prestige combined with political power, is well illustrated by Lorenzo de' Medici's letter of advice to his son, the young Cardinal Giovanni de' Medici; exhorting him to cherish the honour and standing of the Church and the Holy See, he added: 'While doing this it should not be difficult for you to aid the city [Florence] and our house ... I think it is likely that a way will be found to save, as the proverb says, the goat and the cabbages ...'

This emphasis on the secular role of the popes reflected a deep change in the nature of the Papacy, whose spiritual authority and universal character had suffered severely during the unedifying years of the Great Schism, when the rulers of Europe had seized the oppor-tunity afforded by papal weakness to wring concessions from the popes over ecclesiastical patronage and financial contributions to the Holy See. This tendency had not been reversed when the popes returned to Rome in 1423; it had increased as the monarchies of Europe became stronger, more centralized, and unwilling to tolerate papal inter-vention. The Renaissance popes were still acknowledged as heads of Christendom, but their power and resources depended increasingly on their position as secular overlords. While the 'spiritual' income derived from international contributions steadily declined, they became more dependent on the 'temporal' income, which they re-ceived as overlords of the Papal States.

Sovereignty of the Papal States gave the Papacy its status as a major Italian power. The lands of the Church straddled central Italy, stretching from Bologna in the north to the frontier of the kingdom of Naples in the south, and included Emilia-Romagna, Le Marche, and the March of Ancona on the eastern side of the peninsula, Umbria and the papal cities of Orvieto, Viterbo and Spoleto in the centre, and the Patrimony of St Peter in Tuscany and the province of the Roman Campagna and Campagna Marittima to the west and south.

Yet before the accession of Alexander VI in 1492 much of this territory belonged to the Church in name only; to the north of Rome it was split up into lordships varying in size and importance from the prestigious dukedoms of Ferrara and Urbino with their princely courts, to the petty signories of the Romagna and the Marches. They were ruled by local families with the title of papal vicars, theoretically deriving their authority from the pope and obliged to pay a yearly tribute to him, but in practice acting as independent princes with little or no regard for their overlord. The Campagna around Rome was dominated by the great baronial families, the Colonnas, Orsinis, Caetanis and their adherents, who did not hesitate to threaten the pope on his home ground when it suited them, cutting off the city from its food supplies, bringing armed troops into Rome to brawl in the streets, and selling their services to the pope's enemies.

Nonetheless, no one questioned the Church's right to overlordship of the Papal States. For a pope with the will and the resources to assert that right by crushing the barons and overthrowing the *signori*, the Lands of the Church represented a vast potential of territorial wealth. It was this potential which the Borgias, father and son, using every weapon in the papal armoury, were to exploit.

But to do so Cesare and his father would have to confront the Italian political establishment, which was to a considerable extent based on family connections and personal relationships. Behind the power politics of the major states lay an intricate web of dynastic connections linking the members of the signorial ruling class from the north to the south of Italy. A chain of intermarriage joined Orsini to Medici, Este to Sforza, Gonzaga to Montefeltro, branching down to the smallest lordships, so that almost any petty *signore* could claim kinship with the great families. A recent historian has compared this family network with a passage in Dante's *Inferno*: 'So thick was the undergrowth of alliances among the signorial families that to strike one branch was to break another, like the dogs in the wood of suicides.' It was this charmed circle into which Cesare Borgia was to irrupt like a conquistador; this family network which was to feel itself deeply threatened as his sword cut off the branches one by one. It was a world to which by birth he did not belong.

II

THE CARDINAL'S BASTARD

SOMEWHERE in the neighbourhood of Rome in mid-September 1475, Vannozza de' Cattanei, wife of Domenico Giannozzo da Rignano, gave birth to a son. The only certain fact about Cesare's birth is that he was not the son of the obscure Domenico, who conveniently spent his time travelling on business for the Church, but of Rodrigo Borgia, Cardinal Bishop and Vice-Chancellor of the Church, the most powerful figure in the Roman hierarchy after the pope. Although Vannozza, for the sake of appearances, had been married to the complaisant Domenico some time before Cesare's birth, she had been the Cardinal's mistress for at least two years previously and there was no doubt whatsoever that her son was the latest descendant of an extraordinary Catalan family, the de Borjas, or, as they became known to history, the Borgias.

The Borgia story began in the remote town of Borja in the wild hill-country of Aragon. The fifteenth-century Borgias, in the manner of adventurers, later claimed royal descent from Pedro Atarés, great-grandson of Ramiro I of Aragon, who was lord of Borja in the twelfth century, but beyond family tradition there is no evidence to support their pretensions to royal blood. All that is certain is that the early Borgias came from Borja and owed their rise, as did their fifteenth-century descendants, to their courage, aggressiveness and opportunism. In the first half of the thirteenth century eight knights of the Borgia family marched with their King, Jaime I of Aragon, to free Valencia from the Moors. They distinguished themselves in this campaign, being inscribed as *caballeros de la Conquista*, and one of them, Esteban, was granted the towns of Jativa, Gandia and other lands in Valencia, taking as his device the grazing bull, emblem of his home town of Borja. Thus, by right of conquest, the Borgias became one of the leading families in Valencia, where for two hundred years they lived the humdrum lives of provincial nobility, until in 1444 Cesare's great-uncle Alonso, the first Borgia to set foot on Italian soil, set sail for Rome to become Cardinal of Quattro Incoronati.

Alonso owed his career to that combination of intelligence, hard work and luck which characterized the later Borgias. The first two qualities earned him the favour of his King, Alfonso v of Aragon, who succeeded to the throne of Naples in 1442, and brought him the cardinalate, but it was his luck which, contrary to all expectations, gained him the Papacy and founded his family's fortunes. In 1455, eleven years after his arrival in Italy, Alonso Borgia became Pope Calixtus III. He had been elected as a compromise candidate after a deadlock between two Italians; he was seventy-seven, in poor health, and not expected to live long. But Calixtus surprised them all by living a full three years after his election and proving to be an energetic and in many ways admirable Pope: pious, ascetic, frugal to the point of parsimony, and devoted to the cause of the crusade against the Turks. Among his less admirable qualities, however, was a nepotism which flooded Rome with a horde of Borgia relations and their hangers-on, all Valencians, or Catalans, as they were known to the Romans.

Among these Catalan relations two young Borgias enjoyed the Pope's special favour: his nephews Pedro Luis and Rodrigo, sons of his sister Isabella. The doting Calixtus showered them with honours; Pedro Luis, the elder, a swashbuckling arrogant young man whose excesses were only restrained by the prudence of his younger brother Rodrigo, was made Prefect of Rome and Captain General of the Church; his successful campaign in this capacity against the great Orsini barons laid the foundations of a bitter running feud between Borgia and Orsini which was to have a bearing on Cesare's own career thirty years later. While Pedro Luis reaped the honours in the secular sphere, Rodrigo Borgia rose swiftly to a position of power and wealth in the ranks of the Church. He was only eighteen when he accompanied his uncle to Italy to study law at the University of Bologna, twenty-five when Calixtus was elected Pope; within a year his uncle made him a cardinal, two years later he appointed him Vice-Chancellor of the Church, and in June 1458 gave him the see of Valencia, the richest in Spain, with a yearly income of 18,000 ducats.

Two months later, in August 1458, Calixtus lay on his deathbed, and a wave of pent-up Roman resentment broke over the heads of his two young nephews and their Catalan adherents. Pedro Luis fled

Rome to die of fever at Civita Vecchia, but Rodrigo, displaying the physical courage in the face of danger which never deserted him, attended his uncle until the end came on 6 August. Rodrigo Borgia, unlike the hot-headed Pedro Luis, was a survivor; he was determined not to be overwhelmed by the tide of anti-Catalan feeling which had swept away his brother and fellow-countrymen. In the conclave which followed his uncle's death, a contest between the Cardinal of Rouen and the Cardinal of Siena, Aeneas Silvius Piccolomini, his was the casting vote. Piccolomini, the successful candidate, who became Pope Pius II, described the scene at the deadlock: 'All sat in their places, silent, pale, as though they had been struck senseless. No one spoke for some time, no one opened his mouth, no one moved any part of his body, except the eyes, which turned this way or that ... Then the Vice-Chancellor Rodrigo rose and said: "I accede to the Cardinal of Siena!" And his words were like a sword through Rouen's heart ...' Thus Rodrigo's cool judgement not only enabled him to surmount the first crisis of his career, but, through the favour of the next ruler of the Church, ensured the continuation of his power and influence. At twenty-eight his feet were firmly placed on the long road which led to the highest office in Christendom. But the significance of the events of 1458 was not lost upon him; he had experienced the transient nature of papal power, seen how his uncle's death had involved his brother's destruction. It was a lesson he would not forget.

Rodrigo Borgia was a handsome man with a boundless zest for life. He was tall, with a strong, heavy body which never tired, a bull-like neck, and powerful features, black eyes and a great nose arching over full, sensual lips. He had a resilient nature, a boisterous gaiety and a quick sense of humour; easily bored, he loved singing and dancing, hunting and, above all, beautiful women. His tutor, Gaspare de Verona, wrote of him: 'He is handsome, of a most glad countenance and joyous aspect, gifted with honeyed and choice eloquence. Beautiful women are attracted by him in a quite remarkable way, more powerfully than iron ... by a magnet.' Neither as Cardinal nor as Pope did Rodrigo make any attempt to control or conceal his strong sexuality. Yet despite the hedonistic side of his nature, he was a man to be reckoned with. 'Of versatile intellect, great sense and imagination ... above all he is brilliantly skilled in the conducting of affairs,' wrote Jacopo Gherardi of Volterra. He was noted for his personal charm, the eloquence with which he expressed himself, and the dignity, even majesty of his bearing. But this smooth façade concealed an exceptionally able and hard-working administrator who took his duties as Vice-Chancellor seriously, a subtle and devious politician, and a skilful opportunist who was at the same time capable of long-term planning. He was, in short, a man with a quick understanding of other men, of money and the labyrinths which lead to power. He was also single-minded in the pursuit of his great ambition: the Papacy. To this end he exploited two avenues to build up his position: the favour of successive popes, and the interest of his fellow country-man, Ferdinand of Aragon.

Ferdinand, King of Aragon and of Sicily, was a hard-headed Cata-lan like Rodrigo himself, and they shared many of the same qualities. Essentially a pragmatist with a firm grasp on the realities of power, he had that outward-looking attitude to international affairs which had forged the Aragonese empire in the Mediterranean. He was a cautious politician, 'a cunning old Catalan' as Guicciardini later de-scribed him, whose reputation for trickery led Machiavelli to hold him up as a model for princes who wished 'to play the fox'. He was deeply interested in the affairs of Italy; as we have seen, the throne of Naples was occupied by the junior illegitimate branch of his own house of Aragon, but he had hopes of seeing it restored to his own crown. Thus when Rodrigo visited Spain in 1472 as Papal Legate, Ferdinand saw in him a valuable ally to advance his interests at the papal court; while Rodrigo for his part was well aware of the advan-tages that a clever man could gain by playing the field of international politics. Rich rewards might be extracted from Ferdinand in return for favours procured for him at the Vatican. Rodrigo's Spanish Lega-tion cemented a mutually profitable alliance that was to last over twenty years, and he returned to Italy in September 1473 well satisfied with the results of his visit to his homeland.

It was some time after his return from Spain, in the winter of 1473 or the early spring of 1474, that Rodrigo met Cesare's mother, Van-nozza de' Cattanei. He had had many mistresses and fathered three illegitimate children before he met her – Pedro Luis, born in 1462, Isabella, born in 1467, and Girolama, born in 1470 – but Vannozza is the only woman with whom he is known to have had a lasting rela-tionship, and he seems to have cared more deeply for the four children she bore him than for any of the others whom he fathered. She was thirty-two, no longer young by Renaissance standards, when she met Rodrigo Borgia, and she must indeed have been a remarkable woman to have captured and held his affection.

Little is known of Vannozza's origins beyond that she was the daughter of a man described in a document of 20 January 1483 as 'Jacopo Pinctoris [the Painter] of the Ponte quarter [of Rome]', and of Donna Menica, referred to in the same document as his widow. In the secret bull of September 1493 by which Rodrigo as Pope Alexander VI recognized Cesare as his son, his mother is described as 'a Roman woman'. This, however, did not necessarily imply that she was a Roman by birth, only that she was living there at the time Cesare was conceived. Some authorities assert that she came from Mantua, since Cattaneo is a particularly common name there, and point to her daughter Lucrezia's blonde hair as evidence of her northern origin. Yet even such an attentive observer of Borgia family life as the Mantuan envoy Gian Lucido Cattaneo, who would certainly have referred to Vannozza's Mantuan origin had it been known, never made any mention of it. The document of 1483, which refers to two sons of a Magister Antonio da Brescia as her blood relatives, may indicate that her family came from the region of Brescia. Indeed, all the evidence seems to point to the conclusion that even if Vannozza was born in Rome, her family were not native Romans. Had they been so, Vannozza would have had a horde of relations in the city who would have climbed eagerly onto the Borgia bandwagon, but beyond Donna Menica and the two da Brescia brothers, none have come to light. If Vannozza's father Jacopo was a painter, then it was highly probable that he, like hundreds of other artists and artisans from Tuscany, Umbria and Lombardy, would have migrated from a small northern background to the wider opportunities afforded by papal Rome.

The only known authentic portrait of Vannozza hangs in the Congregazione di Carità in Rome, of which she was a benefactress. It shows her well into middle age: her hair is covered by a veil, but does not appear to have been fair like Lucrezia's; her face is oval, with a short chin, small well-shaped mouth, strongly arched eyebrows over almond-shaped eyes, and a long, high-bridged nose which she bequeathed to her son Cesare. Her strong features retained their fineness into middle age, and she must have been strikingly beautiful when young. (In any case it is difficult to imagine that a man with Rodrigo Borgia's taste in women would have been so captivated by an ugly one.) Beyond beauty she must have had character. Rodrigo continued to regard her with respect and to protect her even after their physical relationship had ceased, and her children showed a firm attachment to her throughout their lives. Sensible she clearly was, and possessed of considerable commercial acumen; through her connection with Rodrigo she became a woman of property, owning three hostelries and several houses in Rome. The strong features depicted in her portrait indicate a woman of forceful character with a fierce temper. One unfortunate who crossed her in her commercial dealings called her 'a woman possessed of the devil', and she objected vociferously when some of her jewels were sent to Ferrara on the occasion of Lucrezia's marriage to Alfonso d'Este. Cesare must have inherited his vindictive temperament from his mother: Rodrigo was essentially easy-going.

Vannozza bore Rodrigo three more children after Cesare: Juan, born in 1476, Lucrezia, born in 1480, and Jofre, born in 1481. Domenico da Rignano died soon after Cesare's birth, and in 1480 or 1481 Vannozza married Giorgio di Croce, a Milanese who had been apostolic secretary to Pope Sixtus IV. Her physical relationship with Rodrigo may have been ending by the time of her second marriage; Rodrigo later publicly expressed doubts as to whether Jofre was indeed his son, and did not legitimize him until 1493 after he became Pope, when Jofre was twelve years old. In 1486 both di Croce and Vannozza's son by him, Ottaviano, died and Rodrigo hastened to marry his former mistress to another suitable husband, Carlo Canale, a Mantuan man of letters who had been secretary to Cardinal Gonzaga. A man of education but no means, Canale hoped to make his way in the world through his bride's connection with the powerful Cardinal Borgia. The marriage took place in June 1486, in the presence of the Borgia notary Camillo Beneimbene; Vannozza brought her new husband a dowry of a thousand gold florins and a curial appointment. Canale's expectations were not disappointed; when five years later his wife's former lover became Pope, he was rewarded with an important post as Governor of the Torre di Nona, the city prison. So absorbed did he become with his wife's family that he appears to have acted as unofficial secretary to her illegitimate sons, writing letters to his former patrons, the Gonzagas of Mantua, begging for horses for Juan, to whom he proudly refers as 'my stepson', even signing himself 'Carolus de Cattaneis', his wife's family name, instead of his own.

The Borgia children were not brought up in their father's house; Rodrigo as Cardinal veiled his private life with discretion, and the existence of his illegitimate children seems not to have become public knowledge until after his accession to the Papacy. The bull of September 1493 specifically stated that Cesare and Juan were brought up in the same house; they probably had their own household, as befitted sons of a prince of the Church, and certainly shared the same tutor. Their sister Lucrezia spent the first years of her life in her mother's house on the Piazza Pizzo di Merlo in the Ponte quarter, a few steps from Rodrigo's palace on the Corso. Rodrigo then placed her in the care of his first cousin and female confidante, Adriana de Mila, who was married to an Orsini, Ludovico lord of Bassanello, and lived in the vast Orsini palace on Monte Giordano.

Yet there is little doubt that the children saw a great deal of their father, who loved them deeply. A contemporary described Rodrigo as 'the most carnal of men' in his attachment to his own flesh and blood. And like other fathers he planned for his sons' futures – those plans being simple and in the habitual order of things. Pedro Luis, the eldest son, should take up the sword to win himself lands and fortune; Cesare, the second son, was destined for the Church; Juan, the third, would follow Pedro Luis in a secular career, while Jofre remained to be deployed as a pawn in the family game as opportunity allowed. The girls, naturally, were to make their way through suitable marriages.

But to think of Rodrigo's whole illegitimate brood as a family group would be wrong. Indeed, Cesare can scarcely have known his elder half-brother and half-sisters. By 1483, when Cesare was eight, the dashing Pedro Luis was back in the Borgias' homeland, fighting in the service of Ferdinand of Aragon. He did not return to Rome for four years, and a year later he was dead. Cesare's half-sister Girolama, who had married into the noble Cesarini family in 1482, died in 1483, while her sister Isabella was married in the same year to a Roman nobleman, Pier Giovanni Matuzzi.

It was specifically Vannozza's children, Cesare, Juan, Lucrezia and Jofre, who grew up as a compact family unit, their lives dominated by their father – although in looks they seem to have taken after their mother. None of them seems to have inherited the broad strength of their father's face, nor the powerful curve of his nose. All of them, Cesare and Lucrezia in particular, received from him his physical resilience and strength, his buoyant good spirits and charm. Cesare was tall like his father, but the finely proportioned figure for which he was noted had nothing of Rodrigo's heaviness. No contemporary portrait of Cesare seems to have survived, but the painting generally held to have resembled him and inscribed 'Dux Valentinus' – Duke Valentino – shows a young man with strong, finely cut features, a long, high-bridged nose, dark eyes shaped like his mother's with a watchful look to them, under strongly marked eyebrows, a fresh complexion probably also inherited from Vannozza, and long dark hair tinged with red. 'His head is most beautiful,' the Venetian ambassador wrote of him in 1500 when he was twenty-five. In character he inherited his father's intelligence and great ambition, his deviousness and his skill in diplomacy and intrigue, but although he could exert the famous Borgia charm when it suited him and was capable of outbursts of boisterous high spirits like his father, he did not share Rodrigo's outgoing nature. While appearing outwardly frank, he was inwardly secretive, controlled; his bouts of hectic enjoyment were often followed by periods of apparent lethargy and depression. He had a Spanish pride, and was deeply resentful of slights on his honour, which he never forgave and always avenged. He was suspicious and wary, and – unlike his father – apparently incapable of deep love for anyone, with the exception of Lucrezia. He was self-sufficient, with an almost superstitious belief in himself, that 'high confidence' which Machiavelli later noted in him. Cold, ruthless and unpredictable, Cesare's 'dangerous nature' may have been the reason that Rodrigo, while caring for him deeply, clearly favoured his younger brother Juan, whom he must have found easier to manage.

Juan, 'the spoilt boy' as the Aragonese chronicler Zurita described him, seems to have resembled Cesare in looks, although his hair was lighter in colour. Handsome, vain and self-indulgent, he lacked Cesare's intelligence and self-control. As he grew up observers remarked on the arrogance which was to earn him dangerous enemies. Lucrezia was undoubtedly the darling of the family; both Cesare and his father adored her, Rodrigo it was said 'superlatively'. All her contemporaries agreed in describing her as singularly attractive, with a grace and joyousness that charmed everyone who met her. Niccolò Cagnolo of Parma wrote of her: 'She is of middle height and graceful of form, her face is rather long, the nose well-cut, hair golden, eyes of no special colour [possibly he meant grey-blue]; her mouth is rather large, the teeth brilliantly white, her neck is slender and fair, her bosom admirably proportioned. She is always gay and smiling.' Lucrezia was extremely feminine, intelligent and adept at getting her way through charm. She also had the Borgia inner toughness where emotions were concerned, and her brother's incapacity for lasting deep feeling. She was no cipher and knew what she wanted, but in will-power she was completely dominated by her father and Cesare. Jofre, the baby of the family, appears to have been a complete nonentity and made no mark on his contemporaries apart from invidious comparisons with Cesare – one of them remarked how Jofre 'fits the spurs to the Duke's [Cesare's] boots ...' The only thing he shared with Cesare was their dark hair with the reddish tinge inherited from their mother.

These young Borgias identified closely with their father, their sense of kinship heightened by their Spanish blood and the strongly Spanish character of their father's household. Rodrigo Borgia had lived in Italy for more than thirty years and had only returned to his native land once, yet Spanish remained his first language. He wrote and spoke in Catalan, the dialect of Valencia, or in Castilian; it was the language of the Borgia family inner circle, which they used when conversing with each other on intimate occasions or when they preferred not to be understood by outsiders. Cesare himself always used the Spanish form of his name, signing himself 'Cesar', and his first tutor and lifelong friend, Juan Vera of Ercilla, was a Spaniard.

Cesare would have begun his education at an early age; his contemporary Piero de' Medici, son of Lorenzo, was already writing letters to his father in Latin at the age of seven, and at six he wrote to Lorenzo: 'I have already learned many verses of Virgil, and I know nearly the whole of the first book of Theodoro [the standard Greek grammar by Theodore Gaza] by heart.' Gaza's Greek textbook and Gaspare da Verona's Latin grammar formed part of Cesare's early education; Podocatharo, Rodrigo's Greek Cypriot secretary, undoubtedly helped him with his Greek studies, while Lorenz Behaim, the master of the household, who was a Latinist and member of the Roman classical Academy of Pomponius Laetus, would have introduced him to the classical authors. Cesare wrote and spoke Spanish, Italian, French, Greek and Latin, learned music and drawing, arithmetic and Euclidian geometry. As he grew older he would have been expected to write elegant Latin prose and poetry, and to improvise discourses in Latin, for which Cicero's speeches were the prime model, as were his letters for Latin prose style. The plays of Terence and Plautus were used to teach Latin conversation, and Cesare would have learned history from the works of Tacitus, Livy, Thucydides and Herodotus, poetry from those of Virgil, Horace and Ovid.

This emphasis on classical studies was not merely an academic exercise; the passion for classical antiquity which characterized the Renaissance was of very real significance in Rome, once the centre of the Roman Empire, where the Romans were rediscovering their great past. The classical authors were regarded as sources of know-ledge and as patterns for human behaviour; Cesare's contemporaries took the great figures of classical times as models to be followed, and accepted what they understood to be the ancient Romans' concepts of life as their own. *Fama*, fame or glory, was the goal; to gain it a man must exercise his individual skill and valour, *virtù*, to conquer the unpredictable force of fortune, *fortuna*, which ruled men's lives. This concept of his own power to shape his destiny would have become deeply ingrained in Cesare's mind, as he identified himself with his famous namesake Julius Caesar, whose actions had been guided by a supreme belief in the same idea. The key to the men of Cesare's generation lay in Alberti's famous phrase: 'A man can do anything if he wills ...'

Education was also considered to include the physical side of a child's life, an essential part of the training of the complete man. Alberti wrote: 'Youths should ride for exercise, they should learn the practice of arms, they should run and jump and manage a horse.' Cesare was strong – in later life he was reputed capable of bending a horseshoe with his bare hands – and excelled in all forms of physical exercise with the fierce competitiveness which he applied to every-thing he undertook. He shared his father's enthusiasm for hunting, which he would have practised as early as the age of six, loved horses and hunting dogs, and learned bullfighting from the Spaniards of his father's household, a skill with which he later amazed the Romans.

If Cesare's formative years equipped him mentally and physically for the demanding times ahead, the material side was by no means neglected. As early as October 1481, when he was just six years old, Rodrigo had paved the way to advancement in the career he had chosen for him by persuading the Pope to grant him a dispensation allowing him to hold benefices despite his illegitimacy, while the fol-lowing year Ferdinand of Aragon exempted him from inferiority of status in law deriving from his illegitimate birth, thus allowing him to hold lordships in Spain. The way was now open for Cesare to amass lucrative appointments at the expense of the Church in Spain. In March 1482 Cesare, not yet seven, was made apostolic protonotary by Sixtus IV; in July he was given a prebend and canonry in the cathedral of his father's bishopric of Valencia, as well as becoming archdeacon of Rodrigo's native town Jativa, and rector of Gandia, his brother's future dukedom. In April 1483 he became provost of Albar, while in the next year the new Pope Innocent VIII nominated him treasurer of his father's bishopric of Cartagena, then prebendary of the cathedral of Majorca, archdeacon of the cathedral of Tarragona, and canon of the cathedral of Lerida. The young recipient of all these benefices was not of canonical age to undertake any duties in respect of his offices, whose accruing revenues were used by his father for his maintenance and education.

By 1489 Cesare's Roman boyhood was over; he was fourteen, and for the next three years he would complete his formal education at the universities of Perugia and Pisa. In the autumn of 1489 he was sent to Perugia to study at the Sapienza, and here, while continuing his studies, he was to gain his first experience of the harsh realities of Italian political life, and to make contact with the families of the political establishment outside Rome. Perugia, ancient capital of Umbria, was an important papal city with a town population of 20,000 and some 46,000 in its rich countryside, the *contado*; it was also the most turbulent town in Italy, with a long history of violence stretching back over centuries. The political situation in Perugia was in many ways typical of that pertaining in other papal cities such as Bologna. Officially government was shared between papal officials and the communal magistrates, the ten Priori, but in fact city life was dominated by the tough, unruly Baglioni family, the brothers Guido and Ridolfo and their eight sons, Cesare's contemporaries, of whom Gian Paolo, later to become his condottiere, was the leader. Cesare, as the son of the powerful Vice-Chancellor, must have been frequently in company with Gian Paolo and his brothers, whose houses in the 'Baglioni' quarter of the town near the Porta Marzia were within a stone's throw of the Sapienza building, and he probably went hunting with them on their estates of Bastia and Spello in the *contado* of Perugia. Through them he would have come into contact with the signorial network of Umbria, the Marches and Tuscany – families like the Vitellis, vicars of Città de Castello. At Perugia, Cesare's eyes were opened to the true position within the States of the Church, a valuable lesson for the future.

Meanwhile Rodrigo had not abated his efforts to advance his son's career, and in September 1491 he obtained for him the rich prize of his first bishopric – that of Pamplona, ancient capital of the kingdom of Navarre. While Cesare was no doubt content to be a bishop with rich revenues and no duties, his new flock received the news with mutinous indignation. Their Bishop-elect was only fifteen, and had not yet taken holy orders; his sole qualification for his appointment lay in his being the illegitimate son of the Vice-Chancellor. Rodrigo attempted to calm the defiant Navarrese, ingenuously declaring the reasons for Cesare's elevation to be his 'merits, virtue and doctrine', while Cesare, who was spending his university vacation hunting at the Borgia citadel of Soriano, hastened to write a pastoral letter in Spanish to 'our magnificent and honourable friends' the clergy of Pamplona, commending a certain Martin Zapata to them as his representative. Despite the soothing words of the Borgias, father and son, the Navarrese remained rebellious until Pope Innocent himself was obliged to intervene with a penal admonition against those who might attempt to usurp the see of Pamplona and appropriate its revenues.

And so it was as Bishop-elect of Pamplona that Cesare, after two years at Perugia, went to attend the University of Pisa in the autumn of 1491. There he was to study for his doctorate in law under the famous Milanese jurist Filippo Decio, but the high reputation of the Pisan law school was not the only reason that prompted Rodrigo to send him. At Pisa, Cesare would be entering the territory of the Medicis, a family with which Rodrigo was anxious to be on good terms. In a letter to Lorenzo de' Medici, Rodrigo wrote that he was sending 'the Bishop of Pamplona' to Pisa to be under Lorenzo's 'wing and protection' as a 'means and pledge of the great love' which he bore for the house of Medici. As Rodrigo well knew, Lorenzo's second son Giovanni, Cesare's exact contemporary (born in December 1475), and like him destined for the Church, would be his fellow-student at the University of Pisa.

Lorenzo, who was equally anxious to take advantage of Rodrigo Borgia's influence at the Vatican, had doubtless instructed his son to behave in a friendly manner towards 'il Pamplona' as Cesare was now known, and paternal pressure on both sides ensured that they saw a good deal of each other. But Giovanni's true reaction to the young Borgia was probably reflected in his chancellor Ser Stefano's comments on Cesare's Spanish household: 'It seems to us that these men of his who surround him are little men who have small consideration for behaviour and have all the appearance of "marrani".'

Moreover the style in which the young Bishop of Pamplona lived seems to have exacerbated relations between the Medici and Borgia households. Rodrigo, with some of the instinct of the parvenu, was determined that Cesare at Pisa should outshine the other aristocratic students, and the ostentatious luxury of his life-style was enough to make even a Medici feel inferior. Ser Stefano reported: 'We wished to invite him [Cesare] here one morning to dine, and, if the weather is good it could be this week ... It is true that he has come so well provided with hangings and silver that our not having anything to equal it has left us a little perplexed ...'

The rivalry between the two may have extended to other more serious fields. Cesare was a brilliant student; even the hostile historian Paolo Giovio, who otherwise had nothing but ill to say of him, was forced to admit of his performance at his laureate that 'he had gained such profit [from his studies] that, with ardent mind, he discussed learnedly the questions put to him both in canon and civil law.' In any event he must have gained his laureate before Giovanni was awarded his, since he figured as one of the *arguenti*, disputants, in the debate for Giovanni's laureate. Giovanni, legitimate son of one of the great families of Italy, probably secretly despised and resented the bastard son of the Catalan Borgia as an upstart, and possibly Cesare sensed this, for the two young men were never friends even while both were living in Rome. It was a revealing portent of the reactions of the Italian political establishment to him in the future.

Giovanni left Pisa in March 1492 to take his seat in the College of Cardinals; on his way through Florence he saw his father for the last time. A month later Lorenzo died in his villa of Careggi, attended by his humanist friends Poliziano, Marsilio Ficino and Pico della Mirandola, and a Paduan doctor who pounded precious stones to make a potion which failed to save him. Contemporaries saw his early death at forty-one as a tragedy for Italy, since he more than any other politician had striven to keep peace. Ferrante of Naples remarked with gloomy foreboding: 'This man has lived long enough for his own immortal fame, but not for Italy. God grant that now he is dead men may not attempt that which they dared not do while he was alive.' From Pisa Cesare wrote a letter of condolence to Piero de' Medici, mingling classical references to *virtù* and *fama* with pious references suitable to his ecclesiastical calling, but Lorenzo's loss can hardly have affected him personally. Within a few months the death of another Italian political figure was imminent, an event of infinitely more interest to the Borgias.

Innocent VIII had been Pope for eight years, succeeding Sixtus IV in an election which had marked Rodrigo's first serious attempt on the Papacy. The election was a setback for the Borgias; it was also a triumph for Rodrigo's chief rival, Giuliano della Rovere, Cardinal of San Pietro in Vincoli and nephew of Sixtus. Giuliano, born of a poor Ligurian family in the village of Abizzola near Savona in 1443, owed his career – like Rodrigo – to the elevation of his uncle to the Papacy. He had been made Cardinal at twenty-five, heaped with honours, benefices and abbeys by his uncle, and like Rodrigo he had pursued a policy of collecting strategic strongpoints round Rome. He was intelligent, devious and violent, altogether a formidable opponent.

In 1484, when Giuliano's uncle Sixtus IV died, Rodrigo Borgia was fifty-three, della Rovere his junior by twelve years. The conclave which followed Sixtus' death was Rodrigo's first serious attempt on the Papacy; it was also the first round in a long struggle for power between Giuliano and the Borgias which was to play a part in the destiny of Rodrigo's son Cesare. In the conclave of 16 August 1484, Giuliano and Rodrigo were the two main candidates, but the first ballot ended in stalemate, and Giuliano, recognizing that neither he nor Borgia would succeed in obtaining a majority, worked skilfully behind the scenes to secure the election of one of his party, the Genoese Cardinal Cibo, who spent the night buying votes with signed agreements promising rewards. Rodrigo, recognizing defeat, also came to terms, and on 29 August Gian Battista Cibo was elected as Pope Innocent VIII. It was clear to everyone that Giuliano della Rovere would be the power behind the throne. 'Send a good letter to the Cardinal of San Pietro [della Rovere],' the Florentine envoy Vespucci wrote to Lorenzo de' Medici, 'for he is Pope and more than Pope.' The first round in the contest had ended decisively in favour of della Rovere.

For Rodrigo it was a check, but in no way a final one, to the papal ambitions which he had no intention of abandoning. He spent the years of Innocent's Papacy rebuilding his position, advancing his family, fortifying his Spanish connections and emphasizing his prestige in Rome in the most ostentatious manner. His household itself was indicative of his grand designs, befitting in every way his rank as a prince of the Church and an aspirant for its highest prize. He was the richest cardinal in Rome after the Frenchman d'Estouteville, and his palace on the Corso (remains of which can be seen today in the Sforza Cesarini palace) with its three-storied loggias and Tuscan columns was compared by Pius II with the Golden House of Nero. Jacopo da Volterra, describing Rodrigo's wealth, wrote:

> His papal offices, his numerous abbeys in Italy and Spain, and his three bishoprics of Valencia, Porto and Cartagena, yield him a vast income, and it is said that the office of Vice-Chancellor alone brings him in 8000 gold florins. His plate, his pearls, his stuffs embroidered with silk and gold, and his books in every department of learning are very numerous, and all are of a magnificence worthy of a king or a pope. I need not mention the innumerable bed-hangings, the trappings for his horses ... nor his magnificent wardrobe, nor the vast amount of gold coin in his possession ...

Rodrigo Borgia was a showman, but the object of all his magnificence was not mere display. It was to impress the world with his own importance and thus his suitability to succeed to the chair of St Peter.

Now, in 1492, his hour had come. Pope Innocent's health began to fail in March, and by mid-July it was clear that he was dying. He was too weak to take any nourishment other than human milk, and horrible stories flew round Rome that a Jewish physician had injected the moribund Pope with the life-blood of three ten-year-old children, who had died as a result. The Mantuan ambassador sent home reports of bitter and unseemly rows between Rodrigo and Giuliano della Rovere, who quarrelled like schoolboys over the sickbed of the dying Pope. When Rodrigo urged Innocent to hand the keys of the fortress of Sant'Angelo over to the College of Cardinals for safe keeping, Giuliano insultingly reminded the Pope that Rodrigo was a Catalan. Infuriated, Rodrigo exploded: 'If we were not in the presence of Our Lord the Pope, I would show you who is Vice-Chancellor ...' To which Giuliano angrily retorted that 'if they had not been in His Holiness' presence, he would show him he had no fear of him'. Both men knew that the second round in their struggle for the Papacy was about to begin.

Innocent died on 25 July 1492; on 6 August the twenty-five cardinals present in Rome went into conclave to elect a new Pope. Cesare, who was at Siena preparing his horse for the Palio races, would have been kept informed of events at Rome. He knew that his family's future and his own hung upon the result of this election; Rodrigo was now sixty-one and this might well be his last chance of the Papacy. Cesare must also have been aware that his father's prospects of success were not generally considered high. Rodrigo was not supported by any of the powers principally concerned in the election, France, Naples or Milan, and his Spanish blood was regarded as a handicap in what was traditionally an Italian contest. The College of Cardinals was split into two political alignments. The first, led by Giuliano, was primarily anti-Milanese, and was supported by the French, the Venetians, the Colonna and the Savelli families. Giuliano hoped to block Rodrigo Borgia at all costs and to repeat his previous success by securing the election of a candidate indebted to himself, either the Portuguese Costa or the Venetian Zeno. The second party represented the Milanese interest, led by Ludovico Sforza's brother Ascanio, an old friend and political ally of Rodrigo's, who was supported by the cardinals who opposed Giuliano's pro-French stance, and by the Orsinis and Contis who automatically did the opposite to the Colonnas. Ascanio's candidates were the Neapolitan Cardinal Caraffa and Rodrigo Borgia.

Suspense mounted in Rome during the five days of the conclave. Enemies profited by the interregnum to pay off old scores, while rumours flew as to the nature of the dealings going on within the Vatican, and the diarist Infessura reported that four mules loaded with silver had been seen going from Rodrigo's palace to that of Ascanio. In fact, fear of France and mutual distrust between the two parties was influencing the election in Rodrigo's favour. He was one of the leading candidates from the first scrutiny on; after the third scrutiny, Ascanio Sforza, probably influenced by the prospect of receiving the vice-chancellorship which would be vacated on Borgia's election, switched the votes of his party behind Rodrigo. On the morning of 11 August, under a leaden sky lit by fitful summer lightning, the Romans waiting before St Peter's heard a prelate declaim the traditional formula: '*Pontificem habemus.*' Rodrigo Borgia was now Pope Alexander vi.

At four o'clock that afternoon, a sweating courier brought the news to Siena, having covered the distance from Rome in ten hours. Cesare did not wait to see his horse race, but hurried back to Pisa to wait his father's orders and make his preparations for departure. Ten days later he left for the castle of Spoleto; he was not to attend his father's coronation. But for Cesare, as he rode southward, a new life was about to begin.

III

THE POPE'S LIEUTENANT

'DIVINE Alexander, Alexander the Great!' the Romans shouted as Alexander VI rode through the streets from the Vatican to the Lateran basilica for his coronation on 26 August. 'Anthony was not received with as much splendour by Cleopatra as Alexander by the Romans,' one observer commented. Preceded by thirteen glittering squadrons of men-at-arms, and the cardinals' households dressed in a kaleidoscope of rich stuffs and colours, 'lion-coloured' velvet, crimson silk, cloth of silver, rose damask, Alexander proceeded to the Lateran through streets hung with tapestries, decorated with garlands and triumphal arches. Naturally the most prominent device was the Borgia bull, spouting water and 'most delicate wine' outside the church of San Marco, and proudly displayed on the Pope's personal banner carried before him by Count Antonio della Mirandola, and on the huge papal standard, twelve metres long and four wide, floating over the fortress of Sant'Angelo.

The significance of this rampant family pride was not lost upon the Roman nobility, men like Virginio Orsini, head of his house, who played their traditional parts in the celebrations for the Borgia Pope with some misgiving. 'The Romans and courtiers show little enthusiasm for this promotion,' the Florentine envoy Filippo Valori reported. Proud, turbulent and grasping, the great Roman families, the Orsinis, Colonnas, Caetanis, Savellis, Contis and their adherents, feared a strong Pope above all things, and memories of the first Borgia Papacy were still alive in their minds. They knew Alexander well, as a man of great ability and ambition, with a large family whose advancement could only be at their expense. And accusations of simony flew round Rome, based on Alexander's distribution of offices and benefices to his cardinal supporters, principally Ascanio, who as the man chiefly responsible for his election naturally received the lion's share, the vice-chancellorship with Rodrigo Borgia's own palace and other rich rewards, and moved into the Vatican to take up an honoured position in apartments near Alexander's own. 'He [Alexander] gave all his goods to the poor,' the antipapal diarist Infessura commented sarcastically, while the satirist Sannazaro directed a telling epigram from the court of Naples: 'Alexander sells the keys, the altars, Christ himself – he has the right to sell them, he had bought them first.' But, as a recent historian has pointed out, the distribution of wealth and honours which followed Borgia's election was in line with recently established practice, and Rodrigo differed from his predecessors only in that he had more to give.

In fact, reactions generally were favourable to Alexander's election, and high hopes were entertained of him. The chronicler Sigismondo de' Conti wrote:

> It is now thirty-seven years since his uncle Calixtus III made him a Cardinal, and during that time he never missed a single Consistory unless prevented by illness from attending, which was rare. Throughout the reigns of Pius II, Paul II, Sixtus IV and Innocent VIII he was always an important personage; he had been Legate in Spain and Italy. Few people understood etiquette as well as he did; he knew how to make the most of himself, and took pains to shine in conversation and to be dignified in his manners. In the latter point his majestic stature gave him an advantage. Also he was just at the age, about sixty, at which Aristotle says men are wisest; robust in body, vigorous in mind, he was admirably equipped for his new position.

Wisdom, mental vigour, robust health, international and administrative experience, and a commanding presence – de' Conti made no mention of saintliness or moral worth. The qualities he praised in Alexander VI were precisely those which today would be required of the chairman of a great multinational corporation.

Alexander commenced his Papacy with every sign of good intentions. Even Infessura admired the vigour of his provisions for law and order in the turbulent Eternal City, while the promises he made on his election, including the perennial and never-observed pledge to reform the Church, were designed to calm everyone's fears. The Mantuan envoy Manfredo Manfredi wrote from Florence on 17 August: 'The Pope has promised to do many things towards the reformation of the court, to dismiss the secretaries and many tyrannical officials,

to keep his children away from Rome, and he will make many praise-
worthy promotions, and it is said that he will be a glorious pontiff.'
However, despite Alexander's promises, many seasoned observers like
Valori preferred to suspend judgement: 'The opinion that is held of
the new Pontiff is various: many think that he will occupy this Chair
with great majesty and pomp, since His Holiness is desirous of fame
and glory: and to do this he will be the father of all and maintain
peace. Many are of the opposite opinion: that to dominate everything
properly he will be an intriguing Pope ...'

As far as his children were concerned, Alexander kept to the letter,
if not the spirit, of his election promises – at least for a few months.
On his orders, Cesare remained out of sight in the papal castle of
Spoleto, but his father had not forgotten him and within a week of his
coronation he bestowed upon him his own former archbishopric of
Valencia, worth 16,000 ducats a year. Cesare, aged seventeen, was
quite aware of the change in his circumstances wrought by his father's
election; on 5 October he wrote from Spoleto to Piero de' Medici,
who had succeeded his father as virtual ruler of Florence, asking him
for a professorship in law at Pisa for his follower Francisco Remolines,
in return for which he promised to do all in his power for the Medicis
'at the court of Rome'. Other members of the family also received
their share in the distribution of offices and honours which traditionally followed the election of a new pope, and for the second time within
a century Borgia relations and hangers-on swarmed in the Vatican.
The Ferrarese ambassador Giovanni Andrea Boccaccio wrote sourly
in November, three months after Alexander's election: 'Not even ten
papacies would suffice to content this horde of relations.'

Indeed, within a few months of their father's elevation the young
Borgias were once again reunited with him in Rome. Cesare came
from Spoleto to take up residence in a palace in the Borgo, the recently
built quarter which had grown up round the Vatican. Boccaccio
called upon him there early in March 1493 and wrote this description of the seventeen-year-old Cesare to his master, Duke Ercole
d'Este:

> The day before yesterday I went to find Cesare at his house in Tras-
> tevere. He was on the point of going out for the hunt; he was wear-
> ing a worldly garment of silk and had his sword at his side. He
> had only a little tonsure like a simple priest. I rode at his side and
> conversed with him at length. I am on intimate terms with him.

He possesses marked genius and a charming personality. He has the manners of a son of a great prince; above all he is lively and merry and fond of society; being very modest, his bearing is much better than that of the Duke of Gandia, his brother ...

Significantly he added: 'The Archbishop of Valencia has never had inclination for the priesthood; but his benefices bring him 16,000 ducats.'

But if Cesare had the intelligence not to be seen to allow his newly acquired importance to go to his head, the same could not be said of his brother Juan Gandia, whose bearing, as Boccaccio remarked, was far from modest. Indeed Juan, the favourite, seems to have occupied the limelight of attention at this time. Burchard, the papal master of ceremonies, while making no references to Cesare, frequently recorded Alexander's excursions with Juan, who was dressed in the fashionable Turkish style, and accompanied by Prince Djem, the brother of Sultan Bajazet. Bajazet, having defeated Djem in a struggle for the succession, paid Alexander 40,000 ducats a year to keep his brother as a pampered prisoner in the Vatican, provided with pastimes of all sorts, hunting, music, banquets and wine, of which he was particularly fond. The Mantuan painter Mantegna, who was working in the Belvedere villa of the Vatican when Djem arrived there in 1489, gave a description of him in which the Turkish prince appeared like a great caged wild beast, dignified, somnolent and full of a contained rage: 'He walks like an elephant with a measured step ... he often keeps his eyes half-closed. His nature is cruel, and they say he had killed four people: today he has severely maltreated an interpreter. His people are afraid of him. He takes little notice of what passes, as if he did not understand ... The expression of his face is ferocious, especially when Bacchus has been with him.'

While the Romans had become accustomed to the exotic presence of the Sultan's brother in the Pope's entourage, the circumstances of his daughter Lucrezia's household provoked ribald comment. Vannozza was by now completely in the background, living with her husband Canale in her own house in the Regola quarter, and exercised no influence on Vatican affairs. The backstairs approach to the Pope used by ambassadors and supplicants for papal favours lay through the palace of Santa Maria in Portico at the steps of the Vatican, where Lucrezia lived with the two other women closest to Alexander, his cousin and confidante Adriana de Mila Orsini and her daughter-in-law Giulia Farnese.

Giulia Farnese was of a blonde beauty so dazzling that she was known as 'La Bella'. She had been married at fifteen in 1489 to Orsino Orsini, the son of Adriana and her late husband Ludovico. Little is known of Orsini beyond the facts that he was blind in one eye, nicknamed 'Monoculus', soon became a notorious cuckold, and died an ignominious death in 1500, killed by a falling roof in the country castle where he was kept by his wife's lover at a safe distance from Rome. But Giulia's beauty was to be the foundation of her family's fortunes, the source of the wealth that built the superb Farnese palaces and brought her brother Alessandro Farnese to the papal throne as Paul III. She was the last passion of Rodrigo Borgia's passionate life, her wedding took place in his palace, and he was the first witness to the marriage contract. Their liaison must have begun soon afterwards, for in 1492 she bore a daughter, Laura, whom her brother-in-law Puccio Pucci openly asserted to be not Orsino's but Rodrigo's child. By 1493 the nineteen-year-old Giulia's relationship with the sixty-two-year-old Pope was known all over Italy; contemporary diarists referred to her as 'his concubine' or 'the bride of Christ'. The three women, Alexander's daughter, his mistress and his cousin, lived in the closest intimacy. Adriana actively encouraged Alexander's liaison with Giulia, and seems to have found nothing repellent in the fact of her cousin openly cuckolding her son. The relationship increased her own influence in the Vatican; moreover she was a Borgia by birth, an Orsini only by marriage, and where the Borgias were concerned, blood relationships came above all other ties.

Cesare, Juan and Lucrezia had their place in Alexander's overall plan for his family, altered in its scope, but not in its main essentials, by his accession to the Papacy. The two elder sons were to play a dual role in the interests of the family and the Church; Cesare, the churchman, was to become a cardinal, the first step towards the Papacy, while Juan, as the sword arm, would be appointed Gonfalonier and Captain General of the Church, commander of the papal armies. Rumours of Alexander's intentions were current in diplomatic circles as early as February 1493, when the Mantuan envoy Fioramonte Brognolo wrote to Isabella d'Este, wife of Francesco Gonzaga: 'Many say that the Pope will make Captain General or Gonfalonier the Duke of Gandia [Juan] ... and that they will appoint Cardinals among whom is nominated a brother of this Duke.' Meanwhile

Lucrezia was approaching marriageable age, and a suitable match had been found for her. On 12 February 1493 she was betrothed to Giovanni Sforza, lord of Pesaro, in a formal ceremony in the Vatican. Negotiations for the marriage had been going on in secret since the previous October, complicated by the fact that Lucrezia, according to her father's previous Spanish dynastic schemes, had been betrothed to first one and then another young Spanish nobleman. In fact the last of the two, the Count of Aversa, had arrived in Rome to claim his bride almost simultaneously with Sforza. 'There is much gossip about Pesaro's marriage,' the Ferrarese envoy reported. 'The first bridegroom is still here, raising a great hue and cry, as a Catalan, saying he will protest to all the princes and potentates of Christendom; but will he, nil he, he will have to submit.' Eventually the angry Spaniard, recognizing the inevitable, was bought off with a gift of 3000 ducats, and the thirteen-year-old Lucrezia was safely betrothed to Giovanni, a widower of twenty-six, and as nephew to Ludovico il Moro and Cardinal Ascanio, a member of the Milanese house of Sforza.

The match was a political one, and must be seen against the background of the rapidly disintegrating situation of Italy which Alexander inherited on his accession. Relations between two of the major states, Milan and Naples, were nearing breaking-point in a quarrel caused by Ludovico Sforza's ambitions for the dukedom of Milan, and by his treatment of the rightful heir, his nephew Duke Gian Galeazzo, whom he had confined to the gilded cage of the castle of Pavia, while he managed Milanese affairs in his stead. Gian Galeazzo, an indolent youth, seemed quite content to spend his days hunting and leave business to his domineering uncle, but his spirited wife, Isabella d'Aragona, granddaughter of King Ferrante of Naples, wrote bitter letters to her grandfather complaining of Ludovico's treatment of her husband and herself, and warning of his ambitions for the dukedom. Ferrante was roused to an absolute determination to thwart Ludovico's ambitions at all costs, and the two states were now at loggerheads – with the Pope, for whose favours they intrigued, very much the man in the middle.

Beyond the frontiers of this internal Italian dispute loomed the shadow of two foreign powers, France and Spain, both with dynastic claims to the kingdom of Naples, ruled since 1442 by a branch of Ferdinand's own house of Aragon. The dynastic claims of the dukes of Anjou to Naples had now passed to the crown of France, whose present holder the young Charles VIII dreamed of glory, and thanks to the successes of his predecessor Louis XI had the resources of a great army and a united country to enable him to fulfil his dream.

The glamour of Italy, economically rich and politically weak, was once again exercising the irresistible fascination it had held for foreign invaders since the days of the Roman Empire. Guicciardini, writing his great *History of Italy* in the next century, saw the years up to 1490 as the golden age of the Italian state system:

> Italy had never enjoyed such prosperity, or known so favourable a situation as that in which it found itself so securely at rest in the year of our Christian salvation 1490, and the years immediately before and after. The greatest peace and tranquillity reigned everywhere; the land under cultivation no less in the most mountainous and arid regions than in the most fertile plains and areas; dominated by no power other than her own, not only did Italy abound in inhabitants, merchandise and riches, but she was also highly renowned for the magnificence of many princes, for the splendour of so many most noble and beautiful cities, as the seat and majesty of religion, and flourishing with men most skilful in the administration of public affairs and most nobly talented in all disciplines and distinguished and industrious in all the arts. Nor was Italy lacking in military glory according to the standards of that time, and adorned with so many gifts that she deservedly held a celebrated name and a reputation among all the nations.

It was a rose-coloured picture, but not entirely untrue, of a country whose peace was soon to be brutally shattered in a catastrophe for which the ambition of Ludovico Sforza of Milan was very largely responsible. In order to rid himself of his enemy Ferrante of Naples, Ludovico had conceived the plan of inviting the King of France to invade Italy to assert his claims to the kingdom of Naples, and to that end his agents were bribing and intriguing at the court of France.

Initially Alexander had inclined to alliance with the Sforzas, but as Pope he could hardly encourage the destruction of Naples and the invasion of Italy in the furtherance of Ludovico Sforza's ambitions. Moreover the cause of the house of Aragon in Naples was that of his old ally Ferdinand. Lucrezia's wedding to Giovanni Sforza was celebrated in the Vatican on 12 June 1493, but within a very short time of her marriage there were signs that her father was preparing to switch his allegiances.

Eight days after her wedding, Don Diego Lopez de Haro, the envoy of the Spanish sovereigns Isabella of Castile and Ferdinand of Aragon, arrived in Rome to inform the Pope that Ferdinand considered the Aragonese cause in Naples as his own. His mission initiated a new round of negotiations between Alexander and Ferdinand, described by a Venetian envoy as 'bargaining between Catalan and Catalan'. From Alexander Ferdinand needed not only his support for the Aragonese cause in Naples, but also a decision in Spain's favour over the sovereignty of the new worlds across the Atlantic opened up for Spain by Columbus' voyage of 1492. In return Ferdinand was prepared to receive Juan Gandia at court and to give him Maria Enriquez, his own cousin, fiancée of the late Pedro Luis, to wife. At the same time Ferrante backed up his protector's offer with another Borgia–Aragon marriage: Jofre was to be betrothed to Sancia, a natural daughter of Ferrante's son, Alfonso, Duke of Calabria.

These were offers of the kind which Alexander found irresistible. The famous Alexandrine bulls which assured Spanish New World expansion in the face of Portugal's anterior privileges were dispatched in the beginning of July, one month before Juan, gorgeously equipped, left to claim his Spanish bride. On 6 August the Mantuan envoy Cattaneo reported: 'The Duke of Gandia, nephew of the Pope, has been three days at Ostia ... and this Duke leaves very rich and full of jewels, money and other moveable goods and precious silver. They say he will return within a year, but will leave all that in Spain, and come for another harvest.' A fortnight later Jofre, speedily if somewhat belatedly legitimized by Alexander on 6 August, was married by proxy to Sancia of Aragon. A few days after Gandia's departure, the envoy of Charles VIII of France, Perron de Baschi, arrived in Rome to claim the investiture of the crown of Naples for his master. Alexander answered him in the vaguest possible terms, and he departed empty-handed.

Meanwhile Alexander's plans for Cesare too were nearing fruition. Preparations for the removal of the main stumbling block to the cardinalate, his illegitimacy, had been going on since early February, on the basis that he was not illegitimate but the lawful son of Domenico da Rignano and his wife Vannozza. In line with this pretence, Alexander issued a bull on 20 September 1493 declaring Cesare to be the legitimate son of Domenico and Vannozza (in a second, secret bull issued on the same day he testified that Cesare was his own son). Cardinals Pallavicini and Orsini, who had been charged with the examination of Cesare's status, were thus enabled to conclude that he was legitimate, and therefore eligible for admission to the Sacred College.

Cesare's nomination caused a furore; when Giuliano della Rovere heard the news he gave a bellow of rage and took to his bed with a fever, muttering that he would not allow the Sacred College to be thus 'profaned and abused'. The appointment of Cesare, barely eighteen and not yet in Holy Orders, was certainly scandalous, as was that of Ippolito d'Este, who was only fifteen, and Alessandro Farnese, Giulia's brother, whom the Romans from now on called 'the petticoat cardinal'. But the other appointments were men of worth, including two Frenchmen, one Englishman, John Morton, Archbishop of Canterbury, and the eminent Venetian theologian Domenico Grimani. The real reason for the rage of Giuliano and his followers among the cardinals was because they rightly interpreted the new nominations as a move by Alexander to pack the College with non-Italians and papal partisans in order to stifle their opposition.

The proposed list was put to the cardinals for approval on 18 September. 'Such discord has never been seen,' wrote the Mantuan envoy, who reported that Alexander was furious at the attitude of the opposition cardinals and told them 'that they wanted to slander him and put him in travail, but that he would show them who Pope Alexander vi was if they persisted, and that at Christmas he would make as many again despite them, and nonetheless they would not chase him from Rome ...' When the nominations were put to the vote in consistory on 20 September, the final decision was a close one; Cattaneo reported that ten cardinals opposed, and eleven agreed with the Pope, 'some only by their presence, saying neither yea nor nay...' Alexander had won by the skin of his teeth.

Cesare received the news of his nomination to the cardinalate at Caprarola, where he had gone with Vannozza and Canale to escape the late summer heat and the plague which was rampant in Rome. Described at this time by the Florentine chancellor Ser Antonio da Colle as 'very young in all his actions', he had been spending his time hunting and writing aggressive letters to the councillors of Siena about the disputed result of a race for the Palio. The race had taken place on 16 August, and had been won by Cesare's horse as the result of a trick by his jockey, who threw himself off at the crucial moment, thus lightening the horse and enabling it to win. Francesco Gonzaga, Marquis of Mantua, whose horse came second, not unnaturally lodged a protest which was upheld by the judges. Cesare, who could not bear to be beaten at anything, immediately sat down to write a letter to the governors of Siena enlisting their support, in which he did not fail to hint that his friendship could be more useful to them than that of a simple Marquis of Mantua: 'Have respect to our honour, commanding that the Palio should be given [to us], in which you will give us singular pleasure and we will remain obligated to do things which will be to the pleasure and honour of your Magnificent persons and most noble commune.'

History has not recorded the outcome of the Palio row, but the time had now arrived when Cesare would have more important affairs to attend to than quarrels involving crooked racing; from now on he could no longer afford to be 'very young in all his actions'. On 17 October he made his formal entry into Rome to take up his new appointment as Cardinal of Valencia, prince of the Church and counsellor to his father the Pope. Cattaneo reported: 'This morning they will give the ring and title to the new cardinals and the nephew of the Pope, who was outside Rome in a castle, despite the plague came to the gate and was received by all the cardinals with great pomp, something outside their custom ...' At the same time a testimony to his new importance in the eyes of the world reached him in the form of a letter from Charles VIII of France, invoking his influence with Alexander to obtain a cardinal's hat for his confidential minister Briçonnet, Archbishop of Saint Malo. The letter was emblematic of the future; Cesare's political initiation and his new role as his father's lieutenant were to develop against the threatening background of the French invasion of Italy.

The protagonist of the impending invasion, Charles VIII of France, was neither physically nor intellectually impressive. The Venetian ambassador Contarini described him in 1493 at the age of twenty-two as 'small and ill-formed in person, with an ugly face, large lustreless eyes which seem to be short-sighted, an enormous aquiline nose, and thick lips, which are continually parted; he stutters, and has a nervous twitching of the hands which is unpleasing to watch. In my opinion ... he is not of much account either physically or mentally.' Guiccardini was even more severe on the young King, calling him 'more like a monster than a man'. Not only, he continued:

... was he without any learning or skill but he hardly knew the letters of the alphabet; a mind yearning greedily to rule, but capable of doing anything but that, since he was always surrounded by courtiers over whom he maintained neither majesty nor authority ... Desirous of glory but more open to impulse than advice, generous but inconsiderate and acting without measure or distinction, sometimes immutable in his decisions but often on the basis of a poorly founded stubbornness rather than constancy ...

Guicciardini was naturally prejudiced against the man who brought so much unhappiness to his country. In fact Charles was not entirely lacking in good qualities; contemporary French chroniclers, and especially Philippe de Comines, agreed on his unfailing kindness, his excessive softness of heart. He was not unintelligent and had a capacity for the appreciation of beauty which was aroused when he saw the cities – and the women – of Italy. He was young and naive, with a pathetic desire for glory upon which the ambassadors of Ludovico il Moro had played in their intrigues to entice him to Italy. The French court was divided as to the feasibility of invasion, and feeling as a whole ran against it – except, that is, among those who had been encouraged by Milanese bribes – but the conquest of Naples had become an *idée fixe* with the young King. Ludovico was surprised and somewhat taken aback by Charles' resolution. With his changeable disposition he now began to have second thoughts about the desirability of having a large French army on his doorstep. However, having set events in motion it was too late to turn back; Charles' mind was made up. Having made peace with his three principal enemies, the Empire, England and Spain, he was now intent on the Naples expedition.

The attitude of the Pope was central to the whole question of the invasion and its objective. To reach Naples the French army would have to pass through the Papal States, and it needed a friendly Pope to give them free passage. If Charles succeeded in conquering Naples, the attitude of the Pope was still vital to him, since Alexander alone had the right of investiture to the Kingdom. The Aragonese marriages of Alexander's children, and the diplomatic rebuff he had administered to Perron de Baschi, worried the French, who were nonetheless confident that a combination of force and spiritual blackmail would bring him to heel. As early as September 1493 the King's councillors told the Milanese envoys that there were two ways by which the King, without so much as stirring from his palace, could make the Pope change his tune. One was the threat of a Council, in which the Emperor could easily be induced to cooperate; the other was a refusal of obedience and of the disposition of benefices in France which were worth a considerable revenue to Rome. In other words, if the might of the French armies did not make Alexander tremble, the threat of a Council, which would have the power to depose him, would. But as it turned out they underestimated both Alexander's strength of will and his firmness of purpose in defence of what he believed to be the interests of the Church and of Italy.

Alexander was indeed worried by the threat to his position. The opposition in the College of Cardinals was strong, led of course by Giuliano della Rovere, a personal enemy whom he did not underestimate, and of whose single-minded ambition for the papal chair he was well aware. Such hostility, with the added force of a French army, could indeed mean danger – and moreover there had been mutterings of a schism and of appeals to a Council against him at the time of the cardinals' nominations in September.

During these anxious times Cesare was at his father's side, and at the end of October he accompanied Alexander on a tour of Viterbo and Orvieto. This was in fact a politico-military reconnaissance, since they were key cities of the Papal States through which the French would pass in the event of an invasion. He supported his father too in family affairs; Alexander was deeply worried by reports from Spain of Juan's misbehaviour, and above all that he had not consummated his marriage. He wrote angrily to Juan, reproving him for his 'disorders and excesses', his bad behaviour to his wife, and his alleged non-consummation, accusing him of spending the money he had taken with him 'in gambling and dissolution' and of trying to lay hands on the family revenues in Valencia. Although the charge of non-consummation proved to be unfounded, the other allegations concerning Gandia's behaviour were all too true. From Orvieto Cesare seconded his father with a series of brotherly missives to Juan, saying that although he did not believe the charges made against him, he besought him that his conduct should be such that only good reports reached the ears of the Pope: 'Try to fulfil the hope which His Holiness has always founded upon you, if you wish him a long life, in which is all our good, our life and exaltation; and if you have compassion for me, see that these reports that give His Holiness so much pain should cease ...' The period of Cesare's immaturity was over; as French pressure on the Pope over Naples hardened through

the winter of 1493 and the spring of 1494 he became increasingly involved in politics, privy to all his father's negotiations.

The crux came early in 1494 – 'a most unhappy year for Italy, and
in truth the beginning of those years of misfortune', wrote Guicciardini. On 27 January Ferrante of Naples died, and the need for a decision over the investiture of his successor became acute. Charles VIII
at once dispatched an embassy to Rome, threatening that if Alexander
favoured Ferrante's heir Alfonso he would call for a General Council,
and at the same time he entered into communication with the dangerous Giuliano della Rovere. Alexander, who had hitherto tried to keep
up the appearance of being uncommitted, was now forced to come
out into the open. He had in fact already decided that French control
of Naples would be fatal to the independence of the Papacy, while
his natural inclinations favoured the Aragonese. On 16 March, in
public consistory, he declared himself favourable to Alfonso's claims,
and two days later, against bitter opposition from Giuliano, now
joined by the pro-French, violently anti-Neapolitan Ascanio Sforza,
a bull was read appointing his nephew Juan Borgia, Cardinal of Monreale, as Legate for Alfonso's coronation. The next day Alexander
sent Charles a Golden Rose to palliate this rebuff.

It was too late: on 17 March Charles announced his intention of
invading Italy, and events moved with gathering momentum. The
cardinals opposed to Alexander began to leave Rome to gather round
the French King, which gave the forthcoming invasion an increasingly ecclesiastical character as Alexander's enemies called for a
General Council, reform of the Church, and the deposition of the Pope
on the grounds of his simoniacal election. On 23 April Giuliano, refusing the desperate attempts by Alfonso of Naples and Virginio Orsini
to reconcile him with the Pope, fled from his fortress at Ostia, which
he left in the hands of his friends the Colonnas. From Genoa he went
to his archiepiscopal palace at Avignon, and from thence to the
French court, arriving on 1 June. In Guicciardini's words, 'he was
received by the King with the greatest honour and ceremony, and
joined with the others who were making ready to loose troubles upon
Italy'.

Defiantly, Alexander strengthened his bonds with Naples; in the
first week of April, through the medium of Virginio Orsini, agreement
was reached between Alexander and Alfonso of Naples, by which
Alfonso was made to pay dearly for the Pope's support. In return for
his coronation by the Legate Juan Borgia, Jofre was to be officially

married to Sancia with the title of Prince of Squillace and 40,000
ducats annual income, while Juan Gandia gained the principate of
Tricario and the counties of Carinola and Clarimonte, and Cesare
received numerous rich benefices. Cesare, as he proudly informed
Juan in a letter of 19 April, had taken part in all the negotiations:
'This agreement has been reached ten or twelve days ago, and Your
Grace will be amazed that I should not have informed you of it earlier,
but, finding myself somewhat indisposed when the aforesaid peace
was concluded, in which I have always been concerned from the beginning until the end, I left for the baths of Stigliano, where I have
been until yesterday, returning thence in good health by God's grace
...' The tone of the letter was somewhat condescending and elder-
brotherly, as if Cesare wished to impress upon Juan the relation in
which he now stood to his father: 'We have reason, my lord brother,
to kiss continually the ground on which His Holiness walks and to
pray always for the life of him who has made us so great; and therefore
I pray you to seek continually to serve and please His Holiness, in
a manner that you may show him on our behalf our gratitude in everything that we can.'

Cesare did not attend the double celebrations at Naples in the
second week of May when Alfonso was crowned and Jofre and Sancia
married by Juan Borgia of Monreale; he remained in Rome during
the difficult and anxious months preceding the French invasion. Alexander was isolated: he could expect no help from any of the European
powers, the loyalty of the Papal States was doubtful, and the French
had suborned the Roman nobles. The Neapolitan army, although
commanded by three of the most experienced condottieri in Italy,
Gian Jacopo Trivulzio and Niccolò and Virginio Orsini, could hardly
be expected to defeat the French single-handed; the papal forces were
insignificant, and of the two other major military powers in Italy,
Milan was on the side of the French, while Venice, as was her custom,
remained neutral. Florence, the Pope's other ally, was militarily weak.
Desperate, the Pope even appealed to the Sultan for help, but none
was forthcoming from any quarter, and so on 12 July Alexander and
Cesare rode to Virginio Orsini's stronghold of Vicovaro to meet King
Alfonso and agree on a combined plan of action. Alfonso with part
of the combined forces was to occupy Tagliacozzo, while Virginio
Orsini remained in the Campagna as a check on the Colonnas; the
mass of the allied armies under Alfonso's eldest son Ferrantino were
to march into the Romagna and threaten the territory of Ludovico

of Milan, while a fleet under Alfonso's brother Federigo was to attack Genoa. It was a reasonable plan, but unfortunately it was not put quickly enough into action. On 3 September 1494 Charles VIII crossed the Alps into Italy with the largest army seen in Europe for more than a century.

In his sermons for Lent 1494, the great preacher Savonarola had prophesied from his Florentine pulpit the coming of a 'new Cyrus' who would lead his army through the whole of Italy without breaking a lance or meeting with any resistance; the prophecy was about to come true. Although the Italians, with their appreciation of physical beauty, scoffed at the new Cyrus' dwarfish looks, they were impressed by the size of his army of some 30,000 men, and particularly by his artillery, forty heavy siege pieces which were more mobile and had a greater hitting power than contemporary Italian guns. The Italian princes flocked to do homage to the powerful 'barbarian' as soon as he reached Asti. It was there that Charles received news of the defeat of the Neapolitan fleet at Rapallo by his cousin Louis of Orleans, a victory which created an immense effect in Italy. After a bout of smallpox he resumed his triumphant march southward, stopping at Pavia to visit the sick Duke Gian Galeazzo in the great Sforza castle, where he returned empty words to Isabella's impassioned pleas for the defence of the rights of her ailing husband and his young heir. Ten days later Gian Galeazzo was dead. Ludovico Sforza, amid rumours, probably unfounded, that he had poisoned his nephew, achieved his ambition of the ducal crown.

'God is with the French,' wrote de Comines, who accompanied the expedition, amazed at the ease of their advance. It might have been more true to say that most of the Italians were not against them, and those who were, were physically powerless to oppose them. The bulk of the Papal–Neapolitan forces were stationed in the Romagna in the belief that Charles would choose the easy route down the east side of the peninsula, and that if he did not, the Florentines would hold the Apennine passes. But fortune did not favour Alexander. Due to the lateness of the season Charles and his commanders chose the most direct route south, through Tuscany, thus outflanking the allied forces in the Romagna, while the pusillanimous Piero de' Medici yielded up the Florentine fortresses without a fight. 'The sword has come!' Savonarola cried from the pulpit of the Duomo at Florence on All Saints' Day, 1 November; on the 9th the Florentines, disgusted with Piero, rose against the Medicis and plundered their palace. Two

weeks later Charles entered the city in triumph, welcomed as a liberator by the populace with cries of 'Viva Francia', and as the messenger
of God by Savonarola, now virtual ruler of the city. On 22 November
Charles issued a proclamation from Florence declaring that his object
was the recovery of the Holy Land, and that the possession of his
Neapolitan kingdom was a necessary step towards that goal. He
demanded free passage through the Papal States and wielded the
threat of a General Council and the deposition of the Pope.

At Rome, Alexander refused all attempts to persuade him to desert
Alfonso and win him to France. He declared to the envoys of the Duke
of Ferrara that he would rather leave Rome and give up both his
life and his tiara than become the slave of the King of France, who
was bent upon becoming the master of all Italy. 'And although he
might be a Spaniard, not the less for that did he love Italy, nor did
he wish to see her in the hands of anyone but Italians ...' The Ferrarese envoy reported that he spoke with such vehemence of word
and gesture that they seemed to come from the heart, and that at
times his eyes were brimming as if the tears would flow. In fact the
situation was now hopeless; the Colonnas had deserted the Pope in
mid-September, hoisting the French flag over the fortress at Ostia,
commanding the mouth of the Tiber. In mid-November Giuliano's
brother Giovanni della Rovere captured the papal envoy returning
from his mission to the Sultan, with letters (which may have been
forged) incriminating the head of Christendom with soliciting the
help of the enemy of the Faith against the Most Christian King of
France. By late November the French were pouring into the Papal
States, and their advance was so rapid that on 27 November they
captured Giulia Farnese and Adriana Orsini, Alexander's 'heart and
eyes', as Ludovico il Moro remarked. The French chivalrously
returned the Pope's women on 1 December, and on 10 December
Alexander's spirits were briefly raised by the arrival in Rome of the
Papal–Neapolitan force under Ferrantino. It was a vain hope; on 17
December the French captured Civita Vecchia, and the Orsinis surrendered their fortress of Bracciano north of Rome.

For Alexander and Cesare, waiting helplessly in the Vatican, it was
now a question of days. On the 18th everything was packed for flight
and valuables were sent to the castle of Sant'Angelo. On the 19th
the first French outposts appeared on Monte Mario and from the windows of the Vatican Alexander and Cesare could see the enemy
cavalry exercising their horses in the meadows under Sant'Angelo.

The scarcity of supplies in the city was becoming intolerable, and the Romans informed Alexander that if he did not come to terms with Charles within two days they would open the gates to the French. The allied commanders suggested that the Pope should flee to Naples, and that Cesare should guard the precious hostage Djem in the castle of Gaeta. Alexander rejected the idea. He did not intend to become a prisoner of Naples, and very probably considered that the sight of an empty Vatican would be too much of a temptation to Giuliano and the opposition cardinals who followed the King. He was a man of considerable physical courage, who had already proved that he did not lose his head in a crisis. His enemies in the French camp were pressing for a General Council and for his deposition; in these days of confusion and disaster he knew that to save his personal position it was necessary to come to terms personally with the young King, and being well aware of Charles' nature, he can have had few doubts as to the outcome of such a confrontation.

On the morning of Christmas Day he informed the cardinals and the allied commanders that he had decided to admit the King. The allied forces rode south to defend the kingdom of Naples, accompanied to the Lateran gate by Cesare, who then returned to the Vatican. During the night three French envoys entered Rome. When their suite coolly sat themselves in the places reserved for prelates in the palace chapel, the shocked master of ceremonies tried to oust them; Alexander told him angrily that he wished to destroy him and must let the French sit where they pleased. The Pope's troops, numbering only some thousand horse and a few infantry, occupied the Borgo. Alexander and Cesare shut themselves up in the Vatican with their Spanish bodyguard to await the coming of their conqueror.

Charles chose St Silvester's Day, 31 December, which his astrologers had predicted would be favourable, for his solemn entry into Alexander's capital. As he rode through mud and rain towards Rome, the young King bombarded Alexander's master of ceremonies, Burchard, with questions 'about the ceremonies to be performed, the state of the pope and the cardinals, the power and rank of Cardinal Cesare Borgia of Valencia, and many other things ...' The French army entered Rome through the Porta del Popolo and marched down the Via Lata (the Corso) under the excited gaze of the Romans. Their entry lasted from three in the afternoon until nine o'clock at night, so that torches had to be lit, heightening the impressiveness of the long columns of armed men. The King's German and Swiss mercenaries came first, dressed in short multi-coloured uniforms, with plumed helmets, carrying short swords and the great ten-foot pikes which had made them the most feared foot-soldiers in Europe. They were big, powerful men and marched in perfect time to the sound of trumpets, making a contrast to the following 5000 Gascon cross-bowmen who were small and soberly dressed. After the infantry rode 2500 heavy cavalry, the core of the King's army, the nobles of France with gorgeous silk cloaks over their gleaming armour, carrying lances and maces, riding heavy chargers whose ears and tails were cropped in the French fashion, and behind them some 5000 light cavalry armed with English longbows. Then came the King's guard of four hundred archers, including a hundred Scots, followed by his personal bodyguard of nobles, armed, marching on foot and carrying iron maces over their shoulders. Most impressive of all to the Italians was the artillery which rattled through the streets at a rapid trot, the un-certain light of the torches flickering over the long bronze bodies of the heavy cannon, eight feet long, weighing 6000 lb and with a bore the size of a man's head. Above the clanking armour, the jingle of harness and the rumble of the artillery carriages, the streets rang with cries of 'Francia, Colonna, Vincoli' – the Pope's supporters, if any there were, having the sense to keep their mouths shut. It was a day of triumph for Alexander's enemies. Giuliano and Ascanio, riding in the places of honour beside the King, accompanied him to the Palazzo Venezia where he was to reside.

The King of France was ill at ease in the Borgia capital. The Vene-tian diarist Sanuto, who recorded information from the Republic's envoys and agents throughout Europe, reported that he took stringent precautions against poison: 'He always ate alone with his nobles standing in attendance, while four physicians observed him closely to see whether he ate too much or too little, and whose job it was to test the wine for poison. The wine was served in a cup, stirred with a golden spoon in which was embedded a piece of unicorn horn [a protection against poison], and tasted by the head servitor.' Despite Burchard's careful instructions, Charles showed himself lamentably ignorant of the strict etiquette of the Roman court, and shocked the master of ceremonies by his offhand treatment of the cardinals who flocked to visit him, 'not coming forward to meet them, nor accom-panying them to the head of the stairs as they departed, nor showing them any of the honour due to them ...' Burchard was horrified by the state of squalor to which the 'barbarian' court soon reduced one

of the most magnificent palaces in Rome. Although the French were
provided with plenty of straw beds, he wrote: 'I observed that at no
time were the sacks of straw cleaned. Tallow candles were hung over
the doors of the rooms and in the fireplaces, and, although there were
most beautiful tapestries decorating the walls, everything was like a
pig-sty.' Yet despite the unfamiliarity of his surroundings, Charles was
master of Rome. He sent to Alexander to demand that the castle of
Sant'Angelo and the person of Prince Djem be handed over to him,
and that Cesare should accompany the expedition to Naples; on 6
January Alexander uncompromisingly refused. When the cardinals
carried his reply to Charles, the King replied menacingly: 'My barons
will acquaint the Pope with my will.' That evening Alexander and
Cesare with four cardinals retreated through the underground passage from the Vatican to the safety of the fortress of Sant'Angelo. The
Borgias were at bay.

One wonders what it must have been like for Cesare as he and his
father with their few followers awaited the outcome of events within
the thick walls of Sant'Angelo. This was the first crisis of his career;
in the most anxious moments he must indeed have wondered whether
they would lose everything that they had so briefly enjoyed, the position and the wealth, above all the Papacy and the future which it
afforded him. All the odds were against them. They had no weapons
beyond his father's experience, skill and courage with which to combat their adverse fortune. Yet one of the secrets of the Borgias' success,
which Cesare perhaps learned in this time of crisis, was a refusal to
give up even in the most apparently hopeless circumstances, and, as
events were to show, there can be little doubt that Alexander and
Cesare spent their time discussing contingency plans.

Outside the walls of Sant'Angelo the city was in an uproar. Panic-
stricken citizens buried their valuables to save them from the pillaging
troops. The Mantuan envoy Brognolo wrote on 6 January: 'The discontent of the people is at its height, the requisitions are fearful, the
murders innumerable, one hears nothing but moaning and weeping.
In all the memory of man the Church has never been in such evil
plight.' Charles ordered gallows to be set up in the squares to discourage looting, but the disorders continued. Burchard returned
home one day to find his house requisitioned by some French
noblemen, whose mules were eating up his hay, and on the 8th he
recorded: 'Even the house of Donna Vannozza Cattanei, the mother
of Cardinal Cesare Borgia, did not escape being pillaged.'

Meanwhile Charles menaced the beleaguered Borgias with his artillery, but his cannon proved unnecessary. On 10 January, without a shot being fired, a greater part of the outer wall of Sant'Angelo collapsed over a length of thirty feet from the tower to the gate, killing three guards. Alexander capitulated, and on 15 January agreement was signed. Cesare was to accompany Charles to Naples for a period of three months, Djem was to be handed over to the King's custody for the duration of the expedition against the Turks (but Alexander was to keep the pension), free passage through the States of the Church was to be allowed the French army, and amnesty promised for the churchmen and nobles who had rebelled against the Pope. In return Charles was to profess public obedience to the Pope, to impose no constraint upon him in things either spiritual or temporal, and to protect him against all attacks. The next day Charles met Alexander in the garden of the Vatican with mutual displays of courtesy and respect, and took up residence in the papal palace. On the 19th he made a public profession of obedience to the Pope, whereupon Alexander took him by the hand and called him his first-born son.

The cardinals of the opposition were beside themselves at the sight of this honeymoon between Pope and King. History does not record Giuliano's reaction, but no doubt he fell into one of his fits of bellowing rage; Ascanio and the other Milanese Cardinal, Lunati, left Rome precipitately the day after the agreement. Charles, as if bewitched by Alexander, seemed to have quite forgotten all his propaganda about the reform of the Church. Alexander, the wily diplomatist, had used the only weapons he had, his own personality and the aura of the Papacy, to outwit the inexperienced young King with all his troops and artillery at his back.

On 28 January, Charles came to take his leave of the Pope before setting off for Naples. Burchard described the scene:

King and Pope remained closeted together for a short while, and were then joined for a further quarter of an hour by Cardinal Cesare Borgia, after which His Majesty was escorted by the Pope and Cardinals through the halls as far as the passage leading to the upper apartments of the palace. There the King knelt down, bareheaded, and the Pope, removing his biretta, kissed him, but refused quite firmly to allow him to smother his feet with kisses, which His Majesty seemed to want to do. The King then departed, mounting his horse at the steps of the gate of the private garden, after waiting for a brief period for Cardinal Cesare Borgia to join him. The Pope and the cardinals meanwhile watched everything from the windows of the secret corridor [the passage leading to the castle of Sant'Angelo]. At last Cesare appeared, wearing his Cardinal's cape, and with His Holiness' permission, mounted horse beside the King. To His Majesty he presented six exceedingly beautiful horses which stood ready at hand with bridles but no saddles, and thus both the King and the Cardinal departed, leaving the others watching.

In splendid weather, Charles and his hostage Cesare set off for Naples down the same Roman road taken by Charles of Anjou 220 years before. They spent the night at Marino, where they were joined by the pro-French Cardinals Giuliano, Savelli and Colonna, who obviously preferred not to remain in Rome with a triumphant Alexander, and by Djem with a numerous Turkish retinue. Here Charles received the welcome news of the abdication of Alfonso of Naples. Alfonso, it was reported, thrown into a state of abject terror by the approach of the French, would start up from his sleep crying that he heard the French coming, and all the rocks and trees calling 'France'. Leaving his doomed kingdom to his son Ferrantino, he fled to Sicily, 'out of true cowardice' wrote de Comines, 'for never was a cruel man brave'.

Two days later, however, at Velletri, where the royal party were guests of its titular Bishop, Giuliano della Rovere, Charles received a most unwelcome surprise. 'On January 30th,' Burchard reported, 'news came that Cardinal Cesare Borgia had escaped from the King's hands at Velletri, disguised as a groom of the royal stables, and that he travelled so swiftly that he slept that night in Rome, at the house of Don Antonio Flores, a judge of the Rota.' In order not to compromise his father, Cesare left Rome the next day for the castle of Spoleto. At Velletri, Charles' rage knew no bounds: 'All Italians are dirty dogs and the Holy Father is as bad as the worst of them!' he is reported to have exclaimed. Alexander immediately denied complicity in the escape and all knowledge of his son's whereabouts, although Cesare was in the papal castle of Spoleto. But the escape had almost certainly been arranged between them before Cesare left Rome, and the deception had been carefully planned, as Burchard reported:

In his departure from Rome with King Charles, he had arranged for nineteen mules to follow him, laden with his goods and wearing rich trappings; amongst them were two beasts carrying *credenzas* [chests] with all his valuables. On the first day out, however, when His Majesty and the Cardinal were still on their way to Marino, these beasts had remained behind and returned to the city in the evening, whilst the Cardinal's servants made the excuse at the King's court that the mules had been seized and despoiled by some thieves ...

When the remaining seventeen were examined at Velletri after Cesare's flight, the chests they carried were found to be empty. Cesare's daring escape bore all the hallmarks of his later no less dramatic coups – his fondness for disguise, for secrecy and swiftness of movement. It was also in character that, out of devilry, he should have chosen Velletri for his escape, thus cocking a snook not only at the King of France but at Giuliano, its titular Bishop.

Cesare remained out of the public eye at Spoleto until the end of March, when he returned to Rome to take part in the negotiations for an international alliance between the Pope, Venice, Milan, Spain and the Empire against France. He also found the time to organize a personal vendetta against the Swiss troops of Charles VIII who had remained in Rome; on 1 April a number of Swiss in the piazza of St Peter's were attacked by 2000 Spaniards who killed twenty-four of them and manhandled the rest. Burchard reported: 'Some said afterwards that all these violent acts were ordered by Cardinal Valentino against the Swiss for revenge, because Swiss soldiers in the service of France, with violence and without any cause, had sacked and plundered the house of his mother, robbing her of 800 ducats and other possessions of value.' Cesare never forgot an injury or forbore to repay a wrong; he was already beginning to earn his reputation for vengefulness. And he could now afford his vendetta; on 31 March the alliance of the powers against France known as the Holy League was signed.

Meanwhile Charles, against whom this formidable alliance was directed, was enjoying the delights of the new kingdom he had so easily conquered, which he himself described in a letter to his brother-in-law the Duke of Bourbon as 'an earthly paradise'. 'This King,' reported a Venetian observer, 'was one of the most lascivious men in France, and was very fond of copulation, and of changing his dishes, so that once he had had a woman, he cared no more about her, taking his pleasure with new ones ...' And while the King abandoned business for pleasure, his soldiery did their best to make themselves thoroughly hated by the Neapolitans. According to another Venetian report:

> The French were clownish, dirty, and dissolute people; they were always to be found in sin and in venereal acts; the tables were always kept laid, nor did they remove the cloths nor sweep beneath them; whichever of them entered the house of a Neapolitan first, took the best room and sent the master of the house to sleep in the worst; they stole wine and grain and sold it in the market; they violated the women, with no respect whatsoever, then they robbed them and took the rings from their fingers, and if any woman resisted they cut off her fingers to have the rings; [nonetheless] they spend much time in church at their orations ...

Wine, women, and a new and terrifying disease, syphilis, which the French called *le mal de Naples*, were destroying the discipline of the French army.

Still Charles lingered on, unable to tear himself away, although the armies of the League were gathering in the north of Italy to cut off his retreat to France, and his position in Naples was becoming untenable. He had lost the support not only of the population, but of the barons who had at first welcomed him and then been disappointed in their hopes of honours and rewards. His plans for an expedition to the East had been shattered by the death of Djem on 25 February. (There were rumours that Alexander had him poisoned, but even Sanuto, normally hostile to the Borgias, thought it unlikely, since the Pope would thus have lost his annual pension of 40,000 ducats.)

It was not until 20 May that Charles reluctantly set off homeward, intending to have audience of the Pope en route in the hope that he would grant him the investiture of Naples. But for Alexander there was nothing to be gained this time from a personal interview with Charles, which could only be embarrassing. Determined not to be caught in Rome, he and Cesare left the city on 27 May for Orvieto, accompanied by nineteen cardinals and a considerable body of papal, Milanese and Venetian troops. Four days later Charles arrived in Rome to find the Pope gone; as he marched northward, Alexander and Cesare retreated from Orvieto to the more inaccessible Perugia.

Charles, with all hope of the Neapolitan investiture finally gone, was obliged to make for home as fast as he could. On 5 July at Fornovo on the River Taro he met the forces of the League commanded by the Marquis of Gonzaga. It was a hard-fought engagement, in which both Charles and Gonzaga displayed great personal courage, but the result was indecisive. The Italians suffered the heavier casualties, over 2000 men, but took more prisoners and an immense amount of plunder, including all the booty gathered by the French on their progress through Italy, Charles' helmet, sword and golden seal, together with a book containing portraits of the ladies whose favours he had enjoyed in the cities through which he had passed. Gonzaga claimed a brilliant victory and commissioned Mantegna to paint the Madonna della Vittoria (now, ironically enough, in the Louvre). But a more accurate view of the battle was that taken by the contemporary poet Antonio Cammelli: 'And he [Charles], like a journeying dog, biting now this one, now that, got clean away.'

At the end of June the Borgias returned to Rome in triumph from Perugia where, according to the local chronicler Matarazzo, they had made an unsuccessful attempt to unseat the Baglionis. In July Alexander, to give his son a taste of civil government and strengthen the family hold on a key papal city, nominated Cesare governor and castellan of Orvieto, with the powers of a legate *a latere*. Young and inexperienced as he was, Cesare made several mistakes in his government of Orvieto, dismissing citizens from their posts and substituting them with Spanish familiars. In response to angry protests, he hastened to write the Conservators of the city a honeyed letter of apology, blaming the trouble on false informants, and admitting that 'he knew he was only a man and could thus easily err and be deceived. But on another occasion he intended to use the citizens of Orvieto as brothers and dear companions ...'

The events of the past twelve months had indeed been instructive for Cesare, providing him with first-hand experience of international politics, of the bluff and counter-bluff of diplomacy, and of war. For Cesare, no less than for Italy, the year 1494-5 had been a momentous one. He had witnessed the power of the French army, and the weakness of the Italian political system in the face of force. He had seen the established dynasties of Medici and Aragon fall before the mere threat of French arms. As his father's chief confidant he had played a part at the centre of complex political negotiations, and above all he had watched Alexander, with consummate skill and all the odds against him, outwit the inexperienced young King with a great army behind him, and turn disaster into triumph. Cesare Borgia, aged just twenty, felt himself mature, and for him the game of power, politics and war now exercised an irresistible fascination.

IV

THE ENVY OF BROTHERS

WITH the crisis past, Alexander settled himself firmly in the seat of power. By the spring of 1496 the danger from the French was clearly over, although isolated bodies of troops still hung on in the Abruzzi and at Ostia. The Pope's chief enemies were either reconciled or discomfited. Ascanio and the Colonnas had made their peace with Alexander, Giuliano della Rovere had retired to France, and the Orsinis, fighting desperately in the lost cause of France, were hemmed in by 'the Great Captain' of Spain, Gonsalvo de Cordoba, in Calabria. Without Giuliano, the College of Cardinals, packed with friendly or uncommitted cardinals, was an amenable body which Alexander and his son could manipulate more or less as they liked. Their hold over the College was increased by the creation on 19 February of four new cardinals, all Borgia henchmen, including Cesare's cousin Giovanni Borgia, and their connection with Cesare was made clear to all in that they waited in his apartments during their nomination and dined there with him afterwards. Cesare, as befitted his acknowledged position as his father's right-hand man, had his own suite of apartments in the Vatican, now known as the Raphael Stanze, directly above Alexander's rooms in the Borgia apartments.

Upon his accession in 1492, Alexander had commissioned Pinturicchio to decorate his apartments on the first floor of the Vatican palace built by Nicholas v between 1447 and 1455, and by 1495 the frescoed rooms were completed. It is in these apartments, the only personal monuments to the Borgias which have survived, that Alexander has left his mark on the Vatican. In contrast to the serene piety of Nicholas v's chapel by Fra Angelico nearby, and to the High Renaissance beauty of the rooms on the floor above painted by Raphael for Julius II, the Borgia apartments are an arrogant demonstration of the Spanish origins, personal ambitions and family pride of the Borgia Pope.

Nearly five centuries have passed since the Borgias ruled Rome, but these rooms are still alive with their flamboyant personality. Here, covering walls and ceiling in an almost megalomaniac repetition, are the two Borgia devices, the Aragonese double crown, symbol of the royal house of Aragon, from which they quite fictitiously claimed descent and to which they added sun rays or flames pointing downwards, and the grazing ox of their original emblem, transformed from a peaceful animal into a rampant, virile, pagan bull. Pagan imagery is paramount: lunettes depict the planets, signifying Alexander's interest in astrology; a central plaque shows him as the elect of the sungod; the wild bull, ridden by a cupid, is used as an allegory of bridled force and passion; in other scenes the Borgia device appears in the form of the Egyptian bull-god Apis. Above all, the rooms have an alien, Spanish feeling: the tiled floors blaze with the double crown of Aragon, Pinturicchio's frescoes are inserted in stucco frames of a multicoloured geometric design recalling the Moorish work of Granada and Seville. No Italian passing through these rooms could have failed to be aware of their strangeness in the heart of the Vatican, nor of the family pride and ambition which they represented.

For in that triumphant year of 1496, Alexander no longer attempted to hide his affection for his children. Indeed he proudly and shamelessly flaunted them in the public eye. The Romans were used to papal nepotism, even to papal bastards, but Alexander was the first Pope to live a life of unabashed carnality and pleasure in the full limelight of the Vatican, in the company of his young and beautiful mistress and his handsome, arrogant children. It was this outrageous openness which shocked and amazed contemporaries, and the scandalous rumours which have made the Borgias' lives a byword began to gain momentum as Alexander's children gathered round their father in Rome.

Cesare, in his role as palace Cardinal, was already installed in the Vatican. In April, Lucrezia returned from provincial life at Pesaro to her old palace of Santa Maria in Portico by the Vatican steps. No doubt she was glad to be back in Rome after the confinement of the small court and the unrelieved company of her unloved husband Giovanni Sforza. Far from being the poisoning Messalina of legend, she was a gay, charming, pleasure-loving girl, whose high spirits made her, rather than the beautiful Giulia, the centre of the Vatican circle. Alexander was still infatuated with Giulia, whom even Sanuto described as 'gentle and gracious', and whose obscure young husband

Orsino he took care to keep at a safe distance from Rome as governor of Carbognano and Bassanello. But everyone remarked on his passionate affection, and that of Cesare, for Lucrezia; it was to be the basis of the ugly rumours of incest which later circulated so freely.

The arrival of Jofre and Sancia from Calabria in May contributed much to the gaiety, and to the scandal, of the papal court. Their entry into the city was organized by Alexander and Cesare with all the showmanship of which they were past masters. Entering by the Lateran Gate, they were greeted by the households of all the cardinals, the commander of the Vatican guard at the head of 200 soldiers, the ambassadors of Spain, Milan, Naples, Venice and the Empire, with the senators, nobles and leading citizens of Rome, and by Lucrezia, gorgeously dressed in order not to be outshone by her sister-in-law. Followed by twenty-eight mules carrying their baggage, Jofre, on a magnificent bay horse, and Sancia rode to the Vatican, where, says Burchard, the Pope peeped at their approach through a half-closed shutter before going down with Cesare to greet them. It was Cesare's first sight of his sister-in-law. The atmosphere of sexuality surrounding Sancia, and indeed the Borgia court, comes out clearly in this description of her arrival by the Mantuan ambassador Gian Carlo Scalona:

> In truth she did not appear as beautiful as she had been made out to be. Indeed the lady of Pesaro [Lucrezia] surpassed her. However that may be, by her gestures and aspect the sheep will put herself easily at the disposal of the wolf. She has also some ladies of hers who are in no way inferior to their mistress, thus they say publicly it will be a fine flock ... She is more than twenty-two years old, naturally dark, with glancing eyes, an aquiline nose and very well made up, and will in my opinion not give the lie to my predictions ...

Scalona thought little of Jofre, whom he described as 'dark in complexion and otherwise lascivious-looking, with long hair with a reddish tinge ... and he is fourteen or fifteen years of age'. Neither, it would appear, did Sancia; already in June 1494, one month after their marriage, rumours had reached Rome of the extravagance and disorderly behaviour of the young Squillaces' court. The harassed master of Sancia's household had even found it necessary to testify that no man had been seen entering the Princess' chamber but for 'Messer Cecco, companion of the lady, a worthy man and old, who is above sixty years of age ...' Sancia, brought up in the sensuous atmosphere of the Neapolitan court, could not have been expected to be content with a boy husband several years younger than herself, and she soon found a man more to her taste in his elder brother. As Sanuto reported a year later: 'Jofre, younger than his wife, had not consummated the marriage; he is not a man and, I understand, for many months past the lady Sancia has given herself to the Cardinal of Valencia.' If, as some writers have alleged, Lucrezia's love for Cesare was incestuous, she seems to have displayed no jealousy whatsoever towards his mistress Sancia, and the two girls, whose vivacity and carelessness for outward appearances made them ideal companions, soon became close friends. At a service in St Peter's on 22 May their irreverent behaviour scandalized the congregation when during a long and tedious sermon, which made Alexander restive, Sancia and Lucrezia climbed to the choir reserved for the canons and sat there laughing and chattering with their ladies.

In August, after three years in Spain, Juan also returned to the Borgia family fold, leaving his pregnant wife and young son at the family palace in Gandia. Alexander had wished for his son's return as early as May 1494, but Ferdinand, who did not trust his old ally, had preferred to keep Juan as a hostage for his father's good behaviour as long as the French were in Italy. Juan made a splendid entry into the city on 10 August, received at the Porta Potese by Cesare himself at the head of a numerous retinue including all the cardinals – a signal honour – and their households, the ambassadors, Roman officials and nobility. At twenty, Juan had clearly not outgrown his fondness for ostentatious clothes; he wore a scarlet cap hung with pearls, a doublet of brown velvet the sleeves and breast of which blazed with jewels, black stockings embroidered with the golden crown and rays of Gandia, and a long Turkish mantle of gold brocade. His bay horse was adorned with gold fringes and silver bells which tinkled as he rode, and he was accompanied by six squires including a Moor dressed in gold brocade and crimson velvet, twelve splendid horses ridden by pages, and a crowd of dwarfs and buffoons. At the Vatican, Alexander welcomed the prodigal with open arms.

What was Cesare's reaction to the return of his father's favourite son? In September 1496, only one month after Gandia's arrival, Scalona reported to Isabella d'Este: '... every effort is made to conceal that these sons of the Pope are consumed with envy of each other ...' Certainly Juan was, as his stepfather Canale had described him to the Gonzagas in 1493, 'the eye of His Holiness'. Yet there is no doubt that Alexander loved his eldest son; Scalona's dispatches to the Gonzagas during that autumn and winter are testimonies to the depth of feeling for him. When Cesare, hunting near Tre Fontane, was nearly caught by the Orsinis, he reported: 'If Valencia had been taken prisoner, we would have seen a new Pope in Rome ...' He recommended them to do everything they could to gain Cesare's friendship because he, above all, 'has the Pope in his hand'. And Cesare must have had the additional satisfaction of knowing that his father relied upon him as he could never rely upon Juan.

Yet however sure Cesare may have been of Alexander's loyalty, with his competitive nature and keen sense of his rights he must have resented his father's doting preference for his younger brother, whose qualities of mind and character he felt to be so inferior to his own. Nor can he have relished the sight of that brother whom Zurita described as 'a very mean young man, full of ideas of grandeur and bad thoughts, haughty, cruel and unreasonable', caracoling in the place of honour before his father in public processions through Rome on a horse tinkling with silver bells. More perhaps than the open favouritism, he must have resented Juan's association in Borgia affairs, where before he alone had been his father's right-hand man. And there may have been other more private reasons for rivalry between the two brothers. Scandalmongers whispered that they competed for Sancia's favours, and that Juan had replaced Cesare in her fickle affections. Competition there may have been, but certainly a year later Sancia was still known to be Cesare's mistress. There were enough reasons for sibling rivalry between the two brothers, but no concrete evidence to show that the feeling between them was more dangerous than that. To talk of their being 'consumed with envy of each other' seems to be overstating the case.

And Cesare knew the part he had to play in his father's politico-dynastic plan. Scalona, reporting rumours that the Chamberlain, Raffaele Riario, might be poisoned in order to accelerate Cesare's ecclesiastical career, wrote to Isabella d'Este: 'Ascanio will then be Chamberlain, Valenza Vice-Chancellor, and thus he is preparing a way to the Papacy, to which he has already made great beginnings and by every means attends to it ...' The rumours about the liquidation of Riario were baseless scandal, but that they could be seriously entertained at all indicates that observers in Rome were already conscious of the Borgias' boundless ambitions, and of the ruthlessness with which they were prepared to pursue them. For the moment, however, Alexander's plans centred round Juan, who had been brought back to Rome to be his father's instrument in the campaign he was planning against the Orsinis.

Alexander was well aware that the Roman barons, the Orsinis and Colonnas, were the Achilles heel of the Papacy. Machiavelli, as a good Florentine, formed a very low opinion of them on his legation to Rome in October 1503. 'These men here in the Roman Campagna,' he wrote, 'for the great hatreds between them, are robbers rather than soldiers. And being given up to their own private passions, they cannot serve a third party well. And these truces that they make, last only as long as the next occasion comes to injure each other ...' Indeed the enmity between the factions had traditionally been the weapon used by the popes to play one party off against the other. Nonetheless, since from their lands to the north and south of Rome they controlled the Roman Campagna and the access roads to the city, while leading powerful factions within Rome itself, they represented a perennial threat to the independence of the Papacy, while any power wishing to weaken and intimidate the Pope had only to take into its pay either the Colonnas or the Orsinis, whose swords were always for sale. Moreover, in calling them robbers rather than soldiers Machiavelli was generalizing to an unwarranted degree. Virginio Orsini, Bartolomeo d'Alviano (related by marriage to the Orsinis), and the Colonna chiefs Fabrizio and Prospero were amongst the most skilful and experienced condottieri of their day, and indeed Machiavelli himself was to make Prospero the hero of his *Art of War*. The feud between Borgias and Orsinis was a long-standing one, dating back to the days of Calixtus, and Alexander had not forgiven the family for their treachery in going over to the French in the last days of 1494. Now, in the temporary political lull that followed the departure of the French, it seemed to him that the opportunity had come to crush them once and for all. In July the remaining French troops in Naples capitulated at Atella, and Virginio Orsini, head of the clan, and his eldest legitimate son Giovanni Giordano, or Giangiordano, were thrown into the dungeons of Castel dell'Uovo at Naples.

Alexander had chosen the right moment to move against the Orsinis, but the wrong instruments. The gentle, weakly Duke of Urbino, Guidobaldo da Montefeltro, son of the great Federigo, who had inherited his father's role as condottiere but not his talents, was to be overall commander. As second in command, and Borgia representative in a campaign that was also designed to acquire the strategic Orsini lands round Rome for the family, Alexander nominated the young and totally inexperienced Juan Gandia. Fabrizio Colonna was the only seasoned captain in the papal army intended to crush the fighting clan. On 26 October, to the sound of trumpets, Juan Gandia entered St Peter's with Guidobaldo on his right to be invested respectively with the titles of Captain General of the Church and Gonfalonier. Alexander was quite overwhelmed with paternal affection and pride. As the Mantuan envoy wrote scornfully: 'The Pope is so swollen up and inflated with this election [the Generalship] of his son, that he does not know what to do with himself, and this morning desired to set a feather in his cap with his own hands and sew on a jewel of great value.'

The next day, 27 October, the papal army marched out to lay siege to the Orsini strongholds north of Rome. Initially the campaign was a success – within two months ten castles had fallen – but by mid-December things began to go wrong. The great Orsini fortress of Bracciano held out, commanded by the redoubtable Bartolomea Orsini, sister of Virginio and wife of Bartolomeo d'Alviano, the best of the Orsini captains. Guidobaldo was wounded early in the siege, which left Juan to carry on, with notable lack of success. The Orsinis made sallies up to the walls of Rome, and mocked Gandia, sending a large donkey into the papal camp with the message 'I am the ambassador of the Duke of Gandia' round its neck and a rude letter addressed to him under its tail. At Rome, Alexander, ill with chagrin and disappointment, absented himself from public appearances, and did not attend mass on Christmas Day. But worse was to come: after two futile and costly assaults, news reached the papal camp of the approach of a relieving force under Carlo Orsini, bastard son of Virginio, and Vitellozzo Vitelli of Città di Castello, another noted condottiere. Gandia raised the siege and marched north to intercept the enemy. At Soriano on 24 January the papal forces, in Burchard's words, were 'heavily defeated and in great dishonour': Guidobaldo was captured, Juan, wounded in the face, saved himself by flight, 500 troops were killed and all the artillery lost.

Alexander had no alternative but to make peace, on 5 February. The Orsinis, once more masters of the Campagna, regained all their castles, on payment of an indemnity of 50,000 ducats which they hoped to raise by ransoming Guidobaldo to the Pope. Alexander, always a tricky bargainer, retained the fortresses of Anguillara and

Cerveteri against payment of the indemnity, and refused to ransom the unfortunate Guidobaldo. Publicly, at least, it appeared that his confidence in Juan was undimmed – within a fortnight of the Orsini peace Gandia was dispatched to besiege the fortress of Ostia – but this time the expedition was commanded by one of the greatest military leaders of the day, Gonsalvo de Cordoba, with a body of seasoned Spanish troops from Naples. The fortress capitulated on 9 March, and in the triumphal return of the papal troops to Rome the inept Gandia was accorded equal honours with Gonsalvo. Gonsalvo's Spanish pride was offended; in the splendid Holy Week celebrations which followed he clearly showed his displeasure by refusing to take his appointed place at the ceremonies. 'The cause of this ...' commented Burchard disapprovingly, 'was the Duke of Gandia, the Pope's son.'

In that same Easter Week of 1497, Roman gossips were titillated by yet another Borgia family scandal; Lucrezia's husband, Giovanni Sforza, left the palace of Santa Maria in Portico and fled precipitately and secretly to Pesaro. Stefano Taberna, the Milanese envoy, hinted at Lucrezia's misconduct: 'I suspect that something concerning the reputation of his wife might have led him into a serious quarrel and then to make a departure in this manner ...' Although the immediate cause of Sforza's flight appears to have been that he had received direct or indirect warnings of threats made against him by Cesare, the probable underlying explanation was a change in the orientation of Borgia policy. In 1493 the Sforza–Milan connection had seemed a desirable one; by 1497 Giovanni was seen as an obstacle, even a dangerous one, to their dual objectives of papal independence and family advancement. No one doubted that the political lull was a temporary one, or that the French intended to return to Italy to assert their claims to Naples and now it seemed, through the Visconti inheritance, to Milan. Charles' cousin, Louis of Orleans, had a dynastic right to Milan through his grandmother Valentina Visconti, and should the French decide to assert it Alexander had no wish to be tied to the Sforzas in the event of an invasion. The Borgias had therefore decided on divorce, so that Lucrezia should be free to find a more advantageous partner than the outworn Sforza connection. Giovanni's recalcitrance in the face of Borgia pressure for the divorce was the cause of Cesare's rumoured threats against him, and thus of his precipitate flight. Moreover, Alexander's plans for the advancement of his family had now turned in the direction of Naples, where Ferrantino had been succeeded by his uncle Federigo.

Alexander used the occasion of Federigo's investiture to announce two important appointments for his sons. In a a secret consistory of 8 June, Cesare was nominated Legate for the coronation of the King of Naples, a blatantly nepotistic appointment in view of his youth and lack of seniority. But it was the investiture, in another secret consistory held the previous day, of Juan with the duchy of Benevento and the cities of Terracina and Pontecorvo which caused the greatest resentment. The alienation of these important papal cities as hereditary fiefs to Gandia was widely regarded as an intolerable scandal. Juan, whose arrogance had already earned him powerful enemies, became the primary target of anti-Borgia hostility.

On Wednesday 14 June, exactly a week after his investiture, Gandia disappeared. On the afternoon of that day Juan and Cesare, accompanied by Cardinal Juan Borgia of Monreale, rode out to have supper with Vannozza in her vineyard, or country villa, near Monte S. Martino dei Monti. Returning as night was falling, they reached the bridge of Sant'Angelo leading to the Vatican, where Juan told his brother and his cousin that he must leave them as he must go somewhere alone. Both the Cardinals and Gandia's servants, according to Scalona's report, 'did everything possible so that he should not go unaccompanied': the streets of Rome at night were not safe for a rich young man alone, especially one with the enemies that Gandia had. But Juan was adamant; the most he would do for safety was to send one of his grooms back to his rooms in the Palace to fetch his light 'night armour', and then tell him to wait for him in the Piazza Judea. He took leave of Cesare and Cardinal Borgia and turned his mule in the direction of the Ghetto. As he did so, a masked man wrapped in a black cloak was seen, to mount the mule behind him, and the two rode off together. Cesare and the Cardinal, uneasy, waited for some time by the bridge, hoping that he would return; when he did not, they reluctantly returned to the palace 'with considerable anxiety and doubt in their minds'. Juan's groom was attacked on his way to the Vatican to fetch the armour, and received slight stab-wounds. But 'as he was a strong man', says Scalona, he returned to the Piazza Judea to wait for his master. When Gandia did not return, he too went back to the palace, thinking that Juan was spending the night in the house of some Roman lady, as was frequently his custom. Neither the groom nor Cesare, for the same reason, reported Juan's escapade to the Pope that night. On the morning of Thursday 15 June, Gandia's servants reported to Alexander that he had not returned.

The Pope was disturbed, but not seriously worried; he was used to his son's amorous escapades. But as the day wore on and there was still no sign of Gandia, his alarm mounted, and in the evening he sent for Cesare and Cardinal Borgia and begged them to tell him where Juan was. They told him what they had learned from the groom, whereupon the Pope, according to Scalona, said 'that if he was dead, he knew the origin and the cause'. Then 'seized with mortal terror', in Burchard's words, he ordered a search to be made.

As Alexander's agents scoured the streets on the night of the 15th, the city was in an uproar; many citizens, fearing a wholesale vendetta, closed their shops and barricaded their doors. The Colonnas, Savellis, Orsinis and Caetanis fortified their palaces, while excited Spaniards roamed the streets with drawn swords. Finally, on Friday 16 June, feverish inquiries brought to light the report of Giorgio Schiavi, a timber dealer, who used to unload his wood near the Ospedale of San Girolamo degli Schiavoni, near the conduit used for discharging refuse into the Tiber. Schiavi was accustomed to keep a nightly watch on his timber to prevent it being stolen. When asked if he had seen anything on Wednesday night, he reported:

That night about the hour of two, while I was guarding my wood, lying in my boat, two men on foot came out of the alley on the left of the Ospedale degli Schiavoni, onto the open way by the river. They looked cautiously about them to see that no one was passing, and not having found anyone, returned the way they had come into the same alley. Shortly afterwards, two other men came out of that same alley, also looking furtively round them; not seeing anybody, they made a signal to their companions. Then there appeared a rider on a white horse, carrying a body slung across its crupper behind him, the head and arms hanging to one side, the legs to the other, supported on the right by the two first men so that it should not fall off. Having reached the point from which refuse is thrown into the river, the horseman turned his horse so that its tail faced the river, then the two men who were standing on either side, taking the body, one by the hands and arms, the other by the feet and legs, flung it with all their strength into the river. To the horseman's demand whether the body had sunk, they replied, 'Yes, sir,' then the horseman looked again at the river and saw the dead man's cloak floating on the water, and asked what it was. They answered, 'Sir, the cloak.' Then he threw some stones at it and made it sink. This done, all five, including the other two who had come out of the alley to keep watch, went away by an alley which leads to the Hospital of San Giacomo.

When asked why he had not reported the incident to the authorities, Schiavi answered simply: 'In the course of my life, on various nights, I have seen more than a hundred bodies thrown into the river right at this spot, and never heard of anyone troubling himself about them.'

Following Schiavi's report, all the fishermen and boatmen of Rome were called in to search the river with the promise of reward. First the body of an unknown man was discovered, then, about midday, near the church of Santa Maria del Popolo, a fisherman named Battistino da Taglia brought up in his net the body of a young man, fully clothed, with his gloves and a purse containing 30 ducats still hanging from his belt. Nine stab wounds were counted on the body, in the neck, head, body and legs; it was Gandia.

Juan's body was taken by boat to the castle of Sant'Angelo, where it was washed and richly dressed in brocade with the insignia of Captain General of the Church. At six o'clock on the same evening Juan was carried from the castle by the noblemen of his household to be buried in the family chapel in the church of Santa Maria del Popolo, in a procession led by 120 torch-bearers, all the palace ecclesiastics, the papal chamberlains and shield-bearers, 'all marching along weeping and wailing and in considerable disorder', commented Burchard. He continued: 'The body was borne on a magnificent bier so that all could see it, and it seemed that the Duke were not dead but sleeping,' while another observer remarked that Juan looked 'almost more handsome than when he was alive'.

Alexander's grief for his handsome son was indescribable; even the stolid Burchard was moved:

The Pope, when he heard that the Duke had been killed and flung into the river like dung, was thrown into a paroxysm of grief, and for the pain and bitterness of his heart shut himself in his room and wept most bitterly. The Cardinal of Segovia and some of his servants went to the door, persuading him to open it, which he did only after many hours. The Pope neither ate nor drank anything from the Wednesday evening until the following Saturday, nor from the morning of Thursday to the following Sunday did he know a moment's peace.

By Monday 19th, however, contrary to everyone's expectations, Alexander had recovered himself sufficiently to hold a public consistory in which he announced Gandia's death in emotional terms to the assembled ambassadors and cardinals:

> The Duke of Gandia is dead. His death has given us the greatest sorrow, and no greater pain than this could we suffer, because we loved him above all things, and esteemed not more the Papacy nor anything else. Rather, had we seven papacies we would give them all to have the Duke alive again. God has done this perhaps for some sin of ours, and not because he deserved such a cruel death; nor do we know who killed him and threw him into the Tiber.

In order to scotch the rumours flying round Rome as to the authors of the crime, Alexander went on to exculpate some of those who had been mentioned as principal suspects – Giovanni Sforza, whose motive was held to be resentment over Lucrezia, Jofre, out of jealousy concerning Sancia, and the Duke of Urbino, in revenge for his imprisonment after the Orsini war.

Who did kill Gandia? Within a week of his death, the searchers for the murderer or murderers were abruptly called off, and it seems that Alexander had learned the truth, although he said nothing publicly, in order, as the Florentine envoy Alessandro Bracci put it, 'to catch the authors of the crime in their sleep'. On 1 July he wrote: 'since the Pope no longer shows great curiosity as to the finding of those who murdered the Duke of Gandia, it is held to be certain beyond doubt that His Holiness has now discovered the truth, and that he thinks of nothing else but the manner in which he may safely lay hands on them.' It was the general opinion in Rome that whoever was responsible for the murder was *un gran maestro*, a master-mind, and a man of importance and power. Suspicion first rested on the Sforzas, Cardinal Ascanio and his nephew Giovanni, not only on account of Lucrezia and the divorce but because of a skirmish between Juan's household in which some of Gandia's Spaniards were killed, for which Gandia in revenge had arrested several of Ascanio's grooms and had them hanged from the ramparts of the Torre di Nona. The Mantuan envoy Scalona, in his report of Gandia's death, specifically says that there was bad blood between Juan and Cesare on the one side and Ascanio on the other because of this affair. But Ascanio's letters to his brother Ludovico written in the week after Juan's death give absolutely no intimation of his having had any hand in the crime;

while his nephew Giovanni was not even in Rome at the time, but in Milan, having left Pesaro to seek Ludovico's support. And although Alexander had Ascanio's house searched on 16 June, he seems soon to have come to the same conclusion. At the consistory of the 19th he told the Spanish ambassador, Garcilaso de la Vega; 'God forbid that I should harbour any such horrible suspicions of the Cardinal [Ascanio]. I have always looked upon him as a brother and he will be welcome whenever he comes.' In fact, Ascanio, who had not dared attend consistory because of wild threats made against him by Spaniards of Juan's and Cesare's households, upon receiving friendly assurances from both Alexander and Cesare visited the Pope on the 21st and had long interviews both with him and with Cesare separately, at which the subject of discussion was not Gandia's murder but Lucrezia's divorce.

By far the most likely suspects were the Orsinis, whose names significantly had not even been mentioned by Alexander in his exculpations of the 19th. Of all Gandia's many enemies, they had the strongest motives for a vendetta and, with their connections in the city, the best means of carrying it out. Gandia had been the spearhead of the Borgia attack on them the previous winter, and it was he for whom their lands had been intended. Moreover they held Alexander responsible for the death of their leader Virginio in the dungeons of Castel dell'Uovo on 13 January. Virginio was believed to have been poisoned, since reports alleged that the day before he died he was seen to be in perfect health, and the Orsinis did not hesitate to lay responsibility at the Pope's door. By the laws of the vendetta, Virginio's death called for revenge, and how better could his family avenge themselves on Alexander than by engineering the death of his favourite son?

It seems that the plan for Juan's murder had been laid at least a month beforehand, possibly at the time when Virginio's corpse was brought through Rome from Naples en route for burial at Bracciano at the end of April. Burchard noted that the mysterious masked man who figures in all contemporary accounts of the murder, and whom he averred had had a brief interview with Gandia at Vannozza's supper, had already visited him at the Vatican almost every day throughout the previous month. The bait seems to have been the beautiful and respectable daughter of Count Antonio della Mirandola, with whom Gandia was known to be madly in love. It seems probable that Juan, whose senses had been carefully titillated, was lured to his death with the promise of a final assignation with the lady; in any event his mule was found wandering near her father's house. As soon as the hue and cry against the Sforzas died down, the Orsinis began to be mentioned in connection with the affair, and references to the Pope's suspicions of them recur with increasing frequency during the following months. As early as 8 August the Florentine government received the news that 'the Orsinis were nervous of the Pope, and above all Bartolomeo d'Alviano [Virginio's brother-in-law] to whom the death of the Duke of Gandia is imputed', and Paolo Orsini was also specifically mentioned. On 22 December Manfredo Manfredi wrote to his master the Duke of Ferrara: 'It seems that more than ever the Pope gives signs of blaming the Orsinis for the murder of his son, for which it is thought that he is disposed to revenge the said injury and death of his son . . .' At the same time a Venetian source reported: 'This Pope plotted to ruin the Orsinis because the Orsinis for sure caused the death of his son the Duke of Gandia.' But the Orsinis were powerful enemies, and their punishment was not to be undertaken lightly, as the Borgias had recently learned to their cost. And so they nursed their vendetta patiently and cunningly, biding their time until they could be certain of their prey.

Within less than a year of Gandia's death, in February 1498, a rumour began to circulate in Venice (where, it may be noted, the Orsinis had many friends) that Cesare was responsible for his brother's death. This accusation was later to be embodied in the Venetian envoy's official report of September 1500, at a time when Cesare was openly seen to be guilty of at least one murder, and gained currency at the court of Spain, where he had many enemies. Maria Enriquez, his brother's widow, at least seems to have believed it, as did Queen Isabella, who violently disapproved of Cesare. The story was picked up by Guicciardini, who embroidered it with lurid details. Cesare, he said, envious of Gandia's secular position and jealous that he occupied a greater place than himself in Lucrezia's affections, 'inflamed with lust and ambition . . . had him killed and secretly thrown into the Tiber'. The story gained strength over the years, and formed the basis of the theory put forward by the authoritative German historian Gregorovius, that Alexander's condoning of Cesare's crime was the cause of Cesare's 'satanic hold' over his father.

Cesare was capable of murder if he stood to gain by it, he certainly benefited later from his brother's removal from the scene, but there is absolutely no contemporary evidence that he did do it, and the whole case against him rests on his alleged jealousy of Gandia, his supposedly incestuous relations with Lucrezia, and the fact that over a year later he was seen to have profited by it. Not one of the accounts written at the time of the murder points at Cesare as the author of the crime. Ascanio Sforza, who was close to the Vatican, on bad terms with Cesare, and had every interest in casting suspicion on others than himself, makes not the faintest allusion to such an accusation in his letters to his brother. Moreover there is no contemporary evidence that Alexander was frightened of, or dominated by, his twenty-two-year-old son in the months following Gandia's death, or that Cesare was discontent with his role as an influential Cardinal, a career which might well lead him to the Papacy itself.

Indeed it was as Cardinal Legate for the coronation of King Federigo of Naples that Cesare left Rome six weeks after his brother's death accompanied by a small army of retainers, prelates and camp-followers, including 700 horses, bound for Capua, where the coronation was to take place on 6 August. He reached Capua on 2 August, but fell ill shortly after his arrival, and the ceremony had to be postponed. Sancia, trailed by Jofre, was hurriedly dispatched from Rome to nurse him, but he recovered quickly enough to crown King Federigo on 11 August. Splendid in a grown of crimson velvet 'with more than ducal sleeves', and a flowing mantle of cloth of gold, Cesare was carried in a *sedia gestatoria* into Capua Cathedral, where he performed the coronation ceremony with all the theatrical dignity he had learned from his father; he had a strong histrionic streak, and liked nothing better than to play a part. Yet despite the splendour of the occasion, the ceremony fell rather flat; the Angevin barons of the kingdom of Naples, who opposed the Aragonese dynasty and whom Cesare as Legate had been supposed to reconcile with the King, boycotted it totally, and had it not been for the presence of the Prince and Princess of Squillace the congregation would have consisted almost entirely of ambassadors and the populace.

Cesare failed in his role as peacemaker, but the real object of his visit was to squeeze further advantages for his family from a gratefully dependent King Federigo. There was the question of Juan's rich estates in the Kingdom, whose investiture Cesare was to demand from the King himself in his nephew's name, and there was another more delicate matter to be explored, namely the possibility of a Neapolitan marriage for Lucrezia, as soon as her divorce from Sforza, upon which the Borgias were absolutely determined, could be pushed through. But while bargaining with his host on his family's behalf, the young

Legate was determined to enjoy the delights of Naples, which he reached in company with the King on 14 August. The kingdom of Naples and Sicily had once been the richest territory in Italy, and although it had been in steady decline since the days of the Norman kingdom in the twelfth century, Naples was still a beautiful city, famous for its palaces, its gardens in the Arab tradition (Charles VIII had taken a Neapolitan gardener back with him in 1495), and for its cultivated, sensual and pleasure-loving court. Cesare is said to have fallen in love with Maria Diaz Garlon, daughter of the Count d'Aliffe, and to have spent 200,000 ducats to win her favours. Cesare, with his handsome face and athletic figure, had his father's physical attraction for women and had no need to buy their favours. But his extravagance was already becoming notorious, and no doubt he spent a great deal of money on rich stuffs and Barbary horses. The impoverished King Federigo was forced to bear the expenses of entertaining the luxury-loving Legate and his entire suite throughout their stay in Naples, and must have been heartily relieved when Cesare finally left for Rome on 22 August.

Cesare took with him a lasting memento of the tainted delights of the city which had proved such a fatal honey-trap to the troops of Charles VIII three years earlier. Isabella d'Este's agent, Donato de' Preti, reported to his mistress: 'Monsignor of Valencia has returned from the Kingdom after crowning King Federigo and he too is sick of the French disease.' Cesare's Spanish physician, Gaspare Torella, wrote a treatise on the subject, which he dedicated to his patron, 'because, illustrious prince, you asked me what might be this pestilent malady which some call "the disease of San Semente" and the French say is "the Naples disease" or the great pox, while the Italians call it the French disease, and since you asked me if the doctors have written on the subject and for what reason in so long a time no specific remedy has been discovered ...' Torella condemned the use of mercury in treating syphilis and prescribed a course of ointments, potions and sweating in hot baths. He no doubt claimed credit for curing his master, but in fact his treatments can have made little or no difference: primary syphilis lasts from between ten to ninety days, and within a few months of returning to Rome the disease would seemingly have disappeared of itself, and Cesare would have considered himself cured.

V

CROSSING THE RUBICON

CESARE arrived back in Rome on 5 September, and spent the night in the monastery of his titular church, Santa Maria Nuova. The next day he rode to the Vatican to be solemnly received by the Pope. The formality of his reception by Alexander, who silently bestowed on him the ceremonial kiss, has been interpreted as indicating that the Pope knew that Cesare was responsible for Juan's murder, and could not bring himself to speak to him. In fact his reception on the 6th was a purely ceremonial occasion; Cesare had already reported to his father the previous day.

Father and son must have had important matters to discuss. In the six hectic weeks which followed the discovery of Juan's mutilated body in the Tiber, the Borgias had been obliged to rethink their entire dynastic scheme. Juan was dead. Jofre, not yet sixteen, was too young to play a part in either war or politics. Furthermore it was openly rumoured in Rome that he had not consummated his marriage with Sancia, while there were no doubts as to his elder brother's virility, especially where Sancia was concerned. Clearly, hopes for the establishment of a Borgia dynasty rested with Cesare, but he was a cardinal, and as such was not permitted to marry. The Borgia solution to the dilemma was immediate and simple: if Cesare as a cardinal could not marry, then he must renounce the cardinalate (an unheard-of step), and a wife and state must be found for him.

This project had clearly been discussed even before Cesare left for Naples; on 20 August Ascanio reported in cipher to Ludovico that there was talk of secularizing Cesare and marrying him to Sancia, while Jofre in compensation was to become a cardinal and to exchange his wife for Cesare's benefices. By late September rumours of the Borgias' new plans had reached Venice. Sanuto wrote: 'It was rumoured throughout Rome that Cardinal Valencia, called Cesar, son of the pontiff, who had benefices of circa 35,000 ducats a year, and was the second richest cardinal in terms of revenues, how, desirous of exercising himself in warlike undertakings, wanted to renounce the cardinalate and his other benefices ... The Pope would make him Captain of the Church.' The Borgias looked to Naples to provide a wife and state for Cesare. The Aragonese dynasty was insecure, faced with internal dissension and the omnipresent external threat from France. In the circumstances it was not surprising that they thought that by turning the screws on the helpless Federigo they could obtain what they wanted in return for their support. They were after bigger game than Sancia, who was only an illegitimate daughter of the house of Aragon. Cesare and Alexander had fixed their eyes on the kingdom of Naples for Cesare, and marriage to Federigo's legitimate daughter Carlotta as a necessary step towards the throne. A Neapolitan marriage for Lucrezia was designed to prepare the ground for Cesare, the first move in a Borgia takeover of the Kingdom. Before either of these projects could be realized, it was essential that Cesare should renounce his cardinal's hat, and Lucrezia her husband, Giovanni Sforza.

Lucrezia's divorce, and the Borgias' obsessive pursuit of the matter, became something of a *cause célèbre* in the summer and autumn of 1497. Even in the tragic days following Gandia's death, annulment had been in the forefront of their minds. At the consistory on 19 June, Alexander had announced his intention of starting proceedings on the basis of non-consummation, and had pursued the matter in his long conversation with Ascanio Sforza on the 21st, while Cesare separately told Ascanio that neither of them would rest until the divorce was concluded. The atmosphere surrounding the case rapidly became extremely unsavoury as the Borgias used Ascanio and Ludovico to put pressure on Giovanni Sforza to swear to his own impotence and thus gain an annulment on the grounds that he had been unable to consummate the marriage. When Giovanni, whose first wife died in childbirth, angrily denied the charge of impotence, his uncle Ludovico cynically suggested he should refute it by a public demonstration of his virility. The Ferrarese envoy quoted Giovanni as asserting 'that he had known his wife an infinity of times, but that the Pope had taken her from him for no other purpose than to sleep with her himself'. However, neither Ascanio nor Ludovico was prepared to sacrifice the Pope's friendship for the sake of their expendable nephew, and was the second richest cardinal in terms of revenues, now, desirous was forced to give in. He signed a paper attesting to his non-consummation of the marriage which also obliged him to return Lucrezia's dowry of 31,000 ducats. The divorce was officially promulgated in the Vatican on 20 December, but by the end of September the commission appointed by Alexander to examine the matter had already concluded that the marriage had never been consummated, and that Lucrezia was still a virgin. 'A conclusion,' wrote the Perugian chronicler Matarazzo, 'that set all Italy laughing ... it was common knowledge that she had been and was then the greatest whore there ever was in Rome.'

Lucrezia's reputation was to come into question again within less than two months of the divorce, with the mysterious disappearance of one of the Pope's favourite Spanish chamberlains, Pedro Calderon, known as Perotto. Early in February 1498 Cristoforo Poggio, agent of the Bentivoglio family, wrote from Rome to Mantua that Perotto had vanished, and was thought to be in prison, 'for having got His Holiness' daughter, Lucrezia, with child'. On 14 February Burchard noted dryly in his diary: 'Perotto, who last Thursday, the 8th of this month, fell not of his own will into the Tiber, was fished up today in that river, concerning which affair there are many rumours running through Rome.' Just nine months before, on 19 June 1497, Donato Aretino had reported: 'Madonna Lucrezia has left the palace, where she was no longer welcome, and gone to a convent known as San Sisto ... Some say she will turn nun, while others say many other things which one cannot entrust to a letter.' Lucrezia's exile to the chaste atmosphere of a convent may well have been caused by the discovery of her affair with Perotto, at the very time when her father and brother were anxious to establish her virginity for the purposes of her divorce. There were reports that Perotto's body was found with that of one of Lucrezia's women, Pantasilea, and his death was probably not only an act of vengeance but also the removal of evidence of Lucrezia's misconduct at a time when negotiations for her remarriage were being carried on. Perotto's death was later attributed to Cesare in the most melodramatic fashion, and it is not unlikely that he had a hand in it. Nothing would have been allowed to stand in the way of his plans for Lucrezia, which were so intimately allied with his own. In March 1498 an isolated report from the Ferrarese envoy to the Duke of Ferrara alleged that Lucrezia had given birth to a child, and the whole affair was complicated by the undoubted birth at the same time of the mysterious Giovanni Borgia, known as the 'Infans

Romanus', whose paternity was first attributed to Cesare, but later
in a secret bull of September 1502 admitted to be Alexander's, possibly by Giulia Farnese. As with so many stories about the Borgias,
the truth, concealed beneath a web of gossip, intrigue and deception,
is impossible to discover.

Meanwhile, with the matter of his sister's divorce successfully concluded, Cesare was energetically cooperating with his father in the
plan for his secularization and marriage. On Christmas Eve Ascanio
reported to Ludovico a long conversation he had had with the Pope
on the subject, lasting four hours: 'The principal content was briefly
as follows: Cesare is working every day harder to put off the purple.
The Pope is of the opinion that, if it does come to pass, it must do
so with the least possible scandal, under the most decorous pretext
possible.' For Alexander and Cesare, however, the fabrication of a
decorous pretext for putting off the purple was of less moment than
ensuring that it would be worth his while to do so. He could not take
the irrevocable step of renouncing his great ecclesiastical position and
the 35,000 ducats in yearly revenue which it brought him, without
being sure of a secular position with at least an equivalent income,
and a wife to enable him to found a dynasty.

Somewhat to their surprise, the Borgias found King Federigo to
be a major stumbling-block to their ambitions. Federigo, who knew
both the Borgias well, recognized their takeover plan for what it was.
Although he was prepared to sacrifice an illegitimate member of his
house to the Borgia bull, and offered Sancia's brother Alfonso, with
the title of Duke of Bisceglie, as a second husband for Lucrezia, dynastic pride and political common sense made him obdurate in his refusal
of his legitimate daughter for Cesare. Behind Federigo stood his
powerful patron Ferdinand of Aragon, who had absolutely no intention of allowing the Borgias to annex the kingdom of Naples, which
he meant to regain for the Aragonese crown. By mid-June the Venetian ambassador in Rome reported that there was no more talk of
marriage between Cesare and Carlotta, since King Federigo had said
publicly: 'It seems to me that the Pope's son, the Cardinal, is not
in a condition for me to give him my daughter to wife, even if he
is the son of the Pope,' adding: 'Make a cardinal who can marry and
take off the hat, and *then* I will give him my daughter.'

As a sop to the Borgias, whom he bitterly described as 'insatiable',
Federigo sent Alfonso to Rome to marry Lucrezia. His arrival on 15
July was supposed to be secret, but Ascanio wrote dryly to his brother

that 'the secret of the Duke's presence here is known all over Rome', noting that Cesare's reception of his new brother-in-law was especially cordial and affectionate. Cesare had every reason to be kind to Alfonso, whose wedding to Lucrezia was generally regarded as a stepping-stone towards the greater object of his own marriage to Carlotta of Aragon.

Lucrezia herself was delighted with her new bridegroom, a handsome boy who charmed everyone who met him, and it was soon obvious that the young couple were genuinely in love. The wedding, celebrated in the Vatican on 21 July, was a family affair. The ambassadors, who were not invited, were naturally avid to pick up any titbits of information about the festivities which they could retail to their masters. As usual the Borgias did not disappoint them; the Mantuan envoy reported that an unseemly brawl between Cesare's and Sancia's servants marred the happy occasion. Swords were drawn in the presence of the Pope in the room outside the chapel where refreshments were to be served before the wedding breakfast, and two bishops exchanged fisticuffs. The scuffle caused such confusion that the servitors were unable to bring in the traditional sweetmeats and sugared almonds. When the turmoil eventually died down, the family party were able to sit down to a breakfast that lasted three hours until dusk. In the tableaux presented during the course of the feast, Cesare himself appeared in the strangely inapposite role of a Unicorn, the symbol of Chastity!

As he danced behind the horned mask at his sister's wedding, Cesare's thoughts must have turned optimistically to his own marriage projects. Despite King Federigo's continuing obstinacy, the Borgias had found a new and powerful ally. In fact the summer of 1498 marked a dramatic reorientation of Borgia policy, as Alexander, in his search for a state and a wife for his son, turned away from his traditional friendship with Ferdinand of Aragon towards alliance with France. As spring passed into summer it had become increasingly apparent that Ferdinand represented the main obstacle to the plans for Cesare. Not only did he support Federigo, who was now entirely dependent upon him, in his obstinacy over the Neapolitan marriage, but he had expressed his strong opposition, and that of Isabella, to Cesare's proposed renunciation of the cardinalate, and had adamantly refused to consider the Borgias' demands that Gandia's estates should be transferred to him to compensate for the loss of his ecclesiastical revenues. On 2 March Cristoforo Poggio reported: 'I hear also that the Cardinal of Valencia will not put off the cloth, because he has not received the answer he wanted concerning the state of the late Duke of Gandia, which the King and Queen intend to go to his son, and as catholics are against such a deposition.' Three weeks later he wrote that 'the Most Reverend Valencia' intended to pursue his plan to renounce that cardinalate, despite the opposition of the King and Queen of Spain and their refusal to grant him Gandia's estates, since he was hoping to get what he wanted from Federigo.

The disparity between the two reports is indicative of the hesitations which Cesare felt at the prospect of crossing his personal Rubicon from the safe niche of the cardinalate to the uncertain shore of a secular future. Since the beginning of the year he had been seen more often in the practice of arms than in the exercise of his ecclesiastical duties. 'Monsignor of Valencia every day exercises the practice of arms, and seems resolved to be a gallant soldier,' Poggio wrote to Mantua on 19 January. His appearances in church were so rare as to cause Burchard to note with surprise on 21 April: 'Cardinal Valentino attended the solemn mass in the papal chapel, he has not been seen since Passion Sunday.' It was to be his last appearance: from then on he no longer attended ecclesiastical functions, nor wore the robes of a churchman. But at one point in the summer of 1498 the difficulties raised by Ferdinand and Federigo seem to have made him lose heart and wish to draw back. He was only driven on by the will of his forceful father. In June Ascanio wrote to Ludovico that Alexander was 'every hour more ardent in his desire that this Valentino should change the habit; although Valentino does not want to, His Holiness has decided that he will do so ...'

For the relentless Alexander had found a new avenue which he hoped would lead to a brilliant future for his son. Already in March, faced with Ferdinand's antagonistic attitude, he had sent a friendly mission to Charles VIII of France. Charles made accommodating noises, but negotiations were interrupted by his sudden death at Amboise on 7 April 1498. Charles' demise was a stroke of good fortune for Alexander: his successor, Louis XII, the former Duke of Orleans, had pressing domestic and external reasons for seeking the Pope's friendship. First, he wanted to divorce his wife, Jeanne de France, in order to marry Charles' widow, Anne of Brittany, so as to keep Brittany as an appanage of the French crown, and for this he urgently needed a dispensation from the Pope. Secondly, he had inherited not only the Angevin claims to Naples but also the Orleanist rights to

Milan, and his assumption of both titles on his accession made it abundantly clear that he intended to assert them, in which case the Pope's blessing on his enterprise would be essential to him.

Alexander was not slow to see the advantages which could be extracted from this new situation. As Machiavelli wrote: 'The times served him well, since he found a king who, to separate himself from his old wife, promised and gave him more than any other.' Although contemporaries like Machiavelli saw Alexander's increasingly pro-French stance as motivated solely by his ambitions for Cesare, this was an oversimplification. Alexander was essentially a pragmatist, his policies always adapted to the realities of the Italian and international situation. By 1498 the League that had chased Charles VIII out of Italy lay in ruins. Within three months of Fornovo, in October 1495, Ludovico had hastened to make his separate peace with Charles at Vercelli, a typically turncoat reaction which did not endear him to his former allies. Venice, now violently anti-Milanese, was moving ever closer towards France; Naples, shattered and impoverished, was totally dependent on the arms and support of Spain; while Florence, debilitated and now hardly to be counted as a major power, was equally reliant on France for existence. It was clear to anyone as experienced in international politics as Alexander not only that another French invasion was imminent, but that from henceforward the physical presence in Italy of two foreign powers, France and Spain, was equally inevitable. For Alexander to oppose the French this time as he had in 1494 would have been unrealistic, to do so would have been to place the Papacy squarely in the arms of Ferdinand of Aragon. His aim was to increase the power and influence of the Papacy by playing the two powers off against each other, meanwhile extracting the greatest advantages for himself from either side. In 1498 it was obvious that there was nothing to be gained from Ferdinand, while an alliance with Louis offered a wide range of interesting possibilities.

In June Louis and Alexander exchanged missions. The French envoys were charged by their master to ask for dissolution of his marriage to Jeanne de France on the grounds of his having been constrained to it against his will by Louis XI, and that due to his wife's deformity he had been unable to consummate it. In the last days of the month Alexander's secret envoy, Francisco d'Almeida, Bishop of Ceuta, left Rome for France, where he arrived at court on 21 July. On 29 July, as a token of his goodwill, the Pope signed a rescript constituting the tribunal to examine the case for nullification of the King's marriage. The outcome of d'Almeida's mission is revealed in a document found in the archives at Pau, the text of a secret agreement under which Louis promised to support Cesare's Neapolitan marriage project, and made several important undertakings in his favour:

1 The grant of the counties of Valence and Diois, the former to be raised to the rank of duchy, and the revenues of these estates to be made up to 20,000 gold francs.
2 The appointment of Cesare to the command of a corps of 100 *lances fournies*, to be maintained at the King's expense at Cesare's orders in Italy or elsewhere; this corps to be increased at the King's option to 200 or 300 lances – an army of nearly 2000 heavy cavalry.
3 A personal subsidy to Cesare from the crown of 20,000 gold francs per annum.
4 Upon the conquest of Milan Cesare was to be invested with the feudal lordship of Asti.
5 Cesare would be invested with the collar of the Order of St Michael.

Cesare was to go to France, where Carlotta of Aragon was residing at the French court, for the marriage. To compensate the Pope for the loss of his presence, Louis promised to place at Alexander's disposal in Rome a force of a thousand men, or alternatively 4000 ducats a month to pay for them, a proposal which indicated the extent to which Alexander already relied upon Cesare for security at Rome, especially in face of the renewed hostility from the Roman barons which manifested itself in July 1498.

This document is a significant illustration of Borgia aims and policy in the summer of 1498. Beyond the Neapolitan marriage and the provision of a high secular state and revenues for Cesare, he was to be launched on a career of military conquest in command of a significant body of troops. In return, Alexander tacitly abandoned Milan, Naples and his former friendship with Ferdinand, and held out to Louis the almost certain prospect of the dissolution of his marriage. In August d'Almeida returned to Rome with the news that Louis was sending an envoy, Monsieur de Trans, to Rome with the patents investing Cesare with Valence and Diois, and ships to escort him to France.

For Cesare, the die was cast. On Friday, 17 August 1498, he publicly announced his decision to put off the purple. Burchard reported:

There was a secret consistory, in which the Cardinal Valentino declared that from his early years he was always, with all his spirit, inclined to the secular condition; but that the Holy Father had wished absolutely that he should give himself to the ecclesiastical state, and he had not believed he should oppose his will. But since his mind and his desire and his inclination were still for the secular life, he besought His Holiness Our Lord, that he should condescend, with special clemency, to give him a dispensation, so that, having put off the robe and ecclesiastical dignity, he might be permitted to return to the secular estate and contract matrimony; and that he now prayed the most reverend lord cardinals to willingly give their consent to such a dispensation.

Cesare made his dramatic announcement to a half-empty house. Many of the cardinals, foreseeing an unpleasant confrontation with their consciences or their allegiances (the Spanish cardinals in particular), had absented themselves from Rome on the excuse of *villeggiatura*, the annual escape to the country from the heat and pestilence of the city. Relentlessly, Alexander rounded them up to give the stamp of their consent to this unprecedented step. He arranged for a further consistory to be held on 23 August, and, as the Venetian envoy reported, 'wrote to all the cardinals who were in the neighbourhood of Rome, that they must come to the city, because matters were to be discussed touching the good of the Church and Christianity!' Browbeaten thus by the Pope, the cardinals yielded. 'The Pope,' wrote the same envoy two days later, 'with all the cardinals' votes, has given licence that the Cardinal of Valencia, son of the Pope, could put off the hat and make himself a soldier and get himself a wife.' The news caused scandal in Italy, France and Spain, but Cesare cared little for the world's opinions. On the day of the consistory on the 17th, the French King's envoy, de Trans, Baron de Villeneuve, arrived in Rome bearing the letters patent that would entitle the former Cardinal of Valencia to call himself duc de Valentinois. For Italians, the two foreign titles sounded almost the same; and 'Valencia' became 'il Valentino'.

Cesare, at twenty-three, had crossed his Rubicon. His own consciousness of the importance of the step he was taking and its implications are embodied in the design of a magnificent parade sword made for him during the summer of 1498. The sword is decorated with Borgia emblems, bulls, and the downward-pointing rays, with the

The parade sword made for Cesare Borgia in 1498

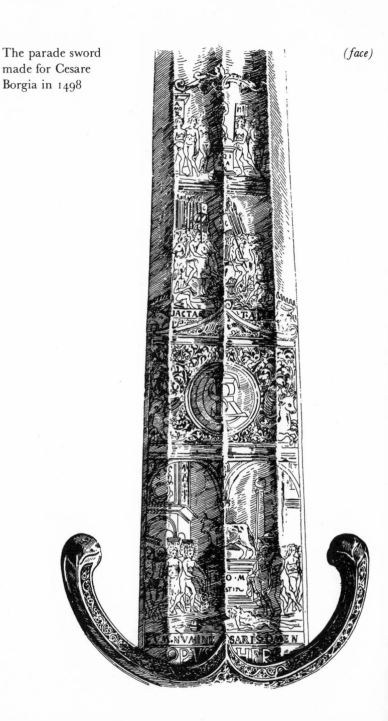

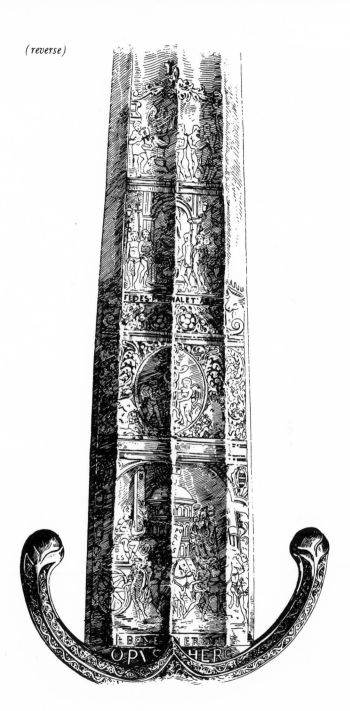

name CESAR arranged as a monogram, and its central theme is illustrated in six classical scenes engraved on the blade. The first repre-
sents the worship or sacrifice of a bull, standing on an altar inscribed
'D.O.M. Hostia' – *Deo optimo maximo hostia*: 'a sacrifice to the most
high god'; underneath it runs the significant inscription: '*Cum Numine
Caesaris Omen*', 'a favourable omen with Caesar's divine good will'.
The second shows Caesar crossing the Rubicon and inscribed beneath
it his famous comment, '*Jacta est Alea*', 'the die is cast'. The third
depicts the triumphs of Caesar, riding in a chariot inscribed D. Cesar
('*Divus Caesar*', 'Divine Caesar', which could also be a reference to
Cesare's own Spanish name and title, Don Cesar); beneath runs the
motto '*Benemerent*', 'to the well-deserving'. The other three vignettes
represent Faith, the Roman Peace, and the worship of Love, frequently used as a symbol in Borgia decoration; while on the equally
elaborate leather scabbard made for the sword (but never used) there
is a scene representing the worship of Venus, who as a planet goddess
was associated with the zodiac sign of Taurus, and thus with the
Borgia emblem. Classical imagery as used in the Renaissance was
never meaningless decoration; the scenes representing Caesar's life
were clearly of great personal significance to Cesare, symbolizing his
own renunciation of the cardinalate and his hoped-for triumph in the
secular world. For him, as for Caesar, arms would be the road to
power. And with the motto '*Cum Numine Caesaris Omen*', Cesare in-
voked his great namesake's protection and help in his new career.

He now concentrated on preparing himself physically for his future
as a man of action. His preparations included bullfighting on horseback, a Spanish sport which amazed contemporary Italians. Cattaneo
reported on 18 August, the day after the consistory in which he had
announced his decision to lay down the cardinalate: 'In these days
Valencia, armed as a janissary, with another fourteen men, gave
many blows and proofs of strength in killing eight bulls in the presence
of Don Alfonso, Donna Lucretia and "his Princess" [Sancia], in Monsignor Ascanio's park where he had taken them remote from the
crowd for greater privacy. In a few days' time I hope to see him fully
armed on the piazza.' On at least one occasion, however, his physical
exercises ended less gloriously; Cattaneo reported on 29 August that
the previous evening Cesare had been practising in the gardens of
the Pope's *vigna* (the Belvedere in the Vatican garden) leaping astride
horses and mules in one bound without touching the harness. He then
'tried to leap in that manner onto a somewhat taller mule and when

he was in the air, the mule took fright and gave him a couple of kicks in the ribs, one on the right shoulder, and the other on the back of his head. He was unconscious for more than half an hour.'

While this violent physical exercise was designed to keep his athletic body in trim, Cesare was seriously worried by his appearance. At this critical moment in his life, when he wished above all to impress the French court and a new bride with his splendid looks, the signs of secondary syphilis began to manifest themselves on his body, and, disastrously for him, on his face. Cattaneo remarked on his departure from Rome: 'He is well enough in countenance at present, although he has his face blotched beneath the skin as is usual with the great pox.' One can imagine the demoralizing shock suffered by a handsome young man of twenty-three at this inopportune reappearance of a disease of which he must have thought himself cured. Syphilis was a new phenomenon at that time, and relatively little was known about it; Cesare would not have known that the unsightly brown rash and dry skin which marked its secondary stage would clear up of itself within two or three months, and he must have been worried about its effect on his matrimonial prospects and his reception at court. The inner doubts and uncertainties which he felt at this testing moment in his life were outwardly revealed by his continuing to sign himself 'Cardinal Valentinus', as if he could not bring himself wholeheartedly to believe in his secular future. As Cattaneo wrote after his departure for France: 'Valencia has certainly left in lay clothes, and having made his preparations as duke, nonetheless he signed himself up to the last moment as Cesar, Card. Valentino ... and this perhaps as a precaution if things did not come out out as he wished or that perhaps, because of that face of his, spoiled by the French disease, his wife might refuse him.'

Cesare was well aware that if his crossing of the Rubicon could lead, as it had for Caesar, to fame and power, it could equally lead to ignominious failure. In turning their backs on the powerful King Ferdinand, and gambling on Louis for Cesare's future, the Borgias were playing a dangerous game. 'The King of Spain [is] extremely displeased with these ways of the Pope and Valencia,' commented Cattaneo. '... However the Pope will disregard this, knowing that anyway there will be a rupture between them for this or for another cause.' Alexander, he reported, said that he cared little for the children of the Duke of Gandia because they were more closely related to the King of Spain than to himself. This declaration of indifference to the children of his beloved Juan indicated the total abandonment of his Spanish dynastic policy and single-minded concentration of all his hopes upon Cesare's future through France. Observers who were less daring and less involved than Alexander warned him of the dangers of his high game, not the least of which could be that Louis might use Cesare's presence at court as a hostage to bend his father to his will. Cattaneo reported that when the Pope boasted to a great cardinal of Louis' desire to have Cesare in his service, the cardinal replied:

> It is true that Valencia is a dexterous man and has practised much in the exercise of arms, horses, and leaping, and uses his physical capacities to the full ... but, believe me, Holy Father, that the King wants him because he doesn't trust you, and Your Holiness is content in order to execute your own designs, but beware that you do not aim so high that, you or he falling, you will break too many bones ...

But the Borgias were gamblers by nature; having weighed up the odds, they considered the prize worth the risk. No doubt Alexander, with his immense skill and experience in the game of high politics, thought that he would be able to handle Louis as easily as he had outmanoeuvred Charles.

Whatever the outcome might prove to be, Alexander and Cesare were determined to astound the French court with the splendour of the Papacy and the family. In an anxious desire to impress, Cesare spent wildly in the months before his departure from Rome. Two hundred thousand ducats had been raised for his expenses, partly from the confiscated goods of Pedro de Aranda, Bishop of Calahorra, who had lately been condemned for heresy, and partly, it was said, from the possessions of three hundred Jews. The money was spent on buying rich stuffs, jewels, gold and silverware to such an extent that the Mantuan envoy reported that Roman supplies were exhausted, and additional luxuries had to be imported from Venice and elsewhere. Cesare wrote to Francesco Gonzaga, asking him to send him horses from his famous stud – 'We find ourselves absolutely destitute of fine coursers suitable to us in such a journey' – and a few days later to Cardinal Ippolito d'Este, requesting 'a courser not unworthy of French esteem', following it up with a demand for musicians. He went to the extremes of extravagance in his determination to bedazzle the French; the Gonzaga coursers were to be shod with silver, while

Cattaneo reported that he took with him a most princely travelling privy 'covered with gold brocade without and scarlet within, with silver vessels within the silver urinals ...'

Thus magnificently equipped, Cesare took formal leave of his father on 1 October, and received from him letters of recommendation to Louis filled with expressions of the most extravagant paternal love: 'We send Your Majesty our heart, that is to say our beloved son, Duke Valentino, who to us is the dearest of all ...' Alexander remained at a window of the Vatican watching Cesare until he was out of sight. Burchard, who continued to refer to him as 'Cardinalis Valentinus', wrote that he departed 'secretly and without pomp'. This was true only in the sense that there was no official procession. Cesare's progress from the Vatican to the Banchi, where he was to embark for Ostia, must have caused a considerable stir. He was dressed in a white brocade tunic, with a mantle of black velvet thrown over his shoulders (the first reported instance of his penchant for dressing in black velvet), a matching cap blazing with large rubies, and boots sewn with gold chains and pearls. Even his bay horse was draped in red silk and gold brocade, the colours of the royal house of France to which Cesare now belonged as Duke of Valentinois, while its shoes and harness were of silver. He was accompanied by Gaspare Torella, his personal physician, his confidential secretary Agapito Geraldini da Amelia, and the Spanish master of his household, Ramiro de Lorqua, later notorious as the ferocious governor of the Romagna, plus a hundred pages, squires and grooms in crimson velvet halved with yellow silk, twelve baggage carts, fifty baggage mules, and a string of *gianette*, Spanish riding horses; the heavier chargers, *corsieri*, had silver harness with silver bells – shades of Gandia – tinkling at their necks. A large suite of Spanish and Roman noblemen embarked with him: the Spaniards were soberly dressed in their national style; the thirty Romans, who included Giangiordano Orsini, son of Virginio, were as flamboyant as their leader in cloth of silver and gold, and had spent a thousand ducats apiece on their wardrobes for the expedition.

While Burchard, used to Italian ways, could describe Cesare's departure as 'without pomp', the ostentation of his dress and equipment was to disgust the French court, accustomed to plainer northern customs. In Renaissance Italy the magnificence of a person's outward appearance was considered an essential manifestation of his standing and importance. Cesare, though half-Spanish, was Italian enough to regard *far bella figura*, 'cutting a fine figure', as of prime importance. But it may be too that his over-ostentation betrayed an inner lack of self-confidence. Later, at the height of his power, he dressed in plain black velvet. The peacock splendour of his attire belongs to this early, uncertain phase of his career. And there was a physical reason for his flashy appearance at this time – the desire to enhance his superb athletic body to distract attention from his diseased face, natural in a young man bitterly conscious that his beauty had been marred, and who had not yet found success to bolster his self-esteem. Torn between the high ambitions expressed on his magnificent sword, and the doubts and uncertainties concealed beneath his splendid clothes and self-confident bearing, Cesare launched himself on his new career, embarking symbolically in a French ship.

His potential as a man to be watched, as distinct from his father the Pope, was now beginning to be recognized by observers at the Roman court. 'All the principal fortresses are at Valencia's disposal by the Pope's will,' the Mantuan envoy wrote ominously on 3 October. 'Above all the castellans are Valencia's men rather than the Pope's . . .' The wary envoys who haunted the Vatican antechambers, political reporters avid for significant news, were becoming aware of the nature of the Borgias, father and son, and of the scale of their ambitions. The significance of Cesare's departure upon a French ship, destined for a military career, was not lost upon them. As Cattaneo wrote with wry foreboding on the day Cesare left Rome: 'The ruin of Italy is confirmed . . . given the plans which father and son have made: but many believe the Holy Spirit has no part in them . . .'

VI

TWO WOMEN

CESARE and his extraordinary suite disembarked in late October sun-shine at Marseilles under the stares of the Marseillais crowding the quays. They met with a royal reception: salvoes of artillery rent the air as the local notabilities greeted them, and Louis XII had sent a guard of 400 archers as a mark of special honour. Cesare spent several days at Marseilles feasting and seeing the sights of the town, including the relics of St Lazaire which were put on show for him. Since syphilis was often referred to in Italy as 'the malady of San Lazzaro', Cesare, who still bore the marks of the disease on his face, must have regarded this somewhat tactless exhibition with mixed feelings.

From Marseilles he went on to Avignon, the city of the popes, now the stronghold of Giuliano della Rovere, who resided there as Papal Legate, and of his nephew Clemente, Bishop of Mende and governor of the city. It was now a year since Giuliano had made his peace with the Borgias, a reconciliation signalled by Alexander's handing back his fortress of Ostia, but he prudently preferred to continue living at Avignon, at a safe distance from Rome. For the moment it suited both men to be on good terms. Giuliano planned to make his way back to power in Rome, while Alexander hoped that Giuliano's influence would help to further his designs at the French court. As he wrote gratefully to him on 1 September: 'We are not unaware with what great effect Your Fraternity has argued our case to the King.' How-ever there is evidence that the devious Cardinal, even while apparently pressing the Borgias' case at court, was secretly involved with Ludovico il Moro in a somewhat pathetic intrigue against them. Evidence of Giuliano's double-dealing is revealed in a letter from one of il Moro's secret agents who was at Avignon when Cesare arrived there. The letter employs code names – Madama Margherita for Ludovico, Lorenzo for Giuliano, Pietro for Cesare and Cristoforo for Louis XII, while the agent signs himself simply 'B'. Ludovico, aware of Louis' designs on Milan, was terrified by the prospect of an alliance between France and the Papacy, and determined to do everything in his power to prevent it. 'B' writes of Giuliano's willingness to accommodate Ludovico, doubtless by throwing a spanner in the works of the Borgia negotiations at the French court:

> Madama Margherita,
> ... You will understand how I came to Avignon to speak with Lorenzo of the matter which we discussed together, so that our interest may be well served in this matter and Lorenzo has received me with the best possible countenance, and has told me that he is all mine, and in the matters in which he may serve me, he will be at my disposition. Thus I believe he will do all that he will ... It seems to me that he has the malady of San Lazzaro in his face. Also Pietro is none too well of his malady, I believe. Lorenzo and Pietro will soon depart from here to do his business with M. Cristoforo.

Giuliano's assurances to Ludovico's anonymous envoy that he was 'all his' may well have gone no further than mere words. Although no doubt he would have been happy to do down the Borgias if he could, Giuliano was adept at picking the winning side, and can have had no illusions as to whose would be the lost cause if it came to a clash between the King of France and the ruler of Milan. And so he prepared a magnificent reception for Cesare, his former colleague in the College of Cardinals and son of his old enemy Rodrigo Borgia. The city council raised 2000 golden crowns to pay for the festivities, which were to include decorations, the presentation of tableaux and gifts of silverware and preserved fruits. Giuliano must have informed the councillors of Cesare's predilection for beautiful women, since the document recording their decisions specifies: 'He must be honoured at the City Palace by ladies and beautiful girls who should know well how to entertain him with dances, because the aforesaid Don Cesare finds pleasure in this...'

While the celebrated *demoiselles d'Avignon* prepared themselves to greet their appreciative guest, Giuliano, accompanied by his nephew and Cardinal Gurck, another anti-Borgia refugee, rode to meet Cesare two miles outside the city. It is difficult to imagine the feelings of the two men as they embraced in the blue light of that Provençal autumn. Cesare had not seen Giuliano since his dramatic escape from

Velletri four years before, since when Giuliano had been living the bitter life of a self-imposed exile in France, well out of his father's reach. No doubt, beneath the cordial greetings, each was deeply wary of the other, but they rode together in apparent amity into Avignon, under a triumphal arch bearing the arms of the Pope, Cesare and the della Roveres. 'Avignon never witnessed such an enthusiastic welcome, never such a splendid procession', wrote a local chronicler. Cesare and his suite were lodged in the archiepiscopal palace as Giuliano's guests for ten days at an estimated cost of 7000 ducats. Among the entertainments provided for him was a reception at the Hôtel de Ville on All Saints' Day, 1 November, when the *moresca*, normally performed by men, was danced by local beauties in deference to his well-known predilections. No doubt Cesare noted the loveliness of the women of Avignon, but for the time being he was limited to a purely passive appreciation. Shortly after his arrival, both guest and host suffered a recurrence of their malady. Il Moro's informant 'B' reported with malicious pleasure: 'Della Rovere has fallen sick of that disease of his: now the flowers are beginning to bloom again [the syphilitic rash]. If God does not help him he will never be quite healthy. They say publicly of Cesare that he has the malady of San Lazzaro on his face, and moreover he is not in a contented frame of mind ...'

The mysterious 'B' guessed correctly when he referred to Cesare's uneasy state of mind. Whether or not he had suspicions of Giuliano's treacherous intrigues, he was restless, made nervous by inactivity, impatient of the protracted delay, and longing to reach the court and get his 'business' done. Almost certainly, on Alexander's orders, he was waiting for news from Rome which would enable him to present the King with the dispensation for his marriage with Anne of Brittany, without which he knew he would not find a welcome at court. And so, fretting with impatience and uncertainty, he dawdled his way northward, trying to find relief from his doubts and anxieties in a constant round of festivities. From Avignon he went to the capital of his new duchy, Valence; when Louis was asked by the Venetian ambassador when they might expect to see the Duke of Valentinois at court, he replied with an enigmatic smile: 'He is in the Dauphinate, in a land where there are beautiful women and good wine, and he is there feasting and dining well.' On 7 November he made a solemn entrance into Lyons, where a gargantuan banquet was held in his honour. But things were going sour; the French were not as impressed by Cesare as he had expected they would be. They found the Italians' ostentatious luxury vulgar, and Cesare's own manners arrogant. He seems to have displayed little of his famous charm, except perhaps to the women. Inwardly unsure of himself, he could be brusque, prickly, apprehensive of slights to his honour and status. When, at Valence during a festive reception in his honour, the King's special envoy Monsieur de Clerieux attempted to bestow upon him the collar of the Order of St Michael, Cesare brushed him aside, saying haughtily that he intended to receive it only from the King's own hands.

At last news came that the sentence of the Divorce Commission set up to inquire into the validity of Louis' marriage to Jeanne de France was ready for delivery. Through the medium of Giuliano, who had ridden ahead to prepare for Cesare's reception at court, it was arranged that he should meet the King at the castle of Chinon in Touraine, where the court was then staying. On 17 December, carefully timing his arrival to coincide with the Divorce Tribunal's pronouncement in favour of annulment, Cesare reached the neighbourhood of the castle. The circumstances of his meeting with Louis raised awkward points of protocol: he was not a prince of the blood, nor the son of a king; no provision had been made under the rules of etiquette for the reception of the son of a pope, nor could he officially be considered as such. It would have been considered improper for the King to go out and meet him. Strictly speaking, Cesare should enter the castle on his own to be received there by him. However, Louis solved the problem by a simple expedient: he went hunting the day after Cesare's arrival, and on his return from the chase met him, as if by chance, the requisite two miles from the town. After giving him the most cordial welcome, he retired to the castle, leaving Cesare to make his solemn entrance on his own.

This was the moment for which he had been waiting, his chance to impress the King of France with the power and wealth of the Borgias, to show the world that the bastard son of the Pope could rival legitimate princes in magnificence. If it was a glorious moment, it was also an anxious one; his entry into Chinon would represent his first step on the international stage. Waiting before the great medieval castle of Chinon which crowned the hill above the town alongside the River Vienne, with the critically expectant eyes of the French court upon him, Cesare must have experienced some of the nervous anxiety of a parvenu.

But Cesare was his father's son, and any pangs of inferiority were camouflaged behind a screen of dazzling display. His entry into Chinon, wrote the Genoese ambassador, surpassed in pomp the triumphal progress of a Roman emperor. An ancestor of the chronicler Brantôme was so impressed by the scene that he left an eye-witness account in the family archives which Brantôme later transcribed:

The Duke of Valentinois entered thus on Wednesday, the eighteenth day of December 1498. Before him marched the Cardinal of Rouen, M. de Ravestain, the Seneschal of Toulouse, M. de Clermont, with many Lords and Gentlemen to the foot of the bridge; he was preceded by twenty-four handsome mules carrying trunks, coffers and chests, covered with cloths bearing the Duke's arms, then again came another twenty-four mules with their trappings halved in red and yellow ... the colours of the King, then twelve mules with coverings of yellow striped satin. Then came six mules with trappings of cloth of gold, of which one stripe was of cloth of gold cut, the other smooth, which made seventy in all ...

And after came sixteen beautiful great chargers, led by grooms, covered in cloth of gold, crimson and yellow ... after these came eighteen pages, each one on a fine charger, of whom sixteen were dressed in crimson velvet, the two others in cloth of gold. These, the people said, must be his two favourites. Then came six fine mules richly equipped with saddles, bridles and trappings in crimson velvet, accompanied by grooms dressed in the same. Then two mules carrying coffers and all covered in cloth of gold. The people said that those two must be carrying something more exquisite than the others, either beautiful rich jewels for his mistress, and for others, or some Bulls and fine Indulgences from Rome, or some Holy Relics. Then after came thirty gentlemen [Cesare's Roman noblemen] clad in cloth of gold and silver, followed by three musicians, two tambours and one rebec, dressed in cloth of gold according to the style of their country, and their rebecs had strings of gold. They marched between the gentlemen and the Duke of Valentinois, playing all the while. Then came four with trumpets and clarions of silver, richly dressed, playing their instruments without ceasing. There were also twenty-four lackeys all clad in crimson velvet halved with yellow silk, and they were all around the Duke; beside him rode the Cardinal of Rouen, conversing with him.

As to the Duke, he was mounted on a great tall horse [one of the Gonzaga *corsieri*] very richly harnessed, with a covering of red satin halved with cloth of gold (in truth I am not very sure what stuff it might be) and embroidered with very rich gems and large pearls. In his bonnet were two double rows of five or six rubies, as large as a big bean, which gave out a great light. On the brim of his bonnet there were also a great quantity of jewels, even to his boots, which were all adorned with chains of gold and edged with pearls.

The collar he wore, wrote Brantôme's anonymous ancestor, was worth a good thirty thousand ducats, and featured a great pendant blazing with diamonds. Even his horse was laden 'with leaves of gold and covered with works of the goldsmith's art' and he had besides 'a beautiful little mule for promenading in the Town which had all its harness... covered with roses of fine gold the thickness of a finger...'

While the people lining the narrow streets of the little town were dazzled by the jewels and strange, glittering materials of Cesare's retinue, the more sophisticated courtiers mocked at this ostentatious display. The King and his nobles, watching Cesare's arrival from the windows of the castle, made jokes at his expense, saying 'it was all too much for a little duke of Valentinois'.

At the castle Cesare dismounted, walked past the royal guard of 200 archers drawn up in his honour, and went into the great hall where the King was waiting with Giuliano and the lords of his court. The Venetian diarist Sanuto reported the scene: 'entering the hall he made a most profound reverence to the ground to His Majesty; then half way across the hall another reverence; and then the King took off his cap; and the Duke, coming up to the King, bent to kiss his foot, but the King preventing this, he kissed his hand, as did the gentlemen of his suite.' After conversing with the King, he was accompanied to his apartments, which were near the King's own, by the Cardinal of Rouen, Georges d'Amboise, attended by lords and gentlemen of the court whom Louis had sent to honour him. After dinner the King sent his guard to escort him to the royal apartments, and 'il Valentino returned to the King, with whom he remained to the fourth hour of night, and was much caressed by him'. At Chinon, the centre of attention of the French court, flattered by the King, and attended by his confidential minister, the great Cardinal of

Rouen, it could be said that 'the little duke of Valentinois' had arrived.

The court's stay at Chinon, the historic medieval fortress where Joan of Arc had her famous interview with Charles VII urging him to save France, was a temporary one. In fact the court was always on the move, rarely staying in one place for more than a fortnight, causing great inconvenience to the foreign ambassadors who complained bitterly, comparing themselves to gypsies. They wandered from château to château through the beautiful valley of the Loire, from Chinon to Louis' favourite Blois, where he was making extensive additions, to Amboise, which his predecessor Charles had loved, and where workmen brought from Italy were still finishing the masonry, decorations and gardens of the palace, sometimes returning to Paris, even going as far afield as Lorraine, Provence, Burgundy, Auvergne. 'When the court descends upon a place,' wrote an irritated ambassador, 'it stays as long as the herons last, and they don't last long, for between the King and the great men in his suite they have more than five hundred falcons.'

The new ruler of France, Louis XII, as the Venetian envoys described him at this time was a tall, thin man of thirty-six, of pleasing appearance, with a large face and nose, and a wiry, athletic body, well conditioned by his passionate devotion to falconry, which he pursued from September to April, and to hunting the red deer in the summer. Wild as a youth, turbulent and rebellious as a young man, as King, Louis seemed to have settled down, and was to lead a blameless private life when he married the strong-minded Anne of Brittany. He was, said the ambassadors, gracious and kindly, and of a merry disposition; he was also more intelligent than his predecessor – although that was not saying much. He was not a fool, but neither was he a very clever man, and lacked the essential capacity to take the long view in politics; he was therefore easily outwitted by his intellectual superiors, Alexander VI and Ferdinand of Aragon. He was abstemious, and almost invariably ate only boiled meats; he dressed simply in black velvet, and was prudent and economical, which earned him the reputation with Italians of being 'avaricious and niggardly'. He was extremely obstinate, with a stubbornness that would allow nothing to deflect him from an object once he had decided upon it; similarly he lacked flexibility and found it difficult to change his plans once made, or to shape them to changing circumstances. In 1498 his somewhat narrow mind was obsessed with the idea of gaining Milan.

The people who exerted influence over Louis were the Queen, Anne of Brittany, and his first minister, Georges d'Amboise, Cardinal of Rouen, one of a long line of ecclesiastical powers behind the French throne. D'Amboise, two years older than Louis, had shared his troubled experiences as Duke of Orleans. Now that he was King, he shared his power. Wise, able, a great administrator and an excellent businessman, he was, by the standards of the times, honest, and personally agreeable. As Machiavelli remarked with surprise, he had 'shown himself to be more pleasant and easy than could have been expected of one who is both a great lord and a Frenchman'. D'Amboise's one weakness, which the Borgias were quick to seize upon and turn to their advantage, was a burning ambition, first for the cardinalate – Cesare brought the cardinal's hat for him in his baggage to Chinon, as the *quid pro quo* for his own duchy of Valentinois – secondly for the Legateship of France, which the Borgias were now dangling as bait for him, and lastly for the papal tiara.

While the influence of d'Amboise was paramount as far as Louis' Italian policy was concerned, that of the Queen was strongest at home. Anne, heiress of Brittany, had been devoted to her hideous husband, Charles VIII, despite his rampant infidelities. She was griefstricken when he died, and at first refused Louis, whom she believed to have rejoiced at the death of her son by Charles. Then suddenly in August 1498 she had changed her mind, and agreed to become Queen of France if Louis could obtain from the Pope the annulment of his marriage to Jeanne and a dispensation to marry his predecessor's widow. Anne, as the Venetian envoys sent to congratulate her upon her marriage immediately remarked, had no pretensions to beauty, but she was intelligent, cultured and elegant. Under her guidance, rather than that of her less educated husband, the French court developed the first glimmerings of the Renaissance splendour which illuminated the glamorous reign of Louis' successor, Francis I. Anne's taste and liberality redeemed the court from the shadow of Louis' 'niggardliness'; she dressed well, and gathered round her the musicians, painters, poets, jewellers and men of letters, also the inevitable crowds of clowns and buffoons, without which no court of the Renaissance would have been considered complete. The nobility of France sent their daughters to Anne, as to a finishing school, to learn taste, manners and the usual court accomplishments, music, singing and dancing – and to find a suitable husband. As Père Hilarion de Coste wrote in his *Éloge d'Anne de Bretagne*: 'The Queen, like another Vesta or another Diana, kept all her nymphs under very strict discipline, but remained nonetheless full of sweetness and courtesy.'

It was among the Queen's circle of 'nymphs' that Cesare met for the first time his intended bride, Carlotta of Naples, daughter of King Federigo. The encounter cannot have been encouraging for him; Carlotta was both plain and determined, making no secret of her repugnance at the idea of marrying Cesare, openly declaring that she had no intention of being known as 'La Cardinala'. Moreover she was in love with a Breton nobleman. But if Cesare failed to alter Carlotta's view of him as a husband, he soon won over the rest of the court, and particularly Louis, over whom from then on he seems to have exercised a potent fascination. As he began to feel at home in his surroundings, his self-confidence returned, and the charm and conviviality which Boccaccio had noted in him aged seventeen conquered the initially bad impression created by his ostentation. His looks and intelligence, fondness for feasting and dancing, skill at hunting and expert horsemanship made him a brilliant and agreeable companion. Moreover he seems to have had an ability, rare among his Italian contemporaries, for getting on well with the French. 'In war he was a good companion and a brave man,' a French fellow officer later wrote of him. Indeed Louis regarded him as a considerable asset to his court, as Giuliano wrote to Alexander on 18 January 1499, in a letter designed to gladden the fond father's heart: 'I cannot refrain from informing Your Holiness that the most illustrious Duke Valentino is so endowed with modesty, prudence, ability and every virtue of mind and body, that he has conquered everybody; he has found so much favour with the King, and all the princes of this court, that everyone holds him in esteem and honour, of which fact I willingly and gladly give testimony.'

Social success, however gratifying, was not enough; Cesare needed concrete results to show for his mission to the French court, and they were not immediately forthcoming. The first cards in the diplomatic game had been already exchanged: Cesare had had his duchy, Louis his divorce, and d'Amboise his cardinal's hat. Cesare's triumphal entry into Chinon was followed by a hiatus as far as the Borgias' plans were concerned, and the early months of 1499 were anxious times for them. For Cesare's sake, Alexander had covertly abandoned his traditional friendships and risked making a number of enemies who, if they should combine against him, could threaten his very position as Pope. Only the positive assurance of a bride, troops and money for Cesare could make the gamble worth while. And Cesare's position at court, despite his outward success, was difficult, even dangerous. He was the target both of secret resentment from those who were jealous of his favoured treatment, and of the concealed hostility of the pro-Milanese faction opposed to the policy he represented. On arrival he had, perforce, to hand over the dispensation for Louis to marry Anne. With this card dealt, how far could Louis be depended upon to carry out his promises? As Cattaneo reported in a dispatch of 10 January: 'The King caresses him extraordinarily and often takes him on his crupper on horseback, according to his letters. All the same a Spaniard who is with him, a man of wit, writes to a Cardinal relation of his, that he is afraid that within a few years it may be like the honours done to Christ on the day of Olives when later on Thursday they placed him on the cross ...'

Louis married Anne of Brittany on 6 January in the castle of Nantes, and in his gratitude bestowed upon Cesare the valuable lordship of Issoudun. But Cesare's own matrimonial prospects seemed uncertain, if not hopeless. Carlotta remained obdurate, despite all Louis' efforts to persuade her. As Giuliano reported to the Pope on 18 January: 'Either on her own impulse or through the persuasion of others, she has until now refused to marry the Duke, unless her father wills it.' Louis, he said, 'seems so perturbed by this feminine perversity, that he has declared that nothing else at the moment is so much on his mind,' while the Bishop of Melfi, sent by Alexander to press Louis over the marriage question, wrote that the King 'has not failed to make every effort that this marriage should come about, having shown signs of wishing to exile her from court'. On 4 February Alexander wrote gloomily that if the marriage failed to take place they would be the laughing stock of Italy, since it was well known that Cesare's main purpose in going to France was to take a wife. Early in February Cesare too seemed to despair, and showed signs of wishing to return to Rome, but he knew that he could not return empty-handed – too much was at stake for the indulgence of offended pride. So he hung on, hoping against hope, relying on Louis' evident good faith in the matter. Louis' treatment of the Neapolitan envoys who arrived at the end of the month seemed to justify his confidence. To the ambassador's offered pledge, in Federigo's name, of his person and realm, Louis answered shortly that the King of Naples could not offer what did not belong to him, that it was already his by right, adding menacingly that when he wanted it he would go and take it. When he then pressed the envoys on the subject of Cesare's marriage, they replied bluntly that 'to a bastard son of the Pope, the King not only would not give his legitimate daughter, but not even a bastard child', and began to speak ill of Alexander. Furious at such impertinence, Louis dismissed them on the spot. To calm the scandal caused by this scene, he made Carlotta dine alone with himself, the Queen and Cesare, in a last public effort to persuade her to yield. News of this dinner raised hopes in Rome to such a point that Burchard reported: 'It was also reported by some that Cesare, son of the Pope, formerly Cardinal Valentinus, had contracted matrimony with the daughter of the King of Naples in France where she now lives.' A few days later, however, Alexander learned the unpleasant truth from Giuliano. 'The marriage of Duke Valentino with the daughter of the King,' he wrote, 'was now totally excluded.'

Cesare's bitterness and disappointment at the definitive collapse of his hopes can only be imagined. Once again he talked of leaving, but this may have been a feint to put pressure upon Louis. He had set his heart upon the French alliance, and in his privileged proximity to the King he could see how firmly Louis had fixed his mind upon the assertion of his Italian claims, and how anxiously he desired a formal alliance with the Papacy. On 9 February, a league between France and Venice was signed at Blois, which it was left open to the Pope to join. Cesare was astute enough to see that the King's obvious need for the Borgias' friendship could only turn to his advantage. His main worry was that before he could achieve his objectives in France his father might weaken under the pressures being exerted upon him at home.

Alexander, holding the Borgia fortress alone at Rome, was beleaguered by enemies, besieged by doubts and anxieties. The announcement of Cesare's journey to France, with its clear implications of a Franco-Papal alliance, had brought a storm of protest down upon his head. The question of a new French invasion of Italy was uppermost in everybody's mind, and the attitude of the Papacy was of vital importance not only to the two threatened states, Naples and Milan, but also to Ferdinand of Aragon. Any formal alliance between Alexander and Louis would involve an open breach with Ferdinand, Federigo, and the Sforza brothers, Ludovico and Ascanio. In Rome itself, Alexander had succeeded in winning over the pro-French Orsinis, but the Colonnas leagued with Federigo in support of

Ascanio, and their attitude was so menacing that on All Saints' Day and other public occasions Alexander appeared with a strong armed guard.

The concerted diplomatic onslaught on Alexander by the anti-French powers began in November, when the Portuguese envoys at an audience with the Pope berated him violently for his nepotism, simony and above all for his French policy, which they said endangered the peace of Italy and of all Christendom. Ascanio reported the incident to Ludovico with malicious satisfaction: 'The demeanour of the Portuguese envoys is all the more unpleasant to the Pope in that he believes Their Spanish Majesties to be at the bottom of it, and that the Spanish envoys, who are daily expected, will say the same things or worse. He thinks that the King of the Romans [Maximilian] also has a hand in it, as he has made similar representations.' In December Alexander and Ascanio had a sharp interchange in consistory after Ascanio declared that in sending Cesare to France the Pope was bringing ruin on Italy. 'Are you aware, Monsignore,' Alexander replied dryly, 'that it was your brother who invited the French into Italy?' The Venetian ambassador was of the opinion that Ascanio intended, with the help of Ferdinand and Maximilian, to convene a Council to dethrone Alexander, on the grounds of simony of which he himself had been the principal beneficiary. On 19 December the Spanish envoys finally arrived and in a stormy interview with the Pope three days later they threatened him with a Council and accused him of gaining the tiara through simony, while he riposted by calling his erstwhile patrons, the Catholic Kings, usurpers. No holds were barred: the Spaniards reproached him for his nepotism, and even went so far as to refer to the death of Gandia as a divine chastisement. Not to be outdone, Alexander hit back well below the belt, retorting 'that the Spanish monarchs were more severely punished than he was, for they were without direct successors...' – a strange boast for a pope!

Despite his brave words, Alexander was deeply worried. He was well aware of the dangerous nature of the game he was playing, and in the early months of 1499 the French connection upon which he had gambled so much appeared to him increasingly as a risky and profitless speculation. The threat to his position as Pope was a real one, with the possibility that Germany and Spain would renounce their obedience to him being openly discussed in Rome. Moreover the alliance with the house of Orleans against the house of Aragon went against his Spanish nature; at heart he could not bring himself to trust Louis, whom he regarded as a foreigner and a barbarian. By February the Venetian ambassador thought that he was losing his nerve, repenting of his alliance with France and wishing to be friends with Ascanio again. At this point the ever-ready Ludovico intervened with a proposal of alliance between the Papacy, Milan and Naples, with the promise of money and lands in Italy for Cesare. On 12 March the Venetian envoy wrote that if Cesare had not been in France he believed Alexander would have allied himself with Milan. It is unlikely that Alexander would seriously have considered binding himself to the losing cause of Ludovico Sforza in the face of the combined forces of France and Venice. More probably his negotiations with Ludovico were intended to gain time and to avoid a breach until the success of the French venture made it inevitable. But there was truth in the Venetian ambassador's reading of the situation to the extent that Alexander suspected Louis of holding Cesare as a hostage, as Ferdinand had Juan. Cattaneo wrote on 26 March: 'In France they joke that the son of God will not be able to escape as he did from Velletri'.

These tense months of 1499 marked a new stage in the development of Cesare's relationship with his father. It was the first time in his adult life that he had been apart from his father, and in playing the diplomatic game on his own at the French court he seems to have been flexing his new-found political muscle independently of him. Cesare, not Alexander, seems to have been the driving force behind the French alliance; it was he who wrote strongly urging his father to reject Ludovico's advances, he who accepted Louis' new proposal of a French marriage for himself with enthusiasm and delight. Perhaps at the distance he was from Rome he did not appreciate the dangers to his father's position; in any case he was always single-minded in the pursuit of his own ambitions. Alexander seems to have suspected his son's independence and resented it; on 27 March, after receiving the announcement of the negotiations for Cesare's French marriage, the Venetian envoy reported him as discontented with Cesare and distrustful of Louis. Perhaps he felt that Cesare was throwing himself too wholeheartedly into the arms of France and dragging the Papacy thoughtlessly in his wake. Almost certainly he would have preferred an Italian bride for his son. In any event the letter which he wrote to Louis on 28 March, giving his consent to the negotiations, was grudging and ungracious. Carlotta's refusal had stung his pride, and he could not refrain from expressing his bitterness. The affair had caused, he said, in the eyes of the world:

> a diminution of our honour and standing, but also that of Your Majesty. . . . May Your Sublimity consider what targets of ridicule are we ourselves and the Duke who, having laid down the honour of the cardinalate and renounced all benefices and revenues, remains excluded from that marriage which the Princess, as Your Majesty writes, from her own perversity and induced by perverse counsels, has refused. However, since Cesare has written that 'that cousin of yours pleases him . . .' willingly we consent to the will and judgement of your Majesty . . .

Cesare had every reason to be pleased with the bride Louis had chosen for him, another Charlotte at the court of France, Charlotte d'Albret. Born about 1483 at Nerac, the feudal castle of the d'Albret family in Gascony, she was the daughter of Alain, nicknamed 'Le Grand', Duke of Guyenne, Count of Dreux, Penthièvre and Périgord, Viscount of Tartas and Limoges, and lord of Avesnes. Her mother, Françoise de Bretagne, was kinswoman to the Queen, while her eldest brother Jean had inherited the crown of Navarre from his brother-in-law François Phoebus, who had died without heirs. At sixteen she was an acknowledged beauty: even the critical Italian envoys called her 'the loveliest daughter of France' and 'unbelievably beautiful', while a later chronicler, Arnold le Feron, wrote that Cesare married her with enthusiasm, 'de grand cœur', not only for her relationship with the royal family but for her beauty, her goodness and the gentleness of her manners. Charlotte's own feelings are unrecorded, but it seems that under the concerted pressure of her father, anxious for Louis' friendship in the interests of the hard-pressed kingdom of Navarre, and from the King and Queen themselves, she cannot have had much choice in the matter.

Negotiations for the marriage dragged on for six weeks, as Alain d'Albret showed himself to be an avaricious, foxy, mistrustful old man, determined to screw all he could out of Louis and the Borgias in return for his daughter's hand. He demanded to see the dispensation allowing Cesare to marry, wanted the 100,000 livres which Louis promised as a royal dowry for Charlotte paid in ducats, and insisted on all sorts of guarantees. Finally, at the end of April, by agreeing to most of Alain's conditions, offering on the Pope's behalf a cardinal's hat for Charlotte's brother Aymon, and suborning his chief representative, the Sieur de Calvimont, with the offer of an office in the Parlement of Bordeaux, Louis brought the negotiations to a successful conclusion. In a letter of 27 April informing the Pope of the impending signature of the marriage contract, he announced his own early arrival south of the Alps. Alexander was to be under no illusions as to the *quid pro quo* of his son's marriage.

Indeed the political background to the match was made quite clear in the contract, signed at Blois on 10 May 1499 in the presence of the King and Queen, d'Amboise, and other high officials of the court. The preamble declared that the King consented to Cesare's marriage with Charlotte, being 'duly informed of the great and commendable services which the high and powerful prince don Caesar de Bourga [sic], Duke of Valentinois, has rendered to him and to his crown, and hoping that the aforesaid Duke, his relatives friends and allies will render them unto him in the future, and likewise for the conquest of his kingdom of Naples and of his duchy of Milan...'

The wedding took place two days later in the chapel of the Queen's apartments at Blois. A simple private ceremony was followed by a magnificent wedding breakfast given by Cesare to the court. Since his own apartments were not large enough, he had great tents of silken cloth set up in the meadows below the castle for the feast. The marriage was consummated that afternoon, and again in the evening, with the usual lack of privacy enjoyed by important couples of the time. Charlotte's ladies spied on them through the keyhole, and reported that Cesare, victim of an embarrassing practical joke, spent an unusually disturbed night. Robert de la Marck, seigneur de Fleurange, wrote: 'To tell you of the Duke of Valentinois' wedding night, he asked the apothecary for some pills to pleasure his lady, from whom he received a bad turn, for, instead of giving him what he asked for, he gave him laxative pills, to such an effect that he never ceased going to the privy the whole night, as the ladies reported in the morning.' Nonetheless, between dashes to the privy, Cesare did his duty valiantly, as he hastened to inform his father the next day. News of his performance reached Rome by special courier on 23 May, and Burchard noted to his diary: 'A courier from France arrived in Rome, who announced to Our Most Holy Lord that his son, the former Cardinal Valentinus, had contracted matrimony with the magnificent lady, and on Sunday the twelfth of this month, had consummated

it: which he did eight times in succession.' Not quite in succession:
Louis, who had supplied the Pope with details of his own wedding
night with Anne of Brittany, wrote to Alexander informing him that
Cesare's performance had surpassed his own. 'Valencia has broken
four lances more than he, two before supper and six at night, since
it is the custom there to consummate the marriage by day,' reported
Cattaneo. Such public relevations of intimate details were a combination of boasting and business. While Cesare naturally prided himself
on demonstrating his exceptional virility, he was anxious to record
that his marriage had been consummated and therefore could not
be nullified, and to assure his father that he had done his duty in
the Borgia dynastic interest. Meanwhile Charlotte wrote a more
modest letter to the Pope, declaring herself to be his devoted daughter,
expressing her wish to come to Rome to see him, and saying that she
was very satisfied with her husband. Alexander was beside himself
with delight. He had all the letters from France read out in public
consistory, and wrote effusively to Louis thanking him for the good
news and for the hundred bottles of excellent claret which the King
had sent him. He had every reason to be content; the long months
of anxiety were over, and the French gamble had turned out to be
a winning throw.

The young couple spent their honeymoon with the court at Blois.
Cesare, who wrote to his father that he was 'the most content man
in the world', lavished gifts on Charlotte, 'brocades, silks and jewels
worth 20,000 ducats', wedding presents that he had brought with him
from Rome intended for Carlotta of Aragon. An inventory later made
of Charlotte's belongings undoubtedly included some of the things
which Cesare gave her· upon their marriage – a great pear-shaped
pearl set in gold, a ruby clasp and five emeralds set in gold, a gold
chain, a 'great long emerald' in gold, a pendant of rubies, a collar
of twenty rubies and eight pearls, a diadem of twelve rose diamonds
and thirty pearls, and quantities of unset pearls, diamonds and other
precious stones. Apart from jewels, there were table services in massive
gold, silver gilt, enamels, rock crystal, all richly worked: salt cellars,
plates, spoons, forks, dishes, jugs, basins, sauceboats, flagons and other
vessels, vases for spices and for wine. There were also fine tablecloths
and elaborate table centres – miniature warships in mother-of-pearl,
a citadel with four towers in silver, and a fountain worked in silver
gilt and enamel in the form of a bell tower which issued forth jets
of rose water.

Cesare's wedding was the subject of ribald comment. The Milanese envoy Cesare Guaschi reported to Ludovico that the students of Paris University 'on the subject of this marriage had put on a farce which tended to the great ignominy of the pontiff''; the King had sent the Chancellor and M. de Ligny to Paris to punish them and there had been a great riot. But at court Louis continued to lavish honours upon him. On 19 May, a week after the wedding, he invested him with the Order of St Michael, the highest order of chivalry in France, while a few days later he formally adopted him and his future descendants, authorizing them to use the name and arms of the royal house of France. From then on Cesare proudly signed himself 'Cesare Borgia of France, Duke of Valentinois, Count of Diois, lord of Issoudun, captain of a hundred lances of the King's ordinance'. It was, he must have reflected, a higher and more exciting-sounding title than the simple 'Cardinal Valentinus' of a year before.

Cesare, as commander of a squadron of heavy cavalry, was to accompany Louis to Italy. By mid-July French military preparations for the attack on Milan were nearing completion, and as the news filtered through to Italy the pro-Milanese casualties of the Borgias' French policy fled from Rome. Ascanio was the first to go, leaving precipitately on 13 July, on the pretext of a hunting trip, for the Colonna stronghold at Nettuno. A week later, Ludovico captured one of Cesare's servants en route from Rome to Lyons with secret letters from the Pope, and communicated their contents to his allies. Ascanio immediately took flight from Nettuno to Milan to join his brother, while on 2 August Alfonso Bisceglie left Rome secretly and took refuge with the Colonnas at Gennazano, leaving Lucrezia in tears and six months pregnant. In the same month Sancia also departed for Naples, abandoning Jofre, who was shut up in the castle of Sant'Angelo and in high disfavour with the Pope on account of a skirmish with the city police in which he had been severely wounded. Alexander, wrote Cattaneo of the affair, 'is much displeased because of his honour, not because he is true son ... he has already said concerning a certain matter that that last one is not his son.' However, by 8 August Jofre had recovered enough to accompany the disconsolate Lucrezia to Nepi. Among the last of Alexander's opponents to leave the city was the Spanish ambassador Garcilaso de la Vega, who departed 'biting and ferocious as ever against the Pope, warning him that he would become the chaplain of the French'.

For Cesare and Charlotte in France, the brief period of their married life together was already over. Towards the end of July, he left his wife and joined Louis at Lyons, prepared to ride the tide of a new French invasion of Italy which, he hoped, would sweep him to fortune.

VII

VALENTINO AND
THE VIRAGO

ON 6 October 1499 Louis rode into Milan as a conqueror, with Cesare and Giuliano in his train. The victory had been easy; Ludovico Sforza had fled from his capital at the beginning of September, as the strongholds of the duchy fell like ninepins before the advancing French, while the Venetians pressed in from the east, capturing Cremona and Ghiara d'Adda. The great lords of Italy, among them Ludovico's father-in-law Ercole d'Este, had hastened to join Louis as they had flocked to Charles VIII five years previously, and rode in his train into Ludovico's capital.

Louis' entry was a splendid one; the French and Italian lords in his suite vied with one another to impress the notoriously luxury-loving Milanese. Baldassare Castiglione, future author of *The Courtier*, and thus no mean authority, noted approvingly that Cesare stood out as 'very gallant'. But despite the magnificence of the occasion, the population received their conquerors coolly. The Venetian ambassadors who rode with Louis noted that there were few cries of 'France', while the populace vented 'their anger on the hated representatives of Venice, calling them dogs, and warning them: 'We have given the King dinner, you will provide him with supper.' Louis entered the Castello Sforzesco, the great Sforza fortress, where he found the oaken jewel chests with their special locking devices designed by Leonardo da Vinci empty. Ludovico had taken with him 240,000 ducats in gold and the best part of his famous collection of jewels and pearls, but enough remained to impress the French with the splendour of the ducal court. The two things which Louis admired the most in Milan were Ludovico's stables with their frescoed portraits of his horses, and Leonardo's *Last Supper* in the monastery of Santa Maria delle Grazie, which he visited, accompanied by Cesare and the other princes, the day after his arrival. But if the French were impressed by the riches

of Milan, the Milanese themselves were contemptuous of their conquerors, whom they soon found justifying their opinion of them as
'barbarians'. Castiglione wrote with disgust that the French had filled
the superb rooms of the Castello with drinking booths and dung hills;
a Venetian reported: 'The French captains spit upon the floors of
the rooms, while their soldiers outrage women in the streets.' French
archers used Leonardo's marvellous clay model for an equestrian
statue of Francesco Sforza for target practice, and soon reduced it
to a heap of rubble.

The ruin of Leonardo's great statue, crumbling under the impact
of French arrows, was an apt symbol of the fall of the Sforza dynasty;
it was also significant of the future fate of the Italian political system.
If the shock of the first French invasion had revealed the cracks in
the edifice, the second was to shatter it. None of the Italian princes
who crowded round Louis at Milan had time to spare a thought for
Ludovico's fate – indeed he could be considered to have brought
about his own fall. They were all too preoccupied with the effect that
French possession of Milan, and above all a permanent French presence on Italian soil, might have on their own fortunes. And so the
endless round of court amusements, the feasting and dancing at
Milan, hunting in the park at Pavia, went on against an undercurrent
of fear, suspicion and intrigue. The ambassadors and princes of every
state in Italy, with the natural exception of Naples, who were on the
alert for any sign that might portend the future, could not fail to note
the exceptionally favourable treatment which the King of France
accorded to the Pope's son, Cesare Borgia. Everyone knew the Pope's
ambitions for a state for his son. It was only a question of the precise
direction they would take.

Indeed, the Borgias' Grand Design for a state for Cesare in central
Italy had been maturing since the early summer of 1499, and was
now ready to be put into execution. A Florentine cardinal who knew
both Alexander and Cesare well once remarked of them that, among
the attributes of great men which they shared was the supreme ability
to recognize an opportunity and to make the best possible use of it.
The guiding spirit of Borgia policy was a planned opportunism. Alexander and Cesare were experts in the art of political camouflage, at
concealing their real aims while making use of others, in this case
Louis, to achieve them. These characteristic features of Borgia policy
began to reveal themselves at the time of the French invasion in 1499.
Alexander had immediately recognized the opportunity offered by

Louis' obsessive desire for Milan, and launched his son's career upon it. Later, the failure of the Neapolitan marriage project had caused a shift in the direction of the Borgias' objectives, and their moves after Cesare returned to Italy were a natural development of that situation. With Naples now out of the question as the base for a Borgia dominion in Italy, their eyes turned towards the Papal States, and to the Romagna in particular.

The Romagna, or rather the Romagna and the Marches (Le Marche), the specific area in which the Borgias were interested, stretched from the borders of the Duke of Ferrara in the north to those of the March of Ancona in the south, bounded by the Apennine mountains to the west and the Adriatic to the east. It was a rich countryside of vineyards, orchards and arable fields, rolling down from the foothills of the Apennines to the flat coastal plains by the sea. Through the heart of these lands, straight as a die, ran the great Roman road, the Via Emilia, and most of the important cities lay along it: Bologna, the most important city of the Papal States after Rome, with a population of around 50,000, which was under the control not of the Church but of the Bentivoglio family; Imola and Forlì, held as vicariates in the name of the Riarios by Girolamo's widow, Caterina Sforza Riario; Faenza, where the Manfredis were exceptional in commanding the loyalty of their subjects; Cesena, under the direct rule of the Church; and Rimini, ruled by Pandolfo Malatesta, worthless grandson of the wicked Sigismondo. To the south lay Pesaro, lordship of Lucrezia's ex-husband Giovanni Sforza, and Camerino, ruled by the Varano family, with the mountain duchy of Urbino under Guidobaldo da Montefeltro to the south-east. All these towns had an extensive *contado*, or countryside, and were essentially agricultural, all trade being in the hands of the Florentines or Venetians. Their lords ruled as apostolic vicars or lieutenants of the Church, which obliged them to pay a yearly sum, known as the census, to their overlord the Pope. In practice they acted quite independently of the Pope, and all politics centred round them and the groups of families supporting them, whose power was based on a mixture of land and local office.

Almost without exception, these Romagnol lords were a worthless lot, heartily detested by their subjects, whom they shamelessly exploited. Machiavelli wrote in the *Discorsi*:

Before those lords who ruled it were driven out by Pope Alexander VI, the Romagna was a nursery of all the worst crimes, the slightest occasion giving rise to wholesale rapine and murder. This resulted from the wickedness of these lords, and not, as they asserted, from the disposition of their subjects. For these princes being poor, yet choosing to live as if they were rich, were forced to resort to cruelties innumerable ... and among other shameful devices contrived by them to extort money, they would pass laws prohibiting certain acts, and then be the first to give occasion for breaching them; nor would they chastise offenders until they saw many involved in the same offence; when they fell to punishing, not from any zeal for the laws they had made, but out of greed to realize the penalty...

But if the Romagna was a lawless, turbulent, disunited province, it was nonetheless a covetable possession. The soil of the Adriatic hinterland was extraordinarily fertile, and moreover, a factor of importance for a fifteenth-century military leader, the people were excellent soldiers. Since the Middle Ages, the condottieri who roamed Italy had drawn upon the Romagna, and particularly the area known as the Val di Lamone, as a source of recruits, and many of the most famous captains themselves, including Muzio Attendolo, founder of the Sforza dynasty, were Romagnols. If Cesare Borgia were able to wield the disunited province into a coherent whole, the strategic importance of the new state would not only put him among the first rank of the princes of Italy, but also offer interesting possibilities for expansion. The addition of Siena and Piombino, for example, would place him firmly astride the centre of Italy. Moreover, in dispossessing the Romagna vicars, Alexander was pursuing his favourite policy of killing two birds with one stone: not only would he thus provide Cesare with a rich lordship, but he would also be strengthening the temporal power of the Church by reasserting control over lands which had hitherto belonged to it in name only.

The opening round in the campaign against the lords of the Romagna was fired even before Cesare reached Italy, with the mission of Juan Borgia of Monreale as Cardinal Legate to Venice in September. The report of Monreale's interview with the Signoria provides an interesting illustration of Borgia aims at the time, with the various alternatives they had in view:

The Legate said that he had a letter in cipher from Duke Valentino saying that he did not want Ferrara since it was a great state, and its lord old and loved by the people, and has three sons who would never leave him in peace if he had it, however he wanted Imola, Forlì and Pesaro, an undertaking which would be easy, or Siena and Piombino whichever our Signoria opined, and to chase out Messer Giovanni Bentivoglio from Bologna, and to reduce that city to the Church.

The Venetians' cautious response to this feeler was to temporize, saying that they must first consult with the King of France.

Indeed Louis held the key to success for Cesare. To achieve their goals in the Romagna, Alexander and Cesare needed both the French King's troops and the power of his name. The papal army was still relatively weak, and Alexander had no wish to employ Italian captains such as the Orsinis, who were unreliable and might make him too dependent upon them; he needed French soldiers and French commanders. On the diplomatic front he knew that the neighbouring powers, Florence and above all Venice, would oppose a direct papal attack on the Romagna, an area which each of them regarded as in their sphere of interest, and where most of the lords whom the Borgias intended to dispossess were under their protection. The enterprise would therefore have to be executed under the aegis of the King of France, whose name carried enough weight to compel both Florence and Venice to acceptance.

While the powers watched anxiously to see what the King would do, Alexander, sure of his man, came out into the open. In October he declared forfeit of their vicariates, on the grounds of non-payment of the census, the vicars of Rimini (Pandolfo Malatesta), Pesaro (Giovanni Sforza), Imola and Forlì (Caterina Sforza in the name of her son Ottaviano Riario), and Faenza (Astorre Manfredi). This two-pronged approach, the wielding of the spiritual weapons, deprivation or excommunication, followed by the temporal, physical attack, was to be the pattern of Borgia aggression. No one doubted that the attack would come, and Alexander's announcement sent the threatened lords scurrying for protection. Giovanni Sforza journeyed to Venice to offer Pesaro to the Signoria, but Venice was prepared to sacrifice Pesaro to the Borgias in order to save Rimini and Faenza, which were both already under their umbrella. From Forlì Caterina Sforza, whose last husband had been a Medici, appealed to Florence for help, but the Signoria, fearful of offending Louis, decided on neutrality, thus tacitly abandoning her to her fate. No one was prepared to risk the King's resentment by aiding any member of the doomed Sforza family, and Louis made his intentions quite clear. In a letter to Giovanni Bentivoglio of Bologna on 5 November he granted Bentivoglio the protection he had requested, but required him to give the Pope any assistance he might demand in recovering states for the Church. 'In response to the request of Our Holy Father the Pope, and ... wishing to aid him in the recovery of his lands and lordships of Imola and Forlì ... we have constituted our dear and well-loved cousin the Duke of Valentinois as our lieutenant,' he declared. Nor were they empty words: before he left Milan for France on 7 November, Louis ordered Yves d'Alègre with 300 lances and the Bailly de Dijon with some 4000 Swiss and Gascon infantry to place themselves at Cesare's disposal.

For Cesare, just twenty-four, this was to be his first real military experience, the test of all the physical preparations he had put himself through since he had first decided to lay down the cardinalate. And it was taking place under the best possible circumstances: although he was personally in command of a company of a hundred French lances, overall responsibility for the expedition was shared with the other seasoned French captains. Moreover, as he had confidently informed the Venetian government, he expected the enterprise of Imola and Forlì to be an easy one. In the fifteen years that the Riario family had held the vicariates of those cities they had succeeded in making themselves almost exceptionally unpopular for the cruelty and rapacity of their rule, and Cesare was therefore well aware that the citizens would be unlikely to lay down their lives in defence of an extortionate dynasty. Moreover their ruler was a woman, Caterina Sforza.

But Caterina was no ordinary woman; admiringly known throughout Italy as 'the virago', she was noted not only for her beauty but for her courage and ruthlessness. She was in many ways as typical a figure of the Renaissance as Cesare himself. The descendant of the Sforzas, one of the great fighting families of Italy, she had had more experience of military affairs than the young man who was to face her. Aged only twenty-one she had held the Castel Sant'Angelo in the name of her husband, Girolamo Riario, during the violent days which followed the death of his uncle, Sixtus IV. Striding the battlements with a steel corselet over her satin dress, a falcon perched on her wrist, 'she was much feared by her men, whether mounted or on foot, because when she had a weapon in her hand, she was proud and cruel'. She had taken a bloody revenge on the murderers of her first husband Girolamo Riario in 1488, and when the citizens of Forlì defied her before the citadel, threatening to murder her children, she is reputed to have raised her skirts and bluntly replied: 'Look, I have the mould to make more.' In time of war she wore a full suit of armour like a man's except for the generously curved breastplate over her full bosom, and her son by Giovanni de' Medici was to become one of the most famous – and the last – of the condottieri, Giovanni della Bande Nere.

And yet the fierce virago was at the same time totally feminine. She was a passionately sensual woman who had had three husbands, nine children and many lovers, three of whom were younger than herself. She was strikingly beautiful, tall, statuesque, naturally blonde, with a fine complexion of which she was particularly proud, and hands which were described as 'soft as sable'. She took great care of her beauty to the end of her life, even after imprisonment by the Borgias had prematurely aged her. In the year before her death she added a new formula for face lotion to her private book of recipes which included everything from sunburn remedies to abortifacients and slow-working poisons. She loved rich clothes and jewels, danced gracefully and spoke wittily with a charming eloquence which could degenerate into a storming tirade when she lost her temper. There was also a practical female side to her character: she was a good needlewoman and kept careful household accounts.

Despite her talents and formidable courage, Caterina's position was precarious, as Cesare well knew. Abandoned by her ally Florence, she had no army to field against him, and was dependent on the doubtful loyalty of her subjects and the walls of her citadels of Imola and Forlì. Although the Rocca Ravaldino of Forlì had been considered in its time one of the strongest in Italy, it had been built in the mid-fifteenth century, was now outdated in terms of modern weaponry, and was unlikely to hold out for long against sustained bombardment by sophisticated French artillery of the type which Cesare had brought with him. In this desperate situation Caterina fought back with every weapon at her disposal. Even before Cesare reached Imola he was forced temporarily to abandon his march southward and make a precipitate dash to Rome – Caterina had attempted to assassinate the Pope. Her method was simple and ingenious and had nothing to do with the complicated formulas from her private book. Plague had been raging at Forlì; Caterina took a cloth that had been wrapped for several days round a corpse until sufficiently impregnated, she hoped, with the deadly germ, and placed it in a cane tube containing letters of surrender purportedly addressed by the citizens of Forlì to the Pope. Caterina's messenger, one Tommasino of Forlì, who was employed at the Vatican, unwisely confided the plot to another servant, also from Forlì. The two Forlivesi were arrested and thrown into the Castel Sant'Angelo, where, under torture, they made a full confession. On 18 November Cesare, according to Burchard, arrived 'secretly' at the Vatican and spent three days there conferring with the Pope before returning north. Eminent historians, including Gregorovius, Burckhardt and Caterina's biographer Pasolini, have seen this story of the poison plot as a Borgia invention designed to justify their attack on Caterina and to blacken her in the eyes of potential allies such as Florence. But there seems to be no reason why such a further justification should have been necessary, and the evidence is that most contemporary chroniclers, including Burchard, Bernardi the historian of Forlì, Cattaneo, and Venetian diarists, believed it.

Whatever the truth of the story, Caterina's machinations were of little avail. Her citizens of Imola and Forlì offered themselves to Cesare 'like whores', as the Venetian diarist Sanuto put it, even before his troops reached their walls. The one exception was the castellan of Imola, Dionigi da Naldo, member of a famous fighting family from the Val di Lamone, who was later to become one of Cesare's most trusted captains, and his decision to resist was almost certainly based on the fact that his wife and children were hostages in the ferocious Caterina's hands in the citadel of Forlì. Cesare entered Imola on 27 November; a week later, after bombardment by his artillery had knocked down part of the wall, the citadel surrendered. Following the example of Imola, the towns and strongholds of the *contado* yielded easily, and on 15 December Cesare left for Forlì, which he entered, lance at rest in the style of a conqueror, on 17 December, under torrential rain and continual bombardment from the citadel. From the rampart of Ravaldino Caterina must have watched with a certain malicious satisfaction the sufferings inflicted by the French soldiery upon her disloyal subjects, which Bernardi the contemporary chronicler of Forlì described as 'similar to the pains of hell'. The Gascon infantry fully justified their reputation as riotous robbers, and the camp followers were if anything worse – 'two thousand priests, friars, hostpickers, and prostitutes, and two thousand other rabble' as Bernardi put it. The French mercenaries answered only to their own commanders, and Cesare was powerless to control them. He could only exhort the loudly complaining citizens to have patience, and told them 'that if he lived to remain their lord, he swore on his word to make it up to them'. Cesare's courteous treatment of the citizens of his towns, his tactful consideration for local officials whom he almost invariably reappointed to their offices, was, as Machiavelli later pointed out, an important factor in their continuing loyalty to him.

There remained the immediate problem of the defiant 'Madonna' in the citadel. The day after Christmas Cesare made two personal attempts to persuade her to surrender, riding 'like a paladin' to the brink of the moat to talk to her on the ramparts, but Caterina would have none of it, and even, according to a Venetian report, attempted to trap Cesare by luring him onto the drawbridge and raising it, but he escaped. So it was to be war to the bitter end between them. On 10 January Cesare set up his siege batteries, which, says Bernardi, he personally directed day and night; by the morning of the 12th a great breach had been opened in the wall and the order for the assault was given. The Swiss and Gascon mercenaries poured through the breach, and were soon engaged in fierce hand-to-hand fighting with the 2000 defenders hemmed in within the walls. In desperation Caterina ordered the stores and magazines to be fired, but the explosions and smoke hampered the defenders rather than the attackers. Caterina herself was seized by a Swiss constable in the command of the Bailly de Dijon, eager for the ransom money. Cesare, with Yves d'Alègre and the men-at-arms, rode through the gate of the citadel to the keep where she was held. Several hours later she reappeared, supported by Cesare and d'Alègre; by the flickering light of torches they waded through the water surrounding the keep, and led her down into the town, to the house of Luffo Numai where Cesare was lodged. For the Lady of Forlì the war was over. The assault, as Cesare reported to Ercole d'Este, had lasted only half an hour and 400 of the garrison had been killed.

Cesare's pleasure in his victory was marred by news of the death of his friend and cousin, Juan Borgia of Monreale, of pneumonia at Urbino on 14 January, and he soon had other troubles on his hands arising from his possession of Caterina. Hearing that Caterina was to be sent to Rome, the Bailly de Dijon marched to the Palazzo Numai at the head of his Swiss mercenaries, seized her and took her back to his lodgings. The French, headed by Yves d'Alègre, who seems to have fallen under Caterina's spell, clearly considered the holding of a woman as a prisoner to be against the rules of war, but the Bailly's motive on this occasion was mercenary rather than chivalrous: he feared that if Caterina were sent to Rome he would lose the ransom due to his company for her capture. Meanwhile his Swiss took this opportunity to strike for a new contract, refusing to undertake the projected expedition against Pesaro unless this was done. After a furious row in the piazza of Forlì, during which Cesare threatened to call the people to arms to cut the foreign mercenaries to pieces, the affair was settled. Caterina was to be handed over to Cesare to be held at the instance of the King of France, and was to be given into the custody of the Pope on that condition. The Swiss got their new contract, and the Bailly 4000 ducats. In Machiavelli's words, 'Madonna was sold to il Valentino.' Cesare was anxious to pursue his next objective, the dislodging from Pesaro of Giovanni Sforza, his erstwhile brother-in-law. On the afternoon of 23 January, having received the oath of fealty from the councillors of Forlì in his own name and that of the Pope, he left for Cesena in company with Yves d'Alègre, taking Caterina with him.

Cesare's relations with his beautiful captive were naturally the subject of titillated speculation. There were rumours that he abused her; Bernardi, who was normally favourable to Cesare, wrote, without mentioning him by name, 'of the injuries [committed] on the body of our poor and unfortunate lady, Caterina Sforza, who was possessed of great physical beauty...' On the other hand, Sanuto, a persistently hostile source, made no mention of rape or outrage in his report dated 18 January 1500: 'There is news that the lady of Forlì has been sent to Cesena; and it seems that Duke Valentino has gone there [in fact Cesare at that time was still at Forlì], and, as I hear, was keeping the said lady, who is a most beautiful woman, daughter of Duke Galeazzo of Milan, day and night in his room; with whom, in the opinion of all, he is taking his pleasure.' Given the reputation which both Cesare and Caterina shared for sensuality, the speculation is hardly surprising, and it is likely that there was a good deal of truth in the rumours concerning Cesare's treatment of her. He was sensual, he also had a streak of cruelty in him, and the piquancy of having his beautiful enemy in his power would have appealed to his cruelty as well as his senses. Whether he actually raped and humiliated her as Bernardi seems to imply is impossible to establish – it certainly cannot be ruled out. He had none of his father's tenderness for women, and his feelings for them never seem to have gone beyond the physical aspect. In a revealing remark to Bishop Soderini, discussing Caterina, he later said 'that he took no account of women, nor did he esteem her, and if it had been up to him he would not have let her leave Sant'Angelo [where she was later imprisoned by the Borgias] ...' On the other hand, Caterina's sexual record suggests that she may not have been an unwilling victim; the Milanese condottiere Trivulzio's reaction when he heard of her capture by Cesare was 'O good Madonna, now you will not lack for f..... f.....' She was thirty-six, and had always had a penchant for young lovers, while Cesare, twelve years younger than she was, was acknowledged to be an exceptionally physically attractive man.

But Cesare was soon in no mood for pleasure. On 26 January, as he was heading for Pesaro, where the nervous Giovanni Sforza had already packed his baggage and was poised for flight, he received news of a serious check to his plans. Ludovico il Moro with 8000 Swiss and 500 Burgundians was marching on Como. From Milan Trivulzio ordered the urgent recall of d'Alègre and the French troops, who left for Lombardy the following day. The departure of the French was a blow for Cesare; he had intended to round off his Romagna campaign by expelling Sforza from Pesaro, and then going on to take Rimini and possibly also Faenza. Now, left with only a thousand infantry and 500 horse, he could not hope to proceed. Like the successful gambler that he was, he knew when to cut his losses and keep what he had already won. Leaving small bodies of troops to garrison the Romagna, he assembled his six remaining companies of German, Gascon and Spanish infantry and a body of 500 horse under Vitellozzo Vitelli, and took the road south for Rome with Caterina in his train.

Rome, in the last week of February 1500, was in the throes of its Carnival, a time when, as a puzzled Turkish envoy reported to the Sultan, 'all Christians go mad'. It was also Jubilee year, and the city was crowded with pilgrims from all over the Christian world, who had journeyed to Rome to receive the special indulgences decreed by the Pope to ease their passage from this world to the next. On the morning of 26 February the city was astir with excitement. The Via Lata, the broad street running from the gate of Porta del Popolo to the Piazza Venezia, was lined with people. The entire population, pilgrims and natives, had come to see the triumphal entry of the Pope's son into the Eternal City. From loggias, windows and balconies the women of Rome, respectable matrons and their daughters, rich courtesans with their dwarfs and Moorish pages, craned their necks to catch a glimpse of the handsome young Duke whom they had known as Cardinal Valentino. Eighteen months after he had crossed his personal Rubicon to the secular life, Cesare, like his namesake, was to make his triumphal entry into Rome.

Even before the appearance of the principal character, the spectacle was worth seeing. Down the street from the Porta del Popolo marched a colourful and varied procession: the city dignitaries and officials of the Roman Curia in their best robes, the cardinals in purple and ermine, with their numerous retainers spectacularly dressed, the ambassadors of every country in the Christian world. The organization of the procession at the Porto del Popolo had driven the precise papal master of ceremonies, Burchard, almost to despair. People had joined the cortège from every village it had passed through from Civita Castellana down to Rome, a milling horde of unruly gawpers. Naturally they had no regard for protocol, and neither had Cesare's foreign mercenaries. Burchard complained bitterly that the Swiss and Gascons, who were grouped in five companies under standards bearing Cesare's arms, refused to recognize his authority, and 'indecently' occupied a rank in the procession which did not properly belong to them. Poor Burchard had trouble too with the diplomats, always touchy on questions of precedence. The ambassadors of England and Naples quarrelled with the envoys of Cesare's brother-in-law, the King of Navarre, and the proud Navarrese withdrew in disgust.

But the people lining the streets had come to see 'the Duke', and at the first appearance of his train, excitement mounted. First came his baggage waggons, including doubtless that silver-lined personal privy, and the mules clad in his colours; behind them marched two heralds, one in the colours of France, the other emblazoned with Cesare's own arms. Then came a thousand infantry in full campaigning gear, and a hundred hand-picked grooms and mace-bearers of his personal guard with 'CESAR' embroidered in letters of silver on their chests. Fifty gorgeously dressed gentlemen of his general staff preceded the cavalry, headed by Vitellozzo Vitelli. Then came Cesare himself, riding between Cardinals Orsini and Farnese, followed by Jofre and Alfonso Bisceglie (who had rejoined Lucrezia at Spoleto in September 1499), one hundred lackeys in black velvet with black batons in their hands brought up the rear, and behind them the confused mass of camp followers, peasants from the villages, gypsies and townsfolk, struggling for a glimpse of the Duke.

Cesare was simply dressed in a robe of black velvet down to the knees, his only ornament the gold collar of the Order of St Michael.

The stark black cloth set off his looks more dramatically than the coloured silks he used to wear. From now on, with a growing confidence in himself, he showed an increasing fondness for dressing in black, a colour which with its outward connotations of drama, its inward feeling of narcissism and introversion, was a reflection of his own personality. The watchful ambassadors to the papal court who remembered the flashy young Cardinal must have noted the difference eighteen months' experience had wrought in him with some disquiet.

The procession marched past the castle of Sant'Angelo, where from the great new tower built by Alexander floated huge standards bearing devices alluding to his son's exploits, while the garrison drawn up on the ramparts saluted him with thunderous salvoes of artillery. Taking the broad new road which had been especially opened up for the Jubilee, they then proceeded to the Vatican, where Alexander waited, leaning anxiously over the balcony of the open loggia of the palace to catch a first glimpse of his son.

Alexander was beside himself with delight at Cesare's triumphal return. Ambassadors reported him as so moved that he cried at one moment and laughed the next. He received Cesare publicly, enthroned in the Sala del Pappagallo, but even here passionate affection and paternal pride overcame papal dignity. Cesare advanced solemnly to the foot of the throne, making a low ceremonial bow, and spoke to his father in Spanish, to which Alexander replied in the same family language. Then, as Cesare bent to kiss the pontifical foot, Alexander, unable to contain himself, raised him and clasped him warmly to him. In his joy, the Pope even received his enemy Caterina with a show of cordiality, and lodged her, in comfort but still a prisoner, in the beautiful villa of the Belvedere in the Vatican gardens.

The celebrations continued the next day when the people of Rome were treated to the spectacle of an allegorical procession whose inspiration so nearly corresponded to the motifs on Cesare's sword that he himself must have had a hand in it. The theme was, of course, the Triumph of Caesar, and among the eleven decorated waggons bearing montages designed and executed by the artists of the papal court were tableaux representing the Crossing of the Rubicon, while in the last chariot Caesar sat enthroned, crowned with the victor's laurels. Cesare accompanied the procession on horseback, as it wound its way from Piazza Navona to the Vatican, where Alexander was so childishly delighted by it that he had it pass twice under his windows.

Cesare did not, as some writers would have it, go to the ridiculous
lengths of representing Caesar himself, but his identification with
his great namesake must have been more than ever in his mind as
he rode through the familiar streets of Rome with the shouts of the
crowd ringing in his ears. Very soon he was to adopt the proudly revealing motto *Aut Caesar, aut nihil* – 'Either Caesar or nothing'

Indeed he had good reason to be satisfied with the results of his
experiences in the time he had spent away from the city. During his
time in France he had married a beautiful, well-connected wife,
whom he now knew to be pregnant, and he had gained valuable first-
hand experience of the French army and court. He now had a personal insight into the mind and character of Louis, the man who
decided the destiny of Italy, and of the most influential men who
surrounded him, like d'Amboise. As far as his military career was
concerned, he had a working knowledge of French artillery and had
marched with most of the principal French captains, such as Yves
d'Alègre. Above all he had learned how to operate on his own, independently of his father, and how to achieve his objectives by navi-
gating the treacherous waters of international intrigue.

Success in France had been followed by achievement in Italy in
his chosen career. Although the campaign in which he had been
engaged had been a minor one, and his victories easily predictable,
he had displayed those qualities of prudence, caution and cleverness
which his contemporaries considered essential in a military commander. Fifteenth-century Italians, regarding themselves with some
justification as the most intelligent and highly educated people in
Europe, esteemed cleverness above all things and looked on the use
of brute force as a last resort. The acquisition of a town by negotiation
and intrigue was sensibly viewed as infinitely preferable to an assault
with its attendant sackings and expensive casualties. Cesare's mode
of operation at Imola and Forlì, which was to be the pattern for many
of his future campaigns, would have been considered admirable by
his contemporaries, as too his careful use of his troops, evidenced in
a letter which he wrote to Ercole d'Este from Forlì: 'The delay has
been caused not so much by the undoubted strength of the fortress,
as much as by the need to arrange things so as to lose as few men
as possible.' Cesare had deployed his artillery in order to spare the
lives of his assault troops; those of the wretched 400 defenders who
died did not count. Also he had drawn several useful conclusions from
his experiences that winter: the indiscipline of the French at Forlì,

and the abrupt conclusion of his campaign caused by their departure, had convinced him of the necessity of raising his own forces with commanders directly answerable to himself. And although he had not gained all that he had hoped for, as acknowledged lord of Imola and Forlì and *de facto* ruler of Cesena he had made a promising beginning, and at twenty-four was clearly a coming man. A new star was rising in the Italian political firmament.

VIII

ROMAN SUMMER

JUST over a month after Cesare's return to Rome, on Sunday, 29 March 1500, Alexander conferred upon him the offices and insignia of Gonfalonier and Captain General of the Church, in a solemn ceremony attended by the representatives of all the Italian and foreign powers. The symbolism of the occasion cannot have escaped the watchful envoys: the Pope's nomination of his son as official commander of the papal armies implied nothing less than a total Borgia takeover of the Church. With the father wielding the spiritual and temporal authority, and the son in control of the papal forces, the beginnings of a Borgia state already laid, who could predict where this move might lead them?

From the moment Cesare returned to Rome after his successful campaign in the Romagna, the objectives uppermost in the Borgias' minds were first to establish Cesare as ruler of a major Italian state, secondly to ensure that he should keep it in the event of his father's death. As regards the first objective, they counted for the present on the continuing support of France and their own daring and skilful opportunism. It was perhaps the second goal that caused them the greatest concern, for two obvious dangers threatened Cesare's maintenance of a future state. They were the election of a pope hostile to him after his father's death, and attack by the most powerful Italian state whose interests, like his, lay in the Romagna – the Republic of Venice. If Cesare could be made hereditary Captain General of the armies of the Church, with secure possession of a great state founded upon Church lands, both dangers might well be avoided, since neither a future pope nor Venice would be powerful enough to harm him. And there was something of a precedent for this plan: in 1434 Pope Eugenius IV had made Francesco Sforza Captain General of the Church and Marquis of the March of Ancona for life. The Borgias, characteristically, were carrying this idea a good deal further; the ceremony of 29 March was the first step towards putting it into practice. A few days later Cesare added the pontifical keys to his personal arms, on which the Borgia bull was quartered with the lilies of France, symbolizing the three sources of his power: his own wit, skill and courage, supported by France and the wealth and authority of the Papacy.

For the moment, however, Cesare could do nothing to further his plans; in that spring of 1500 everything turned on the outcome of events in Milan, where the French under Trivulzio were locked in a struggle for Lombardy with Ludovico, who had returned to his capital in triumph on 5 February. This forced inactivity seems to have thrown Cesare into one of those fits of nervous, almost superstitious, depression which tended to afflict him at such periods. He had presentiments of an early violent death, perhaps brought on by the prospect of his approaching investiture as Gonfalonier, which raised the spectre of his murdered brother Juan, invested with the same insignia only four years before. On 17 March Cattaneo reported: 'Valencia speaks thus, half joking with his companions: "I know that in my twenty-sixth year I stand in danger of ending my life in arms and by arms."'

Cesare, like most of the men and women of his day, was a believer in astrology. While the new education had swept away the old fear of the power of God as the limiting factor in human action, it had substituted the idea of fortune and fate. A man might combat fortune with all his ingenuity, only to be swept away by the evil stroke of a capricious fate. Kings, popes and princes consulted astrologers in an effort to avoid an evil day or to catch fortune at the flood. It is known that Cesare asked the German humanist Lorenz Behaim to cast his horoscope, and that this chart must have predicted a swift rise to power leading to a violent end. This fear in the back of his mind, coupled with the knowledge that his father might die at any time, drove him on with a desperate desire to seize all before a maleficent fate might deprive him of it. And there were other reasons for an uneasiness which he failed to conceal. He was well aware that at this point in his career, with no sizeable army of his own, only Louis' protection stood between his nascent state and predatory, secretly hostile Venice. If Louis failed to recover Milan he would be unable to help Cesare. Cattaneo noted his anxious state of mind on 17 March: 'Whether it is because his state depends on the outcome of events in Milan, or whether it is that, although he will keep those lands for some time, nonetheless he has to be slave to the Venetians, and when it does not suit them, he will be overturned in one blow . . .'

And there were signs that Louis, although he liked Cesare personally, did not trust him; still less did he trust Alexander, whom he rightly suspected to be at heart pro-Spanish and anti-French. For Louis, Cesare was the key to the Borgia combination, and while his wife Charlotte remained at the French court she could be used as a hostage for his good behaviour, and as a reminder that he was bound to the crown of France. While it was natural that Charlotte should not have accompanied her husband to Italy on his first military campaign, it seems clear that the Borgias expected her to join him once the campaign was over. On 22 January 1500, ten days after the fall of Forlì, the Venetian envoy reported that Alexander had contracted a loan of several thousand ducats to send to France to pay for the Duchess of Valentinois' journey to Rome. Charlotte refused to travel on the grounds of her pregnancy – a reasonable enough excuse. However, the Venetian envoy added significantly that the real opposition to her journey came from the court of France, which had forbidden her to go. Therefore 'the Pope, seeing matters beyond the mountains going on in such a manner that he is not without suspicion that she will be forbidden to come', had given orders that the money should not be handed over until permission for the journey had been granted. In May Charlotte gave birth to a daughter, Luisa, and her father Alain d'Albret sent a messenger to Rome inviting Cesare to join his wife in France. Cesare, said the Venetian ambassador, returned him fair words, 'but he cares little for returning to France'.

For by that time Cesare had neither the time nor the inclination to leave Italy, where events had once again turned in his favour. On 10 April 1500 Ludovico Sforza had been captured at Novara while attempting to escape disguised as a Swiss soldier. He was sent captive to Louis at Lyons, and died eight years later in strict confinement in the castle of Loches in Touraine. It was a sad end for the once magnificent Duke of Milan, born as much for his own ruin as that of his country. Leonardo da Vinci wrote in his notebook an epitaph on his former employer: 'The Duke has lost fortune, state and liberty, and not one of his works has been completed.'

Ludovico's downfall and the definitive victory of the French in

Lombardy meant that the way now lay open for Cesare to renew his plans for further conquests in the Romagna. The period of enforced inactivity was over, as the Borgias threw themselves into action on the diplomatic front. Their military objectives were Rimini and Faenza; the two main targets for their diplomatic pressure France and Venice, for without the support of the former and the consent of the latter, Cesare could not hope to extend his operations in the Romagna. In France the Borgias' envoys held out the bait of Naples for Louis and the Legateship for Amboise. The Venetians, who were under increasing military pressure from the Turks, were to be offered papal support for an international crusade against their enemies in return for the withdrawal of their protection from Rimini and Faenza, a declaration of friendship and a condotta, or contract for troops, and money for Cesare. It was the beginning of an obsessively uneasy relationship between Venice and the Borgias, marked by mutual fear, suspicion and hostility, as the Borgias pursued the Republic's friendship with increasing anxiety on the one hand, and Venice watched Cesare's meteoric rise with growing resentment on the other. Pressure on Venice had commenced as early as April, when their envoy in Rome reported 'the Duke of Valentinois has persuaded the Pope to make provisions against the Turks for love of the Signoria', and continued with growing insistence through the summer months of 1500. Venice was extremely reluctant to give Cesare the go-ahead in the Romagna, and above all determined not to make him her captain and give him troops and money to act against her own interests, while Louis, involved in war with Pisa on behalf of Florence, and in negotiations with Ferdinand over the partition of Naples, was at first lukewarm in his support. Nonetheless the Borgias continued their relentless diplomatic campaign, backed by a conviction that events were going their way.

Indeed Cesare, once again confident in himself and his future, seemed determined to enjoy life to the full in this summer of 1500. He had a beautiful mistress, a Florentine courtesan named Fiammetta de' Michelis, who owned three houses in the city, including one on the piazza named after her near the Piazza Navona, and a country villa, or *vigna*, outside the Porta Viridaria. Fiammetta was typical of the rich courtesans of her day, called *cortigiane honeste* – 'honest courtesans' – to distinguish them from the poor prostitutes called *cortigiane delle candelle*, since they often worked out of candlemerchants' shops. The poor whores 'of the candles' ended their lives begging for alms on church steps as soon as they lost their looks, and died as paupers in the Hospital of the Consolazione (Cesare's one charitable endowment). The lives of the fashionable courtesans were very different. Pietro Aretino, who called Rome 'a town of whores', poked fun at the bogus intellectualism of the courtesans of the day, and in one of his plays a mother advised her daughter to advance herself in the profession by leaving fashionable books such as *The Decameron* and Petrarch lying about, and to hire some poor poet to ghost verses for her.

Fiammetta, apart from her other accomplishments, spoke Latin, declaimed Ovid and Petrarch from memory, and sang delightfully, accompanying herself on the lyre. No doubt she lived in circumstances of the utmost luxury, like the girl described by the Sienese Pietro Fortini, who sat 'resembling a glittering sun with her splendid and rich clothes, her jewels and her golden chains' in a room decorated with gilded leather and fine paintings, while her bedroom was hung with silk and had 'a bed with superb curtains, a royal bedspread, and above all sheets so fine and white that they in truth seemed as thin, as fine, as white as the membrane of an egg'. The apartments of Imperia, Fiammetta's contemporary, wrote Matteo Bandello, were so richly furnished that they might have belonged to a princess, and the Spanish ambassador who visited her there preferred to spit in the face of a servant rather than on the floor for fear of spoiling the magnificent carpets. Fiammetta and Imperia, mistress of Raphael's patron Agostino Chigi, earned remission for their profitable sins by building themselves splendid memorial chapels in the fashionable church of San Agostino, frequented by their former friends and clients, the great cardinals, bankers, artists and humanists. Aretino, who saw Fiammetta's chapel there after she died in 1512, remarked of her that 'she made a beautiful end'. In fact little is known of Fiammetta beyond her relationship with Cesare, which was notorious to the extent that her will in the city archives was headed 'the Testament of la Fiammetta of il Valentino'.

While the Romans gossiped about Cesare's relationship with the lovely Fiammetta, they were amazed by his physical feats in public. The Venetian envoy Paolo Capello reported that at a bullfight held in the piazza of St Peter's on 24 June he 'killed seven wild bulls, fighting on horseback in the Spanish style, and he cut off the head of one with his first stroke, a thing which seemed great to all Rome'. But on Monday, 29 June, five days after his triumph in the arena, an accident occurred which was a vivid reminder to Cesare of the tenuous nature of his hold on power. At about five o'clock a violent storm struck the city in a tempest of rain, hail and whirlwinds. A chimney on the Vatican roof fell through the 'ceiling into a room, mortally injuring three people, including Lorenzo Chigi, brother of the famous Sienese banker. The floor collapsed into a room below where Alexander was seated on a dais conversing with Cardinal Lopez and his secret chamberlain Gaspara Poto. Lopez and Poto were hurrying to close the windows against a violent squall of rain when they heard a crash and the room filled with a cloud of dust; the dais where the Pope had been sitting was covered by a heap of fallen masonry. Panic-stricken, they called to the guards outside the door that the Pope was dead. The guards, showing more presence of mind, cleared away the rubble and found the Pope still sitting on his throne, unconscious but alive – a roof beam had saved him from the falling masonry. He had a bleeding wound on his head, bruises, and various cuts and scratches on his right hand and arm, but he was soon able to walk to the neighbouring chamber to be tended by his doctors.

Typically, Alexander's first thought was for politics, and his son's future; he sent for the Venetian ambassador Capello and dispatched a brief to the Venetian Signoria informing them of the accident. From his sickbed, where the ambassador found him devotedly nursed by Lucrezia and her ladies, one of whom he describes as 'his favourite', Alexander pressed Capello on the question of Rimini and Faenza, and above all for a Venetian condotta for Cesare. In France it was rumoured that the Pope was dead, and moves were made to gain the tiara for Giuliano della Rovere. Indeed, his father's narrow escape from death can only have impressed Cesare the more with the urgency of carrying out his plans and securing his future. As the Florentine envoy Francesco Cappello wrote perspicaciously on 8 July: 'Since the Pope is a man of seventy, similar shocks are considered dangerous ... This illness will be the cause of il Valentino arranging his affairs with Venice by whatever means he can, because if the Pope died he is well aware that he would be in a very exposed position ...'

Within just over a fortnight of the Pope's accident a brutal attack on Lucrezia's husband, Alfonso Bisceglie, focused a lurid light of speculation on Borgia family relationships within the Vatican. On the evening of 15 July Alfonso was set upon and seriously wounded as he crossed the piazza of St Peter's on his way from the Vatican to the palace of Santa Maria in Portico where he lived with Lucrezia. Burchard reported:

> On Wednesday 15 July, towards the tenth hour of evening, the most illustrious Don Alfonso d'Aragona, Duke of Bisceglie, husband of Donna Lucrezia, the Pope's daughter, passing by the steps of the basilica of St Peter's, before the first entrance, was attacked by several persons and gravely wounded in the head, the right arm and the thigh. The aggressors fled by the steps of St Peter's where there were awaiting them about forty mounted men, with whom they rode towards the Porta Pertusa.

Alfonso, badly wounded, was carried into the Vatican, where the Borgias' first reactions seem to have been shock and sympathy. Alexander had him placed in rooms near his own and tended by his personal doctors, while Lucrezia was reported to be 'half-dead'. Cesare for his part issued an edict forbidding the carrying of arms in the Borgo.

In the atmosphere of fear and suspicion that surrounded the affair, some people dared not commit their opinions to paper. Alfonso's former tutor, the Florentine humanist Raphael Brandolin, who received a stipend from the papal court, wrote to Ferrara on the day following the attack: 'Whose was the hand behind the assassins is still unknown. I will not, however, repeat which names are being voiced, because it is grave and perilous to entrust it to a letter.' One name, however, was being voiced within twenty-four hours of the attempt on Bisceglie – Cesare's. On 16 July Vincenzo Calmeta, poet and papal secretary, wrote his former patroness the Duchess of Urbino a detailed account of the incident, ending: 'Who may have ordered this thing to be done, everyone thinks to be Duke Valentino.' Alfonso's wounds should not prove mortal, he thought, adding significantly: 'If some new accident does not intervene.' Others, noting similiarities between the attack on Bisceglie and Gandia's murder, saw the hand of the Orsinis in the affair, since Alfonso was a partisan of the pro-Neapolitan Colonnas. And the Orsinis were now on good terms with Cesare, several of their captains having signed up with him for his next campaign. Although the Orsinis were the most likely authors, or rather bunglers, of the assassination attempt, it is feasible to consider that Cesare might have had foreknowledge of it, or at least welcomed it – he had his own personal reasons for desiring the elimination of Alfonso, as we shall see later. He is reported to have said: 'I did not wound the Duke, but if I had, it would have been no more than he deserved,' and he rather than the Orsinis would have had intimate knowledge of his brother-in-law's movements. The one factor which may be seen to exculpate him from the actual planning of the attack was the bungling of its execution; his own henchmen never failed to carry out his orders, as events were soon to show. Whatever the truth of the affair, for the moment the Borgias were not talking, nor it seems were they making any attempt to find the assassins. As the Florentine envoy Cappello wrote on 16 July: 'Who may have wounded him, no one says, and there are no signs of diligent inquiries being made as there should be.'

Alfonso, anxiously tended by Lucrezia and Sancia, recovered relatively quickly from his wounds. On Tuesday, 18 August, just one month after the assassination attempt, he was sitting up in bed in his room in the Torre Borgia overlooking the gardens, chatting and laughing with his wife and sister, when sudden violence shattered the peace of the warm August afternoon. Brandolin gave a graphic account of the scene, moving in its detail:

On the advice of the doctors, the wounds were already bandaged, the sick man was without fever, or very little, and was joking in his bedroom with his wife and sister, when there burst into the chamber ... Michelotto [Miguel da Corella] most sinister minister of Cesare Valentino; he seized by force Alfonso's uncle and the royal envoy [of Naples], and having bound their hands behind their backs, consigned them to armed men who stood behind the door, to lead them to prison. Lucrezia, Alfonso's wife, and Sancia, his sister, stupefied by the suddenness and violence of the act, shrieked at Michelotto, demanding how he dared commit such an offence before their very eyes and in the presence of Alfonso. He excused himself as persuasively as he could, declaring that he was obeying the will of others, that he had to live by the orders of another, but that they, if they wished, might go to the Pope, and it would be easy to obtain the release of the arrested men. Carried away with anger and pity ... the two women went to the Pope, and insisted that he give them the prisoners. Meanwhile Michelotto, most wretched of criminals, and most criminal of wretches, suffocated Alfonso, who was indignantly reproving him for his offence. The women, returning from the Pope, found armed men at the door of the chamber, who prevented them from entering and announced that Alfonso was dead. Michelotto, the author of the crime, had invented the fiction which was neither true nor half true, that Alfonso, distraught by the greatness of his peril, having seen men linked with him by kinship and goodwill torn from his side, fell unconscious to the floor and that from the wound in his head much blood flowed and thus he died. The women, terrified by this most cruel deed, oppressed by fear, beside themselves with grief, filled the palace with their shrieking, lamenting and wailing, one calling on her husband, the other on her brother, and their tears were without end ...

Burchard's laconic report confirms Brandolin's account, using significantly loaded phrases. Alfonso, he wrote, 'refusing to die of his wounds, was strangled at four in the afternoon'. He added: 'There were arrested and taken to Sant'Angelo the dead man's doctors and a hunchback, but were later set free, being innocent, *which fact was well known to those who had ordered their arrest.*'

Six hours later Alfonso's body was carried from the palace to St Peter's and hastily interred in the chapel of Santa Maria delle Febbri. The dead prince was attended only by Cardinal Francesco Borgia, a confidant of Lucrezia's, and his retinue. It was the quietest of funerals; for Alfonso, unlike Juan, there was no lying in state, no processions of chanting priests bearing lighted tapers through the streets of Rome. But the repercussions of his death reverberated through the city and the palace and indeed throughout Italy, quite overshadowing the recent Baglioni bloodbath at Perugia, where half the family had massacred the others in their beds. This time no one doubted that Cesare Borgia was the author of the crime. The question remained – why he had done it?

Some saw it as a purely political murder, motivated by Cesare's desire to show the world that the Borgias were committed to France. Cattaneo reported as early as 30 July, two weeks after the first assassination attempt: 'This matter is a pledge to France on the part of the Pope and Valencia, and to the designs of each, and where first they negotiated to give Valencia a state in Spain, now in everything they are with the French and the Venetians.' But if this was the motive, then the crime was singularly unnecessary. Cesare had no need to make a public pledge of his allegiance to France, and stood to gain nothing by this deep affront to the house of Aragon, which included the King of Naples and Ferdinand. As the next few days were to show, he had already come to an agreement with Louis whereby the King of France promised him military and diplomatic support for renewed action in the Romagna in return for his participation in a French attack on Naples. Moreover France and Spain were not at this moment antagonistic towards each other, since negotiations were going on for the partition of the kingdom of Naples between the two powers which were to culminate in the cynical Treaty of Granada in November. Cesare's brutalities were always calculated: there is not one single recorded instance of his committing an act of violence which he would have considered unnecessary or from which he did not stand to gain.

The official Borgia justfication for the murder, repeated by Alexander to the diplomats, was that it was a necessary act of self-defence. As the Venetian Paolo Capello wrote on the day of the crime: 'The Duke of Bisceglie is dead today because he planned to kill the Duke, when he was walking in the garden, with a crossbow ... And the Duke says that his dead brother-in-law had written to the Colonnesis to come with troops, who had sympathizers in the Castello [Sant'Angelo] and would have cut the Orsinis to pieces.' If the story of the plot were true – and it seems to have been widely believed not only by the Venetians, who were hostile to Naples, but by others including the level-headed Florentine Cappello, who reported it in a cipher letter to his government – it would explain the involvement of the Orsinis in the original assassination attempt. And in such a situation it would have been typical of Cesare to strike first. Yet it still does not provide an explanation of the time lapse between the original attack on Alfonso and his murder one month later.

The real explanation for the murder seems to have lain within the circle of Borgia family relationships in the Vatican, where Cesare's motives were not only political but personal. Cappello wrote on 16 July: 'The rumour in Rome grows that it is a matter between themselves, because in that Palace there are so many old and new hatreds, and so much envy and jealousy for political reasons and others ...' An internal power struggle between the partisans of France and those of Aragon had been waged for some time past within the Vatican, the ultimate prize being the mind of the Pope. There is little doubt that while Cesare was away in France the Aragonese party centred round Alfonso and Sancia had tried to win back Alexander to his old allegiance to Spain and the house of Aragon from which Louis' promises to Cesare had weaned him. We have seen how in the spring of 1499 Cesare feared that his father, exasperated with Louis and at heart hostile to France, might return to his old friendships. When Cesare returned to Rome at the end of February after his prolonged absence, he was quick to sense a concealed undercurrent within the family circle in opposition to his interests. Sancia and Jofre, Alfonso and Lucrezia had lived on terms of the closest intimacy since Alfonso had rejoined the family at Spoleto the previous autumn, and Sancia had been allowed to return to Rome some time during the winter. This close-knit clique would clearly have had Aragonese sympathies; Jofre, a cipher, in the absence of his elder brother was dominated by his strong-willed wife, while Lucrezia, who had wept bitterly when Alfonso fled from Rome, was clearly very much in love with her husband. On 1 November 1499 she had given birth to her son by Alfonso, Rodrigo, and happy as she was in her role of wife and mother, it was not surprising that she should have felt in close sympathy with her husband.

Sancia, the eldest of the family party, was now in open opposition to Cesare; she was not afraid of him, and naturally put the interests of her family, threatened by Louis' claims to Naples, above those of her brother-in-law and former lover. The tension between them had been revealed by a minor court incident in March, shortly after Cesare's return. A quarrel between a Frenchman and a Burgundian under Cesare's command had ended in a public duel on Monte Testaccio which took place in a bitterly partisan atmosphere with Cesare and Sancia taking opposing sides. The Burgundian won; Cesare, leader of the pro-French party, was deeply chagrined and is alleged to have said that he would have given 20,000 ducats rather than see the Frenchman beaten. Sancia was openly triumphant, and to tease her brother-in-law and parade her anti-French feelings she dressed twelve of her squires in the Burgundian colours.

Cesare, with his fiercely competitive temperament and overriding ambition, was not a man to brook opposition within his own family circle, above all when it threatened not only his political interests, his commitment to the French alliance, but also his personal position within the Vatican, and his two closest relationships, with his father and sister. Cesare's relationship with his father was the most important of his whole life. He was dependent upon Alexander as the source of his power at that time, and he was determined that his father should follow the path in which he saw his own interests to lie, and that no one should come between them. As far as Lucrezia was concerned,

Cesare's intense love for his sister was notorious, and while he may have feared that her pro-Aragonese sympathies might influence her father, who doted on her, jealousy of her feelings for her husband fuelled his hatred for Alfonso. Thus Cesare saw Alfonso as a threat to himself, a threat which must be eliminated; moreover in the context of the future French campaign against Naples he was a political embarrassment whose elimination would be an advantage. Cesare was to prove himself adept at using others as his instruments, and in the case of Bisceglie it is likely that he made use of the Orsinis to achieve his object. When the Orsinis bungled the affair, he waited, hoping that Alfonso, badly injured as he was, would die anyway. It was only when it became clear that Alfonso, in Burchard's words, 'refused to die of his wounds', that the need for direct action became necessary, and even then he moved with a certain circumspection, using the excuse of an Aragonese plot to justify his action to his father.

From ambassadorial reports it appears that Alexander was deeply worried by the first attempt on Alfonso, perhaps because of its effect on his relations with Ferdinand, perhaps also because he suspected Cesare of complicity in it. Cappello wrote on 18 July: 'This affair of the Duke has greatly displeased him, and he is in the worst possible disposition.' Cesare needed the justification of the Aragonese plot to convince his father of the necessity of his action, and Alexander seems to have gratefully accepted it. Eager as he was to embrace Cesare's cause wholeheartedly and to close his eyes to an unpleasant past, Lucrezia's incessant tears for her dead husband irritated him, and early in September she was packed off to Nepi. On 4 September Cattaneo reported that the Pope 'has sent away his daughter and daughter-in-law and everyone except Valencia because at the end they were wearisome to him'. Cesare had won. Raphael Brandolin was correct in his final diagnosis of the Bisceglie case; it was, he wrote, motivated by 'the supreme lust for dominion of Cesare Valentino Borgia'.

The assassination of Alfonso Bisceglie marked a new phase in Cesare's reputation for ruthlessness, an intensification of the fear he inspired throughout Italy as the 'terrible' Duke Valentino. 'All Rome trembles at this Duke, that he may not have them killed,' Capello reported dramatically to the Venetian Senate. From that day on any murder of importance was attributed to him, while the belief that he had in fact murdered Gandia gathered strength and echoed down the ages. 'Cesare murdered his brother, slept with his sister, spent the treasure of the Church, and was the terror of his father Alexander,' a contemporary wrote of him. He brought this sinister reputation upon himself, for one cannot escape the conclusion that the murder of Alfonso was a deliberate act of terror. He could easily have eliminated his brother-in-law less publicly, by the use of poison, but he did not, possibly because it suited him to have men fear him. The atmosphere which he created emerges in the cipher letter reporting Bisceglie's death sent by the Florentine envoy to his government: 'I pray Your Lordships to take this for your own information, and not to show it to others, for these [the Borgias] are men to be watched, otherwise they have done a thousand villainies, and have spies in every place.'

But the Borgias, father and son, clearly cared little for public opinion as long as they got what they wanted. The retiring Venetian ambassador, Capello, gave an interesting if highly spiced picture of Alexander and Cesare, a confident, ambitious partnership in this autumn of 1500, in his official report to the Venetian Senate on his Roman embassy. Alexander's natural resilience had left him quite unmarked either by his recent narrow escape from death or the murder of his son-in-law. Giulia Farnese, who seems to have been absent during the summer, had returned in mid-August, shortly after her husband, the wretched Orsino Orsini, had been killed by a falling roof, and was once again at Alexander's side. 'The Pope,' reported Capello, 'is seventy and grows younger every day. Worries never last him a night; he loves life, and is of a joyful nature and does what suits him.' In his natural exuberance and talkativeness, Alexander could keep nothing secret, Capello said. He remarked on his easy-going tolerance; the eighty-four-year-old Cardinal of Portugal, da Costa, spoke openly against the Pope, 'and the Pope laughs and doesn't answer'. His power was absolute: 'The cardinals without the Pope can do zero.' Only Giuliano della Rovere was singled out as 'a very dangerous man'. As far as international politics were concerned, the Pope thought 'more of the Signoria [Venice] than any other power in the world'; he was, Capello said, the enemy of the King of France, and described his relations with Ferdinand of Aragon as 'bargaining from Catalan to Catalan'.

Capello gave his view of Alexander's relationship with Cesare: 'The Pope loves and fears his son, who is twenty-seven [he was just twenty-five], physically most beautiful, he is tall and well-made, better than King Ferrantino ... he is munificent, even prodigal, and this displeases the Pope ...' It is interesting to note that Capello, who must have seen Cesare on innumerable occasions, stressed his physical beauty; the historical picture of Cesare as a monster skulking behind a mask, concealing features hideously ravaged by syphilis, is a lurid fiction based on Paolo Giovio's later description of him as swarthy and disfigured by blotches. After the disappearance of the rash caused by the secondary stage of syphilis, the chances of physical disfigurement would have been very small, and in any case would have appeared many years later. Hostile contemporaries would have been quick to point out any hideous deformation of Cesare's looks, as they did in 1498, but no such accounts exist for this period, and Capello's portrayal of him as a strikingly handsome man seems to have been the true one. Cesare gave the impression of being mature for his age; the Venetian thought him two years older than he actually was. Capello went on to depict him as a sadistic murderer, stabbing Perotto as he cowered under the Pope's cloak so that the blood spurted up in Alexander's face, ordering the death of Gandia, and wholesale assassinations: 'Every day in Rome one finds men murdered, four or five a night, bishops, prelates and others ...'

As to Cesare's relations with Lucrezia, Capello hinted: 'And they say this Duke [sleeps with] his sister.' Lucrezia, formerly the Pope's favourite, was 'wise and generous, but now the Pope does not love her so much, and sends her to Nepi, and has given her Sermoneta which has cost 80,000 ducats, although the Duke has taken it from her, saying "She is a woman, she could not keep it." '

Capello's account of Cesare dominant was unconsciously coloured by the recent sensation of the Bisceglie murder – 'The Pope loves and fears his son ...' Alexander may have feared his son's ruthlessness, but there is absolutely no evidence that he was dominated by him at this point, and Capello's own portrayal of Alexander as powerful and full of life gives the lie to this theory. The relationship between the two men was one of mutual reliance and interdependence, and in fact Cesare at this point in his career depended totally on his father as the source of his power. It was a partnership in which Alexander was the senior member, although Cesare's influence had grown to such a point that they could be considered equals. The crunch would come when their individual outlooks and policies clashed. For the moment they were identical: the furthering of Cesare's career of conquest could be regarded as an extension of the temporal power of the Papacy.

And the time had come for a resumption of that career. In August, five days after Bisceglie's death, a special envoy from Louis XII arrived in Rome, the same M. de Trans who had brought Cesare his letters patent as Duke of Valentinois on the day he renounced the cardinalate two years before. Once again de Trans was the bearer of good tidings, news so important that Cesare could not wait to hear it. De Trans was at an inn outside the city walls when, as Burchard reported: 'There came a certain horseman, masked and riding fast, with one on foot, who dismounted at the inn, and keeping on his mask which he did not lower, embraced the orator and spoke with him: after a short while the masked man returned to the city. They say it was Duke Valentino.' De Trans was the bearer of a formal agreement whose terms must already have been discussed. In return for the Borgias' political and military help in the conquest of Naples, Louis promised to send 300 lances and 2000 infantry under the command of Yves d'Alègre to help in the forthcoming Romagna campaign. Moreover he would instruct the lords under his protection such as Bentivoglio of Bologna to give free passage and assistance to the papal army.

This meant that Cesare could now go confidently ahead with his military preparations; he had already signed contracts with some of the leading Italian condottieri – Paolo and Giulio Orsini, and Vitellozzo Vitelli – and was negotiating a condotta with Gian Paolo Baglioni. There was a desperate need for money. He would require at least a thousand ducats a day to pay his troops on the campaign, and the Venetian envoy reported that he was engaging soldiers and 'getting money like a madman'. Alexander had contributed funds from the Jubilee income, and some of the tithe imposed on the clergy for the Crusade against the Turks, but still more would be needed. In their necessity the Borgias resorted to the simple expedient of milking the College of Cardinals. No secret was made of the fact that nominations of new cardinals would be made for cash; Cesare himself conducted the negotiations, and drew up a scale of payments, while Alexander browbeat the cardinals into acceptance. When the nominations were made on 28 September, among the new cardinals were several members of the Borgia connection, including Cesare's tutor Juan Vera and his brother-in-law Aymon d'Albret, and the sum raised was calculated at about 120,000 ducats. The new creations were not only profitable for Cesare but provided him with still more adherents in the Roman court, as Sanuto recorded: 'After their investiture they went to the Duke, offering themselves to him, and dined there, and settled their accounts and swore fealty to him.'

One of the new cardinals was a Venetian, Marco Cornaro, a sop to the Republic. In fact, by early September the Borgias had the Venetians where they wanted them. Throughout August Alexander continued to press the Republic to withdraw its protection from the vicars of Rimini and Faenza, whom he had recently excommunicated, with Giovanni Sforza thrown in for good measure. He wanted an alliance and a condotta for Cesare, holding out the use of the Spanish fleet against the Turks as token of his goodwill. The Venetian situation vis-à-vis the Turks in the Adriatic was becoming increasingly critical, and the shock of the fall of Modone on 9 September impelled them to lay down their diplomatic arms unconditionally to the Borgias. 'Shocked, terror-stricken and amazed', the new envoy Giorgi, accompanied by Capello, hurried to the Vatican to appeal to the Pope for help without waiting for a formal appointment. Alexander was disposed to aid them but made his position quite clear. He told them, wrote the Florentine envoy Cappello, that:

> The Signoria had until now acted ungratefully towards His Holiness, never having wished to allow him to carry on the enterprises of Rimini and Faenza, favouring rebels and excommunicates ... and if they wished to please His Holiness they should act differently in future. The two orators answered that they were minded to do anything for His Holiness, and to embrace the Duke Valentino, and hold him as their good son, and to give him a condotta on the best and most convenient conditions, and [as to] Rimini and Faenza ... they would be most content for him to carry out his enterprises. The Pope answered that he wanted no more of their fine words, that he had already had too many of them, but now he wanted deeds ...

On 16 September, the desperate Venetian government gave Alexander the deeds he wanted: although they still had the sense to temporize over the condotta, Rimini and Faenza were sacrificed to Cesare, and they promised to make him a gentiluomo, hereditary gentleman, of Venice – an honour which brought with it the gift of a palace in the city.

Thus, by the end of September, Cesare was ready to take the field. Capello reported on the 26th: 'I understand that the order has been given that, after the cardinals have been created, Duke Valentino will depart within two or three days, according to what the astrologer indicates as the favourable moment.' The envoys at the court of Rome watched his departure with foreboding. As Cattaneo had written in July, rumours were already abroad about the scope of the Borgias' ambitions for Cesare. 'The Pope plans to make him great and king of Italy, if he can; nor am I dreaming,' he added, 'but everything can be described and written down, and so that others will not think my brains are disordered, I will say no more ...' Few seasoned observers would have thought Cattaneo mad; opinions as to Cesare's capabilities had changed considerably over the past twelve months. Paolo Capello declared: 'He will be, if he lives, one of the first captains of Italy.'

IX

LORD OF ROMAGNA

On 30 September Cesare and Alexander watched a review of 800 of his Spanish infantry from the loggia above the piazza of St Peter's; the next day the army moved out of Rome, bound for the Romagna. Cesare himself followed on 2 October, riding northward up the Via Flaminia. He was accompanied by his personal staff of young Roman noblemen, many of whom had been with him in France, three bishops who were to assist him in the administration of his new state, his confidential secretary Agapito Geraldini, his doctor Torella, his treasurer Alessandro Spanocchi, Ramiro de Lorqua the master of his household, and the usual signorial retinue of poets, artists and men of letters, including Vincenzo Calmeta, Pier Francesco Giustolo, Francesco Sperulo and the sculptor Torrigiano. The army which he was to command numbered some 10,000 men – 700 men-at-arms, 200 light horse, and 6000 Spanish, Italian, Gascon and Swiss infantry, with an artillery train under Vitellozzo Vitelli. His captains were Spanish professionals – Cesare's sinister familiar Miguel da Corella, Juan de Cardona, Ugo de Moncada – and Italian condottieri Vitellozzo Vitelli and Bartolomeo da Capranica accompanied him from Rome, while Paolo and Carlo Orsini, Gian Paolo Baglioni and Ercole Bentivoglio waited for him in Umbria and the Romagna. It was a professional, mercenary army, and for the first time under Cesare's supreme command.

Cesare moved slowly northward, stopping to visit the disconsolate Lucrezia at Nepi, where she had spent the past two months in deep mourning for Alfonso, signing her letters 'la infelicissma', 'the most unhappy woman', and pointedly crossing out her title 'Princess of Salerno'. For Lucrezia, who was still in disgrace for her public grief at Alfonso's death, the visit was a reconciliation with the brother who had made her 'the most unhappy woman', and some time before

Christmas she was allowed back to Rome. Cesare's leisurely progress was due partly to the weather, as the artillery trains floundered in thick mud and heavy rain, partly to deliberate timing. As in the previous campaign he had laid his plans well beforehand so as to obtain the maximum advantage with the minimum of costly military action, and as he made his way northward his agents were fomenting trouble for Giovanni Sforza at Pesaro, and negotiating with Pandolfo Malatesta for the cession of Rimini. On 11 October mobs headed by the leading citizens of Pesaro marched through the streets and arrested Giovanni Sforza's brother Galeazzo. Giovanni himself fled from the citadel the next night, and made his way to refuge in Venice, preferring not to remain to face his terrible ex-brother-in-law. On the 15th the town opened its gates to Ercole Bentivoglio in Cesare's name, and on the 18th the ducal commissioner Olivieri, Bishop of Isernia, arrived to take over the government. Cesare himself entered Pesaro on 27 October in pouring rain, 'very proudly, both in himself and his company', a Gonzaga correspondent reported. Over their streaming armour the 150 men-at-arms wore the red and yellow of his personal livery, worked with a new device on chest and back, the seven-headed hydra, an apt symbol for future victims of il Valentino's aggression.

At Pesaro Cesare lodged in Giovanni Sforza's apartments in the palace which Lucrezia had occupied during her first two years as Countess of Pesaro. Here he was visited by the first in a series of acute observers who from now on were to watch his every move. Pandolfo Collenuccio, the envoy of the Duke of Ferrara, was favourably impressed by the affability of Cesare's manner: 'With great frankness and amiability His Majesty first made excuses for not granting me an audience the preceding day, owing to his having so much to do in the citadel and also on account of the pain caused by his ulcer' (Collenuccio reported him to be suffering from a sore in the groin the previous day). As a man of letters Collenuccio remarked on the eloquence and precision with which he spoke: 'He answered me in carefully chosen words, covering each point, and very fluently.' He remarked also the eccentricity of Cesare's nocturnal habits, which exasperated his father and were the despair of ambassadors seeking audience of him:

The Duke's daily life is as follows: he goes to bed at the eighth, ninth or tenth hour of night [3–5 a.m.]. Consequently the eighteenth hour [midday] is his dawn, the nineteenth his sunrise, and the twentieth his time for rising. Immediately on getting up he sits down at table, and while there and afterwards he attends to business.

Collenuccio ended his report with a summing-up of Cesare's character:

> He is considered brave, strong, and liberal [by which he meant munificent], and it is said that he sets great store by straightforward men. He is hard in revenge, so I have been told by many; a man of soaring spirit, thirsting for greatness and fame, he seems more eager to seize states than to keep and administer them.

Collenuccio had recognized in Cesare the qualities of a conquistador. The Gonzagas' anonymous correspondent at Pesaro had meanwhile come to the same conclusion. It was no longer, he wrote, merely a question of Cesare taking Faenza, but, if fortune favoured him, Bologna, and even Florence. 'Now,' he added ominously, 'anything is believable ...'

After two days in Pesaro, spent inspecting the citadel, of which he commissioned a painting to be sent to Alexander, who shared his interest in fortifications, Cesare moved on to Rimini, which he entered on 30 October. It was a purely ceremonial entry. Sigismondo Malatesta's grandson Pandolfo had already handed over the city to Cesare's representative Olivieri on the 10th, turning a quick profit by selling the citadel and its artillery, and had loaded his goods onto a boat to take refuge in Venetian territory. The sinful Sigismondo, depicted by Pisanello as a man of reptilian attraction, strong-featured, falcon-nosed, with glittering flat-lidded eyes which gave a snake-like impression, had been a brilliant if unreliable soldier, and an intelligently passionate patron of philosophy and the arts. His son Roberto had been a celebrated condottiere, but his grandson, Pandolfaccio as he was contemptuously known, was no more than a rapacious thug, and his subjects welcomed Cesare as a liberator. But the ease with which he had taken possession of Rimini and Pesaro caused a state of near panic in the neighbouring powers, Florence and Bologna. The Florentine government noted with anxiety that his leading Italian captains were their sworn enemies; Vitellozzo Vitelli had vowed to avenge himself on them for their execution of his brother Paolo, and the Orsinis were linked by marriage with the Medicis and pledged to their restoration. It was known that at the end of October Piero de'

Medici had arrived in Pisa from France, giving out that he had been called to Rome by the Pope, while Alexander for his part began a mounting campaign of protest against Bologna and Florence on the grounds of their sending help to Astorre Manfredi at Faenza.

As the winter wore on the tone of Florentine government dispatches to their envoy Machiavelli, on special mission at the court of France, became increasingly hysterical. Louis, they insisted, must make the Pope understand that Florence was under his protection:

> From all parts come reports of the ill intentions of the Pope and the Duke, having taken Faenza, to attack us and change our constitution, and because there was there a large army under captains most inimical to the city and the Duke full of pride for the taking of Rimini and Pesaro, and having such confidence in his fortune that every undertaking even the most difficult seemed easy to him, and without any respect to attempt everything which he had in mind.

Machiavelli's report of Louis' attitude to the Borgias can have given them little cause for comfort: 'Concerning the matters which may arise in Italy, the King holds the Pope in higher esteem than any other Italian power.' And there were further disquieting reports that Alexander was working on d'Amboise's ambition for the Legateship of France to persuade him to pressure Louis into supporting the Borgias' Italian plans. As early as 26 October Cappello, the Florentine envoy to Rome, wrote in cipher to his government:

> It is said that the Cardinal of Rouen [d'Amboise] has agreed with the Pope that if he works to ensure that the King will send French troops to his aid, the Pope will make him Legate of France. And because he [d'Amboise] had a great desire for this, it is thought he will induce the King to give in to the Pope. And when this happens, Bologna can consider itself lost, and I understand from a trustworthy source that the Pope has great hopes of this.

Meanwhile, unknown to the anxious Italian powers, a momentous change had taken place on the international scene, which made the Borgias' prospects of success even more favourable. On 11 November a secret treaty was signed at Granada which provided for the partition of the kingdom of Naples between France and Spain. Louis was to have Naples, Gaeta, the Terra de Lavoro and the Abruzzi, with the titles of King of Naples and Jerusalem, while Ferdinand took Calabria and Apulia with the title of Duke. This cynical treaty, by which Ferdinand of Aragon abandoned his ally and kinsman the King of Naples on the fatuous pretext of his having sought help from the infidel Turk, was yet another instance of Louis' incapacity to take the long view in international politics. In order to assure himself the undisputed possession of half the Kingdom, he was giving away the other half to the one power who represented the greatest long-term threat to his own interests in Italy. Whether the Borgias had wind of this agreement or not, and with their excellent intelligence service it is feasible to think that they did, from their own point of view it meant that Louis' havering with regard to Italy was over, that the Naples campaign was decided upon, and that he would have need of them.

In the second week of November, Cesare, with a train of easy successes behind him, moved on Faenza, to meet with his first rebuff. In his interview with Collenuccio at Pesaro he had shown himself uncertain whether Faenza would give up as easily as had Rimini and Pesaro. Indeed, in this case his usual methods of subversion had failed; in the first week of November the discovery of a plot to hand Faenza over to him had resulted only in the arrest of the castellan and four citizens. For at Faenza, unlike Imola and Forlì, Rimini and Pesaro, the ruling Manfredi family was popular with the citizens, and the present lord, the fifteen-year-old Astorre III, had been brought up by the city council since the murder of his father Galeotto by his mother Francesca Bentivoglio. Despite the encouraging news on 7 November that the di Naldo brothers, headed by Dionigi, had handed over to him their nine castles of the Val di Lamone, he was now faced with the dismal prospect of a long and expensive siege in exceptionally bitter winter weather, with the campaigning season drawing to a close.

Cesare arrived before Faenza on 17 November, and began bombardment of the town. On the 20th the unexpected fall of part of the bastion led his more zealous troops into a disastrous unplanned assault. Cesare wrote to Guidobaldo of Urbino making light of the affair – only four men, he said, had been killed – but it seems probable that the repulse was more serious than he let on, and its effect on morale disproportionate to the actual casualities. The severe winter favoured the defenders, snug within their walls, while the besiegers shivered in their bivouacs under snow. Food supplies were running short as the roads were blocked, and money too, so that pay was irregular and a steady trickle of soldiers deserted. The Umbrians under Gian Paolo Baglioni carried on a running vendetta against their Spanish colleagues in revenge for the Spaniards' appalling behaviour as they had passed through Umbria en route for the Romagna, graphically described by Matarazzo: 'The Spaniards washed the feet of their horses in wine, and what they could not use they threw away. And when they departed . . . they shat in all the tuns of muscatel wine, and where they ate, shat beneath the tables, and where they found vases of sweetmeats they emptied them and filled them with filth . . .' He concluded in a phrase illustrative of the general Italian feeling about Spaniards: 'There never was a filthier people than these *Spagnuoli marrani*, true enemies of the Italians.' Under the circumstances, Cesare saw no alternative but to suspend the campaign for the winter; having sent a formal demand for surrender into the city which received the discouraging reply that the Faventines were resolved 'to defend the rule of the Manfredi until death', he marched back to Forlì on 26 November, leaving a skeleton force under Vitellozzo to blockade the town.

Cesare spent the winter establishing himself in his new Romagna lordships. His troops were billeted in the various towns, and this time there were no complaints of outrageous behaviour. He was determined to make his rule popular with his new subjects, and made strenuous efforts to maintain discipline, hanging his own men for looting, and issuing edicts that troops must pay for their provisions on pain of death. As usual his life was a mixture of secrecy and swift movement, interspersed with exuberant pleasure. During the first three weeks he spent at Forlì he hardly showed himself. Indeed when Giovanni Vera, Cardinal of Salerno, came to Forlì on 5 December and Cesare rode out to meet him, the local chronicler Bernardi noted: 'This was the first time His Excellency had ever come out of his house to pass through our city . . . It seemed a great marvel, as he had always been a recluse.' Bernardi himself had an interview with his lord on 21 December, when Cesare in front of his whole court granted him a laureate as historian, with exemption from taxes so that he could pursue his literary work. No doubt for Cesare it was a useful exercise in public relations and a nod to posterity, but one cannot help feeling that he and the elegant men of letters of his court, who in Rome formed part of Paolo Cortese's literary circle, regarded the whole thing as a joke, and amused themselves secretly at the expense of the humble barber-historian of Forlì. The poet Francesco Sperulo composed a verse on the occasion, while Cesare's secretary Agapito wrote a few punning lines on Bernardi's skill with the razor and the pen.

Cesare spent Christmas at Cesena in openly festive mood. It was his favourite city, which he intended to make the capital of his new state. He set up court in the former palace of the Malatesta Novello overlooking the main square of the town, under the great citadel on the hill, and here on Christmas Eve he invited the Councillors, the Anziani, and leading citizens to dinner. On Christmas Day the palace was thrown open to the populace, who crowded through the magnificent apartments and even the ducal bedchamber. Afterwards games were held on the piazza, in which the noblemen of his suite took part. There was the *giostra dell'anello*, when a ring was set upon a lance, which the competitors, charging on horseback, attempted to carry away on their own lances, and the *quintana*, when they rode full tilt at a dummy figure of a Turk, points being awarded according to the part of the body struck by their lances. Christmas was followed by carnival and, as in Rome the previous summer, Cesare appeared outwardly intent only on enjoying the festivities, flinging himself enthusiastically into carnival pranks ill-suited to the ducal dignity: on one occasion, with two of his friends, masked and armed with spades, he went through the streets of the town spattering the passers-by with mud. He liked to ride out to the local hill villages and make a show of his strength, running races and wrestling with the tough Romagnol peasants. The local chroniclers were impressed: 'He ran as swiftly as a horse, and many times ran races with the youths, to whom he gave a start and passed them nonetheless. With his bare hands he could break a horseshoe and any thick cord.'

In February Cesare went on to Imola, where his continued round of pleasure was the despair of the *podestà* (mayor) of the Venetian town of Ravenna, whose job it was to spy on the dangerous Duke and to report any suspicious movement to his government. His intelligence reports were dutiful, if repetitive: 'The Duke is at Imola, feasting and hunting . . .' until in mid-February 1501 Cesare really gave him something to write about as he became once again the centre of a *cause célèbre*. On 13 February a beautiful young noblewoman, Dorotea Malatesta Caracciolo, travelling between Cesare's town of Porto Cesenatico towards Venetian territory at Cervia with a considerable escort, was abducted by armed men and several of her retinue seriously wounded. The *podestà* of Ravenna gleaned what he could from the lady's injured chancellor and hastened to set it down with a liberal admixture of his own imagination:

> The attackers who committed the crime rode separate on that night, and found one of our peasants on foot, whom they made their guide. There were ten horsemen, well equipped, armed with crossbows, and well mounted; and there were two ladies, who were protesting and lamenting greatly, their hair dishevelled ... They had themselves guided to Galiano, two miles from Cesena, to the house of Nicoluzzo di Galiano, and burst down the door, ordered the lady to dismount, the fire to be lit and the supper prepared. She asked: 'Where are you taking me?' They answered: 'Do not seek to know; you are in good hands and will be going to better ones, where you are awaited with high desire.' She said: 'Who is it?' They replied: 'Enough my lady, do not seek to know more.' And they set her, weeping and groaning, down to eat. She did not want to eat, they threatened her, and she was forced to take an egg; then she was put to sleep with her companion and the peasant's wife, and she was not molested that night. In the morning, after daybreak, they mounted eight horses and led the mule on which she was riding, and went with a new guide ... in the direction of Franpuollo on the road to Forlì. And they were all Spaniards.

News of the kidnapping roused a storm of indignation in Venice. Dorotea, the twenty-three-year-old natural daughter of Roberto Malatesta of Rimini, was the wife of Giambattista Caracciolo, a Neapolitan nobleman serving as captain of infantry in the Venetian army, whom she had met at the court of Urbino where she had been brought up as a protégée of the Duchess Elisabetta. The marriage had been celebrated by proxy at Urbino, and at the time of the kidnapping Dorotea had been travelling under Venetian protection to join her husband, who was commanding the garrison of Gradisca against the Turks. At the request of Venice, Cesare had provided an armed escort for the lady, and the abduction had taken place just after her company had crossed into Venetian territory.

Who then was the man who awaited Dorotea Caracciolo with such 'high desire' that he would go to the lengths of kidnapping her under the very nose of Venice? To the Venetians the effrontery of the deed pointed unmistakably to the one man in the Romagna powerful enough to defy them – Cesare Borgia. 'All Venice,' wrote Sanuto, 'the following morning after the news was received, displayed great grief. Thus this Duke Valentino, if he has had it done, has been ill-advised.' Furious, the Council of Ten resolved to send their secretary Aloise Manenti that same day to Cesare 'to complain of the matter without making any other salutation', and to demand Dorotea's restitution. They complained to the Papal Legate and the French ambassador in Venice, and sent a strongly worded letter of protest to their envoy in Rome to be shown to the Pope. In its fury and resentment the Venetian government did not mince its words; describing Dorotea as 'one of the most beautiful and notable women in Italy', it referred to her abduction as: 'a case so to be abominated, detested and horrible, that we know not in what part of Hell worse could be imagined. This injury has been openly effected against the person and whole of our State: which you can imagine how it has penetrated to our very soul, seeing this to be the first fruit we gather for the love and our deserts towards the said lord Duke.'

Cesare's reaction was predictable: one of innocent ignorance. At Imola, Manenti was forced to kick his heels waiting for an audience, while Cesare slept late as was his custom, having spent the night 'in pleasures'. He was then received with informal arrogance by Cesare, alone, leaning casually on a balcony, as he protested that he knew nothing as to Dorotea's whereabouts, adding insolently that 'he did not lack for women'. When Manenti's protests were seconded by the French ambassador, he roused himself to a show of righteous indignation against the culprit, whom he declared to be Diego Ramires, one of his Spanish captains. Ramires, he said, had been formerly in the service of the Duke of Urbino, and had had an affair with Dorotea there during carnival time, and in fact Ramires had shown him some embroidered shirts given him by Dorotea, and boasted to him of his passion. Like all good liars, Cesare, in laying the blame on Ramires, was probably telling a story which approximated fairly closely to the truth. Fantaguzzi, the chronicler of Cesena, recorded that Dorotea 'was attacked and abducted ...: by Messer Diego Ramirro, soldier of Duke Valentino and formerly courtier of the Duke of Urbino'. It is certainly believable that the young and beautiful Dorotea should have had an affair with a dashing Spanish officer during carnival time at Urbino while her middle-aged husband awaited the Turks at Gradisca. It is not, however, likely that a Spanish captain on his own would have risked offending both his master the Duke and the Venetian Republic. Nor is it credible that the powerful lord of the

Romagna could not have laid hands on Ramires if he had wanted to; the inescapable conclusion is that he did not.

In Rome, Alexander's reaction, as described by the Venetian envoy, was one of shocked indignation; it was, he exclaimed, 'a brutal, horrible and detestable thing, and I do not know what punishment whoever did it deserves. If the Duke has done it, he has lost his mind.' Alexander's dismay was probably genuine. It seems unlikely that Cesare would have informed his father beforehand of the planned escapade, and if he had, Alexander would certainly have opposed such an unwarranted insult to Venice, with whom he wished to be on good terms. When the envoy showed him the Venetians' letter, he covered his eyes with his hands, dismissed him without a word, and went into an inner room to confer with the Cardinal of Capua. Later, talking with intimates of Cesare's, he must have learned the truth, and decided that the only action he could take was to cover up for his wayward son. He showed the envoy a strongly worded brief to Cesare demanding punishment of the culprit, and declared that his son could not have been responsible since he was at Imola on the night of the incident. However, the envoy reported, 'despite his bold words, nonetheless he showed how it had upset him'.

Letters of protest rained down upon Cesare, from Venice, the Pope, the King of France, even Francesco Gonzaga entered the fray on behalf of his sister Elisabetta; but he did not punish Ramires, nor did he restore Dorotea, whose whereabouts remained a mystery. Searching frantically for information, the *podestà* of Ravenna picked up rumours that she was being kept in the Rocca of Forlì. One of his spies talked to a wood carrier who reported that he had seen 'at a balcony in the Rocca of Forlì two most beautiful women, and few, only those with permission, were admitted there, and the Duke came there often in disguise with two or three horsemen and entered by the Schiavonia gate.' As time went by and there was no definite news of her, the Venetian government were driven to appear to accept the Borgias' story in order to save face, while they nursed a deep resentment against Cesare, biding their time for revenge. The virtual disappearance of Dorotea is illustrative of the secrecy with which Cesare managed to veil his private life, for the evidence is that he did keep her. Over a year later, in December 1502, Sanuto reported briefly: 'With the Duke, when he left Imola, was the wife of our captain of infantry.'

The kidnapping of Dorotea Caracciolo is interesting for the light which it throws upon Cesare's character. It was not a romantic act – romance had no part in his make-up. Rather it was the satisfaction of a whim, motivated by what Machiavelli later called his 'rash self-confidence', executed for the devilry of it, gambling on the assurance that he would get away with it. No doubt it amused him to feel his power, and to twist the tail of the formidable Lion of St Mark. And yet the game was not really worth the candle, fuelling as it did the growing mistrust and resentment which Venice felt towards him. It is one of the contradictions of his complex character that, despite the clarity of his political perception and his own vengeful nature, Cesare seemed incapable of realizing the depth of the enmities which injuries like this could arouse.

It is not surprising that Cesare felt himself strong enough to cock a snook at Venice; as the winter of 1500 wore into the spring of 1501 French support for the Borgias became increasingly evident, and Cesare's thoughts were already soaring beyond Faenza. The next victim was to be Giovanni Bentivoglio of Bologna, whose aid to Astorre Manfredi was partly responsible for Cesare's failure to overawe Faenza. But Cesare wanted more than the cessation of aid to Manfredi, he wanted the frontier fortress of Castel Bolognese, strategically situated on the Via Emilia between Faenza and Imola, to round off his Romagna conquests, and there is no doubt he would have liked Bologna itself. From the Vatican and the court of France the big diplomatic guns pounded away at the unfortunate Bentivoglio, who was well aware that only Louis' expensive protection, which he had purchased the previous summer, stood between him and the threat from Cesare. The arrival of Louis' envoy de Trans on 18 December left Bentivoglio in no doubt as to the danger of his position; de Trans warned him that the King was displeased by his support of Astorre. The Pope, de Trans said, was demanding that Bologna should be restored to the Church, and if he continued to press his claim Louis, despite his promise of protection, would feel himself bound to give the Pope armed assistance. This body-blow was followed up by a letter from Louis at the end of January requiring him to assist 'our dear and beloved cousin the Duke of Valentinois' with arms, men and provisions, and to provide lodging for the French troops who were marching to join him. The opening of the spring campaigning season was approaching and Cesare was beginning his preparations for the final assault on Faenza. Time was pressing: he knew that it would not be long before Louis would recall the French troops to join in the coming campaign against Naples.

All attempts at suborning the defiant citizens of Faenza into surrender having failed, Cesare had no alternative but a direct assault. At the end of February the promised French troops, 2000 horse and foot with artillery, arrived at Forlì. (They were the price of Rouen's Legateship of France, which Alexander forced through an unwilling but cowed College of Cardinals on 5 April.) A month later Cesare set up his batteries round the walls of Faenza while the rest of Italy watched, hoping against hope that the brave Faventines would give the arrogant young Borgia his first bloody nose. As Isabella d'Este wrote on 12 April, their courageous defiance had 'recovered the honour of the Italians', and she prayed God would give them the grace to persevere. Indeed the first assault by the Borgia troops on 18 April was repulsed with heavy casualties on both sides, and only a prolonged bombardment of the town coupled with the desperate supply situation of the defenders induced the citizens to capitulate on the 25th. Cesare, who appreciated their courage and had even gone so far as to hang a Faventine traitor before the walls as a tribute to the citizens, treated them honourably and forbore to make his usual triumphant entrance into the town. The young lord of Faenza, Astorre, and his brother, flattered by the honours Cesare accorded them, took service with their conqueror.

The ink on the documents for the surrender of Faenza was barely dry before Cesare was off in pursuit of his next objective. He had resolved on a swift show of strength against Bologna to wrest Castel Bolognese from Bentivoglio. Having sent a herald to Bologna demanding cession of the fortress, he marched northward up the Via Emilia without waiting for an answer, while Vitellozzo rode on ahead to seize Bolognese strongpoints on the way. The citizens of Bologna were resolved to resist Cesare, but Bentivoglio, intent on saving his personal position, advised them to give in gracefully. On 29 April Paolo Orsini rode into the city to sign an agreement in Cesare's name; Bologna agreed to hand over Castel Bolognese to Cesare and to provide him with a force of a hundred men-at-arms at the city's expense to be employed in any undertaking he might specify, while he for his part promised to return the fortresses he had seized, to remove his troops from Bolognese territory, and to persuade the Pope to confirm the Bentivoglios in their privileges.

On the face of it, Cesare had won hands down; in four days he had forced Bentivoglio to give up the fortress which he had steadfastly refused him over the past four months. However, one condition of the agreement implied a possible future threat to his freedom of action. On Bentivoglio's express stipulation three of the Borgia condottieri, Giulio and Paolo Orsini and Vitellozzo Vitelli, were made parties to the agreement as guarantors of their employer's good behaviour. In simple terms the condottieri were promising to restrain Cesare from a future attack on Bologna, but behind the formal clauses of the treaty there was evidence of a closer understanding between Bentivoglio and the Orsinis which was potentially dangerous for Cesare. As a pledge of this understanding a marriage was arranged between Giacoma, daughter of Giulio Orsini, and Ermes, one of Bentivoglio's sons. And as Cesare marched away from Bologna, Bentivoglio, who had arrested the leading members of the Marescotti family on 27 April on suspicion of being Cesare's partisans, had them brutally murdered.

By early May 1501, after the agreement with Bologna, Cesare felt entitled to call himself 'Lord of Romagna'. His lordships stretched in an unbroken line down the Via Emilia from Imola to Fano in the south; on 1 May Alexander had issued a bull confirming Cesare as hereditary vicar not only of Pesaro but also of Fano, hitherto under the direct rule of the Church. A fortnight later he invested him with the title of Duke of Romagna, and sent him the Golden Rose, for the second year in succession. In effect the Pope had transferred to his son the perpetual overlordship of one of the most important provinces of the Papal States; the first major step towards the achievement of a hereditary Borgia dominion in Italy had been successfully concluded.

But already in the autumn of the previous year, Machiavelli had described the Borgias as 'insatiable', and now it seemed that Cesare, far from being satisfied with his conquests to date, was determined to ride the tide of fortune to the limit. In fact the next throw in the game had been decided upon months ago should the opportunity arise to take it – Tuscany. With true killer instinct the Borgias had recognized the weakness of Florence, and were determined to take advantage of it. As early as January 1501 Alexander had begun to put pressure on Florence for an alliance and a condotta for Cesare. As Buonaccorsi reported:

At that time the city was in dire enough straits since it was destitute of money and still without men-at-arms; and the request made to her by the Pope was for no other end than to demonstrate that the power to attack us lay with him, our not having the wherewithal to defend ourselves, which he knew very well; and moreover we had the army of il Valentino near our borders and openly hostile to us, and the King of France dissatisfied because certain sums of money owed him by the city had not been paid.

(Louis claimed that Florence owed him money for the war against Pisa in June–July 1500.) Indeed the Borgias guessed that Louis might not be averse to using the threat of il Valentino's army to frighten Florence into paying up, although they also knew that he would never allow a direct attack on the city itself. Over the past months the Borgias had been preparing the way for a Tuscan raid, putting pressure on Florence by threats of encirclement. In March Cesare sent one of his condottieri, Oliverotto da Fermo, with two hundred horse to beleaguered Pisa; and on 2 April he signed a league with another Florentine enemy, Pandolfo Petrucci of Siena, while it was public knowledge that he intended to take Piombino on the Tuscan coast. The Florentine government had scented danger as soon as they heard of Borgia flirtations with the Medicis the previous autumn, and the preponderance of the Orsinis among Cesare's captains only underlined the threat. Alexander and Cesare had obsolutely no intention of replacing the weak Republican government with that of the Medicis, a move which would have only served to increase the power of the Orsinis, but they were perfectly prepared to use Medici hopes and Medici partisans as camouflage to further their own designs in Tuscany.

Within a few days' of the agreement with Bentivoglio, Cesare, it was said, received orders from his father to return to Rome by the eastern route down the Via Flaminia. According to his own account given to the Florentines a year later, Cesare was on the point of obeying when Vitellozzo, weeping and on his knees, implored him to march through Tuscany, swearing that he intended no violence to the Tuscan cities and that no thought of restoring the Medicis was in his mind, only that he wished to obtain satisfaction from Florence in the release of his dead brother's chancellor Carbone. To content Vitellozzo and the Orsinis, who had borne the brunt of his Romagna campaign, Cesare therefore turned his army westward across the Apennines, in direct disobedience to the Pope's orders. In view of the documentary evidence of the Borgias' intrigues over the past months, the story simply does not ring true; moreover the game of Cesare's 'disobedience' was one which the Borgias were to play over and over again, whenever they planned some risky undertaking, as a simple means of getting what they wanted while leaving the Pope in the clear. In any case Cesare had intended from the start to take Piombino, whose lord Jacopo d'Appiano had already been deprived of his vicariate by the Pope, and it would simply not have been feasible to do so by returning to Rome and doubling back up the western coast.

Time was running short for Cesare; if he wanted to blackmail Florence into accepting his demands he would have to move fast. On 3 May Yves d'Alègre with the French contingent left to join Louis' forces massing in Lombardy in preparation for the attack on Naples, and Cesare knew that he would soon be called upon to fulfil his pledge to take part in that campaign. He also knew that there was a limit to which Louis could be pushed in his desire to accommodate the Borgias; there were already reports of his displeasure over Bologna, as Buonaccorsi wrote: 'These methods of the Duke and the Pope begin to displease him, considering their importance.' Florence must be terrorized into subjection before her appeals for help could reach the French court.

Cesare, therefore, was careful not to disclose his demands until the last minute. All he wanted was free passage for his army through Tuscany, he told the Florentine envoy Galeotto de' Pazzi soothingly. While de' Pazzi hurried back to Florence with this unwelcome piece of news, Cesare swiftly crossed the Apennines. The three envoys Soderini, Salviati and Nerli, dispatched from Florence on 10 May to concede the Duke free passage on limited conditions, found him already on their borders. Cesare complained of Florentine help to his enemies in the campaigns of Forlì and Faenza, and warned the envoys enigmatically that he would make his mind known to them when he reached Barberino and not before, hinting ominously 'that he wanted some condotta, by friendship or by force ... or some of our places in the Romagna near his ...' At Barberino on the 12th, he disclosed his demands: alliance and a condotta for himself, the restitution of the Vitelli chancellor Carbone, and some sort of satisfaction for the Orsinis. These demands were accompanied by deliberately vague threats, according to Buonaccorsi, 'either to put back the Medicis, or to reduce the present state to a miserable condition, or "to pluck out some evil weed from the present government"'. In fact Cesare had no intention of changing the government, which he knew Louis would never allow, least of all in favour of the Medicis. His real object, here as with Venice, was the condotta, the thin end of the wedge, which would enable him to maintain a standing body of troops at someone else's expense, and give him a measure of control over Florentine affairs.

News of Cesare's approach threw the Florentines into a panic, described by Buonaccorsi: 'The city was in the greatest disorder and with very few armed men, and many citizens fled from fear. The colleges every day produced new rumours, every day new negotiations were begun without any conclusion. Recourse for help was had to the King [of France] who was too distant in so present a danger. The King wrote letters to the Duke and none of them were obeyed. And everything was in suspense and great tumult ...' By 14 May Cesare had reached Campi, some ten miles from the city, and here on the 15th the Florentines capitulated, agreeing to all his demands. An alliance of mutual friendship and defence was signed, by which each promised to help the other against any hostile person or state excepting the Pope and the King of France, while the allies of each were to be permitted to join the league with the specific exception of the Pisans, other enemies of Florence, or of Cesare's. Cesare obtained his condotta for 300 men-at-arms for a period of three years at an annual salary of 36,000 ducats. The Florentines agreed not to aid d'Appiano at Piombino, and finally, as a sop to Vitellozzo, to release the Vitelli chancellor Carbone.

The terms of the treaty must have come as an unpleasant surprise to Cesare's condottieri, and to the Orsinis in particular. Not only was there no mention of the Medicis, but under the terms of the alliance Cesare had promised that no one in his pay should offend Florence, a clear prohibition of any future Orsini–Vitelli initiatives in that direction, while they knew that they themselves came under the heading of 'enemies of Florence' in the agreement. The Treaty of Campi brought home to them the realization that they had been first used and then deserted by Cesare in the pursuit of his own interests, and sowed the first seeds of distrust between them and their commander which were to grow into dangerous dragon's teeth just over a year later.

Campi was worth no more than the paper it was written upon: the Florentines, in Buonaccorsi's words, had signed it 'for no other end than to get him off our backs'. Cesare was no doubt aware of this; as he marched off on the 17th he allowed his troops free rein to sack and burn as they liked, and sent back peremptory demands for an advance cash payment on his condotta. The next day, 18 May, one of the Borgias' most trusted henchmen, Francesco Troches, arrived in camp with a message from the Pope. Louis, bound to protect Florence by his predecessor's treaty of 1494, had commanded d'Aubigny at Parma to take 300 lances and 3000 foot to get Cesare out of Tuscany. On the 22nd letters arrived at camp from the King, ordering Cesare to leave. The game was up. Plundering and pillaging his way through Florentine territory, Cesare turned westward for the Tuscan coast; by 4 June he had set up camp near Piombino. The Tuscan raid was over.

On the face of it Cesare had earned nothing by his gamble; in return for an empty treaty he had made enemies of the Florentines, revealed the direction of his ambitions to the King of France, who was bound to oppose them, and earned himself the resentment of the Orsinis. Nonetheless he had probed the depths of Florentine weakness, tested the limits of initiative which the King of France was prepared to allow him, and led his army unopposed through Tuscany, which the powerful Venetians had failed to do only two years before. Above all, his experience with Bologna and Florence had shown him the results that could be produced by the swift and unexpected use of force.

The check at Campi was followed by success at Piombino. Situated on a rocky promontory, with its satellite islands of Elba and Pianosa, Piombino was a desirable possession, both financially and strategically. It commanded one of the busiest sea routes in the Mediterranean from the great port of Genoa down the western coast of Italy, and dues levied on visiting shipping had made the d'Appiano family rich. With Piombino in addition to the Romagna, Cesare had to a certain extent encircled Florence, while it provided easy access not only into Tuscany in general but to Pisa and Siena in particular, two cities which he had for some time considered as possible lordships for himself. Cesare set up the seige by seizing Elba and Pianosa, thus cutting off Piombino from reinforcement by sea, but he had not time to continue operations in person. By mid-June the advance guard of the Naples-bound French contingent which he was to join had reached Tuscany, and he had much official and family business to attend to in Rome before riding south with the French.

On 17 June Burchard reported: 'About the third hour of night there came to the city the Duke of Valentino, who remained secretly in the Palace.' This time there was no triumphal entry, no cheering crowds or salvoes of artillery. Cesare now had no need of such things to boost his self-confidence or underline his successes. Aged only twenty-five, he had, in the past eight months, ousted Giovanni Sforza from Pesaro, Pandolfo Malatesta from Rimini, Astorre Manfredi from Faenza and Jacopo d'Appiano from Piombino, threatened the great cities of Bologna and Florence into submission, thumbed his nose at Venice and tested the patience of the King of France with impunity. Small wonder that the lords of Italy, in Francesco Gonzaga's graphic phrase, compared themselves with condemned men who watch their friends hanged one by one without being able to help. The question in the forefront of all of their minds was – who would be next?

X

THE TERRIBLE DUKE

'DUKE VALENTINO has already been in Rome six days, and he has not yet shown himself,' the Venetian envoy at Rome reported disappointedly to his government – the only news he was able to glean as to Cesare's activities. In fact, although all projects of conquest were in temporary suspension, Cesare spent a busy three weeks in the Vatican before his departure with the French for Naples.

As Duke of Romagna he had to regulate the civil and military affairs of his new duchy, the appointment of lieutenants, commissioners and civil officials, the drawing up of charters for the conquered towns, the repairing and strengthening of fortifications. With the resources of Vatican bureaucracy at his command, Cesare used trained administrators, invariably prelates, as his lieutenants in the civil government of the province – men like Giovanni Olivieri, Bishop of Isernia, and his beloved former tutor Juan Vera, Cardinal of Salerno, whom he made governor of Fano. He entrusted military government to his fiercely loyal Spaniards, such as Ramiro de Lorqua, who would be unlikely to fall into the trap of local intrigue, and most of the Romagna castles were garrisoned by Spaniards. Yet Cesare regarded castles as a relic of a more static form of warfare, expensive in time of peace and dangerous in time of war, and in July he ordered Castel Bolognese, 'the finest castle in Romagna', to be razed and permanent barracks for troops to be erected on its site. As for local government, he forbore to make innovations, confirming municipal charters and using local officials as far as he could. With the wealth of the Vatican behind him, he could afford to be generous in the matter of taxation, a sure road to popularity; in the case of Faenza he gave 2000 ducats to the peasants of the *contado* to pay for damage suffered during the campaign.

And, as usual, the Borgias had several important family projects in hand at the same time. A new and brilliant marriage had been planned for the widowed Lucrezia; the bridegroom was to be Alfonso d'Este, son and heir of one of the oldest and most prestigious princely families in Italy. The Borgias wanted Alfonso not so much for the glamour of his name but in the interests of the security of Cesare's state of the Romagna. As Machiavelli later wrote in *The Prince*, it was Cesare's policy to make allies of his neighbours if he could, and Ferrara, on his northern border, traditionally nervous of Venice, would be a useful buffer between his own lands and the predatory Republic. Negotiations had been going on since early in the year, but Duke Ercole was lukewarm about the match, while his children, including the prospective bridegroom Alfonso, whose first wife had been a Sforza, and his brilliant and forceful sister Isabella, married to Francesco Gonzaga, positively opposed it. With royal blood in their veins, inherited from their mother Leonora of Aragon, they were shocked at the prospect of the upstart Borgia as Duchess of Ferrara. Moreover Lucrezia, whose previous marriages had ended in a spectacular blaze of scandal, had a far from unblemished reputation.

However, political survival counted for more than the claims of blue blood. Ercole, in disgrace with Louis for his support of Ludovico Sforza in 1500, was anxious to ingratiate himself with the all-powerful King, and at this time, as far as Louis was concerned, what the Pope wanted, within reason, he could have. 'The marriage will be made at the will of the King,' commented a Venetian observer. Moreover, in view of il Valentino's ambitious plans and his dangerous proximity, it seemed more politic to be friendly with him. As Buonaccorsi noted acutely in his diary: 'Having seen so many happy successes of Duke Valentino in Italy, and knowing the Pope's unrestrained ambition to dominate Italy ... by means of this marriage, he [Ercole] secured himself from being molested.' Nonetheless Ercole was determined to set a high price upon his son: 200,000 ducats as Lucrezia's dowry, with remission of his dues as vicar of Ferrara for himself, and the bishopric of Ferrara, which Alexander had bestowed upon a nephew, for his son Cardinal Ippolito. In league with Amboise and Giuliano della Rovere, who had arrived in Milan, Cesare threw his whole weight into the negotiations, and by July it was clear that they would soon be finalized.

When Cesare arrived in Rome in mid-June, Alexander had opened a new round in his campaign to rid himself of the threat of the Roman barons. The previous year he had dispossessed the Caetani family of

Sermoneta; this time it was to be the turn of the Colonnas. While the Orsinis, leagued with France and the Borgias, were untouchable, the Colonnas, fighting for the doomed King of Naples, were clearly in a weak position. On 6 June, Alexander announced in consistory the conclusion of a league between the Papacy, France and Spain. The official justification for his taking part was that the alliance was directed against the Turk; of course the fact that the unfortunate King of Naples whom the three powers proposed to attack was a Christian prince, who had only sought infidel help in the face of the threats of the Most Christian and Catholic Kings, was not mentioned. Within a week of the announcement, Alexander had forced Cardinal Colonna to hand over the keys of the family castles to him, and had dispatched papal chamberlains with a force of crossbowmen to take over the citadel and monastery of Subiaco, held *in commendam* by Colonna, with eighteen other strongholds and abbeys belonging to the monastery.

But while the announcement of the league presented the Pope with a happy opportunity to lay hands upon the Colonna lands, the prospect of a renewed French military presence in Rome did not fill him with enthusiasm. Without Cesare's reassuring presence he showed distinct signs of nervousness. The Florentine orator Pepi reported in cipher on 6 June: 'The Pope is ill-content in the absence of his close and trusted people,' and a week later: 'The Pope attends to the fortifying of the Castle as much as he can, and within two or three days he will have put everything in a state of defence, and reinforced the artillery: and he is furiously making cannon balls, and yesterday afternoon had a review of his guard which is numerous, and his every action tends to a demonstration of fear . . .' While contemporaries continually stressed the extent to which Cesare was dependent for his power on his father's position as Pope, it was perhaps insufficiently realized how much Alexander was reliant on his son's abilities and his troops to maintain that position. With Cesare away from Rome, he felt himself unprotected, exposed to possible retaliation from the Colonnas, while historical precedents for French seizure of the person of the Pope cannot have been far from his mind.

Meanwhile, everything had been prepared for the reception of the French, who were to pass through on their way to take Naples. Shelters were set up for them outside the city walls beyond the Ponte Milvio, where according to Burchard they were to be provided with 150 butts of wine, bread, meat, eggs, fruit and other necessaries, including the services of fourteen prostitutes, which seems somewhat inadequate for a force of 14,000 men. The Florentine merchants in Rome anxiously paid the city governor 200 ducats so as not to have the French nobles billeted in their houses, but, says Burchard, they found that the officers were billeted on them just the same and the governor kept the money. Yves d'Alègre arrived with the advance guard on 19 June. Four days later the commander of the expedition, Berauld Stuart d'Aubigny, made his formal entry into the city to be received by Alexander with a cordiality as exuberant as it was feigned. As the French chronicler Jean d'Auton commented acutely:

> The Pope, notwithstanding that he was Spanish and a bad Frenchman, all the same dissimulated his feelings and with joyous countenance received the captains of the army of France, and talked merrily with them on various subjects. To Messire Berauld Stuart, the King's lieutenant, he gave a grey charger, very powerful, and very light at hand, with harness so rich and beautiful that all marvelled at it ... In the evening Cardinal San Severino, brother of the Count of Caiazzo [the Italian commander of the expedition], gave the French captains a magnificent banquet, with exquisite dishes and pleasures. The banquet was held in the garden which belonged to Cardinal Ascanio, where there were groves of oranges, lemons and pomegranates, and other fruit trees of singular esteem, and scented flowers of various species. And singers, jugglers, tragedians and comedians all in turn exercised their art there ...

Cesare did not appear at the reception of d'Aubigny, who was met at the city gate by Jofre; indeed he was not seen in public until 28 June, when the entire French force of 12,000 infantry, 2000 horse and 36 cannon marched through the streets of Rome to the roll of kettledrums and the blare of trumpets, to take formal leave of the Pope before marching south for Naples. It was rumoured that he would follow them on 1 July, but he did not, and the delay in his departure was not improbably connected with negotiations for the release of his captive Caterina Sforza.

Caterina had now been a prisoner of the Borgias for well over a year, and in the most miserable circumstances. At first she had been lodged in the luxury of the Pope's beautiful garden villa of the Belvedere, with its loggias frescoed by Pinturicchio, and here the Mantuan envoy Cattaneo had seen her 'in a devilish mood and very strong in spirit' when he visited her at the end of February. Three months later, at the end of May, he found her household in the greatest distress and was refused admission; Madonna, he was told, 'during all this day had done nothing but weep and still refused to eat'. The cause of her distress, he discovered, was an unpleasant interview she had had with Cesare, who had come into possession of certain incriminating letters she had written. A month later Cattaneo reported that the Pope had shut her up in one of the *segrete*, solitary dungeons, of Castel Sant'Angelo, and that she was 'sick at heart'. Alexander pressured her to make a formal renunciation of her rights to Imola and Forlì and to reimburse him for the costs of the war, promising in exchange a pension that would enable her to live in style for the rest of her life. From her dungeon in Sant'Angelo, Caterina defied him, as she had defied Cesare from the walls of her citadel of Forlì. Despite craven letters from her spiritless children by Riario, Cesare and Ottaviano, who seemed only interested in obtaining pensions and an archbishopric for themselves from the Pope, whom they described as 'just and clement', she steadfastly refused to sign away their rights. Indeed, she might have remained a prisoner indefinitely, had it not been for her former champion Yves d'Alègre, who on his arrival in Rome went straight to the Vatican and demanded her release. As Cesare told Soderini fiercely a year later, the fact that she was a woman made no difference to him, and if it had been up to him he would never have let her out of Sant'Angelo. But a demand made in the name of the King of France could not be refused, especially at a time when Rome was full of French troops. And so, on 30 June, after sixteen months' imprisonment, Caterina was led out of Sant'Angelo by the Borgias' confidential servant Troches to the house of the Cardinal of San Clemente, where in return for her liberty she signed away her rights to her cities and to the tutelage of her children. Alexander wrote a hypocritical letter to the Signoria of Florence commending 'his beloved daughter' whom he had 'graciously set at liberty', and some weeks later Caterina, afraid to travel by land 'because of her enemies of Imola and Forlì', left by boat for Florence, the home of her late husband Giovanni de' Medici, to spend the remaining years of her life at the Villa Medici in Fiesole. Despite her dark hints as to maltreatment by the Borgias – 'If I could write of anything, I would stupefy the world,' she told a Dominican friar – it seems that she kept her looks to the end. A visitor to the Villa Medici six years after her release from captivity reported her as 'tall of stature and very well proportioned, with a fair and fine complexion, great eyes, and white hair'. Caterina died there two years later, on 28 May 1509, at the age of forty-six.

But as the gates of Castel Sant'Angelo opened for Caterina Sforza, so they closed upon another Borgia political prisoner, Astorre Manfredi. On 20 July, the Mantuan Calandra reported: 'The Madonna of Forlì has been permitted to leave Rome and has retired to Florence. The lord of Faenza has been placed in the castle of Sant'Angelo, and they keep him there locked up and well guarded.' The unfortunate Astorre put his own head into the noose when he took service with Cesare after the surrender of Faenza, but perhaps he had had no alternative. Cesare can have had nothing personally against the sixteen-year-old Astorre, but he was a political animal, and where politics were concerned he had no time for considerations of humanity. The former lord of Faenza, unlike the *signori* of Forlì, Rimini and Pesaro, was loved by his people; he represented a possible threat to Cesare's hold on the city, and as such, since Cesare was about to depart for two months' compaigning in the kingdom of Naples, he could not be allowed to remain at large.

The exact date of Cesare's departure was the subject of puzzled speculation by Vatican observers. As usual his movements were mysterious. Although he rode out of Rome on 3 July with the main body of his troops, he apparently left them on the road to Naples and returned that same evening to the Vatican. A week later, on 9 July, according to a baffled Burchard, he did the same. He was certainly still in Rome on the 10th, as is evidenced by his signature on an administrative edict for the Romagna of that date, and he probably finally left for Naples within the next two days, although there is no report of his departure. It is hardly surprising that Cesare should have been reluctant to leave Rome when he had so much important business on hand, and he must have regarded the expedition as an irritating interruption to the pursuit of his own plans. And campaigning conditions in the southern kingdom in the high summer months of July and August can hardly have been considered ideal for men wearing full armour weighing around 25 kilos. But go he must – Naples was the price of the Romagna. Cesare joined the French camp at San Germano (Cassino) riding with Vitellozzo, Gian Paolo Baglioni and Giangiordano Orsini, at the head of his own troop of 400 Romagnol infantry wearing his colours of scarlet and yellow. He was, said d'Auton, very splendid, clad in cloth of gold and crimson velvet, a

strange choice for high summer in southern Italy, with four lackeys
and numerous gentlemen dressed like himself.

The Naples campaign of 1501 proved as brief and almost as easy
for Louis' army as it had been for that of Charles VIII. Only at Capua,
commanded by Prospero and Fabrizio Colonna, did the invading
French force meet with any resistance, and here the taking of the
town, apparently by treachery, ended in an appalling sack, during
which the German and Gascon infantry ran wild through the streets
of the town, killing, raping and looting. Cesare has been unfairly
blamed for the bloody sack of Capua. The source for his guilt are
the chronicles of Jean d'Auton, who was not present and heard the
story later from French officers who, not unnaturally, were eager to
shed the responsibility onto the shoulders of a man whose ruthlessness
was well known. In fact, the Count of Caiazzo, not Cesare, was in
command of the operation, and the chief culprits appear to have been
units of the French army. It was Guicciardini who first produced the
story of Cesare locking the women of Capua in a tower and choosing
forty of the most beautiful for himself – a colourful picture of cruel
depravity which has appealed hugely to anti-Borgia historians and
nineteenth-century painters alike – but contemporary Venetian
accounts of the taking of Capua make absolutely no mention of the
incident. Cesare entered Naples with the French army on 3 August,
King Federigo having withdrawn to Ischia on the same day, leaving
his kingdom to be a bone of contention for the future between France
and Spain. Cesare can hardly have felt compassion for Federigo,
whose stubborn refusal to accept him as a son-in-law had wounded
his pride two years before, and he had every reason to be satisfied
with the outcome of the Naples expedition. Louis sent his *valet de
chambre*, Edouard Bouillon, to thank Cesare personally for his services,
promising that he would soon see the effects of the royal goodwill in
his affairs thereafter, and would be treated as a good kinsman and
friend. He received a more concrete reward in the form of 40,000
ducats, half of which were to be paid from Louis' revenues in the
Kingdom and half from Ferdinand's, with the title of Prince of
Andria. At the same time the ever-provident Alexander negotiated
with Federigo to buy the major part of his artillery; neither of the
Borgias emerged from the Naples campaign empty-handed.

For the moment, the apparent unity between France and Spain
over Naples offered no opportunities for the profitable sport of fishing
in the troubled waters of international politics. With projects of

further conquest thus temporarily in suspension, Cesare returned from Naples to concentrate on family affairs. Arriving back in Rome on 15 September, he found the Vatican *en fête* for the signing of Lucrezia's marriage contract with Alfonso d'Este at Ferrara on 4 September. Alexander, despite his seventy years, showed no abatement in his zest for life. One of his particular pleasures was to watch beautiful women dancing, and he took great pride in his daughter's grace. One evening he called the Ferrarese ambassadors to him to watch her, remarking laughingly 'that they might see the Duchess was not lame'. Both Lucrezia and Cesare were exhausted by the constant round of entertainments organized by their indefatigable father. On 23 September, Gherardo Saraceni, one of the Ferrarese envoys, reported that Cesare had received them fully dressed, but lying on his bed : 'I feared that he was sick, for last evening he danced without intermission, which he will do again tonight at the Pope's palace, where the illustrious Duchess [Lucrezia] is going to sup.' Two days later he wrote of Lucrezia: 'The illustrious lady continues somewhat ailing, and is greatly fatigued ... The rest which she will have while His Holiness is away will do her good; for whenever she is at the Pope's palace, the entire night, until two or three o'clock, is spent at dancing and at play, which fatigues her greatly.' Only Alexander seemed unwearied; one day when he was suffering from a bad cold and had lost a tooth, he remarked to the Ferrarese envoy: 'If the Duke [Ercole] were here, I would, even if my face is tied up, invite him to go and hunt wild boars.' The ambassador commented primly that, if the Pope valued his health, he had better change his habits and not leave the palace before daybreak and return before nightfall. At night the fever-carrying mosquito, the cause of malaria, was abroad, but Alexander was never a man to worry about his health.

Between 25 September and 17 October, festivities were temporarily suspended as Alexander and Cesare made two tours of inspection of the recently acquired Borgia strongholds in the vicinity of Rome, lands seized from the Gaetanis and the Colonnas which Alexander had transferred to the two young Borgia children. Rodrigo, Lucrezia's two-year-old son by Alfonso Bisceglie, was made Duke of Sermoneta, while Giovanni Borgia, the mysterious 'Infans Romanus', aged three, was honoured with the title and lands of Duke of Nepi and Palestrina. His investiture, on 2 September, was preceded by his legitimization. On 1 September, Alexander, in a manner curiously reminiscent of Cesare's own legitimization, issued two bulls, one public, the other secret. The first described Giovanni as Cesare's son by an unmarried woman, while in the second, secret bull, Alexander admitted himself to be the father.

Control of the Roman Campagna and the access roads to the city was regarded by the Borgias as vital to the strengthening of their position. At Civita Castellana, dominating the Via Flaminia some forty miles north of Rome, one of the great military architects of the century, Antonio di Sangallo, was building a fortress on Cesare's orders, its vaulted rooms adorned with images of the Borgia bull rampant, bearing the proud motto 'Viva Borgia'. In the absence of her father and brother on these tours of inspection, Lucrezia, who seems to have shared her family's administrative ability, was left as regent in the Vatican, with full authority to open all the Pope's correspondence. That Alexander could appoint his bastard daughter to act in his place as Head of Christendom is a supreme example of the carelessness for public opinion which outraged his contemporaries. As far as their public reputation was concerned, the Borgias had only themselves to blame in that sowing the wind, they reaped the whirlwind.

Scandalous rumour surrounded them as they resumed their family pleasures in the Pope's palace in late October. Cesare did what he could to shun publicity, and once again his now customary secrecy and solitude were remarked upon. On 30 October the Ferrarese envoy reported that he never went out without a mask – 'The rest of the time he remains shut up in his apartments.' Nonetheless lurid details of the Borgias' activities within the walls of their private apartments did leak out, providing the eager diplomats with salacious details to fill out their reports. On the same night that the Ferrarese sat down to pen his dispatch, Cesare gave a party in his apartments that became notorious. Here is Burchard's account of the night:

> On Sunday evening, the last day of October 1501, there took place in the apartments of Duke Valentino in the Apostolic Palace, a supper, participated in by fifty honest prostitutes of those who are called courtesans. After supper they danced with the servants and others who were there, first clothed, then naked. After supper the lighted candelabra which had been on the table were placed on the floor, and chestnuts thrown among them which the prostitutes had to pick up as they crawled between the candles. The Pope, the Duke, and Lucrezia, his sister, were present looking on. At the end they displayed prizes, silk mantles, boots, caps, and other objects,

which were promised to whomsoever should have made love to those prostitutes the greatest number of times; the prizes were distributed to the winners according to the arbitration of those present.

If Burchard is to be believed, here was an orgy in the true Roman tradition, held in the palace of the spiritual ruler of Christendom. The story of the naked courtesans crawling after hot chestnuts, and of the virility contest, may have been prurient embroideries, but that Cesare did give a party for his father and sister, which included courtesans, is attested by another source. On 4 November the Florentine orator Pepi reported that the Pope had not attended mass in St Peter's or in the papal chapel on the days of All Saints and All Souls because of an indisposition, 'which', he added cautiously in cipher, 'did not however impede him on Sunday night, the vigil of All Saints, from spending the night until the twelfth hour with the Duke, who had brought into the palace that night singers, courtesans, and all the night they spent in pleasures, dancing and laughter...' Pepi's account of the evening sounds harmless enough, and contains nothing which, in normal circumstances, an Italian of the day would have found especially shocking. Courtesans, the *hetaerae* of fifteenth- and sixteenth-century Rome, were an essential part of a lively informal party, as the pages of Cellini's autobiography record. Yet this supper, which would otherwise have passed unremarked, took place in the Vatican in the presence of the Pope, a fact which gave it an additional piquancy even in the eyes of seasoned observers of the princely courts of the Renaissance.

It is hardly surprising that Alexander's reputation for sensuality should have grown to exaggerated proportions. Agostino Vespucci wrote to Machiavelli in July of that year: 'It remains for me to say that it is known by everyone that the Pope, who is surrounded there by his illicit flock, has brought in from outside every evening to the palace, twenty-five women or more, from the Ave Maria to one o'clock, so that the Palace is manifestly made the brothel of all filth. I do not wish to give you other news from here now, but if you answer this I will send you more and finer ...' Where the Borgias were concerned there was always more and 'finer' news; family vignettes which could be painted into a great canvas of colourful vice by the watchful envoys, waiting with pens poised, avid as gossip columnists for spicy titbits to enliven their dispatches. A few days after Cesare's chestnut supper, Burchard reported what he called 'another incident' on 11

November, involving mares loaded with wood which a peasant had brought into Rome through the Viridaria gate near the Vatican.

When the mares reached the Piazza San Pietro, some of the palace guard came up, cut through the straps and threw off the saddles and the wood in order to lead the mares into the courtyard immediately inside the palace gate. Four stallions were then freed from their reins and harness and let out of the palace stables. They immediately ran to the mares, over whom they proceeded to fight furiously and noisily amongst themselves, biting and kicking in their efforts to mount them and seriously wounding them with their hoofs. The Pope and Donna Lucrezia, laughing and with evident satisfaction, watched all that was happening from a window above the palace gate.

A delighted, Rabelaisian view of life was part of the fifteenth-century Renaissance mentality, a bawdily vital period when manners were not yet cloaked in the cold formal impotence of the later sixteenth-century princely courts. Lorenzo de' Medici wrote bawdy poems, and Machiavelli pornographic letters, to delight their friends. It is illustrative of the atmosphere in which the Borgias lived, and the intense interest and enmity with which they were surrounded, that this crudely earthy incident could be repeated all over Italy, its sexual overtones magnified and distorted, as in Matarazzo's chronicle of Perugia, where he adds: 'And as if this were not enough, [the Pope] returning to the hall, had all the lights put out, and then all the women who were there, and as many men as well, took off all their clothes; and there was much festivity and play.'

One wonders how the Borgias saw themselves, if they reflected at all on the picture they presented to the world. Did Alexander see any dichotomy between the unabashed profanity of his private life and his official position as spiritual head of Christendom, between the majesty of his public appearances and his often undignified postures in private? It is quite evident that he regarded his official position as Pope as having no bearing on his personal life as a man. As Pope, he took his duties as seriously as he had when he was a Cardinal, defending the temporal interest of the Papacy to the utmost of his powers, while in spiritual matters he never compromised on questions of dogma. He was sincere in promoting a crusade against the Turks, and it was largely due to the apathy of the Christian secular powers that his efforts failed. He was also a deeply religious man in the devotional sense, with a particular reverence for the cult of the Virgin, and in this he differed from his son. While Lucrezia was conventionally pious in her religious observances and became increasingly so later in life, Cesare never seems even to have paid lip-service to religion, nor did he, as so many of his contemporaries did, buy remission for his sins by lavish endowments of religious foundations. Whether he was an atheist, as Leonardo da Vinci was, is impossible to know. It is more likely that he never troubled himself over the question of the existence of God. Fortune was his deity, and he relied on his own talents to make his way in the world; God, as far as he was concerned, did not enter into it. He differed also from his father in an obsession with privacy that bordered on mania, rarely leaving his apartments, and when he did so going abroad masked or in disguise; veiling his movements in mystery, planning his moves, receiving spies and informants away from the prying eyes of inquisitive ambassadors.

There are signs that the eccentricity of his ways irritated his father, who liked to contrast Lucrezia's easy accessibility with Cesare's elusiveness. 'When the Pope discovered', wrote Saraceni, 'that we had so far been unable to secure an audience with the illustrious Duke, he showed great annoyance, declaring that it was a mistake which could only injure His Majesty, and he added that the ambassadors of Rimini had been here two months without succeeding in speaking with him, as he was in the habit of turning day into night and night into day. He severely criticized his son's mode of living.' Whereas Lucrezia, Saraceni continued, 'was always gracious and granted audiences readily, and whenever there was need she knew how to cajole ... he also said that Her Majesty always knew how to carry her point – even with himself.' Although it is unwise to accept Alexander's words at their face value, it is feasible to conjecture that there was a certain friction between him and his son. However well the two may have worked together, and however proud Alexander was of his son's successes, the presence of two such strong personalities living side by side for a prolonged period cannot have made for any easy relationship. It is not unnatural that Alexander, accustomed to dominate those around him, and his family in particular, should have been resentful of his son's independence, secretiveness and eccentric way of life. Lucrezia had always been his favourite and, with brief exceptions, pliable to his will, while Cesare, with a growing sense of his own power, was becoming increasingly difficult to manage.

While Cesare shunned the limelight, and his father openly enjoyed it, they were soon made aware of the light in which others saw them. In mid-November one of the most-bitterly anti-Borgia documents ever drafted came into the hands of the Pope. It was written in the form of a letter addressed to Silvio Savelli, a Roman nobleman allied to the Colonnas, whose lands had been seized with theirs, and purported to have been sent from the camp of Gonsalvo de Cordoba at Taranto, probably by a member or partisan of the Colonna family. After congratulating Savelli, who had taken refuge at the court of Maximilian, on having escaped 'the fury and rage of these brigands', the letter went on to accuse the Borgias of being worse than the Scythians, more perfidious than the Carthaginians, and surpassing in cruelty both Caligula and Nero. It included every charge hitherto levelled against them: murder, specifically of Bisceglie and Perotto, robbery and incest, adding the tales of the chestnut supper and the rutting stallions for good measure. Cesare in particular was attacked for having used crusade funds to finance his unjustified Romagna conquests, while the anonymous writer accused him of further aggressive intentions against Urbino and Camerino. The terms in which it referred to Alexander and Cesare are typical of the letter's tone:

> His father favours him [Cesare] because he has his own perversity, his own cruelty; it is difficult to say which of these two is the most execrable. The cardinals see all and keep quiet and flatter and admire the Pope. But all fear him and above all fear his fratricide son, who from being a cardinal has made himself into an assassin. He lives like the Turks, surrounded by a flock of prostitutes, guarded by armed soldiers. At his order or decree men are killed, wounded, thrown into the Tiber, poisoned, despoiled of all their possessions ...

It was typical of Alexander that when he read this diatribe he laughed; when the addressee, Silvio Savelli, came to Rome a year later, he received him with the utmost amiability. In his long years as Cardinal he had become inured to public criticism, which the Romans were wont to express in biting and often obscene satires and epigrams, frequently pinned to the famous statue of Pasquino. Cesare's opinion of the Savelli Letter is not recorded, but his normal reaction to insult was swift and cruel. In the first week of December shortly after the publication of the letter, a man who had been going about the Borgo masked uttering scurrilous language against il Valentino was arrested on Cesare's orders and thrown into the Savelli prison, where his right hand and part of his tongue were cut out and exposed, with the tongue hanging from the little finger, for two days at the window of the prison. Alexander liked to contrast his son's hard vengefulness with his own tolerance. 'The Duke,' he told the Ferrarese Beltrando Costabili, 'is a good-hearted man, but he cannot tolerate insults,' adding, in a remark that was more illustrative of his way of thinking than of his vaunted clemency: 'I could easily have had the Vice-Chancellor [Ascanio Sforza] and Cardinal Giuliano della Rovere killed; but I did not wish to harm anyone ...'

There was perhaps another reason why Alexander refused to take the outrageous charges penned in the Savelli Letter seriously: he had heard them all before. The letter's accusations, even the language in which they were formulated, bear a close resemblance to Capello's *Relazione* of the previous year, recorded by Sanuto, and it is not improbable that the document was concocted as a deliberate piece of anti-Borgia propaganda in Venice. Venice, secretly inimical to the Borgias, gave political asylum to most of the princely refugees dispossessed by Cesare, including Pandolfo Malatesta and Giovanni Sforza. With the Colonnas, the Savellis and the Gaetanis already added to the list of those injured by the Borgias, it is not surprising that they should have wished to blacken Alexander and Cesare in the eyes of the world by drawing up the most sensational indictment possible. As such, the Savelli Letter was successful; its charges against the Borgias not only appeared in contemporary chronicles but were taken up and repeated by historians over the centuries, giving them the currency of truth.

In view of the nature of the scandalous rumours emanating from Rome in mid-winter of 1501, the Ferrarese envoys – who, it may be noted, had mentioned neither the story of the chestnuts nor that of the mares in their dispatches at the time – felt it necessary to reassure Ercole d'Este as to the character of his prospective daughter-in-law:

Lucrezia is a most intelligent and lovely, also exceedingly gracious lady. Besides being extremely graceful in every way, she is modest and lovable and decorous. Moreover she is a devout and god-fearing Christian. Tomorrow she is going to confession, and during Christmas week she will receive communion. She is very beautiful, but her charm of manner is still more striking. In short, her character is such that it is impossible to suspect anything 'sinister' of her ...

In fact Ercole, reluctant to take the final step into the Borgias' arms, had been deliberately delaying the wedding; he postponed the departure of the bridegroom's procession from Ferrara, pleading the onset of winter, and demanded the cession of the castles of Cento and Pieve as guarantees for the payment of the dowry. Alexander told the Ferrarese envoys in a rage that their master was 'behaving like a tradesman', but the matter was finally settled at the end of November by Cesare, who allowed the Ferrarese temporary possession of his own castles of Rossi, Solarolo and Granarolo instead. On 7 December, in the teeth of winter, the procession finally left Ferrara.

In Rome the Borgias were determined to impress the aristocratic Estes. The most extravagant preparations were made for their reception; while Cesare spent with his usual prodigality, even the careful Alexander opened his purse-strings unstintingly to do honour to his beloved daughter. The bourgeois Pepi was shocked by the lavishness of the expenditure: 'The things that are ordered here for these festivities are unheard of; and for a minor feast the shoes of the Duke's staff-bearers are made of gold brocade, and the same for the Pope's grooms: and he and the Duke vie with each other in producing the most magnificent, the latest, and the most expensive things ...' When Cesare rode to meet the Ferrarese procession headed by Alfonso d'Este's brothers, Ferrante, Sigismodo and Ippolito, on their entry into Rome on 23 December, he made an impressive show not only of luxury but of armed power. Two thousand cavalry and infantry marched before him, the same number behind, all superbly equipped and wearing his personal livery. Cesare's own dress is not recorded – perhaps he wore simple black – but his horse made a glittering impression, an echo of the entry into Chinon: 'The Duke rode a most beautiful strong horse, so fine that it seemed to have wings ... and its trappings were estimated at 10,000 ducats because one could see nothing but gold, pearls and other jewels ...'

After a welcoming ceremony with the customary orations, which lasted two hours, the huge procession, swollen by the retinues of the cardinals, ambassadors and city officials, wound its way in the failing light of a winter afternoon through the streets of the city. At the bridge of Sant'Angelo leading to the Vatican so many bombards were fired from the castle that the noise deafened everyone, and the horses were so frightened they could hardly be persuaded to cross the bridge. At the Vatican Alexander greeted the Este brothers with effusive delight; Cesare then led them across the piazza of St Peter's to meet his sister.

With the true Borgia instinct for showmanship, Lucrezia greeted them at the entrance to the palace, leaning on the arm of an elderly cavalier dressed in black, whose age and dark costume enhanced her own youthful beauty and shimmering white dress. Her golden hair, of which she was extremely proud, shone under a gossamer net of green gauze, held in place by a fine gold band and two rows of pearls encircling her forehead. The Estes were charmed by their new sister-in-law, who offered them 'a beautiful collation, and many presents'.

Cesare emerged from his seclusion to celebrate his sister's wedding in a bout of feverish pleasure. Carnival that year was ordered to begin the day after Christmas, and he and the young Ferrarese roamed masked in the city streets where, Isabella Gonzaga's agent Il Prete reported, 'one sees nothing but courtesans wearing masks'. The rich courtesans, splendidly equipped at their lovers' expense, often dressed as boys and rode about Rome throwing gilded eggs filled with rose water at passers-by, and indulging in every kind of escapade until the twenty-fourth hour, when by law they were forbidden the streets. When the courtesans retired, Cesare and the Estes attended a ball at Lucrezia's palace. Il Prete, who had been dispatched to Rome by Isabella with special instructions to report every detail of her sister-in-law's dress, described the scene:

A nobleman from Valencia and a lady of the court, Niccola, led the dance. They were followed by Don Ferrante [d'Este] and Madonna [Lucrezia], who danced with extreme grace and animation. She wore a *camorra* of black velvet, with gold borders and black sleeves; the cuffs tight, the sleeves slashed at the shoulders. Her breast was covered up to the neck with a veil of gold thread. About her neck she wore a string of pearls, and on her head a green net and a chain of rubies. She had an overskirt of black velvet trimmed with fur, coloured and very beautiful. Two or three of her women are very pretty ... one, Angela, is charming. Without telling her, I picked her out as my favourite ...

Over the next days the Borgias and their guests watched the traditional carnival races; on the 27th the races were run by old men and Jews, and on the 19th it was the turn of the prostitutes and wild boars. The race for wild boars, a hilariously perilous event, took place over a course from the Campo di Fiori to St Peter's. According to Burchard: 'They were mounted and those who sat on them used sticks to beat them and kept control of their heads by rings in their snouts, whilst other men guided them along and prevented their running into side alleys.' On the same day, 'a great number' of prostitutes ran from the pyramid in the Borgo to St Peter's. On the 30th, more serious races were held, with sleek thoroughbreds replacing the panting prostitutes and squealing boars. According to Burchard there were three classifications for the races, the first for Barbary horses imported from Morocco through Naples and much prized for their speed, the second for light Spanish mounts, and the third for *corsieri*, the heavier cavalry chargers. As usual the racing was dangerous and crooked: Burchard's account recalls the clash between Cesare and Francesco Gonzaga over a similar race at Siena:

> ... in these contests there was a great deal of violence and injustice. The Marquis of Mantua's Barbary horse came first in his race, but was awarded no prize since it was riderless, having earlier thrown its rider. In consequence, the horse running for Don Cesare Borgia won the prize. One of Don Cesare's riders also won the race for the Spanish horses, but most unfairly. He did not begin the race with the rest in the Campo di Fiori, but ran out by a house adjoining the vice-chancellor's palace ahead of the other horses as they were approaching, and thereby obtained the prize. In the fillies' races, a certain groom from Don Cesare's household again crossed the highway by the bridge of Sant'Angelo, and with his horse obstructed the leading runner and threw its rider on the ground, but the filly nevertheless ran on and touched the *palio* with its forehead ...

Cesare was an expert horseman and prided himself on his stable of 300 horses, many of them bought or wheedled from Gonzaga. No doubt there was a running rivalry between the Borgia and Gonzaga stables whenever races were held, competitions in which Cesare's team certainly emerges as the most unscrupulous. One wonders if on this occasion Francesco Gonzaga raised objections as he had at Siena in 1493 when Cesare was only an unknown papal 'nephew'; if he did, history has not recorded it.

The ceremony of the exchange of rings took place in the Vatican on the 28th, preceded by a lengthy and boring sermon by the Bishop of Adria, which Alexander with typical impatience ordered him to cut short. After Ferrante as his brother's proxy had presented Lucrezia with a simple gold wedding ring, his brother Cardinal Ippolito stepped forward and placed a casket on a table in front of the

Pope. Out of it he drew a staggering display of Este family jewels, rings, collars, head ornaments, pearls, rubies and diamonds, to the value of 70,000 ducats. However, it seems that the Estes considered them not as a gift but a loan; the circumstances behind the handing over of the jewels showed Ercole to be still extremely mistrustful of the Borgias and unconvinced by his envoys' glowing reports of his new daughter-in-law. Two days after the wedding one of the Ferrarese ambassadors, Pozzi, wrote reassuringly to his master: 'There is a document regarding this marriage which simply states that Donna Lucrezia will be given for a present the bridal ring, but nothing is said of any other gift. Your Excellency's intention, therefore, was carried out exactly. There was no mention of any present, and Your Excellency need have no anxiety ...'

The Estes' secret distrust for their new relations was outwardly well concealed, and the wedding festivities proceeded with every appearance of cordiality. After the ceremony the party watched the mock siege of a wooden fortress staged by the gentlemen of Cesare's household in the piazza below, in which, perhaps due to the bravado of his Spaniards, sharp swords were used instead of the customary blunt weapons and five men were wounded. They then moved to the Sala del Papagallo, where the Pope seated himself on his throne with the cardinals on his left and Cesare, Lucrezia and Ippolito on his right. Alexander, reported Il Prete, then asked Cesare to lead the dance with Donna Lucrezia, 'which he did very gracefully. His Holiness was in continual laughter.'

No thought of the murdered Alfonso Bisceglie, whose marriage to Lucrezia had taken place in the same surroundings just over three years before, seemed to trouble the Borgias as they triumphantly celebrated her third wedding. With the emotional resilience characteristic of her family Lucrezia, who had loved him, seemed to have quite forgotten him as she danced radiantly with the brother who had had him killed. Alexander would have dismissed the unfortunate incident from his mind, delighted as he was with the political advantages which this match would imply for Cesare. Cesare, in his haste for the future, never looked at the past; if he considered the case of Bisceglie he would have seen his action as justified by today's celebrations. The political background to the marriage was clearly emphasized in comedies and representations, including an eclogue given by Cesare in his apartments, in which many classical allusions to Cesare and Ercole were made, predicting that through fortune and valour they would overcome their enemies. The Ferrarese envoys, whose native city was famous for its theatre, criticized the dramatic quality of the representations but were delighted by the political allusions to the alliance between the Borgias and the Estes, which they clearly considered a warning to Venice.

By early January 1502, it was time for Lucrezia to leave for Ferrara. Alexander experienced a certain amount of difficulty in finding a suitable escort for her, a problem not entirely unconnected with his own policies towards the Roman barons. Although he can hardly be blamed for the fact that the Roman ladies were not skilful horsewomen, and thus would not be able to go, he was forced to admit that 'there were no Roman noblemen, except the Orsinis, and they were generally away from the city ...' However, Cesare saved the situation by detailing 200 gentlemen of his own suite to accompany his sister, and considerately provided musicians and buffoons to entertain her on the way. At least 150 baggage mules would be needed to carry Lucrezia's splendid trousseau, as described by Cattaneo: 'silverware to the value of three thousand ducats: jewels, fine linen and trappings for horses and mules together worth another hundred thousand' Her wardrobe included one trimmed dress worth more than 15,000 ducats, and 200 costly shifts, some worth a hundred ducats apiece. Il Prete, who doubtless obtained his information from Lucrezia's pretty ladies-in-waiting, wrote to Isabella that she had one dress worth 20,000 ducats and a hat valued at 10,000. Beyond all this Alexander gave his daughter 9,000 ducats as pin-money to clothe herself and her servants, and a beautiful French sedan chair in which she was to travel with the Duchess of Urbino on the journey from Urbino to Ferrara. Alexander's resources were becoming strained under the enormous burden of expense. He therefore ordered that each cardinal should provide two horses or mules for the cavalcade, and twenty of the bishops one horse or mule each. 'None of the animals borrowed in this way was restored to its owner,' Burchard commented. A Venetian observer who drew up a careful account of the men and animals involved in Lucrezia's company, with Cesare's escort, produced a total of 660 horses and mules and 753 people, including cooks, saddlers, butlers, tailors and her personal goldsmith.

On 6 January, Lucrezia took private leave of her father, whom she was never to see again, in the Sala del Papagallo. As she left, the anguished Alexander hurried from window to window to catch a last glimpse of his beloved daughter. It was snowing as Lucrezia rode out of Rome, between Cesare and Ippolito; they accompanied her for a few miles and then returned to the city. It must have been a sad parting; Lucrezia as Duchess of Ferrara would have her own new life to lead, and it was unlikely that she would see much of her brother in the years to come. Constantly together since they were children, they had grown up very much alike. Lucrezia's intelligence impressed close observers like Il Prete, but, dazzled by her golden hair and her famous charm, they failed to divine the Borgia toughness beneath the feminine skin. She shared with her brother the nerves of steel and incapacity for real feeling which had enabled her to survive the experience of the last few years unscathed. Their mutual affection was based on similarity of character and outlook, and strengthened by the sense that the rest of their world regarded them as dangerous outsiders.

But as Lucrezia made her way northward, greeted with carefully organized enthusiasm by her brother's Romagnol cities, there were moments which his ambitions must have made awkward for her. In her twenty-four hours at Pesaro she tactfully kept to her chamber, under the probably necessary pretext of washing her hair. At Urbino, Guidobaldo and Elisabetta gave a splendid ball for her, but a certain nervous strain underlay their civilities since rumours of Cesare's designs on their duchy had been circulating during the past months. At Imola she again insisted on breaking her journey to wash her hair and put her clothes in order. Ferrante reported to Ercole that she had not washed it for eight days and was therefore suffering from a headache. No doubt the real reason was that she wished to prepare for her reception by the Bentivoglios at Bologna, where Cesare's recent threat against the city must still have been fresh in everyone's minds, and Ginevra, wife of Giovanni, was the aunt of the exiled lord of Pesaro, Lucrezia's former husband Giovanni Sforza. The real ordeal awaited her at Ferrara, where she arrived on 1 February, greeted beforehand by the secretly hostile Isabella d'Este Gonzaga, 'burning with resentment' as she later wrote to her husband. Isabella's eyes, so she said, filled with tears on seeing her mother's ruby necklace round her sister-in-law's graceful neck. Despite the formal festivities it was, as an observer remarked, 'a cold wedding', and Lucrezia's confidence in the midst of the unfamiliar Ferrarese court cannot have been helped by the French King's strange choice of a wedding present for her husband: a golden shield on which Mary Magdalene was depicted in enamel was bestowed on Alfonso by the French ambassador with the remark that he had chosen a wife who resembled her in character. It was hardly a tactful gift for the husband of a bride with Lucrezia's past. Lucrezia was miserable in her first months at Ferrara, involved in quarrels with Ercole over her allowance, embarrassed by her family's political and military activities, but like Cesare at the French court, with her intelligence and charm she eventually succeeded in establishing the central position she aimed for.

Lucrezia's wedding provided another fleeting glimpse into the strange story of Cesare's non-relationship with his wife Charlotte. Although in January 1501 he had ignored a plea from Alain d'Albret on his daughter's behalf to come to France, in December he had sent her a lavish present of sweetmeats, wax and other luxuries ordered from Venice. It appears that he had confidently expected Charlotte to join in the festivities at Ferrara, and his gentlemen hung around waiting for her arrival until Ercole, who was heartily sick of the trouble and expense they caused him, packed them back to Rome on the grounds that the Duchess of Valentinois would not arrive before Easter, and that having spent 25,000 ducats on the wedding festivities he could bear no further expenditure.

Although Cesare would doubtless have liked to have his hostage wife safely in Italy, he now had no time to spare for thoughts of a lonely Charlotte or a homesick Lucrezia – he was planning a new campaign. By the early spring of 1502 Spain and France were quarrelling over Naples, and by April it was clear that they would soon come to blows. Although Louis' attitude to himself had been ambivalent of late, and in mid-April he had renewed his protection of Florence, Cesare knew that the French King's obsession with Naples could once again be turned to his advantage. As an experienced military leader, with the best independent army in Italy and the prestige of the Papacy behind him, his help would be precious to Louis, and he intended that the French King should pay a very high price for it. This time he had decided to exploit Louis' need of him to its absolute limits, calculating that bold action would bring profit rather than retribution. In the early summer months of 1502 Cesare was planning his most daring move to date.

XI

'THE PRINCE'

OMINOUSLY, the recently appointed Venetian envoy to Rome, Antonio Giustinian, reported that on his arrival there in the first week of June 1502 he had been unable to obtain audience either of the Pope or his son. Alexander spent hours in secret council with Cesare, while Giustinian picked up reports that he was being browbeaten by his forceful son into handing over still more money for the forthcoming campaign. 'Today the Pope has been in some difficulty with the Duke, who wants a further 20,000 ducats for this expedition of his, in which he had already made great expenses ... yet although the Pope is being difficult about giving him the money, he will nonetheless come round to acceding to the Duke's wishes in this matter, as he does in everything else,' he wrote. Giustinian quickly gained the impression that Cesare was the driving force of the partnership; he tried anxiously to interview him, but failed. Cesare, poised for action, had important secret business on hand. He wanted to keep everyone in the dark until the last possible moment, and especially the inquisitive Venetians.

Over the next few days a series of events exploded with startling suddenness, revealing the long trails laid by the Borgias over the past months. On 4 June the citizens of Arezzo rose against the Florentine government with cries of 'Medici', and prepared to open their gates to Cesare's captain Vitellozzo Vitelli, conveniently awaiting nearby with a force of 3500 men. Simultaneously at Pisa, in revolt against Florence since 1494, Cesare's name was cried through the streets, and an envoy dispatched to offer him lordship of the city. Meanwhile in Rome rumours began to circulate of a brutal epilogue in the tragic life of Cesare's captive Astorre Manfredi. On 6 June Giustinian reported to his government: 'It is said that Thursday night the two young lords of Faenza were thrown into the Tiber and drowned, together with the master of their household.' Contemporaries pointed to Michelotto as their executioner, and no one doubted that he had acted on his master's orders. Cesare, on the point of leaving Rome, wanted to make finally sure that the popular young lord of Faenza would present no further threat to him. On 10 June his army, a considerable force of 6000 foot and 700 men-at-arms, was marching north up the Via Flaminia. Three days later he left to join them at Spoleto, 'but,' wrote Giustinian reporting his departure, 'it is not known what road he will take.'

Although Cesare had kept his plans to himself, observers reading the signs knew, or thought they knew, that his objective was the taking of Camerino and Sinigallia to round off his Romagna conquests. There had been rumours of his designs on Urbino, but no one seems to have taken them seriously. The Varano family of Camerino seemed clearly doomed: on 28 February Alexander had opened the campaign in the now familiar manner by issuing a bull of excommunication against them for non-payment of census. As early as the end of April, Giuliano della Rovere, safely out of reach at Savona, had written to Guidobaldo da Montefeltro recommending that he send him his sister's son Francesco Maria della Rovere, the young Prefect of Sinigallia, for safe keeping. Alexander and Cesare now again recognized Giuliano as a dangerous enemy. Even before Cesare left Rome, Giustinian reported that an attempt by them to lure the Cardinal of San Pietro in Vincoli from Genoa 'into the hands of the enemy' had failed.

But while Alexander, after his son's departure, repeated that Cesare was going against Camerino, the acute Giustinian wondered whether recent events such as the arrival on the 10th of the Pisan envoys had precipitated his departure northward, and caused some alteration in his plans; indeed a descent on Pisa was rumoured as a possibility. In Tuscany Vitellozzo had entered Arezzo on 7 June, to be joined a week later by Gian Paolo Baglioni, followed by Giulio Vitelli and Piero de' Medici. Alexander initially and Cesare some weeks later disclaimed any knowledge of the Arezzo affair, but as early as 7 June Giustinian wrote: 'It has been declared to me that this is an "old intrigue" of the Duke's, but it was not his intention that it should have revealed itself so soon.' If Cesare had any foreknowledge of Vitellozzo's intentions, and it seems impossible to believe, as some experts on the evidence of his own words have argued, that he did not, he would surely have preferred to synchronize the action with his own arrival in the area. Not only the timing but also the success of the Vitelli raid seem to have taken him by surprise – within a few weeks the strategic valley of the Val di Chiana was in the hands of the Vitelli and Baglioni conspirators. Typically, however, he decided not to abandon but to accelerate the execution of the plan which he had in mind, and to make use of his condottieri's success to further his own designs.

Over one hundred kilometres to the north of Cesare's announced objective of Camerino, Guildobaldo, Duke of Urbino, was surprised by the Pope's request for free passage for the papal artillery through his territory at Cagli, and discomfited by Cesare's demand from Spoleto that he should send a thousand foot-soldiers to help Vitellozzo at Arezzo, since he knew that in doing so he would offend Florence, and through her the King of France. Reassured, however, by Cesare's protestations of fraternal love, and the knowledge that the dangerous Valentino was at a safe distance to the south of his duchy, Guidobaldo spent the hot evening of 20 June dining *al fresco* in the park of a monastery two kilometres from Urbino. At eight o'clock that evening a sweating messenger from Fossombrone arrived with the information that a thousand of Cesare's troops from the Romagna were marching swiftly down the Via Flaminia from Fano in the direction of Urbino, while shortly afterwards news came from the tiny state of San Marino on Guidobaldo's northern frontier that a further thousand Borgia troops were massing on its borders. Hastily, Guildobaldo hurried back to his capital, to be greeted by the stunning news that Cesare himself was at Cagli, only twenty miles away, and intended to be in Urbino by tomorrow morning. The wretched Guidobaldo, taken by surprise in a perfect pincer movement, threatened from north, east and south, barely had time to escape, as indeed Cesare had intended he should not. Fleeing from the city that night, he spent a nightmare week dodging Borgia troops sent to catch him, before reaching the safety of Mantua in a state of exhaustion 'with only a doublet and a shirt to his name'.

On the morning of the 21st, only a few hours after Guidobaldo's hasty departure, Cesare rode triumphantly into Urbino. He had every reason to be triumphant, for the taking of Urbino was his most spectacular coup to date, tactically brilliant, if morally questionable. In Machiavelli's words: 'The manner of this victory is entirely founded on the prudence of this Lord [Cesare], who, being seven miles from Camerino, without eating or drinking, presented himself before Cagli which was about thirty-five miles distant ... and at the same time left Camerino besieged ...' At Foligno he had dispatched Oliverotto da Fermo and the Orsini captains to set up the attack on Camerino, and had then proceeded in the normal way as far as Nocera, where instead of turning east to Camerino he had pushed on in a forced march to join his troops at Cagli, intending to take Urbino before the unsuspecting Guidobaldo had the chance to escape.

Cesare's justification for this sudden unprovoked attack was that on his march northward he had discovered evidence of Guidobaldo's treachery, to the effect that he had sent help to Camerino and plotted to seize the Borgia artillery as it passed through Urbinese territory. Whatever the truth of these charges, indignantly denied by Guidobaldo in a long letter to Giuliano della Rovere in which he accused Cesare of a totally unprovoked and treacherous attack on an ally, there is little doubt that plans for the coup were carefully laid before leaving Rome. Without the grant of free passage through Cagli, Cesare's coup would have had no chance of success, since Guildobaldo's fortress there commanded a narrow gorge and could have held up a besieging army – hence Alexander's advance request to Guidobaldo. Moreover, the duchy of Urbino, situated between the Romagna to the north and Le Marche to the south, and commanding the passes into the Romagna and Tuscany, was strategically a logical acquisition for Cesare.

News of his taking of Urbino sent a shock wave through the courts of Italy; the Montefeltros were one of the most prestigious of the signorial families and closely related to all of them. They were popular and established in the rule of their duchy, and the ease and speed with which they had been overthrown left their contemporaries stunned. While Cesare's earlier successes could have been ascribed to French support and the presence of French troops, this time there could be no doubt that his coup was based on his own skill and initiative, commanding his own troops. Cesare's contemporaries could no longer be in any doubt as to his abilities. While deploring Guidobaldo's unwarranted overthrow, they could not help but admire, in Machiavelli's words, 'this stratagem and so much celerity joined with an extreme felicity ...'

It was in this light that Niccolò Machiavelli first saw Cesare Borgia when he interviewed him at Urbino on 24 June, gaining a vivid impression of power, confidence, intelligence and dynamic energy which still coloured his image of Cesare when, years later, he made him the model for Chapter VII of *The Prince*. Machiavelli, Secretary to the Ten, with Francesco Soderini, Bishop of Volterra, had been dispatched by the Florentine government to Urbino at Cesare's request, and arrived there not knowing what they had to expect from him. At the end of their mission they were still uncertain, their dispatches revealing a puzzled admiration for this man whose character and motives they could not fathom. They found him alone in the great ducal palace of Urbino, the doors locked and closely guarded. At twenty-six, six years younger than Machiavelli, Cesare represented the greatest single threat to the Florentine state, yet such was his skill and the force of his personality that the envoys found themselves arguing his case to their government, whose true interest it was that he should be destroyed. This was their first impression of him, recorded in a letter of 26 June 1502, signed by Soderini as head of mission, but composed by Machiavelli:

> This Lord is truly splendid and magnificent, and in war there is no enterprise so great that it does not appear small to him; in the pursuit of glory and lands he never rests nor recognizes fatigue or danger. He arrives in one place before it is known that he has left another; he is popular with his soldiers and he has collected the best men in Italy; these things make him victorious and formidable, particularly when added to perpetual good fortune.

And this despite, or perhaps because of, the fact that Cesare's manner with them during this first interview was tough, direct and domineering. Without mincing his words he went straight to the point, complaining that Florence had not kept the promises made to him at Campi, assuring them that all he wanted was her friendship, and threatening that otherwise he must secure his states at all costs:

> I want from you a good security, and if this is done, you will have me always at your disposal in everything, but if it is not done, I will be constrained to carry on this undertaking and assure myself of you by any means, so that I do not remain in danger. For I know too well that your city is not well-disposed towards me, rather you treat me like an assassin; and have tried to stir up much trouble for me both with the Pope and the King of France.

Brushing aside the envoys' protestations he continued menacingly:

> I know well that you are prudent men and understand me; however I will repeat what I said in a few words. I do not like this government and I cannot trust it. You must change it and give me guaran-

tees of the observance of the promises you made me; otherwise you will soon realize that I do not intend to live in this way, and if you will not have me as a friend, you shall have me as an enemy.

Cesare's blunt words evoked assurances of Florentine good faith, and the envoys, plucking up courage, retorted that in return he should show his good faith by withdrawing Vitellozzo from Arezzo. Their temerity provoked a sharp reply:

Do not expect that I should begin to do you any great favour, because not only have you not deserved it, but actually the reverse; it is true that Vitellozzo is my man, but I swear to you that I never knew anything of the business of Arezzo. I have not been displeased at the things you have lost, rather it has given me satisfaction, and will continue to do so if they take things further.

Then, putting on the velvet glove, he assured them that he had no designs on Florentine territory, having refused his captains' offers to that effect, and that he was 'not a man to play the tyrant, but to extinguish tyrants . . .' However, he added menacingly: 'Make your decision speedily because I cannot keep my army here since it is mountain country which would soon be stripped bare; and between you and myself there can be no middle way: either you are my friends or my enemies.' On this note the interview ended, and the Florentine envoys retired to their lodgings, as Machiavelli wrote, 'with little satisfaction'. Cesare then used Giulio and Paolo Orsini to frighten them further: the two condottieri hinted to the envoys that the King of France had consented to their operations in Tuscany, and advised them to come quickly to terms with Cesare. The next day he delivered an ultimatum: four days for Florence to decide whether she would be his friend or his enemy.

His tactics had the desired effect, on the envoys at least: on the 29th Machiavelli rode off in dramatic haste to carry the ultimatum to his government, leaving the unhappy Soderini to deal with Cesare on his own, a task he found lamentably difficult. Cesare's secrecy made it impossible to divine his true intentions. Discreet inquiries among his household elicited the dispiriting response: 'He alone decides, and at the moment of action, so that his purpose cannot be known beforehand.' And the eloquence and ingenuity of Cesare's arguments made it hard for Soderini to hold his own in discussion, as the bewildered Bishop wrote on 9 July: 'He argued with so many reasons that it would be lengthy to repeat them, because of his mind and his tongue he makes what use he wills.'

However, the Florentine government, beyond the reach of il Valentino's personality and eloquence, saw the question more clearly than their men on the spot. They had no intention of employing a man whom they regarded as their principal Italian enemy as their condottiere, and they knew, as Cesare himself knew, that time was on their side. Louis was once again on the march for Italy to settle the affairs of Naples; they had only to prolong negotiations until his arrival, and again the game would be up for Cesare Borgia, so they instructed Soderini to temporize over the terms of the condotta. The envoy's dispatch reporting the negotiations throws an interesting light on Cesare's treatment of his troops and his methods of recruitment. The Florentine proposals, Cesare argued, would not suit them: 'because I give so much freedom to my soldiers that I know that to you it would seem too much ... And then I want hand-picked men and would sooner give them double pay, and this cannot be done by dozens. I could recruit them collectively to furnish the condotta, as others do, but this would result neither to my honour nor your advantage. I' form the companies of Italians or foreigners as I find good men ...' This statement goes far to disprove the claim that he relied heavily on a loyal Romagnol militia; he used the resources at his disposal to obtain the best men whether Italians or foreigners, and to keep their loyalty by paying them well and treating them generously. Perhaps he consciously followed the dictum of his mentor Julius Caesar: 'If you lack money, you will have no soldiers, but if you have no soldiers, there will be no money.'

Nonetheless Cesare's persuasiveness failed to move the Florentines; on 7 July Louis was at Asti, and on the 10th the Signoria sent a letter consisting of empty words to be shown to Cesare. Soderini noted his reaction:

> I saw him completely change and his first words were: all this is nothing; those men do not want my friendship nor care anything about it; therefore it will be better to remit this negotiation to Our Lord [the Pope] and the King, who will know how to conduct it to my purpose, because I am not a tradesman and I came to you with that freedom that one looks for between good brothers; and to that alliance which I wish to make and your people care nothing for, and want to give me words of the King which I already know,

because they know well that for my honour I cannot climb down from the terms of the condotta and this asking for time is seeking occasion for new disputes; and they do not wish to give me security, but show that they want to deceive me.

With increasing nervousness Soderini observed Cesare's obvious dissatisfaction and tension over the following week, and on 20 July he literally fled from camp: 'To escape from these continual suspicions I came with all speed this evening to Bagno ...'

Soderini had correctly observed the deep disturbance in Cesare caused by the collapse of his hopes for an alliance with Florence, but he misinterpreted its cause. Cesare's inward reaction to the blow was not anger, but fear. Neither Soderini, nor indeed the more astute Machiavelli, dazzled as they were by Cesare's recent success and the strength of his army, perceived the reality of the situation: that in his desperate pursuit of Florentine friendship, Cesare was acting not from strength but from weakness. One of the essential qualities of a successful politician is the ability to scent danger before it overtakes him, and Cesare, with his mind always attuned to the future, had the rare gift of foreseeing the logical consequences of events. Cesare's enemies confidently expected that he would now get his deserts from France; this time, surely, in overthrowing Guidobaldo and threatening Tuscany, he had at last pushed the King too far. Louis at Asti was already surrounded by influential enemies of the Borgias, and it was authoritatively reported in both Florence and Venice that on the 8th, the day after his arrival, he had summoned the Marquis of Mantua to captain a French force to be used against Cesare. But Cesare was not seriously worried by the threat of retribution from France – indeed when Machiavelli and Soderini taunted him with the French King's resentment, he answered sharply 'that he understood French affairs as well as any man in Italy, that he knew he was not deceiving himself, but that they indeed would be deceived'. He was being kept fully informed by daily letters from agents at the French court, and he knew, as he told Soderini, that the King 'thinks so much of the affairs of Naples that he does not care much about anything else ...' Where Louis and Naples were concerned, he knew that he held two trump cards, his own army and the prestige of his father the Pope.

The danger lay not from without but from within his own ranks, a consequence of his own success in the takeover of the lands of the

Church, planned from the day he was made Gonfalonier. By the end of June 1502, most of the former vicariates north of the Campagna were in his hands, Camerino was about to fall, and Sinigallia also marked out for destruction, while in the area round Rome, the lands of all the Roman barons with the lone exception of the Orsinis had been taken over by his family. Within the Papal States only Bologna, Perugia, Città di Castello, Fermo and, obviously, the Orsini lands remained outside his control. The conclusion was obvious: it would be their turn next. The lords of all these cities, with the exception of Bentivoglio of Bologna, who was closely allied with the Orsinis, were captains in Cesare's pay, and thus, if they joined together against him, might have the power to destroy him. Threatened men can be dangerous, as Cesare was well aware, and the overthrow of Guidobaldo had shocked them into a realization of the perils of their situation. Some time towards the end of June, Vitellozzo and Gian Paolo Baglioni held a conference with Morgante Baglioni at Lake Transimene, at which, according to the Perugian chronicler Matarazzo, Gian Paolo 'spoke at length of the great betrayal [Urbino] executed by the Duke, beginning to recognize his *marrano* faith more clearly ...'

No doubt Cesare had originally intended to use his condottieri's Tuscan exploits to pressure Florence into making concessions, but now the extent of their success made them even more dangerous to him. In this perilous situation he needed all the friends he could get, and Florence was the logical choice: her boundaries marched with his states of the Romagna and Urbino, while his potential enemies, Vitellozzo, Baglioni and the Orsinis, were also hers. But with his customary wariness he was afraid to give the Florentines a hint of the truth, for fear of revealing his weakness, nor did he want to arouse his condottieri to precipitate action by any rumour as to his suspicions of them, until the time had come when he would be ready and able to crush them.

While Cesare, solitary and secretive at Urbino, held his tongue, Alexander at Rome talked and the whole court listened. Giustinian remarked that Alexander was 'so self-indulgent in his appetites that he cannot refrain from saying some word which indicates his mind'. As early as 1 July he reported: 'His intention is not to treat these poor Orsinis any better than he has the Colonnesis and others ... and this ... has not been a secret to the Orsinis, nor to all this court.' While a month later he wrote that every action on the part of the Pope indicates 'that the Pope and the Duke have the intention of clipping the Orsinis' wings, so that he alone remains master of the synagogue'. Moreover the Pope showed open hostility towards Vitellozzo: 'Alexander spoke in an ugly manner of Vitellozzo, as he did the day before ... demonstrating that nothing would give him more satisfaction than to see him ruined; and if the King [Louis] wanted to punish him he will help him until his death and total destruction.' Alexander's talkativeness must have irritated Cesare, but his diplomatic skill was vital to him. While letters passed daily between him and his father, secret negotiations were being carried on through the means of the Borgias' confidential agent Troches with the Cardinal of Rouen to persuade Louis to abandon his protection of the Orsinis and Bologna in return for Borgia help in Naples.

Cesare, as behind the safety of locked doors he paced alone through the high cool rooms of the ducal palace of the Montefeltros, must have felt, not perhaps for the first time, the loneliness and danger of the course he had set himself, surrounded as he was by enemies, open and concealed. Even the walls of the palace, with their memories of the great soldier Federigo da Montefeltro who had built it, must have increased his insecurity, reminding him that his hold on Federigo's son's duchy was likely to be tenuous. Doors, pilasters and chimney pieces in marble and creamy limestone were emblazoned with the insignia conferred on Federigo by his grateful employers, the English Order of the Garter, the Neapolitan Order of the Ermine, even the papal keys, for Federigo, like Cesare, had been Captain General of the Church. The walls were hung with magnificent tapestries and paintings by the artists he had patronized, Melozzo da Forlì, Raphael's father Giovanni Santi, and two portraits of Federigo himself, one with his second wife Battista Sforza, by Piero della Francesca, the other showing him reading one of the precious volumes from his famous library to his little blond son, Guidobaldo. Federigo's formidable profile (he always had himself painted from the left since losing his right eye in a tournament) with its great broken nose and deeply indented chin under a hawk's mouth looked down upon the usurper wherever he went, even perhaps on his vast *alcova*, bed, with its three sides of painted gilded wood and brocade curtains, in which Cesare probably slept, and above all his presence would have been alive in his *studiolo*, where marquetry *trompe l'œil* panels depicted his armour hanging in a cupboard, his favourite books piled on a shelf. Cesare, as he looked down over the hostile roofs of the little town towards the bare hills of Urbino and the mountain passes which Federigo would never have been foolish enough to have left undefended, must have reflected that, unlike the plains of his own state of the Romagna where armies could move swiftly, the mountain duchy was guerrilla country where the sympathy of the population was necessary to the security of the ruler – a sympathy which he knew he did not possess.

Cesare certainly did not regard the ducal palace as a permanent home: while referring to himself in certain acts as 'Duke of Urbino', he systematically looted the Montefeltro possessions, valued by contemporaries at 150,000 ducats, and had them taken to the Rocca of Forlì. A local chronicler reported: 'Il Valentino, while he was at Urbino and afterwards, had all the furniture of Guidobaldo taken from the palace and sent to the Rocca of Forlì: so that during an entire month 180 mules were employed each day; thus that so honoured house was despoiled of silver and rich tapestries, with the magnificent and rare library and all the other hangings, also horses, mules and the perfect stud horses.' While Cesare, who had no blood ties with Guidobaldo, had little hesitation in removing his most valued possessions, the unfortunate Duke's own relations also showed few scruples about acquiring his property. His sister-in-law, Isabella d'Este Gonzaga, whose cupidity as a collector overcame her family feelings, wrote to her brother Ippolito at Rome asking him to intercede with Cesare for the Venus and the Cupid which had adorned the ducal palace. She believed both statues to be antique, she said, and did not think her request 'to be an inconvenient idea, knowing that His Excellency [Cesare] does not take much pleasure in antiques ...'

Cesare, whose cultural tastes inclined to literature, and to vernacular poetry in particular, did not share the current Italian passion for collecting antiquities. He was, moreover, anxious to stand well with the Gonzagas, deeply offended by his expulsion of Guidobaldo, who with his Duchess, Francesco's sister, had taken refuge at Mantua. He hastened to send one of his chamberlains to present the statues to Isabella on 21 July, accompanying the gift with a personal letter explaining that the Cupid (which he had given to Guidobaldo years before while still a Cardinal) was not in fact an antique statue as she believed, but the work of the Florentine sculptor Michelangelo. Isabella was enchanted with it. 'The Cupid, for a modern work, has no equal,' she wrote to her husband, who was with Louis in Lombardy. Isabella's true feelings about Cesare were revealed in a letter she wrote to her husband the following day. Sound political common sense prompted

Left: Alexander VI. Detail from a fresco by Pinturicchio in the Borgia Apartments, painted shortly after Alexander's accession to the papacy in 1492

Cesare. Three portrait sketches by Leonardo da Vinci, executed during the period in which Leonardo worked as his Chief Engineer and Architect from the summer of 1502 until about the end of January 1503

Cesare's brother-in-law, Juan d'Albret, King of Navarre, first left, with Ferdinand of Aragon, second left, and Isabella the Catholic, kneeling in front of Ferdinand. Detail from the Retable of Isabella the Catholic by Juan de Flandres (painted *c.* 1505), in the Palacio Real, Madrid

Vannozza de' Cattanei, Cesare's mother, in middle age

Left: Lucrezia Borgia. Traditionally but not authoritatively held to be a portrait of the young Lucrezia depicted as St. Catherine in a detail from Pinturicchio's frescoes in the Borgia Apartments

View of the City of Rome from the Atlas of Sebastian Münster showing the Vatican (B), St. Peter's (C) and the principal monuments of Rome as they were in Cesare's time

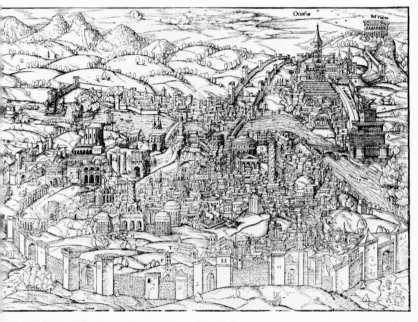

Opposite: Caterin[a]
Sforza. A portrait [by]
Marco Palmezzani[, of]
the beautiful "vira[go"]
defeated and capt[ured]
by Cesare at Forli [in]
January 1500

Above: Charles VIII of
France "more like a monster
than a man" (Guicciardini).
Terracotta bust by an
unknown fifteenth-century
Florentine sculptor in the
Bargello, Florence

Louis XII of France, the
man who, in Machiavelli's
words, "in order to separate
himself from his old wife,
promised and gave Alexander
more than any other,"
and launched Cesare on
his career of conquest

The great condottiere
Federigo da
Montefeltro, Duke
of Urbino, reading
one of the books from
his famous library
to his son, Guidobaldo,
whom Cesare later
dispossessed of his
dukedom. Portrait by
Pietro Berruguete

Niccolò Machiavelli.
Terracotta bust, by an
unknown fifteenth-
century sculptor, of the
man who made Cesare
the model for Chapter
VII of *The Prince*

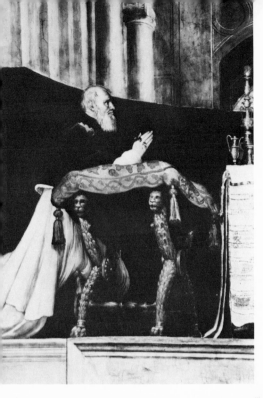

Pope Julius II, the fiery old Pope, depicted by his protégé, Raphael—detail from *The Mass of Bolsena*

Below: Cesare's signature. The development of his character shows in the contrast between the flamboyant 'Cesar' of February 1500 in letter B (*right*), counter-signed by his confidential secretary Agapito Geraldini, and the self-contained elegance of the monogram on letter A (*left*) six years later, written from Pamplona to Cardinal Ippolito d'Este, 7 December 1506

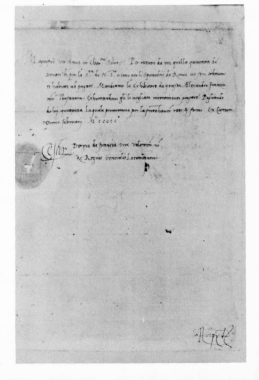

The keep of the fortress of La Mota at Medina del Campo in Castile, in which Cesare was imprisoned for over a year and from which he escaped on the night of 25 October 1506

Modern bronze bust of Cesare as Captain General of the Navarrese Army, beside the Church of Santa Maria in Viana in which he was buried

her in a letter of 23 July to warn the hot-headed Francesco, who was reported to have uttered public threats against Cesare, not to commit himself against il Valentino:

> It is generally believed that His Most Christian Majesty has some understanding with Valentino, so I beg of you to be careful not to use words which may be repeated to him, because in these days we do not know who is to be trusted. There is a report here ... that Your Excellency has spoken angry words against Valentino before the Most Christian King and the Pope's servants ... and they will doubtless reach the ears of Valentino, who, having already shown that he does not scruple to conspire against those of his own blood, will, I am certain, not hesitate to plot against your person ... it would be perfectly easy for anyone to poison Your Excellency ...

July was a tense month; on the 28th Louis entered Milan, surrounded by enemies who were bent on Cesare's destruction – Giuliano della Rovere, Cardinal Riario, Francesco Gonzaga, Guidobaldo da Montefeltro, Giovanni Sforza, one of Bentivoglio's sons, and Cardinal Orsini, who had fled from Rome to join the anti-Borgia chorus round the French King. Cesare, away from the oppressively hostile atmosphere of Urbino, was back in the reassuring surroundings of his camp at Fermignano, where he spent the cool early mornings hunting with leopards in the hills. On the 7th he had a fall from his horse while hunting, and such was his reputation for deviousness that the Venetian ambassador believed it be a deliberate ruse to excuse himself from going to the King to justify himself. But the fall was not serious enough to have prevented him riding to Louis had he wanted to; he continued to hunt 'incognito, among a host of his servants dressed in livery, his face wrapped in gauze'. He had no intention of making a humiliating crawl to the French King under the delighted eyes of his enemies, nor indeed of meeting Louis until circumstances had turned in his favour. Louis had made his displeasure at events in Tuscany abundantly clear to both the Borgias, and to placate him a henchman was to be thrown to the wolves. By 15 July Vitellozzo, who had meanwhile taken Borgo di San Sepolcro 'in the name of Duke Valentino', was ordered to withdraw, a command followed by a threat from Cesare to march on his lordship of Città di Castello if he did not obey. By the end of the month, Vitellozzo and Gian Paolo Baglioni had retreated from Tuscany, raging inwardly at Cesare's desertion of them. Cesare was waiting too for news of the fall of Camerino, which surrendered on 21 July. The seventy-year-old Giulio Cesare Varano and two of his sons were handed over into the custody of Cesare's officers, and few doubted what this implied for the former lords of Camerino.

Alexander was so carried away with delight that in consistory he forgot to have important news from Hungary read to the cardinals and treated them to an exuberant dissertation on his son's exploits instead. 'The cause of such great joy', wrote Giustinian caustically, 'is the capture of those lords, who in everyone's opinion will come to a bad end.' From Urbino Cesare wrote an affectionate letter to Lucrezia, who was having a difficult pregnancy with her first child by Alfonso: 'There could be no more salubrious nor more efficacious medicine for your present indisposition than the reception of good and happy tidings ...' He hoped she would soon be better, for, as he wrote, 'with your illness we can find no pleasure in this news nor in anything else ...', signing himself, 'from your brother who loves you as himself'. With all his other preoccupations Cesare worried enough about Lucrezia to send her his own doctor Torella, and on the 15th he wrote to a famous doctor at Cesena, Niccolò Masini, requesting him to go to Ferrara to consult with Torella about Lucrezia's case.

But the surrender of Camerino, however gratifying, was of minor importance compared with the outcome of the secret negotiations between Louis and the Borgias which were being carried on in Milan behind the backs of the enemy lords. For Cesare, his future plans were dependent on his securing himself from the threat from his own condottieri; for this, and for the extension of his conquests, he was once again dependent on Louis' support. In Rome, Giustinian picked up hints of the behind-the-scenes bargaining; on 1 August he reported that Alexander and Cesare had promised the French King 500 men-at-arms and Cesare to lead them in person, with free passage and supplies for the expedition to Naples. Later in the week, against a background of increasing rumours as to a secret understanding between Alexander and Louis, he wrote that the Pope intended to give Cesare the vicariates of Città di Castello and Perugia. It seems clear that the Borgias had obtained a promise of what they wanted from the King, and were now intent on proceeding with their plans.

It was at this point that Cesare made a typically dramatic gesture. Disguised as a Knight of St John, and accompanied only by three horsemen, including his trusted henchmen Troches and Michele Remolino, he left Fermignano on 25 July and the next day was at Forlì, having covered eighty miles in twenty-four hours. Stopping only to change horses and to dine on chickens and squabs in great number, 'to the scandal of the populace and their own shame' (it was a Friday, when the rules of the Church forbid the eating of meat), they rode on to Ferrara, where Cesare spent two hours at Lucrezia's bedside before going on to Modena. At Milan, Louis kept the news of his impending arrival there secret. Only on 5 August, a few hours before Cesare actually entered Milan, did he impart the news in a manner calculated to give Cesare's enemies, by whom he was sur-rounded, the maximum of disagreeable surprise. According to the chronicler Bernardi, he communicated the news to the governor of Milan in a stage whisper loud enough for everyone to hear, and left to meet Cesare 'with only a small following, since all the rest remained where they were stupefied'. While Cesare's enemies were stupefied by the news of his arrival, they were even more disconcerted by the warmth of his reception. As Isabella's friend Niccolò da Corregio reported from Milan on the 8th:

> His Most Christian Majesty welcomed and embraced him with great joy and led him to the Castle, where he had him lodge in the chamber nearest his own, and he himself ordered the supper, choosing diverse dishes, and that evening three or four times he went to his room dressed in shirt sleeves, when it was time to go to bed. And he ordered yesterday that he should dress in his own shirts, tunic and robes, for Duke Valentino brought no baggage wagons with him, only horses. In short – he could not have done more for a son or a brother.

At Rome, Alexander, the one man who might have been expected to have news of it, was equally surprised and upset by his son's initia-tive. Despite Cesare's honourable reception, Giustinian reported on 9 August: 'The Pope is not content with this journey of his, and is deeply troubled, because from an unimpeachable source I hear that the Duke went without any consultation nor informing His Holiness, urged on by Troches, who was the one who carried on the negotia-tion.' Increasingly in this year of 1502, Cesare acted on his own initia-tive, independently of his father; anticipating his disapproval or fear-ing his talkativeness, he presented Alexander with a *fait accompli* which he was forced to accept. There was, in fact, a deep divergence between them in their attitude to France. While Cesare regarded Louis as the key to the achievement of his personal ambitions, Alexander, Spanish at heart, remained deeply mistrustful of France, and indeed on this occasion he was again worried that Louis might keep Cesare as a hostage, and fearful of the effect Cesare's action would have on his own relations with Spain. By the middle of the month, however, he was slightly reassured by the news that Louis had dismissed Cesare's enemies, the exiled lords, from court. 'He praised the prudence of the Duke, that with the ability of his mind, he had made the king so friendly towards him, when at first he had seemed to regard him as a rebel ...'

Once again Cesare's instinctive grasp of the realities of politics had enabled him to outwit his enemies and triumph despite the apparent odds against him. He knew, as his enemies should have known, that Louis' obsession with Naples would bring him over to the Borgia side. For while the Italian princes who crowded round the King could give him nothing but their personal services, Cesare had far more to offer. As Machiavelli wrote of him some months later: 'The Duke is not to be measured like other lords, who have only their titles, in respect to his state; but one must think of him as a new power in Italy ...'

Even Francesco Gonzaga somewhat belatedly realized this. Although on the day of Cesare's arrival he had boasted to the Venetian envoy that he would fight a hand-to-hand duel with 'that bastard son of a priest' and thus be the one to liberate Italy, two days later he was forced to swallow his bold words in a public reconciliation with Valentino. As he wrote to Isabella: 'Today we have caressed and embraced each other, offering each to the other as good brothers, and thus together with the Most Christian Majesty we have spent all this day dancing and banqueting ...' In seeking Francesco's friendship, Cesare was pursuing his policy of alliance with neighbouring powers, and, as Lucrezia had been the symbol of his relationship with the Estes of Ferrara, so his two-year-old daughter Luisa was to be betrothed to Gonzaga's son of the same age, Federigo, as a pledge of this somewhat hollow alliance. Cesare demanded concrete proof of Gonzaga's goodwill by insisting that he should expel his refugee brother-in-law Guidobaldo from his court. He was well aware of the precarious nature of his hold upon Urbino, and the popular Guidobaldo at large represented a threat to it. Having failed to lay hands upon him in June, the Borgias' solution to the problem of Guidobaldo was ingenious: he was to renounce his rights to the duchy in return for a cardinal's hat and a generous life pension. Having robbed Guido-baldo of his state, Cesare now deprived him of his public reputation as a man. Despite an extremely erotic temperament – Elisabetta was in constant terror lest he endanger his weak health by his frequent passionate advances to her – Guidobaldo was impotent. This sad secret, carefully guarded between them during the fourteen years of their marriage, now became public knowledge. Nonetheless Elisabetta absolutely refused to consider the Borgias' proposal, saying that she preferred to live with her husband as a sister than to be no longer his wife.

Cesare's constant preoccupation with the security of his states was clearly illustrated in his employment at this time of Leonardo da Vinci as his military architect and engineer. From Pavia on 18 August Cesare issued a patent in which he described Leonardo as:

> our most Excellent and Most Beloved Familiar Architect and General Engineer ... [who] has our commission to survey the holds and fortresses of our States in order that according to their necessi-ties and his judgement we may provide for them. They are to give free passage, exempt from all public toll for himself and his com-pany, and friendly reception, and to allow him to see, measure and estimate all he may wish. And to this effect they shall order men on his requisition, and lend him all the help, assistance and favours he may request, it being our wish that for all works to be done in our dominions any engineer be compelled to consult him and to conform to his opinion; and to this may none presume to act in opposition if it be his wish not to incur our indignation.

Leonardo entered Cesare's service some time in the summer of 1502. He was certainly at Urbino at the end of July, and may possibly have accompanied Vitellozzo in Tuscany, since he drew maps of the Arezzo and Val di Chiana areas, and remained in his employ until about the end of January 1503. During the time he worked for Cesare he produced maps which must have been used during the campaigns, towns plans for Urbino, Cesena and Imola, projections for a revolu-tionary system of defences at Imola, and for a canal to connect Cesena with Porto Cesenatico. Cesare, who, like Leonardo, was passionately interested in fortifications, artillery and engines of war, must have appreciated his genius in this respect. One reward which he bestowed on him was recorded by Leonardo in a list of his belongings to be left 'in a crate at the monastery' – 'One cape in the French style, which belonged to Duke Valentino'. The only other reference to Cesare in Leonardo's notes is brief but expressive: 'Where is Valentino?'

It is not surprising that considerations of security and defence should have been uppermost in il Valentino's mind at this time. The danger from his own condottieri, which had haunted him at Urbino, loomed even nearer as the time approached for Louis to leave for France and for himself to take the road again for the Romagna. But Cesare, as Alexander told the Venetian envoy, 'was so circumspect that he knew well how to guard himself against anyone'. Some time before the end of August he reached a secret formal agreement with Louis. No documentary record of its terms has yet come to light, but historians have inferred its content from subsequent events. While Florence was definitely excluded from Borgia hostility, Bologna was to be abandoned to Cesare, who was also left free to deal with his condottieri as his needs might dictate, and to compensate for the loss of their troops Louis seems to have promised a considerable French reinforcement. In return the Borgias repeated the pledge made at the end of July of political and military support for the French cause in Naples. Louis clearly considered the abandoning of most of his Italian supporters hitherto – the Orsinis and Bentivoglios – as a reasonable price to pay for Cesare's support. At Rome in the last week of August, Alexander, the barometer of his son's political affairs, suddenly abandoned his previous anxieties, spoke continually of Cesare, and, reported Giustinian, 'every hour shows himself to be more for the French'.

Cesare left Genoa where he had gone with Louis from Milan on 2 September 1502. On the 7th he was at Ferrara with Lucrezia, who was ill and depressed after the birth two days earlier of a still-born daughter. Despite his own preoccupations he spent two days with her, cheering her up. His affectionate care for her is shown by a letter written by one of her doctors to Duke Ercole: 'Today at the twentieth hour we bled Madonna on the right foot. It was exceedingly difficult to accomplish it, and we could not have done it but for the Duke of Romagna, who held her foot. Her Majesty spent two hours with the Duke, who made her laugh and cheered her greatly.' Lucrezia made a rapid recovery, and knowing her to be out of danger Cesare rode south to Imola to begin a dangerously high game with his condottieri, a game in which the stake could be not only the existence of the states which he had won, but even, perhaps, his life.

XII

'A MOST BEAUTIFUL DECEPTION'

BY 10 September 1502 Cesare was back in the Romagna, setting up headquarters at Imola and attending to administrative affairs and to the assembling of troops for his next campaign. The objective was to be Bologna, which he, as Gonfalonier and Captain General, was to wrest from the control of the 'tyrant' Giovanni Bentivoglio and restore to the Church. Louis, in accordance with the agreement, had withdrawn his protection and dispatched an envoy to Bentivoglio warning him to look to himself, since he, Louis, would not oppose the Pope's wishes. Alexander had summoned Bentivoglio to Rome to answer charges of maladministration, and given him fifteen days to comply. The groundwork for the attack on Bologna was laid, but the question remained whether the Orsinis, as soldiers of the Church, would comply with the Pope's orders to march with Cesare, and if they did not, whether Vitellozzo and the Baglionis would follow suit.

Tension mounted during September as Cesare's suspect condottieri debated whether or not they should obey. Vitellozzo, sick with syphilis at Città di Castello, Gian Paolo Baglioni at Perugia, and the Orsinis in their castles round Rome became increasingly nervous and suspicious as rumours flew that the Borgias intended to dispossess them of their lordships in the name of the Church. On 25 September Giulio Orsini told Alexander to his face that the French had warned Cardinal Orsini at Milan that it was the Pope's intention to ruin his house. Alexander replied fiercely that they lied in their throats, but the next day the Orsinis gathered for an ominous family conference at Todi. The Venetian envoy reported Alexander as being tense and nervous. As was his wont when something was worrying him, he repeatedly asked anxiously: 'What do you think, Lord Orator, that these Orsinis will do?'

It soon became clear what the Orsinis intended to do, and not only the Orsinis. In the first week of October a meeting which boded ill for the Borgias took place at Cardinal Orsini's castle of La Magione, near Perugia. The conference was attended by the Cardinal, as head of the clan, with his nephew Francesco, Duke of Gravina, Paolo Orsini, lord of Palombara, Gian Paolo Baglioni and his brother Gentile, Oliverotto da Fermo, another of Cesare's captains, and even Vitellozzo, who appeared groaning with pain carried on a litter. Other lords who had been threatened or injured by the Borgias were represented. Giovanni Bentivoglio sent his son Ermes, Guidobaldo his nephew Ottaviano Fregoso, and Pandolfo Petrucci of Siena two of his intimates. None of the major Italian powers was represented; Ferrara and Mantua were Cesare's allies, Florence feared the Orsinis and Vitellozzo, while Venice, secretly sympathetic, dared not come out openly against the King of France. Nonetheless the conjunction of these men was dangerous for Cesare: between them the conspirators commanded forces numerically superior to his. Bentivoglio, poised on his northern frontier, was strategically placed for a damaging attack on the Romagna, while Guidobaldo could be the spark to ignite a partisan uprising in Urbino.

Feeling against Cesare ran high at La Magione, with Gian Paolo Baglioni taking the lead. He represented to his fellow conspirators the danger that threatened them 'of being one by one devoured by the dragon', if they did not take preventive action, and told them that he had intercepted a papal brief instructing Cesare to invite himself, Vitellozzo, Oliverotto and the Orsinis to Imola and seize them. Violent words followed, with Vitellozzo and Bentivoglio swearing to kill Cesare if they had the chance. Yet it seemed that the conference would produce little more than words; united as they were in their hatred and fear of Cesare, that fear and their intimate knowledge of him made them wary of undertaking open action against him. There was not a true leader amongst them; they were all subordinate officers with their own lordships to look to, while behind Cesare stood the King of France, so that neither Florence nor Venice would help them. While the Baglionis and Oliverotto were for all-out war against il Valentino, the Orsinis, Bentivoglio and Petrucci were having second thoughts about the wisdom of confronting a man with his proven reputation and backing. Cesare, typically, further disturbed the unity of the conspirators by sending one of his gentlemen, Roberto Orsini, with instructions to win over his relations, and particularly the gullible Paolo, with offers of better conditions for his condotta and hints of Alexander's gratitude. But while Bentivoglio and Fregoso left the conference in disgust, the revolt of the key fortress of San Leo in Urbino against Cesare on 7 October put new life into the conspiracy. On arrival at La Magione, the leader of the rising was told bitterly by Gian Paolo Baglioni that 'against his own opinion, and only through the action of Paolo Orsini, suborned by the promises and words of il Valentino, the League had not yet been concluded, but that the following morning he would speak to the Cardinal and the others to make every effort so that the agreements should be signed'. Gian Paolo, who had known Cesare Borgia longer and better than the others and was not beguiled by his smooth words, was now able to bring the others into line behind him, and on 9 October the league was signed. Cesare was to be attacked on two sides, in the Romagna by Bentivoglio and in Urbino by the Orsinis in support of the uprising. In the exhilaration of the moment the confident conspirators planned the division of Valentino's states between them.

Alexander, when the news of La Magione and the revolt of San Leo reached Rome, was described as 'raging like a bear' against the Orsinis, but Cesare at Imola reacted with amazing calm to a situation which he had doubtless foreseen, at least as far as the conspirators were concerned. To Machiavelli, who arrived at camp on the 7th with assurances of Florentine support, he made a most revealing remark. After showing him a letter from Louis promising him 300 lances against Bologna, he referred to the confederates: 'Believe me that this thing is to my advantage, and they cannot reveal themselves at an hour when it will damage me less, nor can I, to strengthen my states, wish for a thing that will be more useful to me; because I shall know this time against whom I have to protect myself, and I shall recognize my friends. And if the Venetians reveal themselves in this matter, which I do not expect, I shall be the better pleased ...' And when he read Gian Paolo Baglioni's account of the confederate forces, he laughed:

He said that those 600 men-at-arms, of whom those enemies of his boast, would turn out to be less each one on the parade ground: and laughing said to me: 'They do well to say "men-at-arms on paper", which means nothing. I do not want to boast, but I would like the results, whatever they may be, to show what kind of men they are and who I am. And I think the less of them, the more I know them, both themselves and their troops; and Vitellozzo, who enjoys such a reputation, I cannot say I have ever seen him do anything as a valiant man, excusing himself on the ground of the French disease: he is only good at devastating defenceless places, and robbing those who dare not show him their face, and at these kind of betrayals ...'

Yet despite Cesare's contempt for his former condottieri, and his relief that they had at last revealed themselves, the situation to observers on the spot like Machiavelli looked extremely dangerous. His immediately available forces did not exceed 2500 foot and some 750 men-at-arms, and if the condottieri were to make a swift concerted attack they could overwhelm him. The nearest French troops were at Milan, too far away to afford immediate help, and if his cities of the Romagna followed the example of Urbino he would be lost. Machiavelli, unaware that Cesare had been expecting a situation of this kind since June, was amazed at the speed, decision and confidence with which he reacted to the crisis. Urbino for the moment was to be considered lost; he concentrated on securing the Romagna and speedily recruiting new troops and more trustworthy Italian condottieri. Ramiro de Lorqua, military governor of the Romagna, rode through the country putting the towns and fortresses in a state of defence, while Ugo de Moncada on the borders of Urbino was ordered to retreat to Rimini, and Michelotto dispatched to recruit a thousand infantry in the Romagna. Within a few days Cesare had raised 800 of the famous infantry from the Val di Lamone, and according to Machiavelli had inspected a further 6000 foot-soldiers from the Romagna. Meanwhile he sent to engage 500 Gascons at Milan, and 1500 Swiss, the best infantry in Europe. Alexander backed him up by forwarding 18,000 ducats from Rome to pay the troops. Couriers and messengers were dispatched from Imola to Rome, France, Ferrara and Milan to obtain money, troops and invaluable intelligence as to enemy movements. One of the secrets of Cesare's success was the excellence of his intelligence service and the money he was prepared to spend on it. As Machiavelli wrote in what was intended as a backhanded reproach to his government for their short-sighted parsimony in this respect: 'He has spent, in the two weeks since I have been here, as much money for couriers and special messengers as anyone else would have spent in two years ...'

Michelotto and Ugo de Moncada, retreating from Urbino into the Romagna, took cruel revenge on the rebels, sacking Fossombrone and

La Pergola, where Giulio Cesare Varano was strangled in the castle for good measure. At Imola, Cesare revealed the strong streak of superstition in him when he described to Machiavelli 'what Don Ugo and Don Michele had done ... saying thus joyfully that this year the planets showed themselves evil towards those who rebelled'. However, during the second week of October the planets showed themselves favourable to the conspirators as things went from bad to worse in Urbino, and the Orsinis fell upon Ugo de Moncada and Michelotto at Calmazzo and routed them, taking Ugo prisoner and forcing the remainder to retreat upon Fano. On the 18th Guidobaldo, amid general rejoicing, re-entered Urbino, which was now the condottieri headquarters. From Bologna, Giovanni Bentivoglio sent forward 2300 troops to Castel San Pietro, only seven miles from Cesare's headquarters at Imola.

On the face of it the situation looked discouraging, but in fact the worst was over. Over two weeks had passed since the signing of the league at La Magione and the outbreak of the revolt in Urbino, and since then the conspirators had accomplished little beyond the retaking of the duchy. Cesare's Romagna cities had remained loyal to him, and, what was more important, none of his other commanders, Romagnol, Italian or Spanish, had joined the revolt. The Orsinis and their adherents had revealed themselves as an isolated clique. Events had proved Cesare right in his estimate of the confederates and their psychology, or, as he had put it to Machiavelli, what kind of men they were and who he was. Fear of his reputation for luck and invincibility had prevented them from making a direct attack on him and destroying him when he was weak; now with his defensive arrangements in order, with troops and money pouring in from all sides, he was too strong for them. His masterly inactivity as far as the conspirators were concerned, and his prudent refusal to be drawn into the field against their superior forces, had confused them. Machiavelli, considering the situation from Imola on 23 October, thought that Cesare had won the first round:

The state of this Lord, since I have been here, has been governed only by his good fortune; the cause of which is the general opinion that the King of France will support him with troops and the Pope with money, and another thing which is no less responsible for it; and this is the tardiness of his enemies in pressing him. Nor do I think that at this time they are any longer in a position to do him much harm, because he has garrisoned all the important places with infantry, and the fortresses he has provided for most excellently; so that, as their spirits cool in the face of such provisions, he can feel secure enough to wait for reinforcements.

By the end of October, reinforcements in the form of French heavy cavalry were on the march from Lombardy.

Fear had united the conspirators against Cesare, and fear was to disunite them, enabling him to drive a wedge between them. Even while acting against him in Urbino, they continued separately to send him messages of friendship. As Cesare told Machiavelli on 23 October: 'Thus you see how they govern themselves: they keep up negotiations for an agreement, write me friendly letters, and today the lord Paolo is to come to see me, and tomorrow the Cardinal [Orsini]; and thus they play games with me in their way. I, on the other hand, temporize, listen to everything, and bide my time.' Machiavelli failed to note the sinister implications of Cesare's final phrase, and it was not until a week later that the truth began to dawn upon him. Cesare was perfectly content to play a cat and mouse game with his condottieri, building up his strength while pretending to believe in their assurances of friendship. By the end of October he had already succeeded in separating Bentivoglio from the rest: Machiavelli reported on the 30th that there had been constant comings and goings between Cesare and Bentivoglio, and that Bentivoglio 'when he sees he can secure his own affairs with this lord, would be content to leave the Orsinis to his discretion'. At the time of La Magione, Cesare had picked upon Paolo Orsini with unerring instinct as the weak link among the conspirators; now once again he used him as his instrument to induce the others to play into his hands. The wretched Paolo easily fell victim to the charm which Cesare could exert when he wanted to, and hurried to do his bidding with such officious eagerness that Guidobaldo's partisans called him 'my lady Paolo', intimating that he was infatuated with il Valentino. Machiavelli, as Paolo rode back and forth between Imola and Urbino, was at a loss to comprehend the motives of either side in making this agreement. He wrote on 27 October:

As to the suggested understanding, respecting the terms of which I am still in ignorance, I do not augur well of it. For when I consider the two parties concerned, I see on the one hand Duke Cesare, vigorous, courageous, confident in his future, blessed with exceptional fortune, backed by the favour of Pope and King, and now suffering at the hands of faithless servants the loss of a signory [Urbino] which he had just made his own. Confronting him, we have a group of lords who, even whilst they were his friends, were in anxiety for their possessions, and fearful of his growing power; and now, having thus injured him, and become his declared enemies, naturally more apprehensive still. So that I fail to understand how, on the one part, such injury can be expected to find forgiveness, and how, on the other, such fears are to be assuaged ...

Despite his bewilderment, and the difficulty of gleaning information at Cesare's close-mouthed court where 'things to be kept silent are never mentioned to us, and are carried on with wonderful secrecy', Machiavelli's perception enabled him to divine the truth. The agreements were no more than a temporary truce in the high game for survival which both sides were playing. It is hard to see how the condottieri, in the situation into which they had led themselves, could have done anything else but sue for peace. They had rebelled to save themselves and their lordships from extinction; they made peace for the same reasons. For the present, Cesare, surrounded by trustworthy troops and squadrons of French men-at-arms, was untouchable, but there might always be another chance to catch him unawares. With the exception of Francesco Orsini, the condottieri were tough, ruthless, and practised in deceit – men like Gian Paolo Baglioni, whom Machiavelli later reproved for his treachery as 'a stumbling horse whom no one would ride for fear of breaking his neck', and Oliverotto da Fermo, who the previous year had lured the uncle who had fostered him from childhood into a trap and murdered him with all his family and followers in order to seize power at Fermo. It is difficult to believe that such men, knowing Cesare as they did, would ever have expected him not to take his revenge. Cesare, as he had told Machiavelli, let them play their games with him, listened to everything, and bided his time.

The separate agreements with Bentivoglio and with the Orsinis and the rest were finally signed in the last week of November. Cesare was probably sincere, at least for the moment, in making an alliance with Bentivoglio. It was Alexander rather than Cesare who was bent on the acquisition of the former papal city, a huge prize which, according to Machiavelli, Cesare realized would be too difficult for him to digest at present, and whose friendship was essential to him for the security of his northern frontier. Moreover Bologna promised to supply him with troops, 200 men-at-arms and 200 light horse, and to give him a condotta for eight years at 12,000 ducats per annum. Not the least of the advantages of the Bologna agreement from Cesare's point of view was the bad blood which it created between Bentivoglio and his former friends; although it was supposed to be kept secret, Cardinal Orsini got wind of it and raged at the Bolognese envoy in the presence of the Pope.

As far as the terms of agreement with the condottieri were concerned, Cesare's confidential secretary Agapito Geraldini, who knew his master as well as anyone could know so secretive and complex a man, told Machiavelli that 'even children would laugh at such articles' – a remark which perfectly illustrated the seriousness with which Cesare regarded them. Both sides were to end their enmity with remission of all injuries; Cesare would receive all the confederates in perpetual alliance, and promise to defend their states, reserving only the interests of the Pope and the King of France, while the confederates promised to aid him to recover Urbino and also Camerino, which had fallen to Ercole Varano. Cesare promised to keep on all the condottieri in his service, although only one of them at a time was obliged to serve in the field. The controversy between the Church and Bologna, the ostensible cause of the whole outbreak, was to be decided between Cardinal Orsini, Pandolfo Petrucci – and Cesare.

Cesare, through his own cool-headedness, diplomatic skill and knowledge of men, had turned disaster into triumph. He had separated the confederates and brought them to sign agreements with him on his own terms. They had pledged themselves to help him recover both Urbino and Camerino, thus abandoning Guidobaldo and the Varano family, while Cesare had not lost one single city in the Romagna. He had shown himself able, in the face of adverse odds, to confront fortune, to outface and outwit some of the most experienced, tough and treacherous captains in Italy, to divide them and bring them crawling to his feet. Baglioni and Petrucci sent representatives to Imola to assure him that their purpose had been to make him King of Tuscany, while the much-admired Vitellozzo, Machiavelli reported, wrote 'the most submissive and pleasing letters, excusing himself and offering his services, and saying that if he ever spoke to him personally he had no doubt that he would be able to justify

himself absolutely and make him understand that the past events
were never intended to offend him'.

If the condottieri really intended to fool Cesare with fair words they
underestimated him even more than they had at the time of La
Magione. As one of his circle remarked to Machiavelli of Vitellozzo's
letter: 'Here is a man who has stabbed us in the back and then thinks
to heal the wound with words.' In Rome, Giustinian, with more information at his disposal than Machiavelli, had seen clearly which way
the wind was blowing. Alexander was bent on vendetta against the
Orsinis; he had not forgotten Juan Gandia, although he never spoke
of him. The punishment of Vitellozzo and the others was incidental –
for him the real targets were the Orsinis. On 6 November Giustinian
wrote that in signing the agreement the Orsinis 'could be certain of
having taken a terminal poison'. He saw, too, how the Orsinis and
their allies had played into the Borgias' hands; everyone, he said, vitu-
perated them because 'like stupid brutes they took the initiative and
with unconsidered fury, then more stupidly made an agreement with
little security, indeed greater peril to their interests, and also thus
made themselves guilty and deserving of every punishment, which
at some time the Pope may give them: the common opinion is that
with justification he may and should do so'.

As November turned into December, Machiavelli at Imola gained
a sense of impending tragedy, and his dispatches are full of repeated
references to Cesare's 'bad feelings' about the condottieri and his
occasional 'sinister' references to them. They were also full of pleas
for his own recall; he was ill, and he was doing nothing of use to the
city. Cesare was repeating his demands for an alliance and a condotta
from Florence, which the Florentines, as before, had no intention of
giving him. As Cesare perceived this, and his need for Florence
became less pressing as the crisis passed, so his treatment of Machiavelli changed from the intimate frankness of early October when he
had seemed to take the envoy flatteringly into his confidence, admitting his mistakes and asking for opinions, to his usual elusiveness.
Machiavelli's admiration for Cesare remained undimmed, but he was
embarrassed at the false position into which his government's tem-
porizing placed him in his relations with il Valentino:

> I have not tried to speak with the Duke, not having anything to
> tell him that is new, and the same things would bore him. You
> must recall that nobody speaks with him except three or four of

his ministers and some foreigners who have to deal with him about matters of importance, and he does not come out of his ante-chamber except at about 11 or 12 at night or later; and for this reason there is no opportunity to speak with him ever except through an audience appointed; and when he knows that a man brings him nothing but words he never gives him an audience.

But the Florentine government insisted that he remain to spy on Duke Valentino and give them first-hand information as to his intentions. Despairingly Machiavelli pointed out to them the difficulty of such a mission:

> ... this Lord is very secretive, and I do not believe that what he is going to do is known to anybody but himself. And his chief secretaries have many times asserted to me that he does not reveal anything except when he orders it, and orders it when necessity compels and when it is to be done, and not otherwise. Hence I beg that Your Lordships will excuse me, and not impute it to my negligence if I do not satisfy Your Lordships with information, because most of the time I do not satisfy even myself.

It was no use. On 10 December in heavy snow Cesare and all his army left Imola, 'which they have devoured down to the very pebbles', as Machiavelli put it, for Cesena. Machiavelli, still complaining about the hardships and discomforts of camp life, followed in their wake. He was quite mystified as to what Cesare intended to do with the considerable forces now at his disposal – some 5000 infantry, 800 armed cavalry and 400 light horse. With Urbino, which had been abandoned by Guidobaldo on 8 December, once more in his possession, and negotiations for the surrender of Camerino on the point of finalization, what could be his next objective? There were rumours of an attack on Sinigallia, or that Cesare would march to Naples with the French, and scattered hints of vengeance: 'It is thought that he cannot wish to do other than secure himself of those who have done him this villainy,' Machiavelli wrote from Cesena on 14 December. In Rome, Alexander seems to have been equally in the dark as to his son's intentions; he complained of having no letters from him, and increasingly showed his discontent and even suspicion as Giustinian reported on 2 December: 'Speaking of the French, he said that their troops would go to the Kingdom [of Naples], then with a certain sign of pain he said: "And also we strongly suspect that the

Duke will go, although he writes nothing of it." And he added: "It is bad to deal with young men! If he really wishes to go, we do not want to know anything of it, nor have a word in the matter, because he will not do it on our account."' Alexander was nervous that Cesare was committing himself too deeply on the side of the French in a cause whose outcome was far from certain, and dragging the Papacy along in his wake. He was worried by the continual expense which showed no obvious profit; Cesare's treasurer Spanocchi told Machiavelli that in the two months up to December Cesare had spent over 60,000 ducats, while on the 17th Giustinian wrote that the Pope had spent the entire day counting money to send to his son, and would forward 14,000 ducats in cash and letters of remittance. Yet still Cesare made no move: 'The Duke is still at Cesena with the army, to the displeasure of the Pope: and it is most unwillingly that he sends him more money, because it almost seems to him like throwing it away: but he does not know how to say no to the Duke . . .' The days wore on, Christmas approached, and the worried Alexander was reduced to asking every courier for news of Cesare; when on the 23rd a Venetian courier reported him to be still at Cesena, he could not contain his rage and exclaimed loudly at least three times: 'Son of a bitch, whore, bastard! and other words in Spanish, all angry ones.'

But even as, in Rome, Alexander passionately cursed Cesare for his expensive and enigmatic inactivity, two events occurred at Cesena – inexplicable and apparently unconnected as they seemed to observers – which proved to be the sparks of an explosive underground train precipitating him into action. On the evening of 20 December, Machiavelli observed all the French officers in a body come to interview Cesare; by their gestures and excited conversation they appeared to be angry. Interested, he waited for one of the officers of his acquaintance to emerge from the interview, who told him that the cause of the disturbance was that they had received sudden orders, with no reasons given, to return to Milan. The reason for their departure given out by Cesare's officials, and backed up later by the French, though with a slightly different emphasis, was that he no longer had need of their services, and since they were expensive to maintain had dispensed with them. Privately, Cesare's confidants told Machiavelli that 'the Duke could no longer support them, and that if he kept them, he would be more distressed by the arms of his friends than by those of his enemies; and that without them the Duke had enough soldiers left for doing everything . . .' The news caused a sensation not only at Imola but in Rome, as Cesare must have known that it would; there was a general sense of relief, and Giustinian reported: 'The suspicions that the Duke can do anything of great moment have ceased ...' Although Machiavelli on the spot was half-inclined to agree with this opinion, he could not help noting Cesare's continual strengthening of his forces; 600 Romagnol infantry had arrived the previous day from the Val di Lamone, and a thousand of the long-awaited Swiss had now reached Faenza. Moreover the artillery had been sent on ahead and not recalled; he therefore concluded that Cesare did not intend to abandon any plan made up to now.

On the evening of 22 December, the day the French left for Lombardy, five gentlemen of Cesena gave a ball in Cesare's honour, at which he led the dance and appeared to be enjoying himself immensely. According to a local chronicler, he danced many times with Cleofe Marescotti, the wife of one of his hosts, 'with whom he was greatly taken, and it seems that his feelings were returned'. While Cesare flirted imperturbably with the lovely Cleofe under her husband's nose, his chief lieutenant, Ramiro de Lorqua, military governor of the Romagna, who had returned from Pesaro that evening, was summarily arrested and thrown into prison. Three days later, at dawn on Christmas Day, Ramiro, gloved and dressed in a brocade robe, was decapitated in the piazza at Cesena, and his body left exposed, the head displayed on a lance, the bloodstained blade and execution block left by its side. Ramiro, aged about fifty, a stocky taciturn Spaniard with a black beard and a habit of standing with his right hand stuck aggressively into his belt, was unpopular in the Romagna for his ruthless severity, but nonetheless he had been a faithful follower of Cesare's since his student days, and Machiavelli was at a loss to explain his dramatic downfall. 'The reason of his death is not known,' he wrote, 'if not that thus it pleased the Prince, who shows that he knows how to make and unmake men at his will, according to their merits.'

This somewhat feeble explanation cannot account for Cesare's decision to dispense with a competent and trusted official in such a melodramatic fashion. It seems more likely that as far as Cesare was concerned not only was Ramiro's usefulness to him suspect, but his loyalty as well. As early as September he had deprived Ramiro of the civil government, and his official explanation for de Lorqua's disgrace, issued on 23 November, was that the governor was guilty of grave corruption, extortion and rapine in the administration of justice, and also of trafficking in grain. This alone would have been enough to justify Cesare's making a public example of him, but there were rumours that his disgrace was due to other, more secret reasons. On the eve of his execution, the Bolognese chancellor Fileno Tuate wrote that Ramiro had been arrested, it was rumoured, because he had plotted with Messer Giovanni Bentivoglio, the Orsinis and Vitellozzo against the Duke. But of this intrigue Cesare, for the time being, breathed not a word.

For Cesare knew that the time had come for the final round in the contest with his condottieri, and it was vital to the success of his plans that that knowledge should be concealed from them. The stage for the last scene in the drama was already set: it was Sinigallia, a small town on the Adriatic coast fifteen miles south of Fano, which the condottieri had agreed to take in Cesare's name and where they were all encamped with the exception of Gian Paolo Baglioni, who had prudently retired to Perugia. Cesare guessed that the condottieri thought him greatly weakened by the departure of the French contingents, also that they were unaware of the present strength of his forces. He intended that they should remain in confident ignorance; before leaving Cesena he ordered his commanders to proceed southward with small bodies of troops by different routes, while he himself with his personal staff of men at arms set off on 26 December, marching south down the Via Emilia. On the same day Oliverotto da Fermo entered Sinigallia in Cesare's name. Guidobaldo's sister, Giovanna della Rovere, who ruled Sinigallia as regent for her twelve-year-old son Francesco Maria, had already fled, leaving the citadel in charge of the Genoese Andrea Doria.

At Pesaro, which he reached on the 28th, Cesare received the news of the surrender of the town, with the seemingly innocent message that the castellan, Doria, would only hand over the citadel to the Duke in person. From Fano, where he arrived on the 29th, Cesare sent word on the 30th that the next day he would join the condottieri at Sinigallia, and required them to withdraw all their troops from the town to quarters several miles away, leaving only Oliverotto's garrison in Sinigallia, so that he should have room to billet his own men. He also ordered all the gates of the town to be locked, except the one through which he intended to enter. His scattered troops were commanded to rendezvous with him the next morning at the Metaurus river a few miles to the south of Fano. Only then, on the eve of his arrival at Sinigallia, did he reveal his plans to a few trusted henchmen, the indispensable Michelotto among them – plans which depended on a detailed knowledge of the layout of the town. Only then did he let his father into the secret. Alexander, who had been gloomy and fretful over Christmas, suddenly regained his spirits on 30 December, talked of setting up courier staging posts for Sinigallia, and, with ominous cordiality, invited Cardinal Orsini to a private supper party with women and gambling. On the 31st he chatted gaily of Cesare's arrival in time for Carnival; nobody, he said fondly, knew how to celebrate Carnival without him: 'He will do a thousand follies and throw away several thousands of ducats ...'

At dawn on the same day Cesare rode out of Fano down the Via Emilia. It was noticed that he wore full armour, although no fighting was expected. In the cold light of the winter afternoon on that last day of the year 1502, Cesare, surrounded by his armed men, approached Sinigallia with the long sad Adriatic shore to his left and the bare grey hills to his right. His army in their colourful livery of red and yellow, with the polished armour of the men-at-arms and the pikes of the Swiss glittering in the winter sun, made a rare spectacle according to one observer, but it must have been an unpleasant surprise for the condottieri who straggled out to meet him three miles from the town. The Orsinis were the first to come up with him, then Vitellozzo, who had been hanging back, gloomy and apprehensive on his mule. Not seeing Oliverotto, who had remained with his troops in the Borgo, or new town, before Sinigallia, Cesare made a sign to Michelotto, who rode off to fetch him. Cesare received his captains with the utmost cordiality, touching them on the hand in the French manner before embracing them, and having been joined by Oliverotto he rode towards Sinigallia conversing easily with them. A single wooden bridge led across the River Misa to the square of the Borgo before the gate by which Cesare intended to enter the town. His advance guard of heavy cavalry crossed it then divided and wheeled to face each other, forming two lines guarding the bridge through which the rest of the army would pass, and effectively cutting communication between Oliverotto's troops in the town and Vitellozzo's men in the country to the south and east. The infantry, a thousand Swiss and Gascons, marched through into Sinigallia, followed by Cesare and his staff with the condottieri. Behind them, the gate was quietly shut. The only troops in the inner town, apart from Oliverotto's escort, were Cesare's own infantry.

The condottieri, by now extremely nervous and apprehensive, rode as if mesmerized with Cesare to a house which Michelotto had already picked out for him. Here, before dismounting, they made an attempt to take their leave, but Cesare told them he wished them all to come to his room, to consult with him what action should be taken on the morrow and afterwards when this undertaking was finished. Somewhat reassured by the friendliness of his manner, and seeing that they had no alternative, surrounded as they were by his armed men, the captains dismounted and followed him. Accounts vary as to the exact sequence of events which then took place. According to one, they dismounted and went into an inner courtyard, where Cesare began to mount a small stair, and when he was half-way up made a sign with his eyes upon which the soldiers seized the condottieri. 'Paolo Orsini turned towards the Duke calling out to him in a high voice and asking the grace of being able to talk to him before he mounted the stair, but he turned his back and went to the chamber arranged for him.' A Florentine account reported that they had seated themselves in a room with Cesare who, 'having remained a while with them, said that for necessities of nature he must withdraw but would soon return. Hardly had he left the room, than there entered the men deputed for the work, who bound their hands behind their backs and took them prisoner.'

Machiavelli, arriving from Fano as evening fell, found the town in an uproar; the excited Borgia soldiery, out of control, were plundering and killing every citizen presumed to be a partisan of Oliverotto or the della Roveres. Somehow, he contrived to send off a courier to Florence with the news of the condottieri's arrest, adding: 'In my judgement, they will not be alive tomorrow morning.' As far as Oliverotto and Vitellozzo were concerned he was right: at two o'clock on the morning of New Year's Day, 1 January 1503, they were garrotted at Michelotto's orders, seated back to back on a bench. According to Machiavelli, 'They both behaved in a manner unworthy of their past life; for Vitellozzo implored that they ask the Pope to give his sins plenary indulgence; and Oliverotto blamed all the injuries done the Duke on Vitellozzo.' As for the three Orsinis, Paolo, Francesco and Roberto, in Cesare's words, 'we are taking them as prisoners to a similar end.' Cesare himself, riding out in full armour to restrain his troops from sacking the town, caught sight of Machiavelli, and in a few words put the whole Sinigallia affair in its logical perspective. 'This,' he told him, 'is what I wanted to tell the Bishop of Volterra, when he came to Urbino, but I never trusted the secret to anyone, thus, the occasion having come to me, I have known very well how to use it ...'

On the very night of his arrest of the condottieri, Cesare sat down to write the first of a series of letters giving his version of the affair to the world. In a letter to the Doge Leonardo Loredano, which must have given him a good deal of malicious satisfaction since he knew Venice to be secretly in sympathy with his enemies, he recalled their first rebellion against him, and their reconciliation, after which, he said, they planned a second betrayal of him:

> Believing that, by the departure of the French troops who returned to Lombardy, they would be able to effect their former designs, there joined me in my undertaking of Sinigallia, the Duke of Gravina, Paolo Orsini, Vitellozzo da Castello and Liverotto da Fermo, with all their forces, and under the colour and pretence of aid, [they] had plotted against me that in which I, having foreseen and discovered [it], forestalled them and made them prisoner, to put an end to their infinite perfidity and malignity.

The condottieri, it appears, had plotted with the castellan of the citadel, Andrea Doria, who as a della Rovere partisan was naturally hostile to Cesare, to trap him in the inner city and fall upon him on the night of his arrival. The message which Cesare had received from them at Pesaro on the 28th, concerning the castellan's refusal to surrender, was intended to ensure that he came to Sinigallia in person.

Alexander, in a conversation with the Venetian ambassador in Rome, led the trail back from Sinigallia to the execution of Ramiro de Lorqua:

> He began by saying that, being already sentenced to death, Ramiro said that he wished to make the Duke understand something for his own ease, and told them how, having plotted with the Orsinis to give them Cesena, which did not come to pass by reason of the accord between His Excellency and the Orsinis, Vitellozzo had resolved to kill the Duke, and Oliverotto da Fermo was party to this (he mentioned no other names); and, seeing no other way to carry out this intent he had planned with a crossbowman, that when the Duke was riding, he should kill him ...

He went on to say that Vitellozzo, under examination at Sinigallia, had admitted that Ramiro's confession was the truth, and confirmed that Oliverotto was with him in the plot. Giustinian thought that

Alexander was lying, but his version of the plot and Ramiro's treachery was given wide credence, and appears in the account of the chronicler of Cesena, Fantaguzzi. It is feasible that Ramiro, burning with resentment at his demotion in September and aware of Cesare's discontent with his administration, knowing his master as he did, might have plotted against him with Vitellozzo to save himself from inevitable retribution. Cesare's knowledge that Vitellozzo and Oliverotto intended to have him murdered may account for his summary execution of them; the seizure of the Orsinis was part of the overall Borgia plan for their destruction, which Alexander immediately followed up with the arrest of Cardinal Orsini in Rome on 3 January.

Throughout Italy Cesare's trapping of his condottieri was regarded not only as a justifiable punishment for their treachery but as a masterstroke, a supreme example of intelligence and subtlety. Machiavelli called it 'an admirable deed', while Louis of France is reported to have exclaimed that it was 'an act worthy of a Roman hero'. Even Paolo Giovio, a historian bitterly hostile to the Borgias, described Sinigallia as 'a most beautiful deception'. Everyone, even the Venetians with bitterness at heart, hastened to congratulate Cesare on his great coup. Isabella d'Este sent him a hundred carnival masks, 'because we believe that after the strains and fatigues which you have undergone in these your glorious undertakings, you should also find time to amuse yourself ...' Isabella's timely gift reached Cesare when he was already far away from Sinigallia on the road to Rome. Her envoy found him in light-hearted mood: 'He insisted on examining them one by one with his own hand, saying how fine they were, and how much they resembled many people he knew ...'

For Cesare, the elimination of the condottieri was but a necessary step along the road he had planned for himself. Even before the cords of the garrotte had choked the life out of Vitellozzo and Oliverotto, he was making political capital out of their downfall, and preparing to reap the material gains of his success. Cesare was an expert at propaganda; in his letters to the governments of various cities he had represented himself as a public benefactor, in that he had liberated them from these 'public pests ... that swarm of troublesome insects who were ruining Italy'. In an interview with Machiavelli on the evening of the 31st, 'his face lit up with delight, he bade me rejoice at the happy event', and urged the envoy to represent to his government how they too should rejoice at the defeat of her bitterest foes, 'men indeed, who were ... enemies of order and peace throughout Italy'. Two days later he returned to the theme he had introduced at Urbino in June, that his purpose was not to play the tyrant, but to extinguish tyrants. It was in this guise, as the enemy of tyrants, that Cesare, in the name of the Church, proposed to continue his campaign and reap the benefits of the coup at Sinigallia by annexing Fermo, Città di Castello, Perugia and, if possible, Siena.

Cesare was a man in a hurry, and had no time to waste. By noon on 1 January, having received the surrender of the citadel, he had left Sinigallia with all his army 'in the worst weather imaginable in which to make war', and was on the road to Perugia. By the 5th, he was at Gualdo Tadino on the Via Flaminia, where he received news of the submission of Città di Castello – Fermo had capitulated on hearing of Oliverotto's death – and a deputation from Perugia, offering him the city, from which Gian Paolo had already fled. On the 7th he was at Assisi, where he informed the Sienese envoys that they must exile Pandolfo Petrucci and return their city to the lordship of the Church. Cesare was determined to catch Pandolfo, whom he regarded as the brains of the conspiracy against him. He told Machiavelli during a long interview at Torgiano on the 10th: 'Knowing his brains, the money he can get, and the place where he is, he would be, as long as he was in power, a spark from which one would fear great conflagrations ... I want to have him in my hands, and for this the Pope plans to sedate him with Briefs ... meanwhile I move forward with the army: and it is well to deceive those men, who have been masters of deception.' In the case of Siena, as with the other cities, Cesare was careful to stress that he did not want them for himself, but only, in his role as Captain General of the papal army, to rid them of the 'tyrants' and return them to obedience to the Church. Nonetheless Pandolfo proved a harder nut to crack than his fellow conspirators. He was a cunning, tough, self-made man who had forged his way to power through the ruthless use of brains, money, and the elimination of competitors, including his own father-in-law. He had a strong hold on Siena, where his rule was popular, and it was only after a ferocious ultimatum from Cesare on 27 January that Pandolfo, weeping, and accompanied by Gian Paolo Baglioni who had taken refuge there, finally left the city.

The expulsion of Pandolfo was the last in the train of successes that followed Sinigallia. Cesare, always sensitive to political atmosphere, discerned warning signs that the time had come to halt his triumphant progress, or rather to postpone it until the way was again clear. For, as he told Machiavelli at Torgiano on 10 January, he knew that Louis, who was 'the master of the shop' in Tuscany, would not let him have Siena for himself. The pious claim that he sought the lordship of these cities not for himself but for the Church had not deceived Louis, who sent messages to Alexander ordering him to restrain his son. Moreover Alexander, nervous at the outcome of the Siena enterprise, and intent on pursuing his vendetta against the Orsinis, repeatedly and angrily ordered him to return to Rome, orders which Cesare up till now had deliberately ignored.

At Rome Alexander complained passionately in public about his son's disobedience. On 22 January he declared: 'We have done everything in our power to make him give up the enterprise of Siena ... nonetheless he is absolutely resolved to disregard us ... we promise you, that since we have sat in this chair, we have never heard of anything which causes us greater displeasure. And nonetheless we must have patience: he wills it thus, and it seems to him that he can do to us with impunity that which he is doing.' Indeed never had the divergence between Cesare and his father been so apparent. Cesare was by now, Machiavelli was convinced, determined to make himself ruler of Tuscany, and he was unwilling to leave the area until he had pressed his luck as far as it would go, and assured himself of his most dangerous enemy there, Pandolfo. Moreover, although he had Paolo Orsini and the Duke of Gravina strangled in the castle of Sarteano on 18 January, that was for him the final act in the tragedy of Sinigallia. He was not interested in the execution of his father's vendetta. While Alexander, with the temporal interests of the Papacy at heart, saw the final destruction of the remaining Roman barons not only as an act of personal revenge for Juan's death but as essential to his pontifical authority, Cesare was obsessed by his own ambitions and his own career. As always he looked to the future, not the past; the events of that long-dead Roman summer of 1497 no longer aroused any emotion in him. He had been jealous rather than fond of Juan, the favourite son, whose death had brought him all the advantages he now enjoyed. Interested as he was only in himself, his vendettas were reserved for men who had injured him personally or might do so in the future. The remainder of the Orsini clan had not threatened him personally, and moreover, as Machiavelli had remarked perspicaciously the previous November: 'When the Pope dies, he will still need to have some friends in Rome.'

And so it was only at the end of January, when it became clear that his home base in Rome was being seriously menaced by the Orsinis, who attacked the Ponte Nomentana on the 21st, that he reluctantly turned southward, giving his troops free rein to plunder and burn Sienese territory as a warning to anyone who might defy him. Even then, he did not hurry to obey his father; the mere news of his approach was enough to send the Orsinis scurrying back to their castles, which they put in a state of defence. He lingered for ten days at Viterbo, reorganizing his forces and attempting to win over the Savellis and some of the Colonnas, while Alexander bombarded him with angry letters and even sent him a brief threatening him with excommunication if he did not attack and destroy all the Orsinis. He was furious at Cesare's negotiations with the Savellis, which, he told Giustinian, had been done without consulting him, 'because these men were traitors and enemies, and could never be trusted ... and he said that the enmities against all these houses have gone so far that one must see the end of them, and remove all cause for fear.'

The real bone of contention between them was Cesare's stubborn refusal to obey his father's order to attack Bracciano, stronghold of Giangiordano Orsini. The eccentric Giangiordano, who was contemptuously described by the rest of his clan as a 'public madman', had refused to take part in the original conspiracy against Cesare at Todi in September. He, like Cesare, was a knight of the Order of St Michael, whose rules forbade its members to bear arms against each other. In Cesare's complex nature, the concept of honour as an intrinsic part of a man's personal pride and public reputation was of immense importance; even the hostile Paolo Giovio wrote of him that 'he regarded his public honour more than his private interest'. Alexander sneered at this exhibition of chivalry, and announced his intention of carrying out the attack without Cesare if necessary, but his bold words were empty ones – Cesare had the upper hand, and Alexander knew it. The papal army was under Cesare's command, and the Pope could rely on no one else to carry out the campaign. In the face of his son's determined independence Alexander was forced to give in and be content with the siege of another Orsini stronghold, Ceri, defended by Giulio Orsini.

Even then, Cesare initially did not seem to be taking the siege of Ceri very seriously. On 25 February he returned to Rome in time for Carnival, and appeared to be spending the following three weeks occupied with his private pleasures. Giustinian reported that he was never seen without a mask, although he was perfectly recognizable, and grumbled that his caprices were unintelligible: 'Every day he goes hunting, although he does not let himself be seen in the city ...' He spent a brief two days at the siege in mid-March with a team of engineers, while in Rome Alexander anxiously observed the preparation of a huge machine held to be capable of carrying 300 men up to the ramparts, and it was only at the end of the month that he returned to Ceri to direct a prolonged bombardment which resulted in its surrender on 5 April. Palombara, Vicovaro, Cerveteri and the other Orsini castles, with the exception of Bracciano, gave themselves up to Cesare at the same time. On 11 April, through the medium of the French ambassador, a truce was signed between the Borgias and the Orsinis.

But Alexander, despite his public rejoicing at the surrender of Ceri, whose siege, he told the Venetian ambassador, had cost him 40,000 ducats, was far from satisfied with the outcome of his vendetta against the Orsinis. Louis' influence, which he blamed, probably rightly, for Cesare's half-heartedness in the affair, had saved the Orsinis from total destruction. Although their power in the Roman Campagna had been shattered and their estates surrendered, many of the leaders remained unharmed. Cardinal Orsini had died in Castel Sant'Angelo on 22 February, amid strong rumours that Alexander had had him poisoned; Paolo and Francesco Orsini had been strangled on Cesare's orders at Sarteano; but Giangiordano, Giulio, Niccolò of Pitigliano and the others remained very much alive to form a potentially dangerous threat for the future. Alexander spoke very bitterly of Louis in public; Cesare, as usual, held his tongue. 'The Duke shows more reserve than his father,' Giustinian commented. But in private, there is little doubt that he was now in agreement with Alexander. Louis, the man who had helped him win the Romagna, was now the main obstacle to his plans.

XIII

SON OF FORTUNE

'ASTROLOGERS and necromancers called him the Son of Fortune,' the chronicler Matarazzo wrote of Cesare in the summer of 1503. And indeed it seemed to Cesare himself that he was riding the crest of an irresistible wave which would lead him to even greater goals than those which he had already attained. As the year opened Machiavelli had noted his exalted state of mind. 'Duke Valentino', he wrote, 'exhibits a fortune unheard of, a courage and confidence more than human, believing himself capable of accomplishing whatever he undertakes.' While others preferred to attribute his astonishing success to good luck rather than his own abilities, Cesare knew that the seeming ease with which his coups had been achieved was due to intelligent planning, careful preparation, and an instinctive grasp of the realities of politics which enabled him to foresee events and adopt his plans to changing circumstances, so that, in his own words, when the occasion came he knew how to use it well.

During the spring and early summer of 1503, the political outlook in Italy was being transformed by the outcome of the conflict between France and Spain in Naples, where Spain was emerging as the dominant power. Through the autumn and winter of 1502, things had been going badly for Spain in the Kingdom, but early in 1503 Ferdinand's determination to win showed itself in massive reinforcements for his gifted commander, Gonsalvo de Cordoba, who thus felt himself strong enough to take the offensive. On 21 April, d'Aubigny was routed and captured at Seminara, and a week later Gonsalvo won a crucial victory over Nemours at Cerignola. The result of these victories was to lock up the French in isolated units in difficult country, while Gonsalvo reaped the benefit of carefully prepared negotiations with anti-French partisans throughout the Kingdom. Encouraged by his successes, sixty fortified towns offered themselves to him, followed by the key cities of Capua and Aversa. On 13 May he entered Naples, and by the end of the month only the two Neapolitan castles, dell'Uovo and Castel Nuovo, and Gaeta on the coast, held out for Louis. As the star of Spain rose and that of France rapidly dwindled, Alexander became ever more openly pro-Spanish in his public pronouncements. On 23 June he told the Bolognese envoy that if the French would do nothing to help themselves in the Kingdom, 'if they stand looking and want us to make war for them, we are resolved not to lose what we have acquired,' adding piously: 'because we see that it is the divine will that the Spaniards have been victorious; and if God wills it thus, we must not wish it otherwise.'

Cesare, more cautious than his father, made no public commitments. Officially he was in a delicate position, bound as he was by his promise of the previous August to assist Louis in person, should he make an attempt to reinforce the French in Naples. Privately, however, he also regarded the Spanish successes as providential from his own point of view. As Machiavelli was to write of him later in *The Prince*:

> When the Duke had become very powerful and in part secure against present perils, since he was armed as he wished and had in part destroyed those forces that, as neighbours, could harm him, he still, if he intended to continue his course, had before him the problem of the King of France, because he knew that the King, who too late had become aware of his mistake, would not tolerate further conquest. For this reason the Duke was looking for new alliances and wavering in his dealings with France ...

It had become obvious to Cesare that wherever he turned, and whatever new project he attempted, the hand of the King of France, 'the master of the shop' as he had put it to Machiavelli, was the limiting factor. Louis' power alone had prevented him from taking Siena for himself; Louis' protection had enabled Florence to resist his pressure for an alliance and a condotta. France stood between himself and Tuscany, the prize on which he had set his mind. That very spring he had had concrete evidence that France was actively working against him. Too late, as Machiavelli said, Louis had realized that in encouraging il Valentino he had sown dragon's teeth which were now springing up as armed men to harm his interests. During March he had unsuccessfully attempted to repair the situation and cut Cesare down to size by encouraging a league of the Tuscan cities. The only outcome of this intrigue was the return of Pandolfo Petrucci to Siena on 29 March, which was nonetheless a serious blow to Cesare's interests in the area. If Cesare wanted Tuscany, he would have to abandon Louis, and by midsummer there were strong rumours of an understanding by which Cesare would attack Tuscany in league with the victorious Spaniards once they had taken Gaeta.

This drastic reorientation of alliances involved considerable danger for Cesare, but he had never been the man to be daunted by the risk if the prize was big enough. Gaining Tuscany could mean endangering the Romagna; Louis was still the dominant power in northern Italy, where the French forces in Lombardy were well placed to carry out reprisals against Cesare's Romagnol states. Moreover, fear of France was the one restraint on Venice, 'the bold winged Lion of St Mark', as Ariosto called her. Having made her peace with the Turks, Venice was no longer dependent on the Pope for help, and the lion was once more flexing its gilded claws landward in the direction of the Romagna. Cesare had hoped for an alliance with Florence to counteract Venice, but the Florentines had been consistently cool to his approaches. In any case, should he abandon Louis and attack Tuscany, their friendship would be out of the question. Cesare had no illusions as to Venetian hostility towards himself and his states: he had envisaged the possibility that Venice would openly join the condottieri the previous autumn, and although she had not dared publicly to show her support, there had been no doubt of her secret sympathy for the rebel captains. It was probably a Venetian agent who had warned Gian Paolo Baglioni to have no part in the Sinigallia enterprise, and while dispatching official congratulations to Cesare on the success of his coup, a secret letter from the Senate to a Baglioni partisan showed their true attitude. 'Truly,' it ran, 'we have always loved all of the houses of Orsini and Baglioni and all the others of those lords . . .' And Venice gave political asylum to Cesare's enemies, including Guidobaldo da Montefeltro, whom he had succeeded in dislodging from Mantua through pressure on the Gonzagas. In February they had encouraged the two remaining Varano sons to attempt a return to Camerino, but the young men were caught at Rimini and strangled by a nephew of Michelotto's at Cattolica. Recently, during the Orsini war, they had sent Giambattista Caracciolo and Bartolomeo d'Alviano, both Cesare's sworn personal enemies, to the borders of Romagna.

Nonetheless, Alexander and Cesare hoped that political logic would bring the Venetians round. Through the winter of 1502, while Cesare was occupied with the condottieri, Alexander had pressured Venice for an alliance with himself and Cesare. As he constantly pointed out to them, such an alliance would form an Italian bloc strong enough to maintain the independence of Italy between the aggressive intentions of the two rival foreign powers, France and Spain. Alexander was right, but paradoxically the fear which he and his son inspired drove the Italians to mortgage their own freedom to the foreign powers. As the Cardinal of Siena, Piccolomini, told Giustinian bitterly one day that summer: 'The bankrupts of Italy find themselves constrained to help either France, as the majority do, or Spain, in order not to be prey to the wolf ...' The great Venetian Republic could hardly be included among the 'bankrupts of Italy', but the same distrust of the Borgias, and of Cesare in particular, and her greed for his territories, blinded her to her real long-term interests – a lesson which she finally learned six years later on the field of Agnadello, defeated by the army of the League of Cambrai. Early in the spring Alexander proposed an alliance between Venice, the Papacy and Spain, but the Venetians still refused to be tempted. On 26 March, Cesare attempted to exert his charm on Giustinian, who had hitherto succeeded in dodging his invitations to an interview for fear, as he wrote, of the 'blandishments of the *marrano* duke'. It was to no avail; the Venetian attitude to the Borgias was mirrored in the dispatches of their Roman envoy, full of a patrician contempt for these men whom he regarded as dangerous upstarts, to be destroyed at all costs.

Despite the hostile stance of Venice, the risks as far as Cesare was concerned were diminished by his conviction that the Romagna would remain loyal to him as it had during his time of trouble the previous autumn. His government there was strong and popular, and after the punishment of Ramiro de Lorqua there had been no further complaints of corruption or extortion. The cities were no longer plagued by the factionalism that had been rife under their former lords, or the petty ward politics backed up by thuggery which had characterized Perugia under the Baglionis, where even their partisan Matarazzo admitted that their departure had ushered in a period of most unwonted peace and justice. Indeed, Cesare, probably because he was a strong overall power aloof from local politics, had no trouble with the *grandi*, the leading local families. Civil government was largely in the hands of local officials appointed by him; military control was the responsibility of four Spanish commissioners on whose loyalty he could count absolutely. While civil government remained essentially local in character, with the communes enjoying their ancient privileges and systems of taxation and exemption, Cesare took one step towards administrative unity for his state by the institution of a supreme court of appeal, the Rota, modelled on the Vatican court. The Romagnol Rota, presided over by a man of character and ability, Antonio da Monte, sat in the seven principal cities – Fano, Pesaro, Rimini, Cesena, Faenza, Forlì and Imola – its seven auditors or judges were nominated by the seven cities and approved by Cesare, and its expenses paid by a levy of 200 ducats per annum on each judicial circuit, the only known instance of a common impost levied uniformly on the Romagna. The revolt of the condottieri had postponed the setting up of the court, but the situation was now peaceful enough for its inauguration, amid great festivities, at Cesena on 24 June. The one seemingly justified accusation levelled against Cesare in the Romagna by Machiavelli and other observers was that he tended to favour the troops over the civilian population, and allowed his soldiers too much licence. Otherwise even hostile contemporaries such as Guicciardini admitted that Cesare's government of the Romagna was a point in his favour, and attributed the cities' continuing loyalty to him to the fact that 'he had placed in the government of those peoples, men who had governed them with so great justice and integrity, that he was greatly loved by them'.

Confident in the possession of the Romagna, and with his mind on new horizons of power, Cesare went ahead with his plans in order to be ready when the moment came. The most pressing need was to raise money, both to recoup the heavy expenses of the previous winter and the Orsini war, and to maintain his present forces while recruiting new troops. It has been estimated that Cesare's army cost him over a thousand ducats a day, and while Alexander was an excellent money manager, and spent less on his household than either his predecessors or successors, the ordinary papal revenue from the Camera Apostolica could not cover the huge sums involved in military expenditure, and it was obvious that, as before, extraordinary measures would have to be resorted to. Alexander's cupidity was ridiculed by his contemporaries, who sneered at the shameless avidity with which he seized the possessions of cardinals who died intestate, forbade them to make wills so that their wealth should fall into his hands, ransacked the house of the disgraced Ascanio Sforza, and sold cardinal's hats for exorbitant sums. But to Alexander money meant power, and his son's extravagance and taste for luxury constantly pained him – money was to be spent not on costly and useless objects, but on gunpowder, cannon and troops, the sinews of Cesare's career.

Every possible means was employed to raise funds. As the Venetian envoy remarked, Alexander showed the world that the income of a Pope could be just what he wanted it to be. On 29 March in secret consistory eighty new official posts were created, to be sold to candidates at 760 ducats apiece. Alexander, although a Spaniard, had hitherto shown remarkable tolerance towards the Jews, but now, in time of necessity, he too resorted to the time-honoured practice of religious blackmail. Edicts were promulgated against Jews to raise money in fines and confiscations; armed Borgia troops, it was alleged, forced entrance into citizens' houses and arrested them on the pretext that they were *marrani*, secret Jews. In the urgency of their need, the Borgias did not hesitate to resort to the use of poison, probably the famous *cantarella*, or white arsenic, for which they have become notorious down the ages. In fact, the use of poison, as Guicciardini pointed out, was an Italian custom, and Cesare's normal method of disposing of his enemies was the Spanish garrotte. Contemporaries accused the Borgias of wholesale poisoning of wealthy cardinals for their money, among them Cardinals Orsini, Ferrari of Modena, d'Almeida of Ceuta, and Juan Borgia of Monreale; but Italians were prone to suspect poisoning in the deaths of prominent people, and the number of cardinals who died during Alexander's long reign did not proportionately exceed the average deaths under previous pontificates. In only one case, that of the Venetian Cardinal Michiel, can deliberate poisoning be held to have been established beyond reasonable doubt.

Cardinal Giovanni Michiel, nephew of Pope Paul II, Bishop of Porto and Patriarch of Constantinople, died during the night of 10 April after three days of violent vomiting. On the morning of 11 April, a few hours after his death, his nephew, Don Angelo Michiel, told Giustinian: 'Two days ago there came upon him a distemper of the stomach with great vomiting; and some diarrhoea; there is considerable suspicion that he may have been poisoned, and obvious conjectures are not lacking.' As to the 'obvious conjectures' he went on to say that 'as soon as the Pope heard of his death, he sent the governor to the house, and before it was day, it was completely plundered. The death of this Cardinal gives him more than 150,000 ducats.' The late

Cardinal's secretary estimated Alexander's loot at 50,000–60,000 ducats in cash, with the remainder in silver, tapestries, horses, cattle and grain.

What may well have been the true story emerged almost a year later when on 6 March 1504 sentence was pronounced against the late Cardinal's major-domo, Asquino de Colloredo, on the charge of having poisoned his master. Asquino's story, according to the process against him, was that in March of the previous year he had been approached in the Vatican by a certain nobleman whose name he did not disclose with the suggestion that he poison the Cardinal. In April the same man had given him a sweet white powder enclosed in paper to be mixed with the Cardinal's food or drink. Asquino gave the powder to Michiel's French cook, Désiré, who added it to his master's food for the first time on 7 April, when he was seized with pains and vomiting, and then again the following Friday, when he again vomited, lost consciousness and died three days later. At his public degradation in the piazza of St Peter's, Asquino repeatedly cried out, according to Burchard, 'that that violent deed had been commanded of him by Pope Alexander, and that the true delinquent was Duke Valentino ...' Asquino's evidence was suspect on two grounds: first, the dates he gave did not agree with Angelo Michiel's account of his uncle's death, and secondly his examination was part of a general campaign at that time to discredit Cesare. Nonetheless the circumstantial evidence against him is damning: the Cardinal's illness showed every symptom of poisoning, and Cesare's campaign chest profited by his death to the tune of 150,000 ducats.

Once again Cesare had recourse to the Sacred College as a source of funds. On 31 May the nomination of nine new cardinals was announced. Giustinian reported on the same day:

> Five of these are Spaniards, Giovanni Castelar of Valencia, Francesco Remolino, Francesco Sprats, Jacopo Casanova and Francesco Lloris; three are Italians: the Count of Lavagna, Francesco Soderini and Adriano da Corneto; one is German, Melchior Copis von Meckau, Bishop of Brixen. Most of them are men of doubtful reputation; all have paid handsomely for their elevation, some 20,000 ducats and more, so that from 120,000 to 130,000 ducats have been collected ...

Giustinian was justified in his aspersions on the qualities of the new cardinals. Of the nine, only Adriano Castellesi, called da Corneto, was an outstanding churchman; he was a classical scholar, a man of upright life, who had been papal Nuncio to Henry VII of England, from whom he had received the see of Hereford and other benefices. But his chief advantage in Cesare's eyes was that as secretary to the Pope he was a Borgia dependant, a quality which he shared with all the Spanish nominees: Francisco Remolines was an intimate of Cesare's, Casanova was confidential chamberlain to the Pope, and Castelar also a papal familiar, while Sprats and Lloriz were family connections. Soderini, Bishop of Volterra, was known personally to Cesare from the time of his mission at Urbino in June 1502, and he probably hoped to have in him a friend well placed in Florentine circles, since the Bishop was brother to the Gonfalonier of Florence, Piero Soderini. As before, the nominations and the scale of contributions were all made by Cesare, who again entertained the new cardinals to dinner after their investiture. And indeed, beyond the obvious financial profit, the nominations could have been said to have been made entirely in his interest. The fact that six out of the nine new cardinals were committed Borgia partisans reflects his constant preoccupation with his future after his father's death. If he aimed, in his role as Gonfalonier, to exercise some form of permanent control over the Papacy, as seems probable, then a reliable block vote in the election of his father's successor would be vital to him. The nationalities of the nominees revealed the changing pattern of Borgia alliances: the lone German, the Bishop of Brixen, was included to please the Emperor Maximilian with whom Alexander was negotiating for the investiture of Pisa for Cesare; above all five of the nine were Spaniards, and there was not one Frenchman.

Ten days before the announcement of the new nominations, official Rome was startled by the news of the sudden and mysterious flight of one of the Borgia inner circle, Francesco Troches of Avila, the Pope's secret *cubiculario*, a man hitherto entrusted by Alexander and Cesare with their most secret and delicate diplomatic missions. The story of the Troches affair is extremely revealing of the methods used by Cesare in dealing with men who had become dangerous or even no longer useful to him, the subtle, careful pleasure which he took in devising a trap for his victim, and the ruthlessness with which he eliminated him when he had fallen into it. Troches left Rome on 18 May. On the 19th he was at Siena, delivering the strange message to Pandolfo Petrucci that neither Cesare nor Alexander intended to undertake anything in regard to Pisa, which a puzzled Pandolfo retailed to Florence on the 21st, adding that Troches had left for Rome again on the 19th. On the same day that Troches was conferring with Pandolfo, apparently on Cesare's behalf, Cesare himself was issuing letters from Rome ordering his arrest, and stating that he had left without permission for an unknown destination. Somewhere on the road back to Rome two days after he had left Siena, Troches got wind of the danger threatening him and was panicked into precipitate flight, as indeed it was intended that he should be. Reaching Civita Vecchia on the 22nd, he fled by sea to Genoa pursued by papal briefs ordering his detention, and from thence via Sardinia to Corsica, where he was caught and brought back to Ostia on a papal galley. Reaching Ostia on the night of 8 June, he was escorted to Rome by Michelotto, who placed him under heavy guard on a boat moored on the Trastevere bank. A few hours later Cesare arrived to interview the prisoner, then, according to the Ferrarese envoy Costabili: 'His Excellency placing himself in a spot where he could see and not be seen, Troches was strangled by the hand of Don Michele.' Alexander admitted that Troches was dead, but at first said vaguely that he had been thrown into the river at Ostia and drowned, but later, again according to Costabili, he told Cardinal Sanseverino 'the truth of the matter, saying that the Duke had had him killed, by that tower, in the boat, and that His Holiness has had no part in it'.

As the curious envoys struggled to find an explanation for yet another of Cesare's mysterious executions of a formerly trusted henchman, Cesare as usual said nothing and left the talking to his father. Some attributed Troches' death to his bitter disappointment at being left out of the nominations for the cardinalate, which had led him into wild talk against Cesare. Costabili wrote to Ercole d'Este on 11 June: 'I understand that later he complained even more to the Pope of the Lord Duke. And that His Holiness told him he was a madman to speak like that, and that if the Duke came to hear what he was saying, he would have him killed. And it was through the words of His Beatitude that, terrified, in the morning he took flight.' However, the most plausible explanation for Cesare's punishment of Troches was held to be that he had revealed to Louis the extent of Cesare's negotiations with Spain, which undoubtedly gathered momentum as the failure of the French in the Kingdom became apparent after Gonsalvo's entry into Naples on 13 May. Ludovico della Mirandola, one of Cesare's captains, wrote to Francesco Gonzaga that one of Louis' *valets de chambre*, sent by the King to discover the Pope's intentions, had shown

Alexander a letter written by Troches warning Louis 'to have a good care for his own affairs; since His Holiness the Pope was allied to the Most Serene King of Spain, at which the Pope appeared like a dead man'. Yet Louis had been informed by the Venetians as early as 4 April of the Pope's attempts to make an alliance with themselves and Spain. Whether Troches played the informer or not, Cesare probably suspected him of treachery, since for the past few months he had not employed him on important missions. Troches was known to be pro-French, and as such was not only expendable but, with his intimate knowledge of Cesare's affairs, positively dangerous. The elaborate plan to frame Troches was probably intended to convince the Pope and everybody else of his treachery, and to justify his subsequent elimination. The ruthless manner of his death was a deliberate act of terror on Cesare's part, intended as a warning to possible traitors, following the pattern of his action in the murder of Bisceglie and the execution of Ramiro de Lorqua.

As if to underline his message, Cesare had Jacopo di Santa Croce, a leading Roman nobleman generally regarded as a Borgia familiar, executed at dawn on the same day, and his body exposed on the bridge of Sant'Angelo. Santa Croce had been suspected of acting as the Borgias' instrument in the arrest of Cardinal Orsini, but appears to have changed sides during the Orsini war and to have urged Giangiordano to join the others against Cesare. He had been arrested, released on payment of a large sum a week before his death, then suddenly rearrested. No reason was given for his punishment, and the mysterious execution of the two men on the same day sent a shiver of terror through Rome. Giustinian commented maliciously and inaccurately: 'Now they are without those servants who used to execute their affairs. The Duke is left with Remolines and Don Michelotto, who await the same end shortly.'

By midsummer things were going splendidly for Cesare. In Naples the two castles had fallen to the Spaniards and Gonsalvo de Cordoba had moved in person to besiege Cesare's old comrade-in-arms Yves d'Alègre at Gaeta. Cesare's own military preparations were almost complete, and he had an army consisting of some 600 men-at-arms, an equivalent number of light cavalry and over 4000 foot, including bodies of Romagnol infantry whom even Giustinian had to admit were very fine men. His troops were dressed in his livery quartered in red and yellow, with 'CESAR' embroidered in huge letters on their breasts and backs. Matarazzo wrote of him that he was at this time the first captain in Italy: 'All the flower of the soldiery was with him, since he had all the famous condottieri for him ... and he was much followed by the soldiery. And also he was most fortunate and he had so much treasure accumulated and possessions that it seemed there was not as much anywhere in Italy, nor were there in Italy as many soldiers so well ordered in horses and cloth of gold, in infinite number.' On the political front matters were equally satisfactory. Cesare now felt himself strong enough to throw off the pretence that his conquests had been made not for himself but for the Church, and on 8 July Alexander issued a bull conferring the vicariate of Città di Castello on Cesare and requested the Perugians to offer him their lordship. Negotiations with Emperor Maximilian for the investiture of Pisa, Siena and Lucca for Cesare in return for the money raised for the abortive crusade were nearing completion, and the Pisans had offered themselves to him. Arriving in Rome on 3 July, the envoys 'ran like madmen to the palace to have audience of the Pope and the Duke'. In the first week of July Cesare accelerated the pace of his military preparations and over the following days large bodies of troops moved out of Rome bound for Perugia, strategically placed on the borders of Tuscany.

Giustinian, anxiously observing Cesare's activity and straining every nerve to discover his objectives, noted ominously that, although Pisa and Siena were much spoken of, the preparations were for greater undertakings. Everyone, he wrote, 'affirms that, when the Spaniards have taken Gaeta, the Pope must reveal himself, and then, on the wave of such a victory, with many troops, with the preparations they are making here, that all will be in order at one point, so that on the spur of the moment they will be able to make such an attack and proceed so far, that not without the greatest difficulty will it be possible to remedy so great an evil'. No doubt he remembered that after Sinigallia Alexander was reported to háve said: 'What has happened up till now is nothing to that which will soon be seen.' Indeed it seemed to everyone that Cesare was poised for some great coup, perhaps the final achievement of his objectives, to which the intermittent negotiations with Pisa and the raids into Tuscan territory had been leading up. Cesare appeared invincible. Anything could be believed of him. Never before had he appeared so dominant as in this high summer of 1503, acting as if he were an independent power, with the entire weight and resources of the Papacy behind him. Alexander seemed more than ever obsessed with his son's career, to the point where he appeared to make no distinction between Cesare's interests and those of the Church. Even the pretext that his conquests were made only for the Church was now finally discarded. As the month of July drew to a close, Cesare's departure was reported to be imminent, but no one knew when he was going or where. It was officially given out that he was going to review his troops in Umbria but no one believed it and fears of his intentions reached panic proportions. 'Everything is in a panic,' Giustinian wrote on 22 July, 'and everyone hangs on the enterprise of Gaeta, the end of which, which is expected soon, seems to everyone must be the beginning of some novelty.'

July passed into August, and still Cesare deferred his departure. In reality he was in an agony of suspense: the success of his plans depended on the timing of events which had seemed certain in June, but now appeared as if they could turn against him. In the last weeks of July Gaeta had still not fallen, and the French were massing in Lombardy for a descent on Naples. If the Spaniards did not take Gaeta before the French entered Tuscany, his hopes were at an end. And there was the security of the Romagna and his other states to be considered; if he openly took the Spanish side, his enemies might, in the wake of the huge French army, attack him through the chinks in his armour, Urbino and the recently acquired lordships. He had now to take the decision whether to ride northward and await the outcome of events, or remain in Rome and be forced to join the French on their way south. His tension mounted as the sweltering days passed with ever more discouraging reports. On 6 August news reached Rome that the French in strength with 1100 men-at-arms, 1400 light horse and some 8000 foot were on the move from Lombardy, which, wrote Giustinian, 'has put the Spanish, the Pope and il Valentino beside themselves'. The next day the envoy found the Pope worried and preoccupied, talking of the sickness in Rome, depressed by the lack of news from Gaeta; the Spanish ambassador had assured him that it would soon fall, but Alexander told Giustinian gloomily: 'We believe that if they have not taken it before Sunday, they will never have it.' He said that Cesare's departure was now definitely fixed for the 9th, and it seems that Cesare had come to a final decision.

Realist that he was, he recognized that the odds had turned against him. He would make some kind of accommodation with the French and ride northward to join his troops; Gaeta might still fall soon, and after the French passed south he might still be able to make his move; however, it was clearly time to hedge his bets. On 8 August the Mantuan envoy reported that he had summoned the French envoys and assured them that he was only going to review his troops and had no intention of molesting either Florence or Siena. After they left he is reported to have said: 'These Spaniards will be finished if they do not have other help, and it will be expedient to me to be with the French coming in such power, otherwise I would lose everything.' As he prepared to change political horses in mid-stream, he did not, however, appear particularly despondent. It is likely that he regarded the present perilous situation and the postponement of his plans as only a temporary setback. He was accustomed to playing a dangerous political game; he had always been able to extract the maximum advantage from the clash between France and Spain over Naples, and at this moment, with the best army he had ever commanded ready for action, he was in the best possible position to sell his services to the highest bidder. In fact he appeared to be in excellent health and spirits, hunting in the cool of dawn in the countryside round Rome, and writing to Isabella d'Este for more dogs for the chase. No doubt he was looking forward to his departure, to escape from the sweating inaction of Rome, and on 5 August, with his father, he attended a farewell supper party given by Adriano da Corneto in his country villa.

Alexander, on the other hand, was noticed to be uncharacteristically morose, oppressed by the dangerous political situation, the heat, and the prevalence of sickness. Two days after the Corneto supper party he remarked heavily to Giustinian: 'Lord Orator, the fact that so many are sick in Rome now, and every day are dying, preoccupies us to the extent that we are disposed to take a little more care than we are accustomed of our person.' For the first time in a long and healthy life, Alexander, now seventy-three, felt the intimations of mortality. That same year, his last child, Rodrigo Borgia, had been born, but now, weary and apprehensive, with men dying of fever round him, he at last felt the need to take care of his ageing body. He had been greatly depressed by the death on 1 August of his nephew Cardinal Juan Borgia-Lanzuol, after a bout of fever. The Cardinal was excessively corpulent, and as his funeral procession passed beneath the windows of the Vatican, Alexander, thinking of his own heavy body, remarked gloomily: 'This month is fatal for fat men.' August, he well knew, was a fatal month for popes. Of his predecessors,

Calixtus, Pius II and Sixtus IV had all died in August, Innocent VIII at the end of July. This month of August 1503 was exceptionally hot; the envoys attached to the court wrote to their masters complaining of the stifling temperatures and particularly of the dangerously un- healthy air in the neighbourhood of the Vatican. Normally the court would have moved from Rome to the hills to escape not only the heat but the threat of *malaria perniciosa*, the fever borne into the city during the dog days by mosquitoes bred in the swamps of the Roman Cam- pagna, a sickness which struck without warning, accompanied by fits of vomiting and bouts of fever which could raise a man's temperature to over one hundred and six in a few hours. But this was not a normal year; in the present political situation Alexander could not afford to leave Rome, and so he and his court were forced to remain and face the danger.

On 11 August, the anniversary of his elevation to the Papacy, an occasion which he was accustomed to celebrate with gusto, observers remarked Alexander's unusual apathy. Giustinian thought that he was deeply troubled by the political situation, and indeed the Pope after Mass told the Venetian grimly: 'See how disastrous it has been that no understanding should have been reached between your Sig- noria and ourselves.' In fact the true cause of his listlessness and de- pression was that the sickness was already upon him. On Saturday, 12 August, after dining, the Pope was seized with a fit of vomiting and fever which lasted through the night; on the same day Cesare, still in Rome, fell ill with the same symptoms.

For six days father and son lay gravely ill in the Vatican, while doctors fought to save their lives with the crude methods then at their disposal. Of the two, Cesare's case was the more serious, but he was young and exceptionally strong. On the 14th, Alexander's doctors bled him severely; 'ten ounces – which seems too much and remark- able in a man of seventy-three,' Giustinian commented. This seemed to bring him temporary relief, although it can only have served to undermine his physical reserves, and Giustinian wrote that his anxiety about Cesare's illness was making him worse. Cesare's doctors sub- jected him to even more drastic treatment. On the 15th they sub- merged him in a great oil jar filled with iced water, and the skin peeled from his body with the shock. Probably as a result of this, on the 16th he was reported to be in danger of his life, and in a worse condition than his father. The greatest secrecy was maintained about both cases, but the indefatigable Giustinian, questioning the doctors as they hurried in and out of the palace, managed to glean some details: 'Both are still with fever . . . the Duke has it more strongly, with paroxysms of fever following one upon the other, and strange fits; and this past night at midnight he sent for the doctors who are tending him, who are not of the palace, and has kept them there and does not let them leave, and makes even more difficulty in letting his condition be known.'

Yet, even in the midst of his delirium, Cesare's instinct of self-preservation was strong enough for him to send messages ordering a body of his troops back to Rome, and reassuring words to the Romagna. By the 17th, Alexander's life was despaired of. Giustinian reported that evening: 'The Palace was upside down, and everyone sought to save himself and his belongings, however with the greatest secrecy . . .' With the Pope on the point of death, and their protector Cesare desperately ill, the Borgia party made every effort to conceal the gravity of Alexander's condition in order to gain time to save themselves from the fury that they expected to descend upon them the moment the news of his death leaked out.

Alexander died on the afternoon of the following day, 18 August; in the room above his father's, Cesare had surmounted his crisis, and although he was weak and exhausted he had recovered just in time to save himself from total ruin. On hearing of his father's death he dispatched the faithful Michelotto with a body of armed men to close all the doors to the Pope's chambers. Once inside, one of the soldiers drew a dagger and threatened to cut the throat of the Cardinal chamberlain Casanova if he did not hand over the keys to the Pope's closets. In a small chamber behind the Pope's bedroom Michelotto and his men found silver and jewels to the value of 200,000 ducats, with a further 100,000 in cash in two small chests. In their haste they overlooked a further cache of valuables including the tiara, rings and more silver and jewels, but the 300,000 worth they took with them was more than enough to ensure their master's immediate future. The papal servants then plundered the Pope's apartments and wardrobes, leaving only the papal thrones, some cushions and hangings. At four o'clock in the afternoon they opened the doors of the pillaged apartments and announced that the Pope was dead. The reign of the second Borgia Pope was over.

Burchard, summoned to the palace just after four o'clock to supervise the laying out of his third Pope, found the Vatican deserted but for a few officials and servants, with not a cardinal in sight.

Alexander's body, clothed in red brocade vestments and covered with a fine tapestry, was laid on a table in the Sala del Papagallo, scene of so many Borgia festivities in the past, and there spent the night, totally alone, with two tapers burning beside the bier. The next day it was borne on a bier by the customary group of paupers to St Peter's, where fighting broke out inside the church as the palace guards tried to seize the valuable wax tapers from the monks accompanying the body. The monks stopped chanting when the soldiers drew their swords, and fled into the sacristy, and in the confusion the Pope's body was abandoned. Burchard and a few others who kept their heads had the bier dragged behind the railings of the high altar, and shut the iron grille for fear that Alexander's enemies might desecrate his body.

During the day Alexander's corpse began to decompose, and when Burchard went to look at it at about four o'clock he found it a most horrifying sight: 'Its face had changed to the colour of mulberry or the blackest cloth, and it was covered in blue-black spots. The nose was swollen, the mouth distended where the tongue was doubled over and the lips seemed to fill everything. The appearance of the face then was more horrifying than anything that had ever been seen or reported before ...' The dead Pope's putrefying body was hastily buried as the sun set. Francesco Gonzaga, writing to his wife from the French camp at Isola Farnese, described it as a burial so wretched that even the dwarf wife of the cripple at Mantua had a more honourable one. He too gave a lurid description of the body, saying that it swelled up until it had lost all human form and was as broad as it was long; since everyone refused to touch it, a porter dragged it from the bier to the grave with a rope attached to one of the feet. Burchard relates that the corpse was unceremoniously stuffed into its coffin by six porters making blasphemous jokes about the late Pope and his hideous appearance: 'The carpenters had made the coffin too narrow and short, so they placed the Pope's mitre at his side, rolled up his body in an old carpet, and pummelled and pushed it into the coffin with their fists. No wax tapers or lights were used and no priests or any other persons attended his body.'

No sooner had Alexander's body been hurried to its grave than rumours began to spread as to the manner of his end. There were stories of Satanic mysteries surrounding his death, that the devil in the form of an ape had appeared in his chamber on the day he died, and had been seen disguised as a black dog running through St Peter's on the day he was buried. Indeed some said that he had made a

Faustian pact with the devil, a story which Francesco Gonzaga retailed to Isabella:

> When he fell sick, he began to talk in such a way that anyone who did not know what was in his mind would have thought that he was wandering, although he was perfectly conscious of what he said; his words were: 'I come, it is right, wait a moment.' Those who know the secret say that in the conclave following the death of Innocent he made a compact with the devil, and purchased the Papacy from him at the price of his soul. Among the other provisions of the agreement was one which said that he should be allowed to occupy the Holy See twelve years, and this he did with the addition of four days. There are some who affirm that at the moment he gave up his spirit, seven devils were seen in his chamber.

That a man like Francesco Gonzaga should have found such a story credible is indicative of the extent to which dark remnants of medieval superstition lingered on in the back of the most sophisticated Renaissance minds.

There were of course the usual rumours of poison, stimulated by the frightful appearance of the corpse. Four days after the Pope's death, reports that he and Cesare had been poisoned at Adriano da Corneto's supper had spread as far as Florence. As usual with a story concerning the Borgias, it was given a poignant twist: planning to murder the wealthy Cardinal for his money, they had bribed a servitor to poison the wine, and then through a mix-up of the flagons had drunk the poisoned wine themselves. This tale of the Borgias hoist with their own petard spread throughout Europe; it was repeated in the chronicles of Pietro Martire d'Anghiera at the court of Spain on 10 November, and even reached the ears of Luther. Giovio, Bembo and Guicciardini all repeated it in their histories. (Guicciardini's information was so inaccurate that he had Alexander die the day after the Corneto supper.) In fact the story was patently absurd: the famous supper took place on the 5th, none of the participants felt any ill effects until six days later, when da Corneto himself went down with the fever, while Alexander and Cesare and several other guests at the party fell sick on the 12th, a week after the fatal evening.

It is a measure of Alexander's impact on his contemporaries that none of them could regard him with objectivity, even after his death. For many, no words could be bad enough for him. Machiavelli in his *Decennale Primo* described Alexander's soul being transported to heaven followed by 'his three familiars and dear handmaidens, Luxury [by which he meant sensuality], Simony, and Cruelty', and there was a great deal of truth in what he said. Alexander's faults were as great as his abilities. He was possessed of enormous intelligence, farsightedness and administrative ability, besides being one of the ablest diplomats ever to occupy the papal throne. Where the temporal interests of the Church were threatened, he fought with all his powers and with outstanding success. During the twelve years of his Papacy he succeeded in accomplishing what no one else had done before, in crushing the power of the great families who had held the Papacy to ransom in the past, and destroying the independent vicars of the Romagna. Even his enemies admitted that he was more absolute master of Rome than any pope had ever been before him, and when he died the Papacy was a great military power, the only kind of power that really counted in the contemporary context. It is equally true, however, that he could have accomplished none of these things without Cesare; together they formed an irresistible combination of dynamic energy and supreme ability which swept all before it.

On the international scene he had played his cards with consummate skill, so that the great powers of Europe could no longer dictate to the pope as they had in the days of Avignon, but were forced to compete for his friendship. He had been elected as a political pope, as the circumstances of Italy at the time demanded, and on that basis he had more than fulfilled expectations. The open sensuality of his private life and the absolute ruthlessness of his political methods were admittedly shocking in a man who held the office of High Priest of Christendom, but in his simoniacal practices he merely continued and extended fund-raising methods initiated by his predecessors, notably Sixtus IV. The cupidity ridiculed by his contemporaries was inspired not by love of money for its own sake but by the consciousness that money meant power, and that without it nothing could be achieved. He was the most nepotistic of popes, but there is a strong case for arguing, as Machiavelli did, that Cesare's career advanced the temporal power of the Church. Alexander was a supreme example of a man who believed that the end justified the means, and it was the ruthless gangsterism of his methods, for which Cesare must be held largely responsible, which incurred the odium of those who were threatened by them. The charge levelled by the author of the Savelli Letter – 'All men fear him and above all fear his son' – contained a considerable element of truth: Cesare inspired an atmosphere of terror in which prominent people literally feared for their lives. Alexander VI was, in short, the most outrageous and one of the most able popes who ever lived. Most of his contemporaries regarded him with a mixture of hatred, fear and admiration. Guicciardini, no friend to the Borgias, while cataloguing Alexander's vices, could not help admitting his great qualities, winding up with the epitaph: 'He was, in sum, the worst and the most fortunate pope that has ever been...'

One man sincerely mourned Alexander – his son Cesare. Their partnership had been in many ways a unique one, and after the early years it had been quite unlike the normal relationship between father and son. Alexander had been exceptionally young for his age, Cesare in many ways mature for his. It was as if they had been close contemporaries playing together and working together, with the same objectives, the same methods, the same attitudes of mind. Towards the end of Alexander's life it seems that Cesare was the driving force behind the partnership, and that to a certain extent he dominated his father, who loved and admired him, and was perhaps a little afraid of him. This seems, at least, to have been the impression gained of their relationship by contemporaries. While Capello's *Relazione* and the opinion at the French court reported by the Venetian envoy there as to Alexander's fear of Cesare were probably exaggerated, Machiavelli certainly thought that it was Cesare who made the decisions. Giustinian, an observer at the Roman court where Alexander's figure naturally loomed large, tended to see them as a partnership. He habitually referred to them as 'they' and 'the Pope and the Duke', although he made several references to the fact that Alexander could never refuse Cesare anything. Certainly Cesare planned the Sinigallia coup quite independently of his father, who was not allowed to know anything about it until the last moment, and, as Burchard confirms, it was on his orders and not the Pope's that the Orsini arrests were made in Rome on 3 January. Giustinian, who always suspected Alexander to be playing games with him, did not know whether Alexander was feigning his indignation at Cesare's disobedience to his orders to return from Tuscany and attack the Orsinis, but the picture that emerged from his dispatches of Alexander angry and frustrated, powerless to bend his son to his will, seemed real enough. Whether Cesare dominated his father or not, the key to their relationship was that each was indispensable to the other.

And Alexander died before Cesare had reached the point where he could consider himself strong enough to stand alone, at the very moment, as both Guicciardini and Machiavelli agreed, when he was within sight of the final achievement of his goals. Both the Borgias, in the five years since Cesare took up the sword, had been working against time to secure his position before the Pope should die. The blow had always been anticipated, but when it fell it fell with an extreme malignity. As Cesare told Machiavelli two months after Alexander's death, he had thought of everything that could happen when his father died, except for the possibility that when he did so he himself would also be at the point of death.

XIV

LONE WOLF

ALL over Italy Cesare's enemies and former allies watched to see what he would do. There were rumours that he was dead or dying. Twenty-four hours after Alexander's death, he had a relapse; Giustinian reported on the 19th: 'The Duke is more feverish than before, and "the crowd" here are in the expectation and hope that he will soon follow his father.' Men like Ercole d'Este sat on the fence, wondering whether this would be the end of the powerful Duke Valentino, while his enemies, the Orsinis and Colonnas, Florence, Venice, Guidobaldo da Montefeltro, the Baglionis and the other dispossessed lords, moved to the attack. Venice provided Guidobaldo with troops to regain Urbino, Florence gave men to Jacopo d'Appiano to return to Piombino, and the Baglionis with Florentine encouragement took La Magione and presented themselves before Perugia. Venice hovered like a great gilded bird of prey over Cesare's states of Romagna, watching for the moment to swoop. As if this were not enough, Prospero Colonna with a considerable body of Spanish troops sent by Gonsalvo de Cordoba was at Marino, a few hours' march from Rome, while the huge French army commanded by Francesco Gonzaga had accelerated its march southward at the news of Alexander's death and was now nearing Rome.

Cesare knew that precious time had been lost during the six days he had lain delirious. Still weak and exhausted and subject to recurrent bouts of fever, even so he reacted to the situation with speed and decision. He had seized his father's treasure; his troops under Michelotto and Jofre held the Borgo; reinforcements had already been ordered to make their way with all speed back to Rome. He now had three urgent problems to confront: his personal security in Rome, the conservation of his Romagna states, and most important of all, the election of a new pope favourable to his interests. As for his own security vis-à-vis the hostile Roman barons, while he knew the Orsinis to be irreconcilable he had not personally injured the Colonnas, who, backed by Spanish troops, were in any case the stronger party. On the evening of Alexander's death, he had dispatched envoys to Prospero Colonna offering the restitution of the family lands, with the countersigns of their fortresses as a pledge of good faith, while the next day he sent Cardinal Borgia to escort the Spanish ambassador to the Vatican for an interview. On the 22nd, Cesare's loyal right-hand man, Agapito Geraldini, signed an agreement with the Colonnas in his master's name, and on the 23rd Prospero entered Rome. On the same day Fabio and Niccolò Orsini arrived with 400 horse and 1500 foot, but were helpless to do Cesare any harm in the face of the combined Borgia and Colonna forces, and were ordered to withdraw the next day having achieved little beyond sacking the houses of a few Borgia courtiers.

In fact, thanks to his firm handling of the situation, Cesare was still very much the strong man in Rome. He had troops and money, while his nominal masters, the College of Cardinals, had neither. Two hundred of his lances had arrived from the north and were encamped outside the city, while as to money, as Giustinian remarked, the College had not a penny, because 'the Duke has had it all'. He held Castel Sant'Angelo, where the castellan was his partisan, and the Vatican, which he had stripped of all its furnishings, while the Sacred College met nervously in the church of Santa Maria Sopra Minerva. Until Cesare and the Borgia troops left the city, they could not feel themselves safe enough to hold the conclave for the election of a new pope in the Vatican. Protracted negotiations then took place, with the College and the foreign ambassadors, led by Giustinian, attempting to persuade Cesare to leave, while he for his part played for time, pleading sickness and the threats of his numerous enemies. It was not until 30 August that agreement was finally reached and Cesare consented to depart, on condition that the College reconfirmed him as Gonfalonier until the election of a new pope, guaranteed his safety and that of the cardinals dependent upon him, ordered Venice not to molest his states, and wrote to his Romagnol cities urging their continued allegiance to him.

Cesare was determined not to leave Rome until the last possible moment. For him, as for the other powers, the outcome of the forthcoming papal election was of overriding importance. Control of the election of his father's successor had always been one of his principal objectives, and he was not prepared now tamely to withdraw in the face of a situation to which he believed he held the key. Thanks to his policy of nominating his partisans to the cardinalate he controlled the votes of between eight to eleven cardinals, or roughly a third of the voting strength of the College – men who, as Giustinian remarked, 'attended to his wishes with more reverence than they did to Pope Alexander'. Neither the pro-French nor the pro-Spanish parties in the College were strong enough to swing the election on their own, while the 'Italian' cardinals were, in the Venetian envoy's words, 'lost men', leaderless and open to intimidation by all parties. Cesare made every effort to ensure that they should remain so; there were rumours that he had laid ambushes for his two principal enemies, Giuliano della Rovere and Raffaele Riario, at the ports and by land in order to prevent them reaching Rome. Giustinian reported on 26 August that Cesare was 'resolved by whatever means to make one of his own [men] Pope; since without that he sees himself deprived of everything; and the fear is not lacking that, seeing he cannot make one according to his purpose, he will not make some schism in the Church, since he has eight cardinals who follow him in everything'. It was rumoured that the previous Saturday eleven cardinals had sworn on the host in Cesare's presence to make Giovanni Vera pope, or to create a schism.

Cesare was not alone in regarding himself as the pope-maker; both France and Spain, convinced that the success of their respective causes in Naples depended largely on the election of a pope favourable to themselves, competed feverishly for his support. As Ferdinand and Isabella wrote to their envoy in Rome, de Rojas: 'As to the war in Naples, we believe that a great part of the success of that operation or the contrary lies in who will be pope ...' They therefore urged de Rojas to cement an alliance with Cesare and to ensure that 'he perseveres with us'. Both sides were equally eager to have his support in the coming clash in the kingdom of Naples. Cesare had at first seemed to incline to Spain – their army headed by the Colonnas was nearest to Rome, and he was in need of their immediate protection – but he was deliberately vague in his commitment, and as the huge French army approached from the north the Spaniards became increasingly suspicious that he might, in Prospero Colonna's words, 'play them a bad turn'. On 1 September, the eve of Cesare's departure from Rome, the Spanish envoy admitted to Giustinian his dislike and distrust of il Valentino, and equally his need of him: 'He has plenty of good men: he must of necessity be with us or the French in the enterprise of the Kingdom, and to each side it would be a great reinforcement to have him. And you know that the French have tried everything to have him, and have not failed to offer him Siena, and Pisa, and the state of Giangiordano [Orsini], nor am I yet sure that they will not corrupt him with these their large offers ...'

On the very day that de Rojas was voicing his suspicions, Cesare had in fact signed a secret agreement with France. Louis promised to take Cesare and his family under his protection, with all their possessions, lands and lordships, to safeguard the states which he held and to help him recover those he had lost. In return Cesare pledged himself to serve the King against any power save the pope and the Holy See, to place all his forces at the King's disposal and to unite them to the French army for the campaign in Naples. The reasons for Cesare's sudden volte-face are not hard to divine: in the present uncertain state of affairs it was far more important to him to conserve what he already had than to rely on vague promises of future rewards from Spain. Only Louis' friendship could restrain his enemies, notably Florence and Venice, from making inroads into the Romagna, and persuade his potential friends such as Ercole d'Este into active support. Moreover with Gaeta still holding out for France and powerful French reinforcements on the march southward, the issue of the Naples question was still far from certain, and it might well be that the Spaniards would be unable to deliver what they had promised him. Cesare had always had a tendency to favour the French court, which he knew and understood, and had in fact never openly committed himself against them, while he rightly suspected the Spanish sovereigns of a deep hostility towards himself, an animosity shared and ill concealed by their Roman representative, de Rojas.

On the following day, 2 September, Cesare finally left Rome, ostensibly to join Prospero Colonna and the Spaniards at Tivoli. He was accompanied by his family, including Vannozza and Jofre, all his baggage, and 'women of every kind', according to a report of the Mantuan envoy. These women probably did not include Dorotea Caracciolo, whom Giustinian noted on 23 August as having been sent to Castel Sant'Angelo after the Pope's death, and since Cesare from then on repeatedly disclaimed all knowledge of her whereabouts it seems likely that he did not wish to exacerbate Venetian hostility by openly taking her with him. He himself was too weak to ride, and lay in a closed litter with curtains of crimson damask borne by eight halberdiers, followed by his charger in black velvet trappings with the ducal coronet and insignia. It was, wrote the envoy Cattaneo, 'a grave and honourable sight, arousing compassion'. Indeed he was still very ill, and in the last week of August he suffered a further relapse and was reported to be in peril of his life. Cattaneo wrote that he was completely exhausted, his limbs wasted by continual high fever, and the soles of his feet so swollen that he could not walk. It is remarkable that in this condition Cesare could have had the energy left to take the action that he did, but physically feeble as he now was, his will to win and driving ambition never left him. He was still, as d'Amboise had remarked of him that summer, 'possessed of a devil'.

Even now he was strong enough to devise a typical ruse for his departure, designed to lull Spanish suspicion and conceal his agreement with France until he was safely out of reach of Prospero Colonna and his Spanish allies. It had been agreed that Colonna would wait for him outside the city, and that together they would proceed to Tivoli, and in order to strengthen this impression he dispatched his artillery across the Tiber in the Tivoli direction, and his advance guard to the Ponte Milvio. Meanwhile, as the unsuspecting Prospero was waiting for him outside the Porta del Popolo, Cesare was carried out of the Porta Viridaria near the Vatican. Once safely outside the city, after a short private interview with the French ambassador, he took the road to Nepi, to be joined en route by his advance guard, while the artillery doubled back to Castel Sant'Angelo. Furious at this deception, Prospero left for the Spanish camp accompanied by Sancia, who, as Giustinian remarked caustically, would 'give him some consolation'. Sancia, who for some unrevealed reason had been confined in Castel Sant'Angelo since October 1502, showed no regret at being parted from Jofre, who accompanied Cesare to Nepi, and within a very short time she was Prospero Colonna's mistress. As Giustinian wrote: 'She has gone in a high good humour, with the hope of having her states in the Kingdom, and in all events there is little love between her and her husband and they are by nature very unsuited.'

The immediate results of his volte-face were all that Cesare could have wished for. The French, who not unnaturally mistrusted the sincerity of his intentions, waited for this open sign of his good faith before fulfilling their side of the bargain. It was not therefore until 5 September that they dispatched letters to the Romagna with the news that Cesare was once again 'alive, well and the friend of the King of France'. However the news reached Cesare's Romagnol cities in time to stem the tide that was running against him. Guidobaldo had already re-entered Urbino at the end of August, Gian Paolo Baglioni, after an initial repulse, marched into Perugia on 9 September, while the remaining Vitellis triumphantly took over Città di Castello, parading their emblem of a golden calf through the streets. In the Romagna, Venice had occupied Porto Cesenatico on 1 September, sent Giovanni Sforza back to Pesaro on the 3rd, and Pandolfo Malatesta to Rimini on the 6th. They had then attempted, in concert with troops from Urbino, to storm Cesena, but had been stoutly repulsed. Attempts on the part of Giovanni Bentivoglio and the Florentines to help Caterina's son Ottaviano Riario regain Imola and Francesco Manfredi Faenza had equally failed. The Romagna had thus survived the first onslaught, and the news of Cesare's agreement with France caused his enemies to draw back. Venice abandoned the offensive, and Florence sent him offers of help: Lucrezia's father-in-law, the cautious Ercole, came off his fence to write to Cesare offering his congratulations on his recovery and 200 troops for the defence of the Romagna. Cesare's quick reactions had enabled him to survive the immediate crisis.

But Cesare, as he was carried away from the city which he had come to regard as his power-base, must have been in an uncertain state of mind. The agreement with Louis had gained him a breathing space, but no more, and the temporary lull in military and political activity would end with the election of a new pope. For Cesare, as for the other powers, everything seemed to hang on the outcome of that election, and he fretted at being removed from the scene of action. As the Borgia and Colonna troops left the city, and the French and Spanish forces withdrew to a carefully equal distance, the prospective candidates for the tiara began to gather in Rome to begin the tortuous race for the Papacy.

One of the first to arrive was the Borgias' old enemy Giuliano della Rovere, returning to Rome for the first time since he had fled to France in 1497, and determined to make himself pope. Wily politician that he was, Giuliano realized that there was in fact no chance of a Spaniard or a Frenchman being elected in the present situation, and he hastened to divest himself publicly of the French connection and to proclaim himself a good Italian. As he told Giustinian, who favoured him as Cesare's enemy, the day after his arrival: 'I have come here to look to my own affairs, and not to other people's. I shall

not vote for Rouen [d'Amboise].' As an election manifesto it was a
good one, but Giuliano, although a strong contender, could not persuade Cesare's Spanish cardinals to give him their votes despite all
his blandishments, and his newly acquired pro-Italian platform failed
to convince the Italian cardinals. Although they were in the
majority – twenty-two out of thirty-seven – they were divided, some
for Caraffa, others for Pallavicini, while the others like Colonna,
Medici and Soderini followed their French or Spanish masters.
D'Amboise, who saw this as his great chance for the tiara, arrived
on the 10th, with Ascanio Sforza, who had been released from imprisonment specifically to advance d'Amboise's candidacy. However,
d'Amboise was soon disappointed in Ascanio; the warm welcome
given him by the Romans, who remembered the munificent Cardinal
Sforza with affection, encouraged him to think well of his own
chances. Cries of 'Ascanio, Ascanio, Sforza, Sforza' were so deafening
that no one could make themselves heard, reported Burchard, adding
dryly: 'How this must have pleased Rouen, God knows!' Disappointed in Ascanio, d'Amboise probably counted on Cesare to deliver the support of his followers, who were generally admitted to hold
the casting vote.

Cesare's Spanish cardinals had been thrown into disarray by their
master's volte-face in favour of France, but the faithful Agapito had
been dispatched from Nepi immediately after Cesare's arrival there
to reassure them and, as he told the Pisan envoy, 'confirm the Spanish
cardinals to the Duke's will'. The extent of Cesare's control over 'his'
cardinals is difficult to determine; it is doubtful whether he could have
persuaded all of them to vote for d'Amboise as a Frenchman, and
it is probable that in any case he did not want them to, preferring
a more controllable candidate than a representative of one of the
major powers. It seems likely that he would have instructed them to
go through the motions of favouring d'Amboise, as Giustinian
reported them to be doing up till two days before the conclave, to
try for the election of one of their own number, to block at all costs
the candidature of his enemies – Giuliano, Raffaele Riario, and to a
lesser extent Ascanio – and if necessary to vote for the most harmless
compromise candidate. If these were his instructions, then it appears
that Agapito was successful in bringing the Spanish cardinals into line.
The conclave opened on 16 September, and in the first ballot on the
21st the Borgia party voted heavily for each other, but nonetheless
Giuliano came out ahead. D'Amboise, acting in concert with Ascanio,

who was determined to thwart Giuliano, and the cardinals of the French connection, then proposed the Cardinal of Siena, Piccolomini. This compromise was acceptable to the Spanish cardinals, who were equally anxious to see Cesare's most dangerous enemy defeated, and on the 22nd, without further ado, Piccolomini was elected Pope, taking the name of Pius III, in honour of his uncle Pius II, the friend and protector of Cardinal Rodrigo Borgia. In the conclave of 1458 which had made Pius II Pope, Rodrigo Borgia's had been the deciding voice; now, nearly fifty years later, his nephew, thanks to Cesare's Spanish cardinals, was equally obligated to Rodrigo's son.

For Cesare, waiting anxiously at Nepi, the news of Pius' election was not the worst that could have been expected, but neither was it the best. It was clear to everyone that the new Pope's reign could hardly be long. He was a cultivated and able man, who had led a blameless life, but was prematurely old and decrepit, tormented by gout as his uncle had been, and on the morning of his election he was too ill to kneel in St Peter's and had to be carried to the high altar to give thanks. The reign of Pius III was likely to be little more than a breathing space preluding the advent of a new and possibly more powerful pope. For Cesare it was some consolation to know that the new Pope was obligated to him, and to d'Amboise, who continued to show strong support for him, and had indeed moved into his former apartments in the Vatican, as a mark of special favour from Pius. But everything depended on how far Pius would be prepared to go to give substance to his election obligations. He was surrounded by powerful enemies of Cesare's, Giuliano, Riario, the Venetian envoy and agents of Guidobaldo of Urbino, who acted in concert and never ceased to bombard the Pope with requests for permission to attack il Valentino.

Cesare had recovered some of his health and strength at Nepi, and he had lost none of the almost desperate courage expressed in the mottoes on a ring engraved for him at the time: 'Do what you must, come what may' and 'One heart, one way', but his illness had left its mark on him in the form of anxiety and depression. A Pisan envoy who visited him at Nepi at the end of September reported him as well, but very anxious about his affairs, and obsessed with two things, his confirmation as Gonfalonier and the salvation of his Romagna states. Indeed, in Cesare's mind, the two things were synonymous; as Gonfalonier, with the authority of the Church behind him, no one, he thought, would dare to attack him. Pius' first actions on his election seemed to indicate that he was prepared to implement some at least of his promises to Cesare. On the very next day he told a dismayed Giustinian that he was displeased that the Signoria had tried to foment revolt in the Romagna, and when the envoy tried to recommend to him the lords 'wretchedly' dispossessed by Cesare, he replied that 'God willed that they should be castigated with a wretched instrument'. He refused Giuliano a brief for his nephew's return to Sinigallia, and would not listen to Cardinal Riario's arguments in favour of his nephews of Imola and Forlì. Three days after his election he sent a brief to Cesare confirming him in his vicariates and condoling with him on the league formed against him by his enemies at Perugia on 16 September. At the same time he dispatched strongly worded briefs to the Doge, condemning the Venetian raids on Cesare's territories and demanding the withdrawal of their troops, to Perugia complaining of the Baglionis' activities against the Duke of Romagna, and to the Romagnol cities recommending their continued obedience to their lord. These briefs had their effect in that Pandolfo Malatesta was once more expelled from Rimini, Venice refused open support to the League of Perugia, and Florence redoubled her offers of help to Cesare. But this, it seemed, was as far as Pius was prepared to go. As Giustinian reported, messengers of Duke Valentino passed every day from Rome to Nepi and from Nepi to Rome, 'but up till now he has not decided to give him any more favour than briefs'.

Indeed, on 26 September, the day after he had issued these briefs on Cesare's behalf, Pius told Giustinian:

> In consequence of the pressure put on me by the Spanish cardinals I have been compelled to issue some briefs in favour of Cesare Borgia, but I will not give him any further help. I do not intend to be a warlike, but a peace-loving Pope...I wish no harm to the Duke, for it is the duty of a Pope to have compassion for all, but I foresee that by God's judgement, he must come to a bad end...

Pius' reservations about Cesare were understandable; he had no wish to see the Papacy borne helplessly along on the tide of il Valentino's ambition. It was Pius who, only three months before, had described Alexander to Giustinian as 'the wolf', and from certain remarks he let fall to the Venetian at this time it seems that he secretly desired the destruction of the wolf's cub. To the agents of the Duke of Urbino who came to ask permission to take Fano from Cesare in the name of the Church, he is reported to have said that he could do nothing openly against him but that it was pleasing to him that Guidobaldo should do what he could. As Giustinian commented: 'This clearly shows the mind of the Pope to be that they should do to this Duke Valentino the worst they can, as long as it is not seen to come from him.' Cesare, with his excellent sources of information at the Roman court, was not deceived by Pius' outward demonstrations of goodwill. Giustinian noted: 'He has good words from the Pope, but does not trust him.'

It was by now obvious to Cesare that to remain any longer at Nepi was not only useless but even dangerous. The forces he had with him had dwindled to a point where he could no longer feel himself secure against any concerted attack; on learning of Cesare's agreement with France, Gonsalvo de Cordoba had riposted by sending letters ordering all Spaniards in his service to leave for the Kingdom, and he had thus lost much of his heavy cavalry and infantry and some of his best captains, including Ugo de Moncada, who had ridden off to join Gonsalvo in Naples. Moreover, under his treaty obligations to Louis he had perforce to dispatch most of his remaining forces to join the French, who were once again on the march for the Kingdom. He now learned that the most redoubtable of his many enemies, Bartolomeo d'Alviano, was planning to attack him in Nepi in concert with troops from Urbino, Camerino and Città di Castello. On 2 October, Giustinian reported that d'Alviano 'counts it certain to have him in his hands, and appears to intend the greatest vendetta against him'. Faced with this situation, Cesare had two alternatives for action: to go to the Romagna to stiffen the morale of his loyal followers and to block any further deterioration in his position there, or to return to Rome.

Cesare resolved to return to Rome, a decision for which he has been faulted by historians, who assert that he should have gone to the Romagna to consolidate his position there, leaving his supporters in the city to manage his affairs. Rome was full of his enemies, and in going there he could be riding into a trap. But it was for this very reason that Cesare chose to return to Rome. He had always believed that the best way to outwit his enemies was to confront them rather than to turn his back on them. He did not trust Pius to withstand the attacks of men like Giuliano, who openly berated the Pope for his support of Cesare and devoted all his time to intriguing with the Venetian envoy and his other enemies against him. His supporters at the Vatican needed him as much, perhaps even more, than his commanders in the Romagna. Rome had always been his power-base, and he needed to feel himself secure there before riding northward, which, he assured his Romagnol followers, he intended to do immediately after the Pope's coronation. Above all he needed to gain confirmation as Gonfalonier and Captain General, the concrete symbol that he still enjoyed the support of the Holy See, which would discourage his enemies and encourage his friends. He still had enough confidence in himself to believe that his personal presence in the city would counteract the influence of his enemies and intimidate the Pope into fulfilling his election promises. And so his cardinal supporters pressed the Pope to allow him to return to Rome, representing him as gravely ill, threatened on all sides by his enemies, and only wishing to come back to the city to die in peace. The kindly Pius was moved by their descriptions of Cesare's pitiful condition. He told the Ferrarese envoy Costabili: 'I never thought that I should feel any pity for the Duke, and yet I do most deeply pity him. The Spanish cardinals have interceded for him. They tell me he is very ill and wishes to come and die in Rome, and I have given permission.'

On 3 October, Cesare returned to Rome with his family, guarded by 150 men-at-arms, 500 infantry and a squadron of light horse, to be met by Cardinals d'Amboise, Ascanio, Sanseverino and his brother-in-law d'Albret, who escorted him to his palace of San Clemente in the Borgo. He was widely believed to be on the point of death, and it came as an unpleasant shock to his enemies to discover that not only was il Valentino not dying but that he was as confident, arrogant and active as ever. Giustinian wrote sourly on 6 October: 'Duke Valentino is not so ill as was believed; he speaks with arrogance and says that he will soon regain possession of all his states.' Cardinals della Rovere and Riario raged at the Pope for having allowed him to return; Giuliano had never made the mistake of underestimating il Valentino and he was afraid that in person, with his troops at his back, with the Palace guard which was composed of the same men who had served his father, and the castellan of Sant'Angelo well known to be his 'creature', Cesare would intimidate the helpless Pope into acceding to his wishes – which was exactly what Cesare intended. The wretched Pius, menaced by Giuliano's towering figure and fierce temper, could only excuse himself feebly on the grounds of having been deceived. 'I am neither a saint nor an angel, but only a man and liable to err,' he told Giustinian on the 7th. But Cesare, confident and optimistic again, happy to be back at the centre of things, had no need of armed men to intimidate the Pope; his persuasive personality and his money were enough to get him what he wanted. Giustinian reported that he loaned Pius money to pay for his coronation, as well he might, since the unfortunate Pope on his accession had found the Apostolic treasury full of nothing but debts and the Palace stripped of all its furnishings. However that may have been, Cesare achieved the object for which he had come to Rome; on 8 October, the day of his coronation, Pius confirmed him as Gonfalonier and Captain General of the Church.

Cesare was content. He had once again outmanoeuvred his enemies and proved to the world that he still held the Vatican in his hand. He was still Duke of Romagna, and was now once again Gonfalonier and Captain General of the Church. These titles meant more to him than their prestige value, which was considerable. They implied the continuance of his policy of control of the forces of the Church, interrupted by the sudden death of Alexander before it could be permanently established by his nomination as hereditary Gonfalonier. It meant that he would once again be able to maintain the standing army which had made him a major power in Italy, to preserve the states he already had, and possibly, with luck and by a skilful playing of his cards between France and Spain, to resume the plans for the dominion of Tuscany which he had been about to put into execution that summer. For the moment the question of the security of the Romagna was of the first importance. There the news of his return to Rome with the apparent favour of the King of France and of the Pope had had the propaganda effect which Cesare had hoped for; in the first week of October attempts by the Ordelaffis and Manfredis to enter Forlì and Faenza had been repulsed by the citizens, confident that their Duke had re-established his position. But only his personal presence there could definitely quash the signs of possible treachery among some of the leading families, such as the Moratinis of Forlì, which had appeared for the first time since the death of Alexander. Immediately after the coronation, therefore, Cesare made preparations to leave for the Romagna. Pius wrote to the Florentines requesting safe passage for the Duke and his troops on their way, while d'Amboise charged Giangiordano Orsini to see him safely through the family territories north of Rome.

But even as Cesare was making his preparations to leave, his enemies were gathering to destroy him. Before Pius' coronation one

of Giovanni Bentivoglio's sons, Annibale, had come to Rome to intrigue with Cardinals Riario and Giuliano della Rovere 'so that he
may, by secret means, obtain the Pope's permission to damage the
Duke' by attacking the Romagna. On the 10th, Bartolomeo d'Alviano
and Gian Paolo Baglioni, thwarted in their plan to catch Cesare at
Nepi, arrived in Rome bent on the pursuit of their vendetta. That
night they went secretly to Giustinian's house, where they found him
in bed, and told him they had come 'to lay hands on the Duke ...
whom at all costs they desired to pursue to the death'. The next day
Giuliano Orsini and Bartolomeo's brother, the abbot, rode past
Cesare's palace shouting: 'Let us kill the Jewish dog, and plunder
him before the others do.' Cesare's men-at-arms stood on guard outside his palace, but the situation was becoming menacing in the
extreme, and the city seethed with Orsini partisans. While d'Alviano
backed by Cardinals della Rovere and Riario attempted to persuade
the Pope to order Cesare to lay down his arms, the Colonnas signed
a pact with his Orsini enemies. The Orsinis' hatred of Cesare was
such that they agreed to abandon their traditional allegiance to
France, Cesare's protector, and signed a condotta to serve on the side
of Spain in the Kingdom! The agreement was signed in the house of
the Spanish envoy de Rojas, whose hostility to Cesare was well known.
In the midst of all this turmoil the maverick Giangiordano, to the
fury of the rest of his family, arrived in Rome to obey d'Amboise's
orders to escort Cesare to the Romagna. But it was too late; on the
same day Pius, who had suffered a severe operation on his leg on 27
September and had been too ill to kneel at his coronation, was seized
with a fit of vomiting and fever, and it was soon clear that he was
dying. Cesare was now defenceless in the midst of his enemies. The
French army was too far away to help him, his nearest reinforcements
under the faithful Michelotto were at Rocca Soriana north of Rome,
and now his one protector in the city, the Pope, was on his deathbed.

He saw that he must break out of the trap before it closed upon
him. On the morning of the 15th he put his troops in order and was
preparing to march when two companies of his Italian infantry
mutinied, demanding higher pay. Cesare's loyal German foot-soldiers
turned on the rebellious Italians and chased them into St Peter's, but
the Orsinis, having had wind of his plans, broke through the gate
of the Borgo. According to the chronicler Bernardi, Cesare, hearing
this, cried that he would rather die in the saddle than in bed, mounted
his horse and 'rode like a mad dog' to attack the Orsinis, accompanied

by Jofre, his loyal Romagnol commander Giovanni Sassatelli, the men-at-arms, and the Germans. A ferocious fight ensued in which several men were killed, but the Borgia troops were outnumbered and Cesare was forced to retreat to the Vatican for safety. If the Italian infantry had not abandoned him he would have beaten the Orsinis, the Mantuan Cattaneo reported, but now he was in peril of his life, and deserted by the majority of his men-at-arms, only seventy of whom followed him back to the Palace where the German infantry stood guard. Only the intervention of d'Amboise and the Spanish cardinals and the friendship of the castellan of Sant'Angelo saved him from destruction; while the Orsinis stormed through the Borgo, Cesare with his family fled through the covered way from the Vatican to Castel Sant'Angelo. According to Burchard, he had with him the two little Borgia Dukes, Rodrigo and Giovanni, and his two illegitimate children, of whom nothing before had been known. He was now deserted by most of his men, and his palace pillaged by Baglioni and d'Alviano who, says Giustinian, 'raged like a mad dog' against him, and set guards at every gate to prevent his escape. Two days later, on the night of 17 October, Pius died, after a reign of only twenty-six days, leaving Cesare isolated, at bay in Castel Sant'Angelo, apparently at the mercy of his enemies.

In fact Pius' death was timely for Cesare, and changed his position overnight from one of desperation to one of hope. As soon as Pius was dead, no one in Rome thought of anything else than the election of his successor. Cesare with his clutch of cardinals at his disposal could once more play the role of pope-maker. Giustinian reported on the 19th that the cardinals were totally occupied in negotiations with each other, and that the tone of their business was openly that of the market-place. 'Now,' he wrote disgustedly, 'there is no difference between the pontificate and the sultanate, because to those who offer the most, it is given.' Cesare's Spanish cardinals, he reported, were the masters of the place for their numbers and their unity, and every man who had ambitions towards the Papacy would do anything to please them. The Orsinis were soon made aware that their prey had slipped from their grasp; their request that the cardinals should hold Cesare under arrest in Castel Sant'Angelo until the election of a new pope met with a blunt refusal, and they knew that in *sede vacante* they would soon be obliged to withdraw their troops from Rome. They then changed their tactics, and attempted to lure their victim out of the castle and the city with promises of safe conduct. Cesare turned the trick against them by replying agreeably that he was anxious to leave for France, and would do so within eight or ten days provided the Orsinis left immediately. This was quite simply a ruse to get rid of the Orsinis, and to keep them in check while he carried on negotiations for the forthcoming election.

Cesare had absolutely no intention of leaving Rome, where his position seemed to be growing stronger by the hour. He had now recalled Michelotto with his infantry from Rocca Soriana, and Baldassare da Scipione of Siena and the Imolese Taddeo da Volpe from the French camp with his men-at-arms. The cardinals, eager to accede to his every wish, allowed him not only to retain possession of Castel Sant'-Angelo but to keep his troops with him there. The prospective candidates for the Papacy vied with each other in the lavishness of their promises to him, in the hopes of winning the votes of his cardinals who, as Giustinian wrote sourly, 'have more regard for the convenience of the Duke than anything else'. It is not surprising that Machiavelli, arriving in Rome on 27 October to observe the outcome of the conclave, reported to his government that Cesare was in a confident state of mind: 'He is more in hopes than ever of doing great things, presupposing that there is a pope according to the wishes of his friends.'

And there, despite Cesare's renewed confidence in himself and his future, lay the rub. The race for the Papacy that took place on the death of Pius III was in reality very different in character from that which had been run on the death of Alexander. There was really no question of either a French or Spanish candidate being elected; everyone was agreed that it must be an Italian, and among the Italians one man appeared in a very strong position: Giuliano della Rovere. In the six weeks he had spent in Rome Giuliano's powerful personality had dominated affairs. His vociferous rejection of the French connection had succeeded in convincing the Italians, who, in Prospero Colonna's words, were 'fed up with the barbarians', and even Ferdinand and Isabella, who, it was rumoured, now supported his candidature. Thus Cesare was really much less of a free agent than he liked to believe. Moreover, a few days before the conclave his position was seriously undermined by bad news from the Romagna, where the report of Pius' death and his own flight to Sant'Angelo had encouraged his enemies and weakened the morale of his friends. On the 22nd the Ordelaffis entered Forlì, and on the 26th the Manfredis were back in Faenza, while Malatesta returned to Rimini and

Giovanni Sforza captured the citadel of Pesaro, which up till now had held out for Cesare. Of all his Romagna cities, only Cesena and Imola remained to him, with a handful of scattered castles including the Rocca of Forlì.

The sudden crumbling of his Romagnol states seriously depressed Cesare and forced him to face up to reality. Although he had hitherto favoured d'Amboise, and had obtained five of his cardinals' votes for him, the favour of France had in fact done nothing to stem the tide against him in the Romagna, and in the interests of keeping what still remained to him he thought it better to bow to the inevitable. On Sunday, 29 October, a meeting took place in the Vatican between Cesare and his cardinal followers and Giuliano della Rovere. A signed agreement was drawn up by which, according to Burchard, della Rovere promised that, once elected Pope, he would nominate Cesare Gonfalonier and Captain General, favour him and leave him in possession of his states; in return, all the Spanish cardinals promised to vote for his elevation to the Papacy. The outcome of the election was now a foregone conclusion: on 1 November, after the shortest conclave in the history of the Papacy, Giuliano della Rovere became Pope Julius II.

Cesare has been seriously criticized by historians, including Machiavelli, for his last-minute decision to support Giuliano, but in the circumstances it is hard to see what else he could have done. He could perhaps have held his hand and ordered his supporters to block Giuliano's nomination in the hope of electing yet another compromise candidate, but with a probable majority of the College against him the likelihood was that Giuliano would have been elected anyway. Of the total of thirty-seven cardinals who took part in the conclave, Cesare could have counted on the votes of five 'French' cardinals, d'Amboise, Ascanio, Sanseverino, Medici and Volterra, to block Giuliano, while his own supporters numbered about eleven, together less than half the total voting strength of the College, and in the event he could not have been sure that some of the Spaniards might not either be suborned by promises or decide to obey the orders of their King and support Giuliano. Instead of fruitlessly banging his head against the wall, Cesare obviously thought it more sensible to come to terms with the man who was likely to win, and to extract firm promises from him before his election. Giuliano had the reputation of being a man of his word, and Cesare perforce clung to the hope that he would not break it. Giustinian, who had a private word with Giuliano on the eve of the conclave, formed a different opinion. 'Necessity,' Giuliano told the envoy, 'constrains men to do that which they do not wish, even to place themselves in the hands of others; but once free afterwards, they act in a different manner ...'

On the day after Julius' election, Cesare moved from Castel Sant'-Angelo to the Vatican, where he was attended by forty servants and lodged in the apartments reserved for distinguished guests in the Camera palace built by Innocent VIII overlooking the square of St Peter's. But this outward pomp meant nothing to him without the certainty that the promises Julius had made him were going to be fulfilled. Indeed it must have been a strange and unnerving experience for him to live as a guest in the palace in which for the past four years he had been master. From the windows overlooking the courtyard at the back of the Camera palace, he could see the apartments that had been his father's and his own, in which he had lived the fullest years of his life with his family. But Alexander was dead, and Lucrezia far away at Ferrara; the Borgia apartments were occupied by Pope Julius. Now Cesare was indeed a lone wolf, whose future depended upon his relationship with the man whom he had helped to put in his father's place.

XV

CONFRONTATION

JULIUS II was sixty years old when he attained the object of his lifelong ambition. Men said of him that he had the soul of an emperor, and his appearance was as imperial as his temperament was imperious. Age had whitened his scanty hair, but his tall figure was still erect, and his impressive features had lost none of their impact in the thirty years since Melozzo da Forlì had painted him as Cardinal with his uncle Pope Sixtus. He was a man of volcanic temperament, who never joked, and seemed often absorbed in deep thought; when he acted it was with a dynamic energy, and he was given to fits of violent rage, driving envoys out of the room with his curses whirling round their heads, or striking at unlucky servants with his cane. Guicciardini wrote of him that he was notoriously difficult by nature and formidable with everyone, that he had spent his long life in restless action, in great enmities and friendships and constant intrigues, but that in his loftiness of spirit and magnificence he had always surpassed everyone else. The Venetian envoys Lippomanno and Capello described him as extremely acute, but added:

> He has not the patience to listen quietly to what you say to him, and to take men as he finds them ... No one has any influence over him, and he consults few or none ... One cannot count upon him, for he changes his mind from hour to hour. Anything he has been thinking of overnight has to be carried out immediately the next morning and he insists on doing everything himself. It is almost impossible to describe how strong and violent and difficult to manage he is. In body and soul he has the nature of a giant.

Such a man well deserved the epithet 'terrible' which contemporaries used to describe Duke Valentino. An unwavering ambition combined with a subtle feeling for the winding currents of politics had enabled him to survive the difficulties and dangers of a long life to emerge as the triumphant holder of the papal tiara. His explosive temperament led men to underestimate his political abilities, as they confused the violence of his nature for openness. Guicciardini wrote that he had so long enjoyed the reputation of a generous and veracious man that even Alexander, his bitter enemy, admitted him to be a man of his word. Julius, unlike the Borgias, 'knew very well that no one can more easily deceive others than one who usually had the reputation of never deceiving anyone'.

Machiavelli, at the end of his life, having known the principal kings, emperors, princes and soldiers of his time, considered Julius II and Cesare Borgia as the two most able and exemplary political figures of the age. Now the two were face to face: Julius at sixty in a position of supreme power, Cesare, just twenty-eight, walking the precarious tightrope between success and disaster. Despite the obvious inequality of their respective positions, Cesare at the outset was in a mood of feverish confidence and hope. At twenty-eight he had already survived crises which would have overwhelmed most men, and still, despite the bewildering events of the past two months, he who had been called 'Fortune's son' could not bring himself to believe that his luck had turned against him. His almost superstitious belief in himself and his ability to confront and outface fortune was the wellspring of the unshakeable self-confidence that had been the secret of his success and had so far sustained him on the dangerous course he had set himself. He still had money, and he counted on the fact that Julius, without money or troops, would have need of him. Julius had promised that he would confirm him as Gonfalonier of the Church and Vicar of Romagna, that he would send him to recover his Romagna states with his pontifical blessing as support, and that, as an outward pledge of their alliance, Cesare's daughter Luisa, formerly promised to the young Gonzaga, should be betrothed to the Pope's nephew, Francesco Maria della Rovere of Sinigallia. And so, as Machiavelli remarked: 'The Duke lets himself be carried away by that spirited self-confidence of his, and believes that the word of others should be better kept than his own.'

Cesare, like his father, believed in Julius' reputation, and was buoyed up by the hope that he would keep his promises to him. Indeed, at the outset of his pontificate Julius treated him with the greatest show of cordiality, and Cesare took these demonstrations at their face value, possibly because he so desperately needed to believe in their sincerity. At first his hopes seemed justified; two days after his election Julius dispatched a brief to Faenza exhorting the citizens to obey Cesare, 'our beloved son', ending 'we who love him with a paternal love'. Cesare, pathetically hopeful, wrote to Imola on 7 November expressing the hope that very soon all his states of the Romagna would be reunited, adding: 'And this through the medium of His Holiness, in whom we truly deem that he has revived for us the happy memory of Pope Alexander ...' But of the nature of that paternal love, and the memory which Julius himself retained of Alexander, Machiavelli, a more objective observer than Alexander's son, took a quite different view. Reporting the various forecasts on the development of the situation between Cesare and Julius he wrote:

> Others, who are no less sagacious [by which he meant himself], think that, inasmuch as the Pontiff had need of the Duke in his election, and having made him great promises therefore, he finds it advisable now to feed the Duke on hope; and they fear that, if the latter should not decide upon any other course than to remain in Rome, he may be kept there longer than may be agreeable to him; for the Pope's innate hatred of him is notorious. And it is not to be supposed that Julius II will so quickly have forgotten the ten years of exile which he had to endure under Pope Alexander VI.

Cesare, it seems, had forgotten – or preferred to forget – those years. Throughout his life he evinced a curious blindness as to the effect of his own actions in the past, strange in a man so sensitive to political atmosphere. Like most men he subconsciously believed that others saw things as he did; for him politics were politics and emotion played no part in them, thus only the present or future advantage mattered, and in that light past injuries should be forgotten. He therefore seems to have been unaware of the depths of suspicion with which he was regarded by the powers of Italy, and by the Pope and the Florentines in particular, the two paths by which he hoped to make his way back to his former position. He saw the Pope intent on the recovery of the Romagna, yet without troops, captains or money, while he himself had the remnant of an army, considerable funds, and a name which would instantly attract the best men from all over Italy; moreover he still held several key fortresses in the Romagna, where the people had demonstrated a remarkable loyalty to him. As far as the Florentines were concerned, he saw their jealously and hostility towards Venetian aggression in the Romagna and thought that they would be happy to make common cause with him against the Republic of St Mark. He discounted the bitter hatred of the ordinary citizens of Florence for his actions against them. Obsessed with the future, he seems not to have realized that he must reap the fruits of his successes in the past, and of his reputation as the 'terrible Valentino'. He therefore planned to leave for the Romagna as soon as Julius had confirmed him as Gonfalonier, and to do so with the promise of safe-conduct and support from the Florentines, but, in Machiavelli's words: 'Whoever believes that with great men new services wipe out old injuries, deceives himself.'

Yet Cesare was not entirely wrong in his reading of Julius' mind and his situation. Beset by problems on his accession, the Pope had seemingly not yet decided how he should deal with the problem of Cesare and of the Romagna, where Venice was steadily encroaching in the vacuum left by Cesare's difficulties after his father's death. As far as the territorial power of the Papacy was concerned, Julius' view was that of Alexander – the Papal States must remain under the control of the Church – but for the time being, with an empty treasury and no army at his disposal, he was physically powerless to reassert his supremacy. Julius therefore was strongly tempted to make use of Cesare as an instrument against the Venetians, and thus to fulfil his election promises to him. As Machiavelli wrote with his customary perspicacity:

> He does not love il Valentino, but nonetheless he strings him along for two reasons: one to keep his word, of which men hold him most observant, and for the obligations he has towards him, being recognizant to him for the good part of the Papacy; the other, since it also seems to him, that His Holiness being without forces, the Duke is better placed to resist the Venetians.

Nevertheless, although Cesare was the obvious weapon to employ against Venice, Julius was in two minds as to the wisdom of letting him go. Cesare's enemies bombarded him with pleas for his destruction, but Julius was not a man to listen to other people's advice, nor did he need to be reminded of Cesare's proven potential for causing trouble. Julius knew Rodrigo Borgia's son as well as anyone, and like most of his contemporaries he regarded him as dangerous and unpredictable. Like a caged leopard, once set free there was no knowing which way he would jump, nor where he might pounce. And as a weapon he was a two-edged one, which could easily turn to injure the man who employed him: there were too many historical examples of popes helpless at the dictation of their powerful Captains General, as Eugenius IV had been in the face of Francesco Sforza. And so, as the first week of November passed, Cesare obtained nothing more concrete from Julius than kind words. By the second week, there were signs that the Pope's attitude towards him was hardening; he had made up his mind that neither Cesare nor Venice should be allowed to take possession of the Romagna; the province should return to the direct rule of the Church. Referring to Cesare's hopes of him in an interview with Giustinian on 11 November he said: 'We do not wish that he should persuade himself that we will favour him, nor that he shall have even one rampart in the Romagna, and although we have promised him something, we intend that our promise should extend only to the security of his life and of the money and goods which he has stolen ...'

Cesare, experienced as he was in the labyrinthine paths of Vatican politics, felt the quicksands shifting under his feet. Within a few days of Julius' accession, Giustinian reported with satisfaction that Cesare had lost importance since the election, although it had been only a week ago, and Cesare with his trained political antennae can hardly have failed to sense this, however much he subconsciously refused to recognize it. His confidence was ebbing and his state of mind deteriorating under the uncertainties he faced. The strain of two months of crises following upon a near-fatal illness was telling upon him. In a long and painful interview with Cesare towards the end of the first week of November, Machiavelli found him greatly changed. In place of the self-controlled, masterful figure whose progress he had followed with an awed admiration from Imola to Sinigallia, he saw a man uncertain of himself, breaking into outbursts of bitter, almost hysterical anger. Cesare, having heard reports of the fall of Imola and the advance of the Venetians on Faenza, blamed the Florentines for not supporting him, and alternately stormed and threatened, saying that Florence too would be ruined and he would laugh at it, 'and here he went on at length with words full of poison and anger ...' Machiavelli, whose favourable reports of Cesare had aroused suspicions in Florence that he had been corrupted by him, was at first surprised, then bored, tried to calm him down, and longed to get away from the spectacle of his ruined idol – this, he wrote, 'seemed to take a thousand years'.

Part of Machiavelli's mission to Rome was to discover Cesare's intentions as to the Romagna, and whether there was any serious prospect of his being used against the Venetians there. At first his reports had recommended support for Cesare, but as he watched the deterioration in the man he washed his hands of il Valentino's fate, and his dispatches concerning him took on a note of disillusioned detachment tinged with disgust. His nostrils were quick to scent the smell of doom and failure that now seemed to hang over Cesare like an aura, as he sensed the Pope's secret desire to destroy him, and perceived that even his protector d'Amboise, bought off by the promise of the renewal of his Legateship to France, was weary of him. According to Machiavelli, d'Amboise, when told of Cesare's behaviour at the interview, exclaimed angrily: 'God has not up to now left any sin unpunished, and he won't leave so those of that fellow!'

Still Cesare continued to raise troops and make plans for his departure to the Romagna, almost as if he did not know what else to do. As the Romagna slipped from his grasp so its recovery became an even greater obsession with him. He clutched at the hope that he would be confirmed Gonfalonier and Captain General in the first consistory to be held on 9 November, and it seems that Julius had encouraged him in this, outwardly favouring him although secretly working against him. Giustinian reported on the day of the consistory: 'His Beatitude intends to propose in Consistory this matter of the Captainship for the Duke, but not with the intention that it should take place; since from a good source I hear that he has given to understand to those cardinals to whom he çan speak confidentially, that they should oppose it, because, although he might propose it, it is not his will, but he does not wish to be seen to break his faith with the Duke ...' When the meeting took place, not a word was said about Cesare or his nomination. Cesare was disappointed, but not yet despairing; he continued to hope that he would be nominated in the end, and Julius seems to have been encouraging him to leave, even promising to lend him papal galleys for his journey by sea to La Spezia, and writing a brief to Florence recommending that they grant him a safe-conduct for his troops through Tuscan territory.

Giustinian was puzzled by these demonstrations of favour. 'I find the Pope's mind ambiguous,' he wrote on 11 November, 'for in conversation with me it seems he is badly disposed towards the Duke and desires his ruin ... on the other hand ... he lends him galleys to take him where he wills, recommended in no otherwise than if he were his own son.' Julius' true attitude to Cesare's departure emerged a week later when he told the Venetian that he was letting him go 'because we believe that perhaps he will be attacked and pillaged ...' Cesare, however, convinced of the Pope's sincerity, was once again full of hope; he had promises of troops from d'Amboise and the Duke of Ferrara, and still counted on help from the Florentines. Machiavelli, in an interview with him on 11 November, found him calm and conciliatory, urging Florence to forget the past and join with him in action against Venice. He planned to send his cavalry under Michelotto by land through Tuscany, and to go himself with the infantry by sea to Livorno or Piombino to join up with the cavalry in Florentine territory, before proceeding via Ferrara to the Romagna. The feasibility of the entire plan depended upon the attitude of the Florentine government.

But Florence, much as she hated Venice and was jealous of her success in the Romagna, was even more afraid of il Valentino. The citizens, the Ten wrote to Machiavelli, would never consent to allow Cesare into Tuscany again 'because it would renew the memory of that other passage of his, and the fear occasioned by his behaviour at that time'. Cesare, they continued, was not desirable as a neighbour and could not be counted on for long, and they urged their envoy to explain their decision to the Pope on the grounds of 'the dangerous nature of the man'. No doubt Machiavelli's dispatches had given the Florentines good reason to think that their refusal of a safe-conduct for Cesare would not be displeasing to the Pope, and in fact Julius admitted as much to Machiavelli on 18 November: 'He said it was well thus and that he was in agreement with you.'

The news that Florence had refused the safe-conduct, which Cesare received on the 14th, came as a stunning and unexpected blow, throwing him down from his precarious heights of confidence. Now, perhaps for the first time, he was forced to admit to himself the strength of the forces against him, and the depth of their ill will. He realized that the two powers on whom he had counted for support, Julius and Florence, far from helping him were actually working against him. This last blow to his hopes seems to have had a catalytic effect on him, releasing all the fears, despair and tension which he had held down within himself over the past three difficult and dangerous months. He had been under continual pressure since his father's death and his own illness, which had given him no chance of recuperating his strength sapped by fever. He had managed to build up for himself a fragile edifice of confidence and hope. Now that it was shattered

he lost his self-control and power of decision, plunged in a whirlpool
of self-doubt and irresolution. If he was not on the verge of a break-
down, he was near to it. Men found him unrecognizable: Soderini
described him to Machiavelli as 'inconstant, irresolute, and suspicious, and not standing firm in any decision'; even his friend the
Cardinal of Elna told the envoy 'that he believed the Duke out of
his mind: not knowing what he wanted to do, he was confused and,
irresolute ...' Machiavelli, hearing their reports, wondered whether
he had been wrong about Cesare all along, whether the picture he
had built up of him had been nothing but a mirage, and that the
real Cesare was not the man he had seen at Urbino, Imola and Sinigallia, coolly confronting Fortune, but the bewildered, near-hysteri-
cal creature of that Roman November. He could not decide 'whether
he was so by nature, or because these blows from Fortune have
stunned him, and since he is unaccustomed to receive them, his mind
is confused ...' Cesare's behaviour in an interview with Machiavelli
on the 18th was indeed that of a man who has lost touch with reality.
He raged at the envoy, threatening that if the Florentines did not
give him a safe-conduct, 'he would come to an agreement with the
Venetians or with the devil, and he would go to Pisa, and all the
money and friends he had left he would employ in doing [them]
harm'. Machiavelli cynically assured him that Florence was only
delaying in order to have details of an agreement and encouraged
him to send his agent there. 'I have assured the Duke,' he wrote to
the Ten, 'only to give him a bit of hope, that he may not have to
delay, and the Pope will not therefore have to urge you to give
him a safe-conduct. Your Lordships, when the Duke's man comes,
can treat him negligently, and conduct yourselves as you think
best. ...'

Cesare, who had always shown a supreme ability to adapt his plans
to changing circumstances, now seemed incapable of finding an
alternative, blundering blindly down the road he had set himself
because he could not think what else to do. He had already made
a dangerous mistake in sending off his cavalry by land without a
definite safe-conduct from Florence: without that safe-conduct and
assurances of a friendly reception for himself and his forces from the
Florentines, his whole plan for going to the Romagna was no longer
feasible. The Tuscan route was the only way open to him by land;
to go through Umbria and Urbino, held by the Baglionis and Guidobaldo, was clearly unthinkable. Now that it was no longer safe, he

should have abandoned the idea. In fact by then it was probably too late to go to the Romagna with the few forces he had; he had lost most of his cities and the Venetians were attacking in strength and about to take Faenza. He would have been better advised to take the safe course, join the French in the Kingdom and wait for better times in the future. But Cesare had still not lost his will to fight against Fortune. He was still a gambler; he could not bear to give up the idea of his Romagna dukedom, and possibly, like an animal in a trap, he instinctively longed to be among his own people, on his own ground. It was the blind reaction of the Borgia fighting bull at bay to charge, head down, at the enemy; he could no longer bear to remain inactive in hostile terrain. He felt now as he had when he had ridden out against the Orsinis in October: 'Better to die in the saddle than in bed.' And so, on 19 November, he left Rome for Ostia, 'to the pleasure of all this city', wrote Machiavelli, adding that, since he had already sent off his cavalry without a safe-conduct, 'everybody here laughs at his affairs'.

Even as Cesare was waiting at Ostia for a favourable wind to carry him northward to Tuscany, a further stroke of bad luck befell him. On the 20th news reached Rome of the surrender of Faenza to the Venetians, who were blockading Imola and overrunning its *contado*. The report shocked Julius into a sudden overnight decision: the fortresses still held by Cesare in the Romagna must be placed in the hands of the Church. On the morning of the 21st a messenger was dispatched to Ostia ordering Cesare not to leave, and on the 22nd Cardinals Soderini and Remolines were sent there to demand the cession of the fortresses. Cesare, buoyed up by the prospect of departure, bluntly refused to give them up. His refusal threw Julius into one of his violent rages; a messenger was dispatched to Ostia to order Cesare's arrest, and the Pope's anger was such that Machiavelli thought that Cesare in refusing to hand over the castles had signed his own death-warrant. There were rumours that he had already been murdered: a courtier told Machiavelli on the 26th that the previous day two men had arrived from Ostia, and that on their arrival everyone had been ordered out of the room, but that they had been overheard telling the Pope that Cesare had been thrown into the Tiber as he had ordered. Machiavelli did not know whether or not the story was true, but, he wrote: 'I do believe that if it has not happened, it will. And now we see how honourably this Pope is already paying his debts, and how he wipes them out as with a sponge ...' He

regarded Cesare as finished: 'Since the Duke is taken, whether dead
or alive, we can now act regardless of him ...'

On the 29th Cesare was brought back to Rome under strong guard,
and lodged, a virtual prisoner, in the apartments occupied by d'Amboise that had once been his own. It was the beginning of a long cat-
and-mouse game to be played between Julius and Cesare, in which
the prizes for the Pope were the Romagna castles, and for Cesare his
life and liberty. On 1 December news came that Michelotto with
Carlo Baglioni and Cesare's cavalry had been surrounded and
captured by Tuscan peasants near Arezzo. This report, wrote
Machiavelli, threw the Pope into ecstasies, 'since it seemed to him
that by the capture of that man he had the chance to uncover all
the cruelties of robberies, homicides, sacrileges and other infinite evils,
which over the past eleven years ... have been done in Rome against
God and man.' Julius told Machiavelli merrily that he was looking
forward to talking to Michelotto 'to learn some tricks from him, so
as to enable him the better to govern the Church' and that he hoped
to have him in Rome in good time in order to make use of him in
his coronation procession. It was not only for the imperial pleasure
of seeing his enemy's chief executioner marching captive in his
triumphal procession that Julius was so anxious to have him in his
hands. Michelotto, more than any man alive, knew the darkest secrets
of Cesare's past, and no doubt his evidence could have condemned
his master a hundred times over. For the moment, however, the
Florentines kept Michelotto, and Julius could not make use of him.

For Cesare, the capture of Michelotto and the cavalry was the final
blow which destroyed his hopes and his will to resist. In his desperation to find a friend amongst the enemies who surrounded him, he
even turned to the man whom he had injured most of all, Guidobaldo
da Montefeltro, who had arrived in Rome to press claims for indemnity against Cesare. The interview between the two men took
place on 2 December, and the only detailed account of it appeared
in a letter sent from Rome to Urbino a few days later, which depicted
Cesare as grovelling cap in hand before the Duke of Urbino, begging
his forgiveness and cursing and blaming his father for the taking of
the duchy, while Guidobaldo, with Christ-like magnanimity, raised
Cesare from his knees and embraced him. Cesare was a desperate
man; he was also a consummate actor, and it is not out of character
that he should have put on such a show to arouse pity in the kind-
hearted Guidobaldo. However, Giustinian, who was informed of the

interview by Guidobaldo himself, and who would have been the first to retail the enjoyable spectacle of a grovelling Valentino, makes no mention of such a story. The letter to Urbino was probably an imaginative illustration of the discussion which certainly took place, when Cesare promised to restore all the treasures which he had looted from Urbino with the exception of the famous Trojan tapestries which he had presented to d'Amboise. He also promised to hand over the countersigns (the equivalent of passwords) of his Romagna castles to Guidobaldo in the Pope's name, which he did on the next day. On 4 December, the papal commissioner, accompanied by one of Cesare's men, Pedro de Oviedo, set out for the Romagna, armed with the countersigns. In return, Cesare got nothing from Julius beyond the promise of liberty and immunity of person and goods, a pledge which the wily d'Amboise understandably refused to guarantee. Machiavelli now thought that Cesare had played his last card, and that nothing stood between him and the abyss. 'It seems to me,' he wrote on 3 December, 'that this Duke, little by little, is slipping down to the grave.'

Machiavelli, when he left Rome in mid-December, thought that Cesare was not long for this world, and Giustinian, with deep satisfaction, was of the same opinion. Indeed things looked extremely black for him. On 6 December his admittedly unwilling protector, d'Amboise, left for France; Cesare had hoped to go with him, but as yet no news had been heard from the messengers sent to take over the Romagna castles, and he was not allowed to leave. Now, in Giustinian's words, he was bereft of everyone, and his enemies gathered like vultures to strip the fallen Duke of all he had left. Encouraged by the Pope, they put in huge compensation claims for damages against him – the Riarios asked for 50,000 ducats, Guidobaldo for 200,000, and Florence and Bentivoglio joined in the game. Julius for his part was eagerly gathering evidence to justify legal proceedings against him. On 14 December the late Cardinal Michiel's majordomo was arrested on suspicion of poisoning his master on Cesare's orders; Machiavelli noted in his dispatch: 'Now they are beginning to investigate these affairs ...'

Giustinian hastened to claim Dorotea Caracciolo, who it appears had been placed in a convent after Alexander's death, although, according to the Mantuan envoy Cattaneo, Cesare continued to disclaim all knowledge of her. Giustinian reported that she feared for her life, and requested some form of guarantee from Venice, otherwise she preferred to remain there for the rest of her days. Dorotea herself, according to Sanuto, wrote to Venice thanking them for their envoy's efforts for her release 'from the hell in which she had been for the past three years', begging them to see that her husband would promise to treat her well, else she would return to her mother's house. Dorotea's nervousness as to her reception was understandable; she had been with Cesare for over two years as his mistress, willing or unwilling, and no doubt feared that reprisals might be taken against her for her liaison. However, some guarantee must have been given her, for she later left Rome, and on 4 February 1504 arrived at Faenza, where 'the captain her husband received her joyfully'. Caracciolo, who was now approaching his mid-fifties, and must have known himself a cuckold, presumably tactfully refrained from questioning his young wife about her experiences with Cesare Borgia, for she later bore him four children.

Dorotea's alleged abductor, Diego Ramires, with his brother Pedro, were castellans of the citadel of Cesena, where the envoys bearing the countersigns arrived in mid-December after a dreadful journey through the snowy Apennine passes. The Ramires brothers refused to recognize the countersigns, accused the wretched de Oviedo of treachery to his master, beat him, and hanged him from the castle walls. They then dispatched the papal envoy back to his master with the message that, having held the fortresses for the Duke in the time of his prosperity, it did not seem to them the office of good servants to break faith with him now that they saw him detained and pressed to do that which he did not wish. They would only give them up if Cesare was set free and ordered them to do so, and added, as a warning to Julius, that 'as long as the Duke is detained, they are resolved not to give the fortresses in to the hands of his enemies [by which they meant the Pope himself], but to others . . .' The castellans' proud answer nearly cost their master his life. Julius 'raged like the devil', threatening to throw Cesare into Castel Sant'Angelo to end his days there, and only the pleas of his friends the Spanish cardinals saved him once again. Instead, as a concession to the growing power of Spain, on 20 December he was locked up in the Torre Borgia, in the same room in which three years before Alfonso Bisceglie had been strangled on his orders, a grim reminder, perhaps, that he might well come to the same end.

Cesare's detention threw the Borgia party in Rome into panic. Cardinals Ludovico Borgia and Remolines da Ilerda fled to Naples with Jofre, taking the young Borgia Dukes and possibly Cesare's illegitimate children with them. The news that her son had been brought prisoner back to Rome on 28 November had already caused Vannozza, with the cautious instincts of a woman of property, to transfer the deeds of her house on Piazza Pizzo di Merlo to the church of Santa Maria del Popolo, reserving the use of it during her lifetime. The act was signed on 4 December, and was undoubtedly a precaution against the possibility of a general confiscation of Borgia possessions by the Pope. At about the same time she must have persuaded Cesare to perform the only known pious act of his life, the founding of a ward for elderly and infirm women (many of whom were superannuated prostitutes), attached to the Hospital of the Consolazione, a charity with which Vannozza herself was much concerned. Cesare, with the possibility of sudden death before him, may have seen this donation in the nature of a bribe to the heavenly power to whom he had hitherto paid scant attention. Meanwhile the Borgias took care to protect his earthly possessions. Two convoys of waggons loaded with his goods, one from the houses of Vannozza and the fugitive cardinals at Rome, the other from Cesena, were dispatched for Lucrezia's safe keeping at Ferrara. Neither reached its destination: the Florentines seized the Roman train as it passed through Tuscany, while Giovanni Bentivoglio fell upon the Cesena convoy and had the goods taken to his own house. Bentivoglio's loot included many of the things seized by Michelotto in Alexander's room on the day of his death – the jewel-studded mantle of St Peter, altarpieces, tabernacles, cups worked in gold and emeralds, eighty huge pearls, and 'a cat in gold with two most noble diamonds as its eyes'.

Cesare himself, shut up in the Torre Borgia, in the face of the apparent final ruin of his hopes and in very real danger of his life, seemed not to feel this new blow of fate. He had recovered his mental balance, and his courage and calm strength of spirit impressed even his enemies. Giustinian admitted with grudging admiration that, despite Julius' pressure and his own desperate situation, 'his spirit does not bend'. Cesare, he reported, spent his days watching his friends and servants gambling as if nothing else mattered in the world. Cesare's courage was never questioned, but it is here, in prison, that we have a glimpse of those other qualities that made him the man he was: a refusal to give up even under the worst possible circumstances, a sardonic intelligence that enabled him to take a detached view of life, even his own, and to joke about it. Cattaneo reported that on 10 February a group of Vatican courtiers went to sup with Cesare in the Torre Borgia and that after supper they began to play a game in which each one in turn said the thing that amazed him most. A Roman named de Margano, who had once been imprisoned for taking one of Cesare's women, began: 'I marvel that a man who is in here can be in such good humour . . .' Cesare, who, says Cattaneo, never lost his wit, answered: 'You ask me why I am here, I am so in memory of you and of some others whom I made in a worse humour.' Then they drew lots as it were for the parts of a sheep, each to say his part, one saying my wool will be cut off, the other my tail will be cut off and so on; the head fell to Cesare, who hesitated and seemed not to want to say his piece, then he too said 'my head will be cut off', as if defying fate. And while they were dining, he told them: 'Don't be afraid of being poisoned!' To one of Julius' men who said to him: 'Lord Duke, you were always full of confidence,' he gave a telling reply: 'The more I am in adversity, the more I fortify my spirit.'

Cesare was clearly a man capable of inspiring devotion and loyalty in the men who were close to him. Hated, feared and mistrusted as he was by the princes of Italy, his followers did not desert him in the time of his deepest disgrace, when he was a dangerous man to know, whose favours counted for nothing and whose friendship could bring ruin. It needed something more than the charm which had fascinated Louis XII to hold men to him at a time like this. And the men who followed him were not only his Spanish 'Mafia' and Michelotto, the tough adventurer from Navarre, known as his executioner, whom Guicciardini described as a 'monster of iniquity' and an 'enemy of God and man'. They included the cardinals who stood by him against the Pope, men like Giovanni Vera, his beloved tutor who had known him all his life, and his secretary, the humanist Agapito Geraldini. Nor were they all Spaniards, like the castellans of the Romagna who defied the Pope and Venice on his behalf, but there were also Italians, such as Taddeo della Volpe of Imola, who was captured by the Florentines with Michelotto and preferred to remain in prison rather than enter their service, and Baldassare Scipione of Siena, who later challenged Gonsalvo de Cordoba in his defence.

Cesare was a born leader, a man of superior and instinctive intelligence, who knew what he wanted in life and never faltered in his pursuit of it; those qualities alone were enough to enable him to dominate others, even men twice his own age. But it was above all his deep confidence in himself that inspired the same feeling in others; when that confidence failed him, as it did only once, briefly, in November, it surprised those who knew him to the extent that Machiavelli doubted his whole reading of the character of the man, and his friend Elna thought him out of his mind.

Indeed it was the continuing loyalty of Cesare's Spanish cardinals and the castellans of the Romagna which made his position during the period of his imprisonment stronger than it appeared. Two days after he was placed in the Torre Borgia, the cardinals went to the Pope and attempted to obtain his release, pointing out to Julius the danger that if Cesare were not set free the castellans might hand the castles over to the Venetians. Julius retorted that the Venetians might take them by force, but he was on weak ground, and he knew it. The castellans for their part wrote to Cesare assuring him that they could hold out against the Pope or any power in the world, and that they would never give up the fortresses until they saw him completely at liberty. Moreover the decisive defeat of the French by Gonsalvo de Cordoba on the Garigliano in the last week of December meant that French dominion in Naples was at an end, and the Spaniards were now the power to be reckoned with in southern Italy. Consequently the influence of the Spanish cardinals at the Vatican was immeasurably increased, and Julius dared not move against Cesare. As far as the castles were concerned, he had not the troops to take them, and he was indeed very much afraid that Cesare's castellans might hand them over to Venice in revenge for his treatment of their master. While Cesare professed to have no control over his commanders, Julius was convinced that he sent them secret messages urging them to stand firm.

Cesare no doubt enjoyed the spectacle of Julius' difficulties, but he was anxious for his liberty, and on 18 January his cardinals came to an agreement with the Pope, promising that he would order the cession of the castles within forty days in return for his freedom and the security of his goods. Rumours of his impending release were enough to send Giustinian hurrying to the Palace to warn Julius:

> That Duke Valentino was a person of evil nature; that he still had
> sufficient funds, however much he might pretend to be poor; he
> still enjoyed credit and great goodwill with the soldiers, for the great
> liberty he allowed them to rob and do what they willed, while he

also paid them well; therefore he, once set free, would easily be able to gather together many men, and cause enough commotion, that he would cause His Holiness more trouble than perhaps he thought.

Julius did not need Giustinian to tell him what a dangerous man Cesare was, but he wanted the Romagna castles, and it seemed that only by setting him free could he lay his hands upon them. He was weary of the long game he was playing with il Valentino; irritation at his helplessness made him ill, and he complained bitterly of Cesare's deviousness, saying that 'he was false, and that he could find no reality in him, and that in this matter he had made so many double plays that His Holiness did not know what foundation to put on it'. Cesare's cardinals complained equally of the Pope. Giovanni Vera, who was in charge of the negotiations, told Giustinian that he could find no firmness in Julius, that what he said one day he unsaid the next. Giustinian commented exasperatedly: 'These affairs of il Valentino are more complicated than a labyrinth.'

Indeed they were; on 8 February Giustinian reported that Cesare's case was desperate, and no one could be sure of his life. Cesare wore a sword at his belt all day and slept with it at the head of his bed by night. Yet a week later he was seen boarding a galley for Ostia, the cardinals having succeeded in persuading Julius to allow him to go there in custody of Bernardino Carvajal, Cardinal of Santa Croce, to be released once the fortresses were handed over. Cesare, delighted at the prospect of liberty, raced his horse up and down the banks of the river before boarding the galley, but once he reached Ostia he found himself under even more rigorous confinement than before. He was not allowed out of the walls of the citadel and alleviated his boredom by firing the castle cannon himself over the empty shore and the desolate valley behind. Once again, at the end of February, the castellans sent envoys back to the Pope with the message that they would not surrender the fortresses until the Duke was a free man. Julius, said Giustinian, told them to go and give them to the Turk, the Venetians or to whom they wished, chased them out of the chamber and went raging into his bedroom.

The matter seemed at deadlock, but Cesare was by now desperate to be free. He was in touch with the Borgia cardinals in Naples, and had plans in mind for his future. On 10 March a new agreement was made, with Cesare again promising to surrender the castles of Cesena and Bertinoro, and to pay the castellan of Forlì 15,000 ducats to give up the Rocca. As far as Cesena and Bertinoro were concerned, he meant what he said, for on payment of 3000 ducats each the Ramires brothers handed over the castles in mid-April. Forlì was another matter. Cesare did not intend to give up his last card yet; moreover the castle contained valuable goods, including the furnishings looted from Guidobaldo, and he did not trust Julius to return them. News of the surrender of Cesena and Bertinoro reached Ostia before it reached Rome, as Cesare's custodian Carvajal had ensured that it would. Carvajal, who suspected that Julius had really no intention of letting his prisoner go, had already made arrangements for ships and a safe-conduct from Gonsalvo de Cordoba to carry Cesare to Naples, and released him without waiting for permission from the Pope.

The Spanish galleys had been detained in Naples by unfavourable winds, but Cesare was not prepared to wait. On the morning of 19 April he rode out of the castle of Ostia and galloped south to Nettuno, where he took a small rowing-boat, hugging the coast to a point of thirty miles from Naples, making the rest of the journey on horseback. On the 28th he rode into Naples to the house of Cardinal Ludovico Borgia, and was enthusiastically received by the cardinals and Jofre. Even Sancia, who had finally quarrelled with her husband and refused to have him in her house, invited her brother-in-law to dinner. Cesare went, apparently in the role of mediator, but the fiery princess was adamant and the attempt at reconciliation failed.

Cesare, however, had other things to think about than his brother's marriage problems. The months of imprisonment had told upon him, and he was still not well. Carvajal told Giustinian on 26 April that at Ostia Cesare had been in pain – 'the French disease in his opinion' – that his face was ravaged and blotched with pustules, and that he had mocked those who feared him in such a condition. Carvajal was probably mistaken in his diagnosis of syphilis as the cause of Cesare's condition; tertiary malaria is a recognized modern treatment for the disease, and Cesare's violent bout of it the previous August should have cured him. The after-effects of his illness and prolonged confinement could well have been responsible for his state. At Naples he was at last free and full of hope; life seemed to have begun again for him in the warmth and liberty of that early Neapolitan summer, and nothing mattered to him now but the pursuance of his plans.

He had begun his preparations for action even before reaching Naples; from Gaeta he had dispatched letters of credit for his captains in Rome, who hired ships and set off to join him. Giustinian reported on the 25th that 'the clan' were leaving every day. Giovanni Vera sent funds to the amount of over 12,000 ducats, while Baldassare da Scipione arrived in Rome to recruit cavalry, declaring publicly that his lord 'would soon return to good standing and give his enemies food for thought ...' Cesare planned to go by sea either to Pisa, still in desperate straits in her struggle against Florence, or to Piombino, where d'Appiano's rule seemed insecure. He had given his word to Carvajal not to cause trouble, and specifically not to disturb the States of the Church, but it is impossible to believe that he did not secretly intend to return to the Romagna, where Gonsalvo de Mirafonte still held out for him in the great Rocca of Forlì. He was counting on the support of the Viceroy of Naples, Gonsalvo de Cordoba, who had granted him the safe-conduct to come to Naples. Gonsalvo had done him the honour of a formal visit on the evening of his arrival in Naples, but since then his attitude towards him had been enigmatic. Cesare had high hopes of Gonsalvo and bombarded him with requests for ships, supplies and artillery, but to dispassionate observers it seemed that the 'Great Captain' was stalling, 'stringing him along and feeding him with hope' as Julius had done. However, on 24 May the Florentine envoy at Naples, Pandolfini, who was extremely worried by Cesare's obvious intentions concerning Pisa, reported that Gonsalvo had absolutely promised to let him go to Piombino and Pisa with 3000 foot, eight ships and artillery, and that Giulio degli Alberini, one of Cesare's Roman gentlemen, had been preparing the artillery on the quayside for embarkation. Everything was ready, therefore, when on 26 May, the eve of his departure, Cesare went to the Castel Nuovo to take leave of Gonsalvo. There, that night, as he made to leave, one of Gonsalvo's gentlemen intimated to him that he was under arrest. Cesare, in surprise and disbelief, 'gave forth a great cry "Santa Maria! I am betrayed! With me only has my Lord Gonsalvo dealt cruelly."'

Cesare, the great deceiver, had been himself deceived, and by the man from whom, perhaps naively, he had least expected it. Years ago, Collenuccio had noted of him that, paradoxically, 'he set great store by straightforward men'; he had trusted Julius as a man of his word, and he had trusted Gonsalvo, who enjoyed a reputation for being the soul of honour. It may at first sight seem strange that the

concept of honour should have had such importance in an age of
political and moral unscrupulousness, and to a man like Cesare; less
strange, perhaps, if one considers that the same is true of the Sicilian
Mafia today. It was a concept handed down from the mythical age
of chivalry, which still had a strong hold on the Renaissance imagination. Lies, intrigue, deception and betrayal were one thing, stratagems
to be applauded if they succeeded; public honour and the keeping
of a solemnly given word were quite another. *Mancanza di fede*, breaking faith, was the most serious accusation which could be levelled at
a man, the charge which the desperate Paolo Orsini had screamed
at Cesare at the time of his arrest at Sinigallia, while Cesare himself
had justified his action by retorting that the condottieri had been
guilty of repeatedly breaking their faith with him. Gonsalvo had given
Cesare his sworn safe-conduct to come to Naples, and it is therefore
not surprising that Cesare should have relied on it. Gonsalvo's contemporaries condemned him for thus violating his faith, and Gonsalvo
himself was deeply conscious of it. He sent immediately to recover
the safe-conduct from Baldassare da Scipione, who had taken refuge
in the house of Prospero Colonna, and according to his biographer
Giovio his breach of faith with Cesare was one of the three actions
of his life which he regretted on his deathbed.

Gonsalvo, the gallant, brilliant soldier, had lured Cesare into a web
of international intrigue which stretched from the Vatican to the court
of Castile and Aragon. Julius, as everyone at Rome noted, despite
the brave face he put upon it, was deeply worried by Cesare's escape
and extremely afraid of what he might do, and he remained obsessed
by the idea that he could not be secure as long as il Valentino was
at large. The Spanish sovereigns for their part desperately needed two
things from the Pope, a dispensation enabling Catherine of Aragon
to marry Henry VIII of England and their own investiture with the
kingdom of Naples. On the one hand, therefore, they were prepared
to do anything to please the Pope, while on the other, since they suspected him of being pro-French, they were content, as the Spanish
ambassador at Rome told the Venetian envoy, 'to keep the Pope in
this fear of il Valentino ...' Cesare was a card in the international
game, an ace up the Spanish King's sleeve. The threat of putting him
into play would be enough to bring the Pope to heel. And the
Spaniards were afraid of what Cesare might do if he joined the
French; one of Gonsalvo's motives for bringing him to Naples was
to keep him out of their hands.

Gonsalvo, too, may well have been playing a double game as far as Cesare was concerned. His protectress, Isabella of Castile, was slowly but inexorably dying of terminal cancer of the womb, and he knew that Ferdinand regarded him with jealousy and suspicion. Gonsalvo was an independent man of high ambitions, commanding the absolute loyalty of his troops, and Ferdinand suspected him, not without reason, of aiming at establishing a state for himself in Italy. Gonsalvo had already considered a move against the French in Tuscany through Pisa in concert with Cesare the previous year, and it seems that Cesare at least believed that this plan had been renewed. But as early as March of that year Gonsalvo contemplated undertaking the expedition in person, and it is not beyond the bounds of possibility to conjecture that he saw Pisa as a possible lordship for himself. A Pisan envoy, Francesco del Pitta, was negotiating with both Cesare and Gonsalvo simultaneously but independently in Naples in May, and at the end of the month he referred back to his government asking whether they preferred to have the lordship of il Valentino or that of Spain. The government replied on 1 June that, although they would have preferred Spain, 'if Valentino should come in good order before Spain he would be accepted ...' Pitta was to inform Gonsalvo of this, and if he made no move then they would have il Valentino.

Gonsalvo must have known of these negotiations, and resented them. Perhaps too he now realized that Cesare's incalculable quality made him impossible even for him to control. He knew that if il Valentino should cause trouble for the Pope in the Romagna he would be blamed for it. At any rate it is clear from a letter which he wrote to de Rojas in Rome on 17 May that he had already made up his mind how to deal with Cesare at least a week before the actual arrest, and certainly before he had finally promised him troops and permission to depart. In this letter he confirmed that he understood the Catholic Kings' attitude to the Pope and his recovery of the Romagna, and that since they had ordered him to help the Pope he had decided that Cesare should be detained until he surrendered the Rocca of Forlì, and, if necessary, sent in custody to Spain. 'I desire to be assured of two things,' he wrote, 'first whether such a procedure commends itself to your judgement; secondly whether the Pope is willing to request me in writing to carry it into effect.' He asked for an immediate reply:

... because the Duke of Romagna is pressing me to allow him to depart for Pisa and Piombino, and begs for my aid in ships, men and guns ... and I have given him no reason to suspect it will not take place, and we have agreed that next Monday he will depart, and I am keeping him dangling, asking what security he will give me that he will do no disservice to Their Highnesses nor to the Pope, and thus we are carrying on this negotiation ...

He ended by warning the envoy that if the Pope agreed to his proposal to arrest Cesare the greatest secrecy must be preserved, 'because these Cardinals [Borgia and Remolines] have many intimates within His Holiness' Chamber, and are advised of everything'. The secret was well kept; on this occasion the Borgia network within the Vatican failed to detect the trap which was being prepared for their leader.

Cesare's despair at finding himself once again behind bars after a brief month of liberty can only be guessed at. Three days after his arrest he was placed in a room known as 'the Oven', which had always been used as a maximum security prison for important captives. His mistress was taken away from him and he was forbidden all communication with the outside world, with the exception of envoys from Gonsalvo who pressed him for the surrender of Forlì. While Cesare sweltered in solitary confinement in 'the Oven', the faithful Michelotto suffered under torture in the Roman prison of Torre di Nona. He had been brought to Rome on 21 May, and Cesare before his own arrest had been making every effort for his release, offering Julius 10,000 ducats to let him go, but now, as the Mantuan envoy remarked, 'it is another question in both their cases ...' Michelotto was interrogated about the deaths of a long list of people, including Gandia and Alfonso Bisceglie, but even on the rack he apparently refused to implicate Cesare. An official of the Senate wrote to a secretary of Ercole d'Este informing him that they had begun to examine Michelotto with torture concerning the crimes, 'but up till now he has remained silent and has confessed nothing, I do not know if he will do so ... He said that it was Pope Alexander who ordered the death of Don Alfonso [Bisceglie].' In implicating Alexander, who was beyond harm, Michelotto was undoubtedly shielding Cesare, and it seems that Julius did not succeed in extracting anything incriminating from him, for nothing was made public and he was eventually released. Michelotto's loyalty contrasted strongly with the callous behaviour of Cesare's brother Jofre who, Pandolfini reported, was seen every day with Gonsalvo 'and rides with him in triumph; and to complete his felicity he only needs to recover his wife who refuses to hear anything of it'.

In Rome Julius was of course highly delighted at Cesare's arrest and showered the Spanish envoy with favours – 'It is thought,' Giustinian commented, 'perhaps to induce them to the death of Valentino...' Julius remained obsessed with Cesare almost to the exclusion of other business. 'The Pope', wrote Giustinian contemptuously, 'makes a considerable demonstration of every little thing or nothing at all, neglecting that for which he should have a care.' Attempts were made to trap Alessandro Spanocchi, Cesare's treasurer; his mother's house was searched, and his goods and messengers pounced upon by the papal agents wherever they could be found.

Meanwhile throughout June Cesare refused to surrender Forlì, despite constant pressure from Gonsalvo. The castle was not only his last remaining possession in the Romagna, and as such of a desperate symbolic significance to him, but it also contained valuable goods which the Pope refused to promise to restore to him. On 29 June the Florentine envoy in Naples reported Cesare as more obstinate than ever on the question of Forlì. Then suddenly in the first week of July he gave in, perhaps because he realized the hopelessness of holding out any longer; on 4 July the castellan's nephew was dispatched to Venice to fetch the 15,000 ducats for the surrender of the castle, and on the 29th the capitulation agreement signed by Cesare reached Forlì. On 11 August, Cesare's loyal castellan Gonsalvo de Mirafonte marched out of the fortress, riding in the defiant stance of a conqueror with his lance at rest on his thigh, preceded by a herald proclaiming the Duke of Romagna. As he rode out, the heavens opened in a deluge of torrential rain, due, says Bernardi, to an eclipse of the sun and other 'malign celestial aspects that occurred during the day'. For Cesare, the celestial aspects were indeed malign: Guidobaldo, with tears in his eyes, entered the castle to receive, among other things, his beloved library; Julius' agents seized the rest; for the Duke of Romagna nothing was left.

Cesare did not regain his liberty in return for the Rocca di Forlì. Within a few days of its surrender he was put in the charge of Prospero Colonna and, with only a page for company, placed aboard a galley bound for Spain. Julius had won, but his fear of Cesare was such that he could not bring himself to be generous in victory towards his fallen enemy. Although he had promised Cesare's cardinals to write a brief recommending Cesare to Ferdinand, he told Giustinian that after further consideration he had rescinded the brief, since the King might misinterpret it and favour Cesare too greatly and think of restoring him to his states. Cesare's enemies hoped that he was going to Spain to answer criminal charges concerning Gandia and Bisceglie which would bring him to his death, but none of them, knowing il Valentino as they did, could be sure that he would not return.

XVI

'EITHER CAESAR OR NOTHING'

It was ironic that Cesare should disembark at the very same Valencian port, Villanueva del Grao, from which his great-uncle, Alonso de Borja, had set off sixty-two years before, launched on the career that brought him to the Papacy and the Borgias to Italy.

For Cesare it was a wretched return to the land of his fathers; there was no triumphal reception for Alonso's great-nephew. He disembarked 'very poorly', an observer reported, at the end of September, and was immediately transferred under heavy guard to the fortress of Chinchilla, 700 feet up in the mountains of Valencia. Here, in strict confinement, with only his squire Juanito Grasica to attend him, he had plenty of time to reflect on the destiny which had brought him for the first time, as a prisoner, so near to the lands from which his family had sprung, to Jativa, where his father was born, and to Gandia, where Juan's widow Maria Enriques nursed her hatred of the brother-in-law whom she regarded as the murderer of her husband.

The shadows of Juan and Alfonso Bisceglie lay darkly across Cesare's future as he saw it from within the walls of his prison: Even before he left Naples it had been reliably reported that the Catholic Kings intended to put him on trial for his life for their murders. He cannot have been unaware of his sister-in-law's vindictive feelings towards him, and moreover he knew that she was a favourite at court, where the sovereigns regarded him with extreme hostility. 'We have always abhorred him for his crimes,' they had written to de Rojas in May. Nor could he hope for help from France, where Louis in his anger at Cesare's last betrayal had stripped him of his titles to the duchy of Valentinois and the lordship of Issoudun. Moreover, since France and Spain had signed a truce over Naples he could no longer play his usual game between them. For both sovereigns, Cesare, a prisoner, the enemy of the Pope, and without an army at his back, had lost both his credibility and his usefulness. And although Cesare spoke Spanish as he spoke Italian, Spain for him was a foreign land. Never can he have felt so isolated as in the first months of his lonely confinement in Chinchilla.

However, his friends had not forgotten him. His Spanish cardinals, his sister Lucrezia and his brother-in-law Jean d'Albret, King of Navarre, bombarded the Spanish court with pleas for his release. Their efforts at least succeeded in easing the severity of the conditions under which he was held. At the end of October Giovanni Vera received letters from Cesare's major-domo Requerenz reporting that he had now been allowed eight servants. Requerenz had spoken to the King about his master's liberation, and Ferdinand had answered that he had not ordered the Duke's imprisonment but was holding him because of the things of which Gonsalvo had accused him, and when these were proven groundless he would doubtless accede to the Spanish cardinals' pleas for his release. Everything, however, must wait until Queen Isabella regained her health.

In fact it was clear to everyone that Isabella, Cesare's implacable enemy, was on her deathbed, and the news of her death at Medina on 26 November 1504 raised the Borgia party's hopes that he would be released. Ferdinand had no love for Cesare, indeed he was largely indifferent to his fate, but he was essentially a pragmatist and saw him as a possible instrument to serve his own ends in Italy. As Giustinian, who shared the Pope's nervousness about Cesare, divined: 'It seemed to him that il Valentino would be the perfect instrument to upset the affairs of the Florentines, and at the same time to give the Pope such embarrassment that the troubles he would have on his hands would prevent him from meddling in the affairs of others ...' Early in 1505 rumours were current in Rome that Cesare had been honourably received at court, and that Ferdinand intended to 'make use of his person in Italy'. At Ferrara, Lucrezia received letters to the same effect. Cesare's partisans in Italy were overjoyed, but it soon became clear that their hopes, like Giustinian's fears, had been exaggerated. Hard on the heels of the reports of his release came definite news that he was even more strictly confined than before. Cesare, typically, had taken matters into his own hands and attempted to escape.

The most widely told story of his escape attempt was a colourful one. Cesare invited the governor of the castle, Don Gabriele de

Guzman, to join him on the ramparts of the tower in which he was imprisoned. While the governor was occupied in pointing out various landmarks on the horizon, he attacked him and put his arms around him with the idea of throwing him off the tower. However, his famous strength had been impaired by long imprisonment, and de Guzman, no mean wrestler himself, succeeded in pinning him to the ground. Recognizing himself beaten, Cesare attempted with sang-froid to gloss over the incident as a simple trial of strength, a temptation he had been unable to resist. While it might have amused Cesare to test his pent-up energy on a man with a reputation for strength, he would not have been stupid enough to have thought that a murderous attack on his jailer would have led to his own escape. In fact the true account of his abortive escape was probably that given out by the Spanish envoy in Rome, who told one of Isabella d'Este's correspondents that Cesare had used the more prosaic but no less dangerous method of knotting his sheets together and lowering himself out of the window, but the improvised lifeline broke and he fell heavily into the fosse of the castle, fracturing his shoulder, whereupon he was carried back to his room and kept under strict surveillance. But whatever the manner of his attempt at escape, the fact that he tried to do so indicates that he saw a future for himself outside the walls of Chinchilla. Even under the isolated conditions in which he lived, he had still not lost his hope nor his courage – nor it seems any of his effrontery, for in May 1505 he authorized his brother-in-law d'Albret to request the payment of Charlotte's dowry from Louis XII.

Some time after midsummer of 1505, Cesare was taken from Chinchilla and imprisoned in the great keep, the Torre de Homenaje, of the castle of La Mota at Medina del Campo in the heartland of Castile. La Mota was considered a maximum security prison, a Spanish Colditz; no one, it was thought, could either escape or be rescued from the castle with its central keep, four enceintes, single access gate and deep defence ditches. The castle stood across the River Zapardiel facing the town of Medina, the great emporium of Castile, where the fairs held four times a year brought merchants, bankers and traders from all over Europe to barter for the precious spices which came from the East via Portugal, and the fine Merino wool of Castile. More important from Cesare's point of view, Medina was also one of the seats of the Spanish court, and indeed his arch-enemy Isabella had died there the previous November.

According to a Venetian report, Cesare passed the time watching

the falcons from the windows of his room in the keep, symbolic perhaps of his dreams of freedom. For his thoughts, like the falcons, were
soaring beyond the fierce walls of La Mota. The circumstances of
Spanish internal politics after the death of Isabella had opened up
interesting possibilities for him, avenues which led beyond the
frontiers of Spain, through his brother-in-law's kingdom of Navarre,
to the courts of the Emperor Maximilian in Germany and of his son,
the Archduke Philip, in Flanders. Even from the isolation of Chinchilla he had succeeded in maintaining contact with his friends outside; the document of procuration for d'Albret's requisition of Charlotte's dowry, which had been drawn up in Navarre in May, had been
authenticated by a signature executed by Cesare at Chinchilla, and
carried, no doubt by secret messenger, to Navarre. At Medina, within
a bowshot of the busy town and the court, communication between
the prisoner and his partisans was easier, and Cesare was soon back
at his old game of high political intrigue.

Isabella's death left her daughter Juana, the wife of Maximilian's
son the Archduke Philip, as heiress to the throne of Castile. But Juana,
called 'La Loca', the Mad, was mentally unstable, a melancholic,
deeply neurotic and obsessively in love with her handsome husband,
whose life she made impossible with her psychopathic jealousy. The
Venetian envoy described Philip in June 1506: 'He was twenty-eight
years old, handsome in body, gay and happy, an apt jouster, a skilful
horseman, prudent and skilled in war, and capable of supporting all
manner of fatigue. His character was good, moreover he was magnificent, liberal, affable, and sweet, familiar with all and opposed to etiquette.' Juana, said the envoy, although she was very beautiful, of
the highest lineage and heiress to a great kingdom, tormented her
husband with her jealousy to such an extent that he never succeeded
in contenting her. She was silent, withdrawn from the world, never
addressed a word to anybody, and, avoiding feasting and pleasure,
consumed herself in her jealousy, and never allowed any woman
round her, whether Flemish or Spanish, young or old. Nonetheless,
he said, she was intelligent, spoke well when she wanted to, and had
great dignity. In the absences of her husband she would retreat into
one of the huge chimney places in the palace kitchens at Medina del
Campo, plunged in melancholy and tortured by her obsessive jealousy. Only Isabella had had any influence over her, and her death
aggravated her daughter's illness. Isabella, aware that Juana would
probably be incapable of ruling, had in her will appointed her

husband Ferdinand as Regent of Castile, with the proviso that this should be so as long as he did not remarry.

But Ferdinand was appalled by the prospect of a Habsburg take-over of Spain, implied by the fact that Juana's son, the future Charles V, was heir not only to the Spanish throne but to the Empire and the Netherlands as well. Moreover his own position as Regent was insecure; the great Castilian nobles had always resented their Catalan King, and followed Philip as representing the interests of Castile. Thus the court was split into two parties, one for Philip, led by the Count of Benavente, the other for Ferdinand, headed by Fabrique de Toledo, Duke of Alba. Ferdinand's reaction to the threat of the Habsburg interest had been to draw closer to Louis of France. Negotiations between the two powers were carried on through the summer of 1503. They culminated in the signing of a treaty at Blois on 12 October 1505 which provided not only an ingenious solution to the question of Naples but also a young bride for Ferdinand who might give him the male heir he desired and, thus turn the political future of Spain in his favour and against the Habsburgs. Louis promised the fifty-four-year-old Ferdinand the hand of his niece, the beautiful eighteen-year-old Germaine de Foix; her dowry was to be the half of the kingdom of Naples ceded to France under the Treaty of Granada, which was anyway in the *de facto* possession of Spain. Louis further promised to help Ferdinand conquer the kingdom of Navarre, which on his death should go to the crown of France through Gaston de Foix, the brother of Ferdinand's bride Germaine. On 18 March 1506, Ferdinand married Germaine at Dueñas, near Valladolid, the Spanish Cortes having set aside the remarriage clause in Isabella's will. But Philip had already declared his rights to the Regency from Flanders and set sail for Spain, where he arrived at Corunna six weeks after his father-in-law's marriage. On 27 June Ferdinand surrendered his government of Castile to Philip and Juana, with the proviso that Juana should not be allowed to govern on the grounds of her instability. On the face of it Philip had won hands down.

But Ferdinand, the cunning old Catalan, had no intention of allowing the Habsburgs to rule Castile. His attitude to political trickery is well illustrated by the story that, when he heard that Louis had complained that he had cheated him once, Ferdinand promptly riposted: 'He lied, the drunkard, I cheated him three times.' On the same day that he signed the treaty with Philip, he indited a private statement to the effect that the agreement was invalid since it had been extracted from him under compulsion, and that he would never consent to deprive his daughter of her rights as heiress to Castile. Clearly the old fox intended to leave the way open for his government of Castile through his daughter should the occasion arise. But for the moment he was content to leave Castile to Philip while he journeyed to Naples to ensure his hold on that kingdom, which by rights belonged to the crown of Aragon. For some time past Ferdinand had been increasingly jealous and suspicious of his viceroy Gonsalvo, whose loyalty had been to Queen Isabella and not to himself. He again suspected Gonsalvo of acting independently of himself in Tuscany, as he had the previous year, and of entering into correspondence with his arch-enemy the Emperor Maximilian. He contemplated using Cesare against Gonsalvo should the necessity arise, and he certainly did not want to leave such a dangerous weapon as Duke Valentino in the hands of his son-in-law Philip.

Philip, however, had every intention of using Cesare himself, and his transfer to Medina in midsummer 1505 was probably connected with the Archduke's arrival in Castile. A struggle then developed between Philip and Ferdinand for possession of the prisoner. Ferdinand sent Don Pedro de Ayala to Medina to demand that Cesare should be handed over to him against the assurance that he would hold him prisoner in the castle of Ejerica in Valencia until his own departure for Naples, when he would take Duke Valentino with him. Philip refused to surrender him, and referred the question to the Council of Castile, which decided that Cesare should remain in the custody of the Council until the decision of the Gandia process against him. Ferdinand refused to accept this and made a direct request to Don Bernardino de Cardenas, in whose charge he had placed the prisoner, to release Cesare into his hands. De Cardenas was tempted to obey, but told Ferdinand's messenger that if he tried to hand over Cesare without Philip's consent, then Philip would remove him by force. Ferdinand did not consider himself beaten; he appointed an envoy to make a formal request for the prisoner to Juana's court, and set sail for Naples on 6 September, still determined to have him.

Cesare was far from being a helpless pawn in the struggle between Ferdinand and his son-in-law, and had already made up his mind which party he would support. He did not trust Ferdinand, whose cunning and political cynicism easily matched his own, and who would never allow him free rein for his adventurous spirit. Between Ferdinand and his new ally Louis, who had definitively turned against his former protégé, Cesare knew that he would indeed be helpless, and might easily be offered as a political sacrifice to his old enemy Pope Julius. He was therefore in close touch with Philip's party at court, and furthermore an active participant in an intrigue with the Emperor Maximilian and his own staunchest supporter, his brother-in-law Jean d'Albret, King of Navarre.

The tiny independent kingdom of Navarre, the key to the gates of the Pyrenees, was clearly marked out as the victim of the recent alliance between France and Spain. Jean d'Albret, who had gained the throne through his marriage to Catherine de Foix, sister of the late King François Phoebus, who had died without heirs, was now threatened by both Louis and Ferdinand under the terms of the Treaty of Blois. While Ferdinand had his own pro-Castilian party within Navarre, Louis was actively encouraging Catherine's cousin, Gaston de Foix, in his claims to the Navarrese crown. Cesare, from within the walls of La Mota, was promoting an alliance between Philip and Maximilian on the one hand and d'Albret on the other. For Cesare, Navarre was to be the step towards a new career in the service of the Emperor, a path which he hoped would lead him back to Italy. An agreement between d'Albret and Philip had been signed at Tudela in August, and close connections established with Maximilian during September, when Philip died suddenly of a chill at Burgos on 25 September.

Philip's premature death changed the situation overnight. With Philip dead and Juana now in a hopeless condition, aggravated to the point of a macabre mania by his loss, the power in Castile would be that of Ferdinand, who, fortunately for Cesare and the pro-Habsburg party, was now in Italy, where it was noted that he showed no signs of mourning his son-in-law's death. The heir to the throne, Charles v, was a child of six, far away in Flanders. But Philip's cause was now the cause of the infant Charles, and the pro-Habsburg party at the Spanish court concocted a plan with Cesare and the imperial ambassadors by which Cesare should go via Navarre to Flanders to bring Charles to Spain. Navarre was to be the Habsburgs' gate to Spain, and Cesare their instrument. According to the Spanish historian Zurita, Cesare was the moving spirit of the intrigue; he was in close touch with Maximilian's envoys de Vere and Andreas de Burgo, who had given him signed guarantees that in the case of any future agreement between the Emperor and King Ferdinand, the Emperor would not hand him over to the King.

For Cesare, the plan, if it was to succeed at all, must be put into immediate action. He knew that Bernardino de Cardenas, wishing to ingratiate himself with Ferdinand, had intimated to his envoy Ferrer that he was now willing to hand over Cesare. Ferrer had accepted the offer in principle, but said that he must write to Ferdinand to find out what he wanted done with the prisoner. For Cesare, his future with Maximilian represented his last chance of the power and destiny he still believed in, a chance which might be lost if he waited until Ferdinand's orders reached Medina. In conjunction with his partisan, the Count of Benavente, he therefore planned to dare the impossible – an escape from La Mota.

Benavente, says Zurita, was so determined to get Cesare out of La Mota and Ferdinand's hands that he was prepared to attack the castle and murder the governor to achieve it. However, it was undoubtedly Cesare who planned the method of his escape – more secret, and also he thought more sure, than a bloody skirmish which might fail in its purpose. It also required more personal daring, a quality which he had never lacked. The plan was to follow the lines of his abortive escape from Chinchilla, but it was more carefully prepared, and made easier by the fact that since Philip's accession to the regency the governor de Cardenas had regarded Cesare as a possible future commander of the royal troops; in agreement with Philip he had therefore provided him with numerous servants and a personal chaplain. The chaplain now acted as the go-between for Cesare and Benavente, while Cesare had succeeded in suborning one of the servants of Don Gabriel de Tapia, the administrator of La Mota, to provide the ropes for the escape.

On the night of 25 October, at the appointed hour, three men, one of them the chaplain, waited for Cesare in the darkness of the fosse beneath the keep. A rope was let down from the narrow pointed window of the room at the top of the tower in which he was lodged. One of his servants was first down the rope, but it was too short for the great height, and on reaching the end he fell, injuring himself severely. Cesare followed, but the alarm had been given and the rope was cut from above, precipitating him into the fosse. It was a brutal fall; unable to stand, Cesare had to be carried to the waiting horses and lifted on to the saddle. There was no time to rescue the wretched servant, who was found by the castle guards lying in the fosse and executed on the spot. Cesare, unconscious from his fall, was unable to hold himself on the horse, but his companions somehow managed to support

him and galloped off with him into the night to the safety of Benavente's lordship of Villalon.

Cesare lay low at Villalon for a month, recovering from his injuries,
before setting out for Navarre towards the end of November. Accompanied by two guides, Martin de la Borda and his brother-in-law
Miguel de la Torre, Cesare rode out of Villalon on a big bay horse
with a white star on its forehead. They made straight for the Atlantic
coast, since the direct route to Pamplona, leading through Burgos
where the court was, was considered too risky. The three men rode
hard, and by the time they reached Castres, a little town outside Santander, their horses foundered and they were forced to make their
way into Santander on foot. At Santander, Cesare sent de la Torre
to find an inn and order dinner, while he went to negotiate with the
owner of a boat for the journey to Navarre. Although the alarm for
his escape had not yet been given, Cesare's ill-concealed urgency, his
strange desire to undertake a perilous journey on the stormy
December seas, and the large sums of money he was prepared to pay
for a boat, aroused the suspicions of a witness who hurried to inform
the *corregidor*. Cesare and his companions were sitting down to a welcome meal of 'three fowls and a large joint of meat', when the *corregidor*'s lieutenant arrived hot-foot to question them. On being
questioned separately the three men told the story which they had
previously concocted to explain their obvious urgency and the large
sums of ready cash which they had with them. They were, they said,
corn merchants who had been to Medina to collect money owing
them, and had come to Santander to meet one of their ships loaded
with grain from France. Now they had discovered that their ship was
at Bernico, further up the coast, and they must make their way there
with all haste lest the corn should be spoiled. The sight of their money
convinced the *corregidor*'s lieutenant that they were men of standing,
and, having no reason to suspect them, he let them finish their dinner
in peace.

Later, when the royal hunt for Cesare was on (for some reason no
official attempts to find him were made until 14 December, when
Juana signed a royal warrant for his arrest at Burgos), witnesses, their
imagination sharpened by the knowledge of the identity of the fugitive, gave strange descriptions of him to the inquiring officials. The
innkeeper at Santander said that one of the three was clearly distinguished from the others, kept himself all wrapped up in a cloak, that
he was short and heavy with flaring nostrils and big eyes, and that

one of his hands was bandaged. A witness at Castres, where they abandoned the horses, described him as 'a man doubled up, with an ugly face, a big nose, dark ...' Poor Cesare, once the handsomest man in Italy, now perhaps still crippled by his fall, with his looks ruined by illness and imprisonment, struck a simple Spanish villager as ugly. But he still stood out from his companions by his bearing and his air of a *grand seigneur*; another witness corroborating the evidence of the Santander innkeeper said that he did not seem to be 'of the same race' as the two other men.

The *corregidor*'s visit impressed the fugitives with the need to leave Spanish soil as soon as they could, and at two in the morning they were on the quayside, hoping to embark, but the sea was so rough even within the harbour that they were forced to wait for sunrise to depart. Once outside, conditions were so bad that the captain refused to take them beyond Castro Urdiales a few miles to the west of Bilbao, and still short of their objective, Bernico. Castro Urdiales was a poor fishing village, and horses could not be found, so that Cesare, chafing with impatience, was obliged to spend two days there, until his men managed to persuade a neighbouring monastery to hire them three mules. Followed by an anxious muleteer who besought them not to ruin his animals, they rode hard to Durango and then by devious routes through mountain villages to Pamplona, where Cesare appeared 'like the devil' on 3 December.

Pamplona, the fierce walled capital of the kingdom of Navarre, set on a high plateau ringed by mountains, defied the great kingdoms of France to the north across the Pyrenees, and of Castile and Aragon to the south beyond the Sierras. Its people were tough independent Basques, fighting men who welcomed Cesare as a man after their own hearts. It was ironical that he should now appear in Pamplona as a leader in the cause of Navarrese independence; fifteen years previously he had been their Bishop, resisted by his flock as the symbol of foreign interference in their affairs. In September 1491, when he was just sixteen, Cesare had been nominated Bishop of Pamplona by Innocent VIII, at the instigation of his father Rodrigo, backed by Ferdinand of Aragon, anxious to extend his own influence in Navarre. His appointment had roused the furious opposition of his future brother-in-law, Jean d'Albret, who had not been consulted, and saw it not only as an infringement of his rights as sovereign but as yet another instance of the thin end of the Spanish wedge within his kingdom. Indeed, Cesare's first vicar-general, Martin Zapata, had been a familiar not only of Rodrigo Borgia but also of King Ferdinand. The teenage absentee Bishop's tenure of his see had been brief and unmemorable; after only twelve months he vacated it for the wealthier archbishopric of Valencia, and not one single act in the cathedral archives at Pamplona bears his signature as Bishop. Now, at thirty-one, Cesare was setting foot for the first time in his former diocese to wield the sword for Jean d'Albret against the cause of Ferdinand of Aragon in Navarre.

But Cesare was not really interested in Spanish politics. He regarded Navarre as merely a step towards the future he yearned for. From Pamplona his thoughts strayed far away to the centre of the international stage – to Italy, where he was determined to return. Through the favour of the Habsburg party in Spain, and that of friendly cardinals such as Carvajal, who was in close touch with the Emperor, he hoped to enter Maximilian's service and thus return to Italy. Already in August of that year Maximilian had announced to an appalled Julius II his intention of making an armed expedition to Rome for the purpose of his coronation as Emperor. Cesare knew too of Maximilian's extreme hostility towards Venice, an attitude which was shared by the other powers, France, Spain and the Papacy, and that the possibility of a League against her had already been discussed. Fighting in Maximilian's service he might have the chance to revenge himself on Venice, which had taken from him his states of the Romagna.

Four days after he arrived in Pamplona, he sat down to write a flood of letters to Italy, announcing his escape from Medina and his safe arrival at the court of Navarre. He wrote to Francesco Gonzaga, to Ippolito d'Este and doubtless to Lucrezia, who had already heard the news in late November, for an entry in her household expenses for 20 November 1506 reads: 'To Garzia, a Spaniard, to go to Venice concerning the news of Duke Valentino who has escaped from prison,' and on the 27th she wrote to inform Francesco Gonzaga, with whom she was now on very intimate terms. According to Bernardi, Cesare, with the dream of a return to the Romagna always in his mind, also wrote to Antonio da Monte, once his right-hand man there and President of the Rota, now in the service of Julius II. He signed his letters from Pamplona in his usual style, 'Cesar Borgia de Francia, duca di Romagna', but in fact they were empty titles: Cesare had not, in Julius' words, 'one rampart in the Romagna', and Louis had stripped him of his French titles and lordships. And he had lost almost all his fortune; Julius had seized the deposits which his treasurer Spanocchi had carefully distributed among the Italian banking houses, and sequestrated the treasure which Florence and Bentivoglio had seized from him. He was desperate for money; in November he sent his major-domo, Requerenz, to the French court at Bourges to request the restitution of his duchy of Valentinois, and to ask permission for him to come to court and take up his sword once again in Louis' service. Charlotte almost certainly travelled from her château nearby at La Motte-Feuilly to support Requerenz's mission, but both were met by a blunt refusal. As far as d'Amboise and Louis were concerned, Cesare had changed sides once too often; he was an enemy of their new ally Ferdinand, and, they thought, a finished man, thus no longer of use to them.

Cesare's mission to Louis shows that experience had not changed him; he still would not recognize the truth in Machiavelli's dictum: 'Whoever believes that with great men new services wipe out old injuries deceives himself.' His supreme belief in himself made him an admirable con-man; penniless and landless as he was, he convinced others that, despite the fact that his luck seemed to have turned against him, he was still a man to be reckoned with. Navarre was a remote kingdom in the north-eastern corner of the Iberian peninsula, and the court of the genial easy-going King Jean poor and unsophisticated in comparison with the splendours he had been accustomed to in Italy, but to Cesare, alive and free in the heady upland air of Pamplona after three years of almost continuous imprisonment, everything once again seemed possible.

He was not alone in his belief. News of his escape caused consternation in Italy, and especially to his old enemy Pope Julius, who at that very moment was engaged at the head of a small army in ousting Cesare's former antagonists Gian Paolo Baglioni and Giovanni Bentivoglio from Perugia and Bologna and asserting his control over those parts of the Romagna not held by the Venetians. In the words of Ferdinand's historian Zurita, the news of il Valentino's escape 'put the Pope in great consternation, because the Duke was such a man that only his presence was sufficient to raise new trouble in all Italy; and he was greatly loved, not only by the soldiery, but also by many people of Tuscany and the States of the Church'. For Julius, triumphantly ensconced in Bologna, the news that the popular Duke of Romagna whom he had thought safely locked away in a Spanish prison was once again at large came as an extremely disagreeable surprise. He was immediately on the alert for signs that il Valentino might be planning to stir up trouble for him in the area, and when the bearer of Cesare's letters, his chancellor Federigo, after an interview with Lucrezia at Ferrara on 28 December, unwisely came to Bologna bringing his master's letter for Gonzaga, he promptly had him seized. Lucrezia, always energetic in defence of her adored brother's interests, wrote to Gonzaga, now Captain of the papal forces and also very probably her lover, pleading for Federigo's release in the most ingenuous terms. Federigo, she said, had come to Italy simply to inform them of Cesare's escape, and with no intention of doing anything which might displease or injure the Pope. Cesare, she said, 'would never countenance nor would he dare anything of this sort against His Holiness'; Federigo's arrest was excessively displeasing to her 'because it will injure my brother the Duke, making it appear that he is not in His Holiness's favour, and the same may be said of myself . . .' Lucrezia can hardly have thought seriously that Julius would look on her brother with favour after what had happened between them in the past, and knowing Cesare as she did, neither she nor anyone else can have been under any illusion that he did not intend to return to Italy and fight for what had once been his.

However, before Cesare could think of planning a return to Italy he was bound to play his part in bringing back the infant Charles v to be recognized as ruler of Castile under the tutelage of Maximilian. Cesare was anxious to put this ambitious plan into execution, but before he could do so civil war erupted in Navarre, precipitated by the insubordination of the leader of Ferdinand's party there, Luis de Beaumonte.

Luis de Beaumonte y Luza, Constable of Navarre and Count of Lerins, was a typical Navarrese, a fiery little man, 'with a small body and a high heart' in the words of a contemporary *cancionero*. Although he was nearing seventy he was still restless, turbulent and insatiably ambitious. Since 1505 he had held the castle of Viana in Ferdinand's name, and made of his territories a petty kingdom within a kingdom, raiding and annexing his neighbours' lands, ignoring the edicts of the royal council, regarding himself as answerable only to Ferdinand of Aragon or to himself, and generally behaving as though King Jean did not exist. When, towards the end of 1506, Jean and Cesare resolved to put the country on a war footing in anticipation of trouble from both France and Spain, the King ordered de Beaumonte to surrender the fortress of Viana. De Beaumonte beat the royal envoy, threw him into prison and refused to give up the castle. The King then sent three times to summon him to appear at court and answer for his actions, and when after the third summons he still refused to appear, condemned him on the grounds of *lèse majesté* and sentenced him to death with loss of all his lands and titles. With Ferdinand far away in Italy, the moment was obviously opportune for d'Albret to crush his party's leader once and for all. With this object in mind, he appointed Cesare Captain General of the royal troops.

Early in February 1507, at the head of the royal forces, Cesare took the field again for the first time in four years to teach the rebel count a lesson. It was not, by Italian standards, a large army – some 200 light cavalry, one hundred and thirty men at arms, 5000 infantry and some artillery – and could hardly have been compared with the eight or nine thousand trained troops under his command in that last glorious summer of 1503. But it was an army at last, and Cesare, with the memory of his Italian successes behind him, was confident that he would be able to deal swiftly and easily with a belligerent provincial count. Many years later an old man remembered seeing Cesare pass through his village of Mendigorria at the head of his troops on his way to besiege Beaumonte's castle of Larriaga. He was, he said, 'a big man, strong, handsome, and *soro*', an untranslatable word used to describe young falcons. He was carrying a short, thick double-pointed lance, a most unusual weapon which is specifically mentioned by other chroniclers of Cesare in Navarre. Thus it seems that Cesare, towering above the short Navarrese knights, was once again in the fullness of health, strength and confidence as he found himself again at war. But the castle of Larriaga resisted fiercely, and he decided to raise the siege and to make a direct attack on the Count himself. 'The impatience of the Duke suffered no delays,' recorded the Navarrese chronicler Padre Moret, 'it being his mind to finish speedily with this war in order to undertake as soon as possible his journey to Flanders.'

And so, in the first week of March, Cesare joined King Jean at Viana, a fortified frontier town built in honey-coloured sandstone on a hilltop dominating a rich flat plain stretching southward to the borders of Castile on the River Ebro. Beyond the Ebro, the high Sierras loomed dark against the sky, the edge of the Castilian *meseta*, a constant reminder of the brooding power of Spain. To the east of the town stood the castle of Viana, garrisoned by de Beaumonte's eldest son Luis, and from the castle to the south-east a sad, barren stretch of country of low flat-topped sandstone hills, broken by deep gullies, *barrancos*, divided Viana from Mendavia, where the Count himself was encamped.

For the man who had taken the great Rocca of Imola from Caterina Sforza, de Beaumonte's castle of Viana presented an easy target. It was, Cesare knew, weakly garrisoned and short of provisions, and if the Count attempted to rescue his eldest son, then Cesare from his headquarters in the town could fall upon him and cut him to pieces. Both sides expected reinforcements from their respective partisans in Castile, and from their dominating position on the hilltop the royal troops were well placed to intercept help for de Beaumonte coming from the south. But Cesare was overconfident; his summing-up of the situation was correct, but his contempt for this provincial warfare relaxed the wariness which had always been his first line of defence. After only three months in Navarre he underestimated the ingenuity and persistence of his adversary de Beaumonte, the fighting qualities of the Navarrese, and the sudden ferocity of the weather in early spring on the Navarrese uplands. Accustomed to command highly paid mercenaries and to care for their comfort, he was unused to the conditions of a guerrilla civil war in which the participants were tough native partisans, fiercely loyal to their respective leaders and hardened to the vagaries of the weather.

The weather in that early spring of 1507 was exceptionally bad. On the night of Wednesday, 11 March, a storm of biting winds and torrential rains hit Viana. Cesare, with his usual consideration for his troops, and thinking that the Count was unlikely to make a move on a night such as that, withdrew his sentinels into the town. It was the opportunity for which de Beaumonte had been waiting. Under cover of the stormy darkness he led a convoy of mules loaded with flour and bread escorted by 200 lances and a body of infantry to a point within reach of the castle of Viana. Here he waited with the main body of his troops and sent on the mule train with an escort of sixty horse to enter the castle, which they succeeded in doing unobserved. As the escort were returning from the castle at dawn they made out a body of cavalry coming up the Logroño road, and thinking them to be the reinforcements promised by their Castilian ally the Duke of Najera, raised the cry 'Beaumonte, Beaumonte!'

The alarm was given in the town, where the confusion on that dark, windy dawn was tremendous. Accounts of what followed are conflicting, but it seems that Cesare, hastily dressed in light armour, a corselet and helmet by his squire Grasica, leapt on his horse, followed by seventy horsemen, leaving a message for the King to follow him. As he galloped out of the Solana gate his big chestnut charger slipped in the mud and nearly fell. Cesare, swearing, picked up his head with a strong pull on the reins and rode on in a blind fury in the direction of Mendavia, shouting: 'Where is he, this little Count?' Better mounted, and a more daring horseman than the rest, he outdistanced his followers, and soon caught sight of the de Beaumonte rearguard retreating to where the Count was waiting. Riding with a furious impetus he did not realize that he was alone. De Beaumonte, observing a lone horseman armed with a great double-pointed lance galloping in pursuit of his rearguard, sent forward three of his knights, the brothers Garcia de Agreda and Pedro de Allo, with some foot-soldiers to intercept him. Waiting in ambush in a narrow ravine, they fell upon Cesare, and as he raised his arm to strike them Ximenes Garcia ran him through the body with a lance thrust under the arm at the point unprotected by the corselet. Unhorsed and mortally wounded, but still grasping his huge lance, Cesare fought desperately against his attackers until he fell, overwhelmed by a mass of men stabbing at him from all sides. At least twenty-five wounds were later found on his body. De Beaumonte's men stripped him of his brilliant armour, and made off, leaving him lying naked and bleeding in the mud; one of them had the pious thought to cover his genitals with a stone. It was the morning of the twelfth of March, three days short of the Ides which had been fatal to his hero and great namesake, Caesar.

His attackers were unaware of the identity of the man they had killed, until Cesare's squire Juanito was found searching desperately for his master. On being shown the armour, Juanito recognized it instantly and burst into tears. De Beaumonte exploded in rage at having lost such a valuable prize as Duke Valentino alive, but there was nothing to be done, the King's men were approaching and de Beaumonte retreated towards Mendavia, leaving Juanito to lead the royal troops to his master's corpse. The King had Cesare's naked, bleeding body covered with a cloak of rough wool and carried to Viana, where the once terrible Duke of Valentinois and of Romagna, ex-Cardinal of Valencia, was buried in the simple parish church of Santa Maria, a corner of the remote kingdom of Navarre. Cesare was only thirty-one when he died, and in those brief years he had achieved the most brilliant successes and known the most stunning reversals of fortune. The inscription on the elaborate marble tomb which was later erected for him was simple and to the point: 'Here, in a scant piece of earth, lies he whom all the world feared ...'

Cesare's short life had the proportions of classical tragedy: a meteoric rise to pride and greatness, followed by a dizzy fall to an obscure and violent death. Contemporaries compared his career to the brief, fierce blaze of a sun across the heavens, ending in darkness. Geronimo Casio of Bologna, who had known him, wrote this epitaph:

> *Cesare Borgia, che era della gente,*
> *Per armi et per virtù tenuto un sole;*
> *Mancar dovendo, andò dove andar sole*
> *Phebo, verso la sera, a l'occidente.*

'Cesare Borgia, whom all for force of arms and valour regarded as a sun, dying, went where sets the sun Phoebus, towards the evening, to the West.'

He was looked on as a supreme example of the fragility of human ambition, and indeed his life was a failure in terms of achievement. Nothing concrete remained of the years of pride, blood and intrigue, of the driving force of his ambition; even his bones were ejected from the church by a vengeful bishop of Calahorra. His skeleton was interred by the steps of the church, under the Calle de la Rua, the pilgrims' road to Compostela, where the remains of this godless man were to be trodden by the footsteps of the pious. When the grave thought to be Cesare's was opened in 1871, the skull crumbled to dust. In death his enemies mocked him with satires playing on his ambitious motto: 'You conquered all and hoped for all, O Cesare. Now you have lost everything; you have begun to be nothing ...' Yet while he was alive his contemporaries had seen him as more than life-size, because his ambitions were as great as his will to attain them. He was the epitome of an age which believed that 'a man can do all things if he will'.

The question must be asked whether Cesare's ambitious vision of a central Italian state, possibly supported by the hereditary Gonfaloniership which would have given him some form of permanent control over the Papacy, was a feasible one, or merely a megalomaniac fantasy, incapable of realization. The answer, as Machiavelli saw it, was that he would have achieved it, and was on the point of doing so, if only he had had the time. Cesare and his father perceived very clearly that the collapse of the Italian state system and the conflicting ambitions of France and Spain had created a vacuum into which a new Italian power, backed by military force, could be inserted. The Italian states, with the exception of Venice, were too weak and disunited to oppose such an attempt, and Cesare, as the ruler of a central state with a considerable army at his back, could have held the balance between the two powers of France and Spain, who were inevitably doomed to clash.

Alexander VI, in identifying Cesare's interests with those of Italy and the Church, was not entirely mistaken. He saw that only a strong Italian power holding the balance could prevent Italy from either being divided between the two barbarians or being swallowed up by one or the other of them. He was sincere in his urgent appeals to Venice in the winter of 1502 to ally herself to the Papacy to prevent this. Venice reaped the fruit of her jealous blindness six years later on the tragic field of Agnadello, when she was brought to her knees by an alliance of all the powers against her, a defeat which sealed the fate of the last independent Italian state. Alexander was proved right when Charles V's troops sacked Rome in 1527, an event which signalled the end of the Renaissance Papacy, and it is ironical to think that Cesare, had he lived, might have taken part in that brutal and definitive event, as did his former captain Ugo de Moncada. It is for this reason that historians at the time of the Italian Risorgimento saw Cesare as the symbol of Italy united against the barbarians, a mistakenly flattering conception, since his motives were purely acquisitive. From the historical standpoint Cesare's achievements were not entirely a failure: he proved that the States of the Church could be held and administered by a single power determined enough to do so, and Julius II's success in this respect could not have been attained if Cesare had not prepared the way before him. In the short time during which he ruled the Romagna he succeeded in imposing a form of unity on the province which it had never previously enjoyed, and his one administrative innovation, the Rota, persisted in Urbino at least after his fall.

Why then did he, from his own personal standpoint, fail so absolutely? Machiavelli, in a famous passage from Chapter VII in *The Prince*, diagnosed the cause of his fall as being principally the extreme malignity of fate:

So having summed up all that the Duke did, I cannot possibly censure him. Rather, I think I have been right in putting him forward as an example for all those who have acquired power through good fortune and the arms of others. He was a man of high courage and ambition, and he could not have conducted himself other than the way he did; his plans were frustrated only because Alexander's life was cut short and because of his own sickness ... If when Alexander died, he had been well himself, everything would have been easy for him.

But Machiavelli, despite the fact that he considered his own frustrated life to be due equally to an extreme malignity of fate, knew very well that where human beings are concerned human failings must enter into the question, and he pointed, mistakenly I think, to Cesare's support of Julius' election as his fatal error. It is certainly right to argue, as Machiavelli did, that the combination of three unusual strokes of bad luck was enough to cause Cesare's downfall: the death of his father at a crucial point in his career, above all when combined with his own incapacitating illness; the presence of the armies of France and Spain in the neighbourhood of Rome, which meant that Cesare's own troops were not, as they might have been and were always intended to be, the deciding force; and finally the existence of an Italian candidate for the Papacy with the qualities of a Julius II.

Cesare fought back with all his resources aganst these blows of fate, confident that he could once again master Fortune, but in the end it was his own character which was principally responsible for his downfall in 1503. The myth which he himself had created, that 'dangerous nature of his', inspired a depth of hatred and mistrust to which he himself seems to have been fatally blind. His own ruthless successes inspired a conspiracy of fear against him, and a determination to destroy him, much the same motives which drove Brutus and his fellow conspirators to the murder of Caesar.

It has been suggested that Cesare, like Caesar, deliberately went to meet his death in the fields of Viana because, subconsciously, he no longer saw the point of living. Or else that syphilis had affected the motor centres of his brain so that he was to all intents and purposes mad. The syphilitic explanation of his death is dramatic but untenable. Cesare contracted syphilis in 1497, when he was just under twenty-two years of age; the tertiary stage can appear at any time from five to twenty years after the first, and in any case the chances of serious damage from untreated tertiary syphilis appear to be no more than one third. Cesare was thirty-one when he died, and it is extremely unlikely that in ten years the disease would have progressed so as to damage his brain. There is absolutely no evidence of madness in his actions up to the day of his death, and indeed it is not at all certain that he still had syphilis. The only documentary evidence that he did is Giustinian's statement of 26 April 1504, that Cardinal Carvajal told him that Cesare 'was not very well for certain pains of the French disease which greatly impeded him: he said his face was ravaged and blotched ...' Syphilis at that time was a new disease, and relatively little was known about it. People tended to attribute almost any illness to it, and indeed it is still known as 'the great imitator' for the variety of symptoms which it manifests. As has been pointed out, Cesare's near fatal illness and his long imprisonment could certainly have caused his ulcerous condition and pains, while there is a strong possibility that the violent bout of tertiary malaria which he suffered in August 1503 finally cured him of the disease.

That Cesare subconsciously willed his own death implies that he had finally given up and lost faith in his future, but there seem to be no grounds for believing that he did any such thing. Cesare had never lost hope even under the bleakest circumstances; alive and free in Navarre with the certainty of a career with the Emperor before him, there was even less likelihood that he would do so. Nonetheless the explanation of his odd and useless end at Viana remains a difficult one. The Spanish and Italian accounts of it vary substantially if not essentially, so that after nearly five centuries have passed it is impossible to arrive at the truth. Cesare was a man of reckless physical courage and vengeful nature; one has only to recall Bernardi's description of him on 15 October 1503, riding 'like a mad dog' at the Orsinis with the cry 'Better to die in the saddle than in bed', to get a picture of Cesare galloping furiously out of the Solana gate of Viana against 'this little Count'. Bored with the pettiness of small-scale civil war, contemptuous of the provincials who were holding up his return to the international scene, Cesare charged his enemy with the headlong speed and deadliness of the Borgia fighting bull.

All that can be certain about Cesare's end is that he died as he had lived, violently, alone, fighting against the odds. He died, and therefore he failed, but he might have succeeded. Few men are born, as he was, with a sense of their own destiny and a will to achieve it so strong that they are prepared to sacrifice anything to that end, and it is not necessarily a recipe for inevitable failure. The lust for power is as strong and all-consuming as the compulsion of creative genius. Cesare was ruthless, amoral, in many ways a political gangster, if a brilliant one, but the single-minded drive and ability with which he pursued his destiny gave him the qualities of genius. The essence of the man who was Cesare Borgia is expressed in his own prophetic motto: 'Either Caesar or nothing.'

EPILOGUE

THREE women mourned Cesare's death: his wife Charlotte, his sister
Lucrezia and his mother Vannozza.

Charlotte d'Albret remains a shadowy figure, and her relationship
with her husband mysterious. At the news of his death she plunged
herself into a rigid mourning to which she clung for the rest of her
life. At the Château of La Motte Feuilly where she lived, the hangings
and furniture in the yellow and crimson colours of the Duke of Valentinois were replaced with sombre black cloth, her bright gowns carefully put away in a chest. From then on she wore widow's weeds and
slept in a bed draped in black; even the trappings on her daughter's
Luisa's pony were changed to the colour of mourning. When Cesare
died she was only twenty-five, beautiful and an heiress, but she never
remarried, nor did she return to court, but lived out her days in
seclusion at La Motte Feuilly, occupying herself with the administration of her estates, charitable works, and occasional visits to her friend,
the divorced Jeanne de France, in the Convent of the Annonciades
at nearby Bourges. Charlotte was gentle, kindly and pious, her goodness was remarked on by more than one observer, and she was a careful administrator who took great interest in her estates and had an
acquisitive eye for property (she later bought the lordship of Chalus
for 17,000 crowns). But she seems to have been a narrow-minded
woman; the few books she owned were all devotional works, and in
her enshrinement of her husband's memory it is possible to see more
than a touch of obsessive neurosis.

She had never made any attempt to go to her husband, even when
in the later years of their marriage she was free to do so. The Mantuan
envoy to the French court, Jacopo d'Atri, reported that in July and
early August 1503 repeated efforts were made to induce her to go
to Italy and join her husband, but in vain. Cesare sent a messenger,

Artese, to persuade her, and his efforts were strongly seconded by Louis, who at that moment was very much afraid that Cesare was inclining to Spain, and extremely anxious to accommodate him. Louis even threatened to deprive her of her honoured position as governess to his daughter by Anne, Madame Claude, and promised to send Cesare his daughter Luisa, but the envoy said that Charlotte 'did not want to go to her husband'. She had been deeply shocked by the events at Sinigallia, wrote Francesco Gonzaga, and doubtless by many other reports of Cesare's activities, including his abduction of Dorotea Caracciolo. And although at a distance she was prepared to do her dutiful best for her husband – in January 1504 the Venetian diarist Sanuto stated that she had come to court specifically to plead for Cesare's release – she did not join him even when he was at her brother's court at Pamplona. It would seem that she preferred the mythical memory of the handsome, dashing young husband she had known for those few summer months of 1499 to the harsh reality of the ruthless impious man whom all reports indicated him to be. Cesare's disgrace after his father's death no doubt made her position at the French court an embarrassing one, for some time in the autumn of 1503 she negotiated the purchase of the Château de la Motte Feuilly in Touraine, and moved there in 1504. Absorbed in her widowhood, she lived there in retirement until her death on 11 March 1514, aged thirty-two. The inscription on the stone above the place where her heart was buried in the chapel of La Motte Feuilly was perhaps the best expression of Charlotte's short, unhappy life: 'Here lies the heart of the most high and powerful lady Charlotte d'Albret, in her life the widow of the most high powerful prince Dom Cesar, Duke of Valentinois, Count of Diois, seigneur of Issoudun and of La Motte Feuilly ...'

Cesare's daughter by Charlotte, Luisa Borgia, was just under seven when he died. He never saw the little girl whose marriages he had planned, first to his godson of the same age, Federigo Gonzaga, then to Pope Julius' nephew, Francesco Maria della Rovere, the boy Prefect of Sinigallia. Luisa was fourteen at the time of Charlotte's death, when she was given – unwillingly it appears from a pathetic appeal she made to her hard-hearted old grandfather Alain d'Albret – into the tutelage of the formidable Louise of Savoy, Madame d'Angoulême, mother of the future Francis I. Luisa kept up her Italian connections, corresponding with Isabella d'Este and doubtless too with her aunt Lucrezia; indeed in 1516 the project of her marriage to

Federigo Gonzaga was again briefly revived, and when that fell through a match with Piero de' Medici's son Lorenzo was discussed. But il Valentino's daughter was destined never to see Italy; in April 1517, aged seventeen, she was married to a widower of forty-one, Louis de la Trémouille, lord of Thouars, a brilliant, honourable soldier who was the veteran of many Italian campaigns. De la Trémouille was killed fighting for Francis I against the troops of Charles V on the field of Pavia in 1525. Five years later Luisa married Philippe de Bourbon, lord of Chabannes. By him she had six children, four sons and two daughters; of their descendants the Bourbon counts of Bussett and Chalus still exist today, direct heirs to Cesare Borgia.

Luisa died in 1553, at the age of fifty-three, signing herself to the end of her life 'Louise de Valentinois', with the titles she inherited from the father whose connection with her everyone tried to suppress. When her first husband, de la Trémouille, was asked why he was taking the infamous Borgia's daughter to wife, he is reported to have answered that he was marrying Luisa because she was a lady of the house of d'Albret, whose women had always been known for their virtue. The only known description of her, recorded by Anne of Brittany's biographer Père Hilarion de Coste, declared that she was 'a very noble and virtuous lady, heiress to the perfections as well as to the riches of her mother, whose manners and disposition she made her own; a lady in short, as chaste, virtuous and gentle as her father was possessed, cruel and wicked'.

Luisa was Cesare's only legitimate child. He also had an illegitimate son and daughter, Gerolamo and Camilla Lucrezia, both born between 1501 and 1502, and may well have had others whose existence is unrecorded. Gerolamo and Camilla Lucrezia, whose mother or mothers were unknown, were probably the two children of whom Burchard records that Cesare took them with the little Borgia Dukes Giovanni and Rodrigo into Castel Sant'Angelo with him in October 1503. Since a document of 8 August 1509 legitimizing Camilla Lucrezia refers to her as having been born of Cesare, married, and of a married woman unnamed, it is possible to conjecture that her mother might have been Dorotea Caracciolo, although there is absolutely no evidence to support this. Camilla Lucrezia was brought up in the Convent of Corpo di Christo in Ferrara, under her aunt's protection, and became a nun there in 1516, taking the name of Suor Lucrezia in her honour. Probably due to her connections with the Este family, she eventually became abbess of the convent, and died there in 1573, aged just over seventy. She inherited her father's intelligence and spirit, being described as of a 'grande animo', but not, it seems, his character, since she died with a reputation for saintliness and good works.

Gerolamo, like his sister, was sent to Lucrezia at Ferrara; in June 1505 Lucrezia placed him under the tutelage of Alberto Pio, lord of Capri, a celebrated Maecenas, and patron of Ariosto. As the nephew of the Duchess of Ferrara he moved in noble circles, and in 1537 he married a daughter of the lord of Capri, by whom he had two daughters, named Lucrezia and Ippolita in honour of the Estes. Apart from the record of his marriage, the only reference we have to Gerolamo shows him, unlike his saintly sister, to have inherited some of his father's more sinister characteristics. On 4 March 1542 the Bolognese chronicler Jacopo Ranieri recorded: 'Three Ferrarese were executed ... because they had come into the Bolognese at Poggio, on the orders of a son of Duke Valentino, to kill a man named Chastron...' The assassination attempt failed, but four years later the wretched Chastron was stabbed to death at Ferrara, where Gerolamo was living; il Valentino's son had his father's capacity for nursing a long vendetta. Other claimants to descent from Cesare were of dubious authenticity: in 1550 a correspondent of the Estes reported the appearance in Paris of a priest who claimed to be the natural son of il Valentino, having come from Rome with the strange idea of requesting a subsidy from the King of France on the grounds of his father's death in Navarre fighting in the service of France! And according to Aretino's *I Ragionamenti*, Roman courtesans in the sixteenth century liked to give themselves airs by pretending to be the illegitimate daughters of Duke Valentino.

Cesare's squire, Juanito Grasica, reached Ferrara with the news of his master's death on 22 April 1507. Ippolito d'Este, who received him, knowing, as one of Isabella d'Este's correspondents put it, that Lucrezia 'loved her brother as much as if she were his mother', was afraid to tell her, and the unpleasant duty was deputed to a certain friar Raffaele. Lucrezia received the news with remarkable stoicism – one imagines that by that time she may already have heard rumours of it – exclaiming sadly to the monk: 'The more I try to follow God's will, the more he visits me with sorrows. I thank his divinity, I am content with what pleases him.' She retired to a convent for two days to mourn her brother in private. No doubt she knew that she would receive little sincere sympathy from the rest of the world for her loss, and was too proud to reveal the misery it caused her. While Cesare was alive, and particularly in his time of trouble, she had never ceased to work for the brother whom she loved more than any other human being, and after his death the world must have seemed an empty place for her. Nonetheless, Lucrezia was no Charlotte d'Albret, but a true Borgia. As Duchess of Ferrara she enlivened her husband's court with her charm, gaiety and sophistication. Alfonso was a cold husband, who continued to regard his Borgia wife with a certain suspicion as he pursued his passions for artillery, pottery-making and other women. He seems to have resented his wife's passion for physical exercise and dancing, and claimed that it was responsible for her difficult pregnancies; indeed she had lost her first child by Alfonso in the autumn of 1502, and her first son Alessandro, born in 1505, survived only a month. The birth of the heir Ercole in 1508 established her position, and he was followed by a succession of children; Ippolito, born in 1509; Alessandro, born in 1514; Eleonora, born 1515; Francesco, born 1516; and Isabella Maria, born in 1519.

Lucrezia consoled herself for her husband's lack of appreciation with the adulation of the literary men who surrounded her, including Ercole Strozzi, who dedicated his *Epicedium* to describing Cesare's death. She was still the same light-hearted Lucrezia, craving admiration, and very soon after her marriage, some time in the autumn of 1502, she entered into a relationship with the poet Pietro Bembo which almost certainly went beyond pure literary interests. In 1505 Bembo dedicated his masterpiece *Gli Asolani* to Lucrezia, but he had already been supplanted in her affections by her sister-in-law Isabella's husband, Francesco Gonzaga. Their intimacy began in the autumn of 1505, initiated probably by Lucrezia's desire to enlist Gonzaga's help for Cesare's release. Clandestine correspondence began between them through the medium of Ercole Strozzi until Strozzi's murder in 1508, and seems to have continued until at least 1513. There was no love lost between Lucrezia and her haughty sister-in-law, who regarded each other with mutual jealousy and cold dislike, and the affair with Francesco must have had an added piquancy for Lucrezia in its implied humiliation of Isabella. However, she became increasingly pious in her later years, and when she died after the birth of Isabella Maria in 1519 it was rumoured that for some years she had secretly worn a hair shirt.

Vannozza died in Rome on 26 November 1518, at the advanced age, for those days, of seventy-six, having outlived three husbands and all her children by Rodrigo Borgia save Lucrezia. Tough, tenacious, a true *bourgeoise*, Vannozza survived all the tragedies of her family to become a respected member of Roman society. The Borgias' enemy Paolo Giovio wrote of her that apart from having been Cesare's mother she was otherwise an upright woman. She was also an extremely astute and acquisitive lady with a keen commercial acumen, owning several hostelries and houses which she rented out, and running a profitable sideline in pawnbroking by lending money against the security of jewels. She was not above sharp practice and had used her Borgia relationships for all they were worth; in 1514 one Nardo Antoniozzi was forced to sue her for the return of a silver cross which she had ordered twelve years ago in 1502 and neglected to pay for. He had done nothing about it at the time he said, 'because Duke Valentino dominated the city and all Italy ...'

Forceful character that she was, Vannozza had always had the respect of her children and maintained a close relationship with them; she had sustained Cesare after Alexander's death by accompanying him to Nepi, and kept up a frequent correspondence with Lucrezia until she died. Determined to occupy as comfortable a place in the after life as she had enjoyed on earth, she made many charitable donations, and was a member of the Confraternity of the Gonfalone to which most of the highest Roman society belonged. When she died, Pope Leo x, Giovanni de' Medici, Cesare's fellow student at Pisa, ordered all his court to attend her funeral, which rivalled in pomp the obsequies of a cardinal. Vannozza was buried beside Juan Gandia, her husband Giorgio di Croce and Ottaviano, her son by him, in the family chapel she had prepared for herself in the fashionable church of Santa Maria del Popolo. Rodrigo Borgia's mistress was proud of her Borgia connections to the end; her funerary chapel was adorned with a painting, which has since disappeared, depicting her with her lover and their children, while the inscription on her tomb, ignoring her more obscure relationships, proudly proclaimed her the mother of Rodrigo's children, Cesare, Juan, Jofre and Lucrezia.

Of the remaining members of Cesare's family, Jofre, last heard of callously caracoling in Gonsalvo de Cordoba's train after his brother's arrest, made an abrupt end to an insipid life early in 1517, having married a noble Neapolitan girl Maria Milan de Aragon y Villahermosa, after the death of his estranged wife Sancia in 1506. Strangely enough, one of Cesare's great-nephews, grandson of the dissolute Juan

Gandia, became a saint, St Francis Borgia, third General of the Jesuits.

Cesare's most unsaintly follower, Michelotto, 'that most cruel, terrible, and much-feared man', as Guicciardini described him, reappeared briefly on the Italian scene while the master he had served so faithfully was still in prison in Spain. On 1 April 1506 he signed a condotta with Florence; Machiavelli, who remembered Michelotto's abilities as a leader of Cesare's Romagnol militia, had secured his appointment as commander of his new militia army in Florence, 'since he was used, when he was with the Duke, to command and manage similar men'. Michelotto's employment raised fears in Florence that the Gonfalonier Soderini intended to follow the sinister methods of il Valentino. However, it appears that Michelotto was principally employed to spread terror on the borders of the Romagna, where no doubt the fear of his name was as effective as the actual cruelties he committed. After May 1506, Michelotto, the man who more than any other knew the darkest secrets of the terrible Valentino, vanished from historical records, leaving only his dread reputation as Valentino's 'executioner' across its pages. Possibly he joined his legitimate brother fighting in the service of Spain; he may even have returned to his distant native town of Corella, in Navarre. The date of his death is not known, but Miguel da Corella being the man that he was, one can conjecture that he, like his master Cesare, died fighting.

Julius II, the man principally responsible for Cesare's downfall, died on the night of 20 February 1513, at the age of seventy, still as formidable, restless and energetic as ever. He died triumphant, having mastered the States of the Church, humbled the proud Republic of Venice, and driven the French out of Italy. In him the greatest artistic geniuses of the Renaissance had found their most liberal and appreciative patron. When he died, Michelangelo's Sistine Chapel had been completed, and Raphael's masterpiece, the Stanze della Segnatura, obliterated all memories of il Valentino in the Vatican apartments that had once been his, while the new St Peter's, designed by Michelangelo and Bramante, was rising on the site of the old basilica, destined to be the greatest cathedral in the world, and an astounding monument to a religion founded upon poverty. Michelangelo created the perfect memorial to the towering personality of his patron in the statue of Moses which stands above Julius' tomb in the church of San Pietro ad Vincoli. Moses is shown not so much as the high priest and law-giver but as the resolute leader, a fiery, powerful man of action, whose angry eyes seem to dart flame at those who might dare to oppose him. It is the final expression of the man who was Julius II, in many ways the greatest, and certainly the most successful of the popes of the High Renaissance.

No magnificent memorials remain to Julius' predecessor, his old enemy Alexander VI, his children, or their mother. Fragments of the monument which Alexander raised to the memory of his uncle Calixtus remain in the Vatican crypt, but, characteristically, Alexander had still not envisaged a tomb for himself when he died. He was interred in the chapel of Santa Maria delle Febbri in St Peter's, beside Calixtus and his murdered son-in-law, Alfonso Bisceglie. When the chapel was destroyed in 1586 to make an entrance for the pedestal of the obelisk, the bones of both Popes were removed to the interior of the basilica near the choir. In 1610 the Spanish cardinals at the Vatican had them transferred to the Spanish church of Santa Maria de Monserrato, where they were deposited in a wooden box in the wardrobe of the sacristy. Here they were seen in 1864 by the Prussian minister to the Vatican, Kurd von Schlozer, who recorded the simple label affixed to the box: 'The bones of two Popes lie in this chest, and they are Calixtus and Alexander VI, and they were Spaniards.' This remained the only epitaph to the two Borgia Popes until 1889, when a group of Spanish noblemen resident in Rome erected a modest monument in a side chapel of the church, and even then the sculptor put the wrong names under their portraits.

Poor Vannozza's careful provisions for the preservation of her memory were in vain: in 1760 the name of Alexander's mistress was deleted from the roll of commemoratory masses of the confraternity to which she had belonged; some time later her tomb and the painting of herself with her lover and her children also disappeared from the church. All that remains in Santa Maria del Popolo of her optimistically magnificent donations is a holy water stoup carved with the Borgia arms. The inscription with her name and those of her children by Rodrigo has been moved to the Basilica of San Marco. Lucrezia's tomb at Ferrara is a simple marble slab.

Almost no trace of Cesare remains in Italy. In Rome the serene beauty of Raphael's frescoes has effaced his memory in the Vatican apartments where he lived; the rooms which once echoed to the Borgias' laughter are now filled with tourists staring reverently at the walls. In the Romagna, the Rubicon which was of such symbolic importance to him still trickles, an insignificant stream with an over-poweringly evocative name, between Cesena and Rimini, and the Rocca of Forlì, his last stronghold, still bears his half-effaced arms – the Borgia bull, the lilies of France and the batons of Captain General of the Church – but otherwise his dominion of the Romagna has fulfilled the nun of Mantua's prediction that it would be 'as a straw fire'. White turkeys gobble peacefully in the precincts of Cesare's citadel of Cesena, where once he held Caterina Sforza prisoner; Caterina's arms, not his, decorate the interior of the fortress of Imola, although one building there is traditionally held to have been designed by Leonardo da Vinci, and if so must have been executed during his time in Cesare's service. At Sinigallia, the scene of one of his greatest coups, a shabby square before the citadel bears the name 'Piazza del Duca', but that is all. Italy is a land overcrowded with the ghosts of history; only the memories of the men who built great monuments remain alive. Cesare, in his brief, frenzied years of power, had no time for immortality, and the terrible Valentino has faded into the rich tapestry of the past as if he had never been.

It is in Navarre, where the ghosts of history are few and far between, that Cesare is still remembered as the hero of the fight for independence which failed but remains a tenacious dream. In 1512, five years after his death, the Duke of Alba marched across the frontier and annexed the kingdom for the crown of Castile, but Navarre is a country where the past is yesterday, and lost causes remain alive. At Viana, on 27 August 1945, the grave presumed to be Cesare's was reopened: excavating under the surface of the Calle de la Rua in front of the steps of the church of Santa Maria, they found a grave hollowed out of the rock to fit a human body, covered and protected with bricks. In this rough grave lay the incomplete skeleton of an adult human, mingled with the bones of a child and fragments of domestic animals. The skeleton was lifted out and examined by two experts, who found nothing which invalidated the tradition that it was Cesare's, and several factors which might indicate that it was indeed his. The skeleton was that of a man of between twenty-five and forty years of age, which had lain in its present grave for at least two hundred years. In life the man's height had been approximately 1·73 metres, tall for the period; the left shoulder bone showed clear evidence of a lance wound 2 centimetres in diameter received while the man was alive, the right shoulder evidencing extensive osteitis, a lesion consonant with fractures due to a heavy fall. If the skeleton was Cesare's, the lance wound could have been one of those he received on the day of his death, the shoulder injuries those which he suffered in his escape from La Mota.

The bones remained in the municipal archives of Viana until 3 December 1953, when they were reinterred with considerable ceremonial in the presence of the civil and military governors of Navarre, a representative of the provincial government of Valencia, home of the Borgias, and other dignitaries, permission for their burial having been given by the Bishop of Calahorra, successor of the sixteenth-century bishop who had expelled Cesare's impious bones from the church. Preceded by the municipal band, the bones, enclosed in an urn specially made for the occasion, covered with red carnations brought from Valencia, were attended to the church of Santa Maria by the uniformed dignitaries and children waving flowers, to be reinterred in front of the main door. Valencian soil and red carnations, with flowers from the gardens of Viana, were laid over the urn before the grave was closed; inset into the pavement above it they placed a marble memorial tablet with the resounding inscription: CESAR BORGIA GENERALISSIMO OF THE NAVARRESE AND PONTIFICAL ARMIES DIED IN THE FIELDS OF VIANA 11 [sic] MARCH 1507.

In 1965 the Diputación Foral de Navarra commissioned a local sculptor to execute a bust of Cesare to be placed on a pediment beside the church. Today his idealized features in bronze, calm, commanding, ascetically beautiful, look down on a quiet leafy square in Viana, in the guise of a hero of Navarrese independence, a reincarnation which would have evoked in Cesare himself a self-mocking Borgia smile.

SELECT BIBLIOGRAPHY

I   PRIMARY SOURCES

The following list includes the principal printed manuscript sources, ambassadors' dispatches, contemporary chronicles, and collections of documents. Further documentary collections are to be found in the appendices of authoritative general works under the Secondary Sources, books section.

Alberi, E., *Le Relazioni degli ambasciatori veneti al Senato durante il seculo XVI* (Florence, 1839–63).

Anonimi, *Commentario*, ed. F.Madiai, Archivio storico per le Marche e per l'Umbria, vol. III (1886).

Auton, Jean d', *Chroniques de Louis XII*, ed. Société de l'Histoire de France (Paris, 1889–95).

Bernardi, Andrea, *Cronache forlivesi dal 1476 al 1517*, ed. G.Mazzatinti, 2 vols (Bologna, 1895).

Branca Tedallini, Sebastiano di, *Diario Romano dal maggio 1485 al 6 giugno 1524*, Rerum italicarum scriptores, XXIII (Città di Castello, 1907).

Brom, G., 'Einige Briefe von Brandolinus Lippus', *Romische Quartalschrift*, vol. ii (1888).

Buonaccorsi, Biagio, *Diario de' successi piu importanti seguiti in Italia ... dall'anno 1498 in sino all'anno 1512* (Florence, 1568).

Buonaccorsi, Biagio, 'Summario di cose seguite da dì 6 di giugno 1498 fino a dì X di settembre 1508', in *Niccolò Machiavelli, Legazioni, Commissarie, Scritti di Governo*, ed. Fredi Chiappelli, 2 vols (Bari, 1971).

Burchard, Johannes, *Diarium*, ed. L. Thuasne, 3 vols (Paris, 1883–5).

Burchard, Johannes, *Liber notarum*, ed. E.Celani, Rerum italicarum scriptores, XXXII, 2 (Città di Castello, 1907 ff).

Commines, Philippe de, *Mémoires*, ed. J.Calmette (Paris, 1924).

Conti, Sigismondo de', *Le storie dei suoi tempi dal 1475 al 1510* (Rome, 1883).

de Roo, P., *Materials for a History of Pope Alexander VI, his Relatives and his Times*, 5 vols (Bruges, 1924).

Diario Ferrarese 1409–1502, Rerum italicarum scriptores, XXIV (Bologna, 1934–7).

Fantaguzzi, *Caos, cronache cesenate del Seculo XV*, ed. D.Bazocchi (Cesena, 1915).

Giovio, Paolo, *Gli Elogi* (Florence, 1554).

Giovio, Paolo, *Illustrium Virorum Vitae* (Florence, 1551).

Giovio, Paolo, *Istorie del suo Tempo*, Prima Parte, trans. L.Domenichi (Venice, 1555).

Giovio, Paolo, *Le Vite del Gran Capitano e del Marchese di Peschara*, ed. Panigada (Bari, 1931).

Giustinian, Antonio, *Dispacci*, ed. P.Villari, 3 vols (Florence, 1876).

Guicciardini, Francesco, *Storia d'Italia*, ed. C.Panigada (Bari, 1929).

Guicciardini, Francesco, *Storie Fiorentine dal 1378 al 1509*, ed. Palmarocchi (Bari, 1931).

Infessura, Stefano, *Diario della Città di Roma*, ed. O.Tommasini (Rome, 1890).

Luzio, A., *Isabella d'Este e i Borgia* (Milan, 1915).

Luzio, A., and Renier, R., *Mantova e Urbino* (Rome, 1893).

Luzio, A., and Renier, R., 'Relazione Inedita sulla morte del duca di Gandia', *Archivio della Società romana di storia patria*, vol. xi (1888).

Machiavelli, Niccolò, *Il Principe*, ed. G.Sasso (Florence, 1963); trans. G.Bull (London, 1961).

Machiavelli, Niccolò, *Legazioni, Commissarie, Scritti di Governo*, ed. Fredi Chiappelli, 2 vols (Bari, 1971).

Machiavelli, Niccolò, *Legazioni e Commissarie*, ed. S.Bertelli, 3 vols (Milan, 1964).

Machiavelli, Niccolò, *Tutte le Opere*, ed. G.Mazzoni and M.Casella (Florence, 1929). For English translations see Gilbert, A., Detmold, C., in Secondary Sources, books section.

Matarazzo, F., 'Cronaca della città di Perugia dal 1492 al 1503', ed. A. Fabretti, *Archivio storico italiano*, xvi, 2 (1851).

Menotti, M., *Documenti inediti sulla famiglia e la corte di Alessandro VI* (Rome, 1917).

Pélissier, L.G., 'Sopra alcuni documenti relativi all'alleanza tra Alessandro VI e Luigi XII 1498–9', *Archivio della Società romana di storia patria*, xvii–xviii (1894–5).

Pius II (Aeneas Silvius Piccolomini, Pope), *Commentarii* (Rome, 1584);
English translation by F.A.Gragg with introduction and notes by
L.C.Gabel, *Smith College Studies in History* (Northampton,
Mass., 1937–57).

Priuli,G., *I Diarii*, Rerum italicarum scriptores, XXIV, 3 (Città
di Castello, 1921–41).

Sanuto, M., *Diarii* (Venice, 1879 ff).

Strozzi, Ercole, *Caesaris Borgiae Ducis Epicedium* (Venice, 1513).

Verona, Gaspare da, *Le vite di Paolo II*, ed. G.Zippel, Rerum italicarum scriptores, XVI, 3 (Città di Castello, 1904).

Volterra, Jacopo Gherardi da, *Diaro Romano*, ed. E.Carusi, Rerum
italicarum scriptores, XXIII, 3 (Città di Castello, 1904).

Zurita, Geronimo, *Historia del Rey Don Hernando el Catolico* (Zaragoza,
1610).

II   SECONDARY SOURCES

I   BOOKS

The best biography of Cesare in English is W.H.Woodward, *Cesare
Borgia* (London, 1913); in other languages Gustavo Sacerdote, *Cesare
Borgia* (Milan, 1950), is the most complete, Edoardo Alvisi, *Cesare
Borgia, Duca di Romagna*, is authoritative and well documented, while
C.Yriarte, *César Borgia, sa vie, sa captivité et son mort*, 2 vols (Paris, 1889),
remains useful. The most up-to-date and fair account of the Borgias
in general is Michael Mallett, *The Borgias: the Rise and Fall of a Renais-
sance Dynasty* (London, 1969).

Ady, C.M., *The Bentivoglio of Bologna* (Oxford, 1937).

Alberti, L.B., *I primi tre libri della famiglia*, ed. Pellegrini (Florence,
1911).

Aleson, F.de., *Anales del Reino de Navarra, compuestos por el Padre José
de Moret*, vol. VII (Tolosa, 1890).

Alvisi, E., *Cesare Borgia, Duca di Romagna* (Imola, 1878).

Aretino, P., *I Ragionamenti* (Rome, 1911; trans. London, 1967).

Ariosto, L., *Orlando Furioso*, trans. G.Waldman (London, 1974).

Aubenas, R., and Ricard, R., *L'Eglise et la Renaissance 1449–1517*, vol.
15 in *Histoire de L'Eglise*, ed. A.Fliche and V.Martin (Paris, 1951).

Bandello, M., *Tutte le Opere*, vol. II (Milan, 1934, 1952).

Bellonci, M., *Lucrezia Borgia; sua vita e suoi tempi* (revised edition,
Milan, 1960; abridged English edition, London, 1953).

Beltrami, G., *Leonardo da Vinci e Cesare Borgia* (Milan, 1916).

Boissonade, P., *Histoire de la Réunion de la Navarre à la Castille* (Paris, 1893).

Braudel, F., *The Mediterranean and the Mediterranean World in the Age of Philip II*, 2 vols, trans. Siân Reynolds (London, 1973).

Breisach, E., *Caterina Sforza, a Renaissance Virago* (Chicago, 1967).

Bridge, J.S.C., *A History of France from the Death of Louis XI*, vol. II 1493–8, vol. III 1498–1507 (Oxford, 1924, 1929).

Brinton, S., *The Gonzaga – Lords of Mantua* (London, 1927).

Brosch, M., *Papst Julius II und die Gründung des Kirchenstaates* (Gotha, 1878).

Burchard, J., *At the Court of the Borgia*, selections from the *Diarium* ed. and trans. G. Parker, Folio Society (London, 1963).

Burckhardt, J., *The Civilisation of the Renaissance in Italy*, trans. S.G.C. Middlemore, 4th ed. revised (London, 1951).

Caracciolo di Torchiarolo, A., *Un ratto di Cesare Borgia* (Naples, 1921).

Cartwright, J. (Mrs Ady), *Beatrice d'Este, Duchess of Milan, 1475–1497* (London, 1920).

Cartwright, J. (Mrs Ady), *Isabella d'Este, Marchioness of Mantua, 1474–1539* (London, 1903).

Castiglione, B., *Il Cortegiano*, annot. V. Cian (Florence, 1929), trans. G. Bull (London, 1967).

Cellini, B., *The Life*, trans. A. Macdonnell (London, 1960).

Cipolla, C., *Storie delle signorie italiane dal 1313–1530* (Milan, 1881).

Clementi, F., *Il Carnevale Romano* (Rome, 1939).

Collison-Morley, L., *The Story of the Sforzas* (London, 1933).

Cortese, P., *De Cardinalatu* (Castrum Cortesium, 1510).

Croce, B., *Storia del Regno di Napoli* (Bari, 1944).

De Gaury, G., *The Grand Captain, Gonzalo de Cordoba* (London, 1955).

Delumeau, J., *Vie Economique et Sociale de Rome dans la seconde moitié du XVI siècle*, 2 vols (Paris, 1957).

Detmold, C., *Niccolò Machiavelli, Historical, Political and Diplomatic Writings* (Boston, 1882).

Dumesnil, A.J., *Histoire de Jules II, sa vie et son pontificat* (Paris, 1873).

Elliott, J., *Imperial Spain 1469–1716* (London, 1963).

Ettlinger, E.D., *The Sistine Chapel before Michelangelo, Religious Imagery and Papal Primacy* (Oxford, 1965).

Fumi, L., *Alessandro VI e il Valentino in Orvieto* (Siena, 1877).

Fusero, C., *Vita di Cesare Borgia* (Milan, 1966).

Gancedo, E., *Apuntes Historicos de Viana* (Madrid, 1933).

Garin, E., *L'Educazione in Europa 1400–1600* (Bari, 1957).

Gilbert, A., *Niccolò Machiavelli, The Chief Works and Others, selected and translated* (N. Carolina, 1965).

Gnoli, U., *Le Cortigiane Romane* (Arezzo, 1941).

Gregorovius, F., *History of the City of Rome in the Middle Ages*, trans. A.Hamilton (London, 1900).

Gregorovius, F., *Lucretia Borgia*, trans. J.L.Garner (London, 1903).

Hauser, H., and Renaudet, A., *La Renaissance et la Réforme*, in *Peuples et Civilisations*, vol. 8, 1489–1559 (Paris, 1929).

Hale, J.R., *Renaissance Europe 1480–1520* (London, 1971).

Hay, D., ed., *The Age of the Renaissance* (London, 1967).

Jacob, E.F., ed., *Italian Renaissance Studies* (London, 1961).

Jedin, H., and Dolan, J., eds, *Handbook of Church History, From the Middle Ages to the Eve of the Reformation*, vol. IV, trans. A. Biggs (London, 1970).

Klaczko, J., *Jules II, Rome et la Renaissance, Essais et Esquisses* (Paris, 1898).

Lacarra, J.M., *Historia Politica del Reino de Navarra, desde sus origines hasta su incorporacion a Castilla*, vol. 3 (Pamplona, 1973).

Lanciani, R., *The Golden Days of the Renaissance in Rome* (New York, 1906).

Larner, J., *The Lords of the Romagna* (London, 1965).

Lavedan, P., *L'Architettura in Roma nel Quattrocento* (Rome, 1942).

Lemonnier, H., *La France sous Charles VIII, Louis XII et François I*, in *Histoire de France*, ed. E.Lavisse, vol. V (Paris, 1900).

Leti, G. (pseud. Tomaso Tomasi), *La Vita del Duca Valentino* (Monte Claro, 1655).

Muntz, E., *Les Arts à la cour des Papes Innocent VIII, Alexandre VI, Pie III, 1484–1503* (Paris, 1898).

Litta, P., *Famiglie Celebri Italiane* (Milan, 1819).

Madrazo, P.de., *Navarra y Logroño*, vol. III (Barcelona, 1886).

Mallett, M., *The Borgias: The Rise and Fall of a Renaissance Dynasty* (London, 1969).

Mallett, M., *Mercenaries and their Masters, Warfare in Renaissance Italy* (London, 1974).

Masson, G., *The Companion Guide to Rome* (London, 1965).

Mattingly, G., *Renaissance Diplomacy* (London, 1955).

Maulde de la Clavière, M., *Histoire de Louis XII* (Paris, 1890–3).

Medin, A., *Il duca Valentino nella mente di Niccolò Machiavelli* (Florence, 1883).

Merriman, R.B., *The Rise of the Spanish Empire*, vol. II *The Catholic Kings* (New York, 1918).

Miron, E.L., *Duchess Derelict: A Study of the Life and Times of Charlotte d'Albret, Duchesse de Valentinois* (London, n.d.).

Monteverde, G., *Astorre Manfredi, storia dei tempi del Duca Valentino* (Milan, 1852).

Partner, P., *The Lands of St. Peter, the Papal State in the Middle Ages and the Early Renaissance* (London, 1972).

Paschini, P., *Adriano Castellesi, tre illustri prelati del rinascimento* (Rome, 1957).

Paschini, P., *Roma nel Rinascimento* (Bologna, 1940).

Pasolini, P.D., *Caterina Sforza*, 3 vols (Imola, 1893).

Pastor, L., *The History of the Popes from the Close of the Middle Ages*, ed. F.I. Antrobus (London, 1898).

Pecchiai, P., *Roma nel Cinquecento* (Bologna, 1949).

Pepe, G., *La politica dei Borgia* (Naples, 1946).

Plumb, J.H., ed., *The Horizon Book of the Renaissance* (London, 1961).

Prescott, W.H., *History of the Reign of Ferdinand and Isabella the Catholic* (London, 1962).

Rival, P., *César Borgia* (Paris, 1931).

Rodocanachi, E., *Courtisanes et Buffons* (Paris, 1894).

Rodocanachi, E., *Histoire de Rome, Une Cour Princière au Vatican pendant la Renaissance* (Paris, 1925).

Rodocanachi, E., *Rome au temps de Jules II et de Léon X* (Paris, 1912).

Rodriguez Villa, A., *Cronicas del Gran Capitan* (Madrid, 1908).

Rodriguez Villa, A., *Don Francisco de Rojas* (Madrid, 1896).

Rolfe, F.W., *Chronicles of the House of Borgia* (London, 1901).

Ross, J., *The Lives of the Early Medici as told in their Correspondence* (London, 1910).

Ruano Prieto, F., *Anexion del Reino de Navarra* (Madrid, 1899).

Sabatini, R., *The Life of Cesare Borgia* (London, 1913).

Sacerdote, G., *Cesare Borgia, la sua vita, la sua famiglia, e i suoi tempi* (Milan, 1950).

Sasso, G., *Machiavelli e Cesare Borgia, Storia di un giudizio* (Rome, 1966).

Schlumberger, G.L., *Charlotte d'Albret, femme de César Borgia* (Paris, 1913).

Schüller-Piroli, S., *Die Borgia, Die Serstorung einer Legende, der Gesichte einer Dynastie* (Freiburg, 1963).

See, H., and Rebellion-Preclin, A., *Le XVI Siècle*, Clio series (Paris, 1950).

Simeoni, L., *Le Signorie* (Milan, 1950).

Symonds, J.A., *The Renaissance in Italy* (London, 1906–7).

Tomei, P., *L'Architettura a Roma nel Quattrocento* (Rome, 1942).

Trease, G., *The Condottieri* (London, 1970).

Ugolini, F., *Storia dei Conti e dei Duchi d'Urbino* (Florence, 1859), trans. de la Sizeranne, R., *César Borgia et le duc d'Urbino 1502–3* (Paris, 1924).

Villari, P., *La Storia di Girolamo Savonarola e dei suoi tempi.* (Florence, 1887–8).

Villari, P., *Machiavelli e i suoi tempi*, 3 vols (Florence, 1877–82).

Von Reumont, A., *Lorenzo de' Medici the Magnificent*, trans. R.Harrison, 2 vols (London, 1876).

Wind, E., *Pagan Mysteries in the Renaissance* (London, 1958).

Woodward, W.H., *Cesare Borgia, a Biography* (London, 1913).

Yriarte, C., *Autour des Borgia* (Paris, 1891).

Yriarte, C., *César Borgia, sa vie, sa captivité, son mort*, 2 vols (Paris, 1889).

2 ARTICLES, OFFSETS, MONOGRAPHS

Acton, Lord, 'The Borgias and their Latest Historian', in *Historical Essays and Studies* (London, 1919).

Batllori, M., 'Alejandro VI y la Casa Real de Aragon 1492–8', in *Madrid Real Academia de la Historia* (1958).

Black, C.F., 'The Baglioni as Tyrants of Perugia 1488–1540', *English Historical Review*, 85 (1970).

Blair, C., *Cesare Borgia's Sword-scabbard* (Victoria and Albert Museum, London, 1969).

Bonardi, A., 'Venezia e Cesare Borgia', in *Nuovo Archivio Veneto*, 20 (1910).

Campana, A., 'Dal Calmeta al Colucci', in *Tra Latino e Volgare, Per Carlo Dionisotti*, ed. G.B.Trezzini and others, vol. I (Padua, 1974).

Cansacchi, C., 'Agapito Geraldini da Amelia, primo segretario di Cesare Borgia 1450–1515', in *Bolettino della Deputazione di Storia Patria per L'Umbria*, LXI (1961).

Celier, L., 'Alexandre VI et ses enfants en 1493', in *Mélanges d'Archéologie et d'Histoire*, vol. XXVI (1906).

Chambers, D.S., 'The Economic Predicament of Renaissance Cardinals', in *Studies in Medieval and Renaissance History*, vol. III (Lincoln, Nebraska, 1966).

Cian, V., Review of Pastor in *Giornale Storico della Litteratura Italiana*, vol. 29 (1897).

Clough, C.H., 'Niccolò Machiavelli, Cesare Borgia and the Francesco Troche Episode', in *Medievalia et Humanistica*, Fasc. 17 (1966).

Clough, C.H., 'Niccolò Machiavelli's Political Assumptions and Objectives', reprinted from the *Bulletin of the John Rylands Library*, vol. 53, No. I (Autumn 1970).

Clough, C.H., 'The Chronicle 1502–1512 of Girolamo Vanni of Urbino', in *Studi Urbinati*, Anno XXXIX, Nuova Serie B, No. 2 (1965).

Dionisotti, C., 'Machiavelli, Cesare Borgia and Don Micheletto', in *Rivista Storica Italiana*, 39 (1967).

Dupre-Theseider, E., 'L'Intervento di Ferdinando il Cattolico nella Guerra di Pisa', in *Congreso de Historia de la Corona de Aragon*, Estudios 3 (Zaragoza, 1954).

Ehrle, F., and Stevenson, H., *Les fresques du Pinturicchio dans les salles Borgia au Vatican* (Rome, 1898).

Feliciangeli, B., *Sull'acquisto di Pesaro fatto da Cesare Borgia* (Camerino, 1900).

Filippini, F., 'Liverotto Euffreducci', in *Atti e Memorie delle Marche* (1895).

Galbete, V., 'Bosquejo Historico-Urbanistico de la Ciudad de Pamplona', *Revista Nacional de Arquitectura*, No. 102 (Madrid, 1950).

Galbete, V., 'Vida y Andanzas del Coronel D. Cristobal de Villalba', *Revista Principe de Viana*, XXV (1946).

Garnett, R., 'Contemporary Poems on Cesare Borgia', *English Historical Review*, vol. i (1886)..

Goñi Gaztambide, J., *Los Obispos de Pamplona del Siglo XV y los Navarros en los Concilios de Constanza y Basilea*, Estudios de Edad Media de la Corona de Aragon (Zaragoza, 1967).

Hermanin, F., 'L'Appartamento Borgia in Vaticano', in *Monografie Artistiche dei Musei e Gallerie Pontifiche*, vol. I (Rome, 1934).

Hernandez, A.P., 'Fano e Cesare Borgia negli scritti politici di Niccolò Machiavelli', in *Fano, Studi in memoria di G. Grimaldi* (Fano, 1974).

Idoate, F., 'Como trataban los Condes de Lerín a los de Allo y una semblanza de Cesar Borgia', in *Rincones de la Historia*, vol. III (Pamplona, 1966).

Jones, P.J., 'The End of Malatesta Rule in Rimini', in *Italian Renaissance Studies*, ed. E.F. Jacob (London, 1960).

Juaristi, V., and Becerra, S., 'Informe "Cesar Borgia" ', *Revista Principe de Viana*, XX (1945).

Larner, J., 'Cesare Borgia, Machiavelli and the Romagnol Militia', in *Studi Romagnoli*, xvii (1966).

Lisini, A., 'Relazioni fra Cesare Borgia e la Repubblica Senese', in *Bullettino Senese di Storia Patria*, vol. 7 (1900).

Menotti, M., 'Vannozza Cattanei e i Borgia', *Nouva Antologia*, clxxi (1916).

Michelini Tocci, L., 'Agapito, Bibliotecario "Docto, Acorto et Diligente" ', in *Collectanea Vaticana in Honorem Anselmi M. Card. Albareda*, vol. III (Vatican City, 1962).

Olivier y Hurtado, 'Don Rodrigo Borja, sus hijos y descendientes', *Boletin de la Real Academia de la Historia*, vol. ix (1886).

Partner, P., 'The "Budget" of the Roman Church in the Renaissance Period', in *Italian Renaissance Studies*, ed. E.F.Jacob (London, 1960).

Perez Goyena, A., 'Cesar Borja, obispo de Pamplona', *Revista Razon y Fe* (Madrid, June 1934).

Picotti, G.B., 'Ancora sul Borgia', *Rivista di storia della Chiesa in Italia*, VIII (1954).

Reti, L., 'Leonardo da Vinci and Cesare Borgia', in *Viator*, IV (1973).

Rubinstein, N., *Lucrezia Borgia*, Istituto della Enciclopedia Italiana (Rome, 1971).

Sanguinetti, F., 'La fortezza di Civita Castellana e il suo restauro', *Palladio*, IX (1959).

Saxl, F., 'The Appartamento Borgia', *Lectures*, vols I and II (London, 1957).

Schulz, J., 'Pinturicchio and the Revival of Antiquity', in *Journal of the Warburg and Courtland Institutes*, XXV (London, 1962).

Van der Put, A., *The Aragonese Double Crown and the Borja or Borgia Device* (London, 1910).

Volpe, G., 'Intorno ad alcune relazioni di Pisa con Alessandro VI e Cesare Borgia (1499–1504)', in *Studi Storici*, vols VI (1897) and VII (1898).

Weiss, R., 'Scholarship from Petrarch to Erasmus', in *The Age of the Renaissance*, ed. D.Hay (London, 1967).

Whitfield, J. H., 'New Views upon the Borgias', *History*, xxviii (1943).

Ybarra, G., 'Guevara Buscador de Epitafios', *Revista Principe de Viana*, XIX (1945).

Italy in 1494

Cesare Borgia's Romagna Campaign of 1499–1500

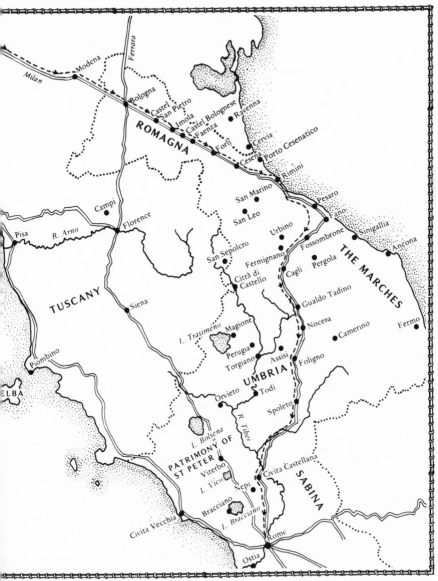

Cesare Borgia's Romagna Campaign of 1500–1

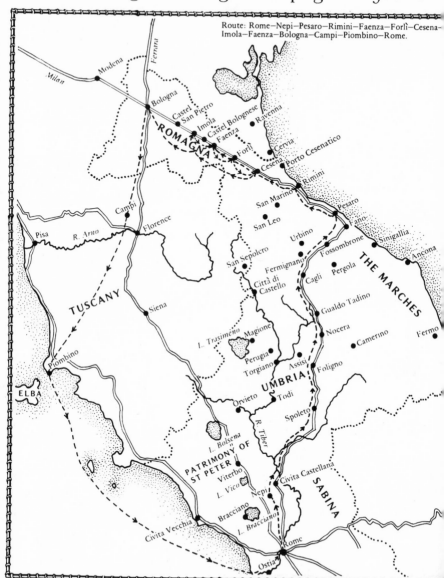

Route: Rome–Nepi–Pesaro–Rimini–Faenza–Forlì–Cesena–
Imola–Faenza–Bologna–Campi–Piombino–Rome.

Cesare Borgia's Romagna Campaign of 1502–3

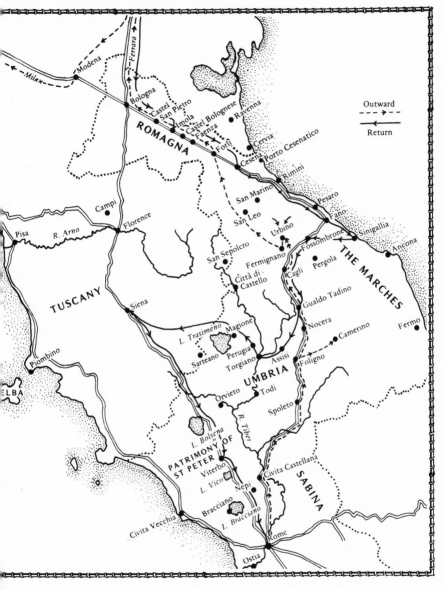

Outward -- -- --
Return   ←——

INDEX